The World of
Musical Comedy

The World of

The story of the American musical stage as

STANLEY GREEN

Musical Comedy

told through the careers of its foremost composers and lyricists

FOREWORD BY DEEMS TAYLOR

GROSSET & DUNLAP Publishers NEW YORK

by Deems Taylor

STRICTLY SPEAKING, a book such as this one—like the guest of honor
at a banquet—needs no introduction. Today, the American musical is admittedly without an equal anywhere in the world, although as recently as during
the Gay Nineties it was the Viennese operetta that ruled the entertainment
world. The evolution of this strictly American art form has taken place
within the space of one lifetime—mine.

I witnessed many of the events chronicled in this book and knew many
of the men who made these events possible. Victor Herbert encouraged me
to study music and become a composer when he heard a college show that
I had written; my first professional work was a show that was actually produced on Broadway by Charles Dillingham; I distinguished myself by
delivering a tribute to the music of Jerome Kern over C.B.S. in 1941 in which
I stated that I had long been a devoted "Fern can;" and not too long ago I
wrote one of the ever-growing list of biographies of Richard Rodgers and
Oscar Hammerstein II. Under these circumstances, I will have to leave the
facts, biographical sketches, and critical estimates to the book itself and make
this foreword a completely personal one.

One thing I will say before I dive into my memories, and that is that the
people you are going to read about are musicians and deserve to be taken

seriously as artists. The creators of musical comedy in America are a body of men (and some women) who have consistently refused to do less than the best that was in them. Anyone who works in a popular medium is constantly faced with pressures from his investors not to experiment, not to innovate; to write down, to compromise, and to be safe. If the creators of musical comedy had allowed themselves to have this sort of view of what would be successful, there would be no American musicals today—we would still be listening to Viennese operettas.

I remember an evening after World War I when I was one of a group of delighted guests at a party given by Neysa McMein, the illustrator. The reason for our delight was another guest, a young man who enjoyed the double distinction of having written some Yale football songs and of having actually joined the Foreign Legion. He played and sang some of his latest songs (one, I remember, was entitled "The Bandit Band") which received loud acclaim. We agreed that they were tuneful and absolutely charming. But many of us, myself among them, also agreed that his tunes were far too tricky and his lyrics much too sophisticated ever to have any popular success. The young guest of honor denied both accusations, and he was right. His name was Cole Porter.

There was an afternoon in the thirties when I was equally dubious and equally wrong. George Gershwin had telephoned to suggest that we have lunch together and then go to the ball game. During lunch he remarked that he was just finishing an opera about Negro life in the South.

"A *what?*" I said.

"You heard me."

So back to his house we went, and he played me all four hours of the score of *Porgy and Bess.* He was right. It *was* an opera—and we never did get to the ball game.

My acquaintance with musical comedy began long, long ago, when I used to spend part of my summer vacations with my Philadelphia cousins. Among the season's attractions were the concerts in Willow Grove Park given by Victor Herbert and his orchestra. There were four of these every day, two in the afternoon and two in the evening.

One cousin and myself were Herbert idolators, and we wanted to hear all four concerts. But the question of money reared its ugly head. Each of us was given fifty cents to cover all expenses. Trolley car fare to Willow Grove and return was thirty cents. Admission to the park was another fifteen. This left us exactly five cents for dinner, if we wanted to stay for the evening. We did, naturally, so eventually we solved the problem. We would each buy five cents' worth of the cheapest and most villainous candy we could find. This, when eaten, would render the thought of any dinner abhorrent, whereat (slightly green but smiling bravely) we would happily sit through the two evening concerts, hearing excerpts from such Herbert scores as *The Wizard of the Nile, The Idol's Eye,* and his latest, *Babes in Toyland.*

Incidentally, in after years, Victor Herbert told me that if it were physically possible, he made it a point to compose at least one tune every day. I doubt if any other composer has ever equalled that record.

One important event that this book neglects to mention is the production in 1911 of a musical comedy called *The Echo,* for which I wrote the original score. In those bad old days, it was the custom for numbers to be interpolated in musical productions at the producer's whim. *The Echo* was produced by Charles Dillingham, who promptly proceeded to hire all the dancers in the world to perform in it, all of whom brought their own music. To liven up the proceedings further, Mr. Dillingham commissioned several young song writers to write individual songs which were then scattered through the production. By the time the show opened, only three of my original numbers were left in the score (although an over-optimistic publisher had already published four).

One of the young writers who had a song in *The Echo* was Jerome Kern, who was to become one of my closest friends. On opening night, legend has it, Kern was standing nervously at the back of the theatre, where he was seen by Bruce Edwards, Dillingham's manager.

"I hope your show goes well tonight, old man," Bruce said kindly to Kern.

Fourteen men said, "Thanks."

Shortly before his death in 1945, Jerry Kern came East for the rehearsals of the revival of *Show Boat.* While he was here, he was able to attend the formal meeting of the National Institute of Arts and Letters at which he was made officially a member, and thereby became the second popular composer ever to be elected to that honorary body. The only musical comedy composer to gain that honor before him was Victor Herbert, and there has been only one since—Richard Rodgers.

But popular composers have had their fans among so-called "serious" musicians nonetheless. One of the most ardent admirers of Vincent Youmans' music was Sergei Rachmaninoff, who never tired of playing his scores. You don't have to be told that Youmans was an equally ardent admirer of Rachmaninoff's music!

He was a passionate devotee of orchestral music, and the larger the orchestra the better. He thought nothing of hiring forty musicians for one of his revues (the usual allotment is twenty-eight). On the other hand, he was deeply suspicious of librettists and lyric writers—doubtless because he had suffered so much at the hands of hack collaborators. All this led to his last folly, a revue without a book. It was a potpourri of songs, (concert) dances, and pantomimes. I played a part in it, to the extent that a four-foot dummy of myself lolled against the proscenium arch doing a sort of narration job (he finally did consent to have a book, and a holy terror it was, too).

I went down to Baltimore to attend the matinee following the opening, and arrived at the theater about halfway through the performance. The book, I discovered, had been junked overnight, but what was left was pretty awful. People were stumping indignantly up the aisles, on their way to demand their money back, to all of which Youmans paid not the slightest attention. I caught his eye, and he beckoned me to stand beside him. He was radiant. "You hear that?" he murmured. "Fifty men in the orchestra pit!"

That disaster cost his backers one hundred and ninety thousand dollars.

The ranks are thinning. Of the composers who flourished during the tens-twenties-thirties-forties, very few are left. Most of them died at ages that we would consider merely middle-aged. Of the great ones, the most untimely departure was that of George Gershwin, who died at thirty-eight. Vincent Youmans died at forty-seven, Jerome Kern at sixty, and Victor Herbert and Oscar Hammerstein II at sixty-five. As this book goes to press (1960), perhaps the oldest survivor of the formative years of musical comedy is Rudolf Friml, at eighty-one.

Friml, by the way, has a system of composing that is, I think, unique. As he described it to me, he first turns on a tape recorder; then, going to the piano, he improvises for an hour. After this he listens to the playback and jots down whatever tunes he might be able to use.

Another system of composing is attributed to Irving Berlin. He is so unbelievably prolific, both as to words and music, that a rumor was started in Tin Pan Alley by jealous composers to the effect that Berlin's songs are all written by "A little colored boy" who plays them to him. I didn't know that Irving knew this story until one day, several years ago, when I was going through the MGM studios with him. As we entered his office he waved a careless hand toward an ancient upright piano that huddled in one corner, observing, "That's where the little colored boy lives."

Irving Berlin is a man whose achievement is solidly based on an appraisal of what he does and does not know. He is anything but conceited. One of the eagerly awaited events in the musical New York of the twenties was Walter Damrosch's annual New Year's Day party, to which one and all flocked, there to imbibe wassail and other beverages. You rang the bell of the Damrosch home, the front door opened a crack, revealing a hand holding a glass, and a voice said, "Drink this." You did, the door opened, you entered, and you spent a happy afternoon. It was not, incidentally, a rowdy afternoon.

At one of these, Berlin was among the guests. I heard Damrosch say, "Irving, with your talent you ought to study music seriously."

"Doctor Damrosch," said the composer, "I have a very slender talent; and if I were to study music I might end up by despising my own stuff."

"You are quite right," said Damrosch.

I have written so much about Richard Rodgers that there is little left for me to say here about him, except that he is a dear friend. But I can't write about musical comedy without at least mentioning one of our contemporary giants. Rodgers is a compartmentalist. When he is working on a show, he works literally day and night. But otherwise, he doesn't go near the piano, and never whiles away an evening playing for friends. (In this respect he is totally unlike George Gershwin, about whom Oscar Levant once said, "An evening with Gershwin is a Gershwin evening.")

It has been a privilege for me to know, and sometimes to work with, all these men. After all, there have only been three forms of musical stage entertainment in the history of Western culture that in their day have been huge money-makers and also perfected art forms. These three are Italian grand opera, the Viennese operetta, and the American musical comedy. We can be proud that one of these belongs to us.

Preface

THE WORLD OF musical comedy covers the vast, vaguely defined area between opera and vaudeville and, at times, incorporates elements of both. "Musical comedy" is, of course, a generic term that refers to the various forms of entertainment included under the more formal designation of "American musical theatre." It covers operetta, comic opera, musical play (now frequently merely called "musical"), musical comedy itself, revue, and, in the past, spectacle or extravaganza. These forms are difficult to define precisely, as they usually overlap. However, in general, the terms operetta, comic opera, and musical play denote a greater dependence on music in the telling of a story than does musical comedy. Revue and spectacle are closest to vaudeville, as they usually consist of unrelated songs, dances, and sketches.

The growth of the American musical theatre has been in the development of all its component parts, but principally the libretto. No show can succeed today on the quality of its music and lyrics alone; they must be part of the over-all fabric of the production. And that fabric is made up of all the theatrical arts that have evolved through the years.

Because music is the one essential ingredient of the musical stage, I have chosen to tell the story of *The World of Musical Comedy* through the careers of its most significant composers and lyricists. Of all the arts that are mobilized in the creation of musical comedy, music changes the least through the years; a good song is a good song whether it was written in

1900 or in 1960. It has the power to affect people's emotions long after the particular work for which it was composed has been forgotten. Indeed, it is because of their music that shows written during the early years of this century can still be revived successfully, and even the most recent attractions are known to countless people throughout the world only through the appeal of their songs.

The cooperation of many people in the preparation of *The World of Musical Comedy* has been both heartening and indispensable. I am especially indebted to four alert and knowledgeable individuals, Charles Gaynor, Irma Hunt, Frank Jacobs, and Alfred Simon for their painstaking reading of the manuscript. In addition to the writers discussed in this book who responded willingly to my requests for assistance, information has been supplied by Edward N. Waters, Helmy Kresa, Hilda Schneider, Tom Weatherly, Irving Brown, Edward Cole, Richard Maney, Chester Kopaz, and James J. Fuld. The staff of the Theatre Collection of the New York Public Library, particularly Paul Myers and William Anderson, has also been most cooperative.

For help in obtaining photographs, I wish to thank Theresa Hart of ASCAP, John Walsh of C.B.S., Lynn Farnol, Edward Jablonski, Grace McCabe, John Springer, Jay Culver of Culver Pictures, Inc., and Harry Collins of Brown Bros.

I am also most grateful to Richard Rodgers and Oscar Hammerstein II for allowing me to reprint the lyric to their first song, "Room for One More."

Most important, to my wife, Kay, my gratitude is boundless.

STANLEY GREEN

Contents

The World of
Musical Comedy

CHAPTER ONE
Prologue

ALTHOUGH THERE WERE earlier attempts to present dramas on the same program with music and dancing, *The Black Crook,* in 1866, was the first successful venture in America to combine the two forms of entertainment. This distinction, however, was achieved entirely by accident. In that year a French ballet company had been signed to appear at the Academy of Music in New York City, but was left without a theatre when the Academy burned down shortly before the scheduled première. At the same time, *The Black Crook,* an incredibly ridiculous melodrama loosely based on the *Faust* legend, was scheduled to be presented at Niblo's Garden. As the play seemed to have little chance of succeeding without some added attraction to lure the public, the producer hired the ballet company (and its scenery) to perform in those sequences which could utilize the services of dancing demons and spirits. The grafting may have been crude (the opening night performance lasted from 7:45 P.M. to 1:15 A.M.), but the sight of one hundred bare-limbed dancers proved to be irresistible to post-Civil War audiences. *The Black Crook* ran for sixteen months, was revived almost continually, and toured the United States for more than forty years.

Such a phenomenal success encouraged others to present similar attractions. These early attempts, however, bore little resemblance to the

1

musical theatre as we know it today; musical interludes were either forcibly inserted into dramatic sequences or performed between scenes. Moreover, the music was usually gathered from many different sources, though *Evangeline*, in 1874, did have all of its songs composed by one man, Edward E. Rice. Many of the productions of the late 1800's relied heavily on spectacular scenic effects. The leaders in this field were the Kiralfy brothers, whose *Around the World in Eighty Days* and *Excelsior* became successful because of their dazzling settings rather than the attractiveness of their melodies. *Excelsior*, presented in 1883, was the first production to feature electric lighting, an innovation that required the personal supervision of Thomas A. Edison.

During this period, many European operettas were being imported and found a large following. At the same time, however, American writers were beginning to find new and native models for characters in their plots. In 1879, Ned Harrigan and Tony Hart introduced recent-immigrant types in their series of shows about the rowdy Mulligan Guards. Soon afterward, Charles Hoyt discovered the great appeal of various regional characters. Hoyt's biggest success, *A Trip to Chinatown*, featured three remarkably durable songs, "The Bowery" and "Reuben and Cynthia" by Percy Gaunt, and "After the Ball" by Charles K. Harris.

Away from the "legitimate theatre," Tony Pastor's Music Hall, which had opened on the Bowery during the Civil War, was the nation's leading variety theatre when it moved uptown to 14th Street in 1881. Pastor's type of entertainment soon led to vaudeville and, eventually, the Broadway revue.

The twentieth century began with Victor Herbert and George M. Cohan as the leading American figures in the musical theatre. In the second decade, despite many foreign operettas imported after the success of Franz Lehár's *The Merry Widow*, Guy Bolton, P. G. Wodehouse, and Jerome Kern achieved a wide following with their intimate, well-constructed Princess Theatre musicals.

The 1920's introduced such major talents as George and Ira Gershwin, Oscar Hammerstein II, Vincent Youmans, Rodgers and Hart, and Cole Porter. Nevertheless, it was not a period distinguished by many changes in the *structure* of the musical comedy theatre. Of all the musicals written and produced during that decade, only *Show Boat* was able to offer a truly adult libretto combined with superior music and lyrics.

The Thirties were years of experimentation. *Strike Up the Band* introduced political satire. In Kern's and Otto Harbach's straightforward love story, *The Cat and the Fiddle*, the music and plot were indispensable to each other. The following year, Kern and Hammerstein accomplished the same thing with *Music in the Air*. The "folk-opera" *Porgy and Bess* was the most ambitious creation of the decade; it still remains the most universally acclaimed operatic work by an American composer. The plot of *On Your Toes* was the first to have integrated ballet sequences. *Knickerbocker Holiday* made a genuine attempt to fuse a philosophical book with songs pertinent to the play's action.

The librettos of the Forties continued to show maturity. *Cabin in the Sky* made imaginative use of Negro folklore. *Lady in the Dark* probed the subconscious with more daring than was customary even in the nonmusical theatre. An unsavory character was the hero of *Pal Joey*. The most impressive work of the decade was *Oklahoma!*, the first Rodgers and Hammerstein collaboration, which artfully blended libretto, score, and dances. Its tremendous success encouraged other writers to risk unusual themes. *Bloomer Girl* was concerned with equal rights during the Civil War period. *Street Scene* took a compassionate view of the inhabitants of a New York tenement. *Finian's Rainbow* blended Irish whimsy with the sad plight of southern sharecroppers. *Brigadoon* related a tender, evocative Scottish legend. Even the writers of more traditional musical comedies kept up with the trend. Irving Berlin's *Annie Get Your Gun* and Cole Porter's *Kiss Me, Kate* were entertaining, adult stories with music and lyrics that perfectly complemented their subject matter. The decade ended with *South Pacific,* probably the most universally popular of all Rodgers and Hammerstein's works.

In the Fifties, there was an even greater dependence on themes of substance. Marcel Pagnol, Sidney Howard, John Steinbeck, George Bernard Shaw, James Hilton, Voltaire, Eugene O'Neill, Jane Austen, and Sean O'Casey provided inspiration for some of the decade's musicals. This was the period that also saw the emergence of the director-librettist and the director-choreographer. George Abbott* and Joshua Logan had been staging and writing musicals for many years, but it was not until the Fifties that they became dominant figures. Abbott's *The Pajama Game, Damn Yankees, New Girl in Town,* and *Fiorello!*, and Logan's *Wish You Were Here* and *Fanny* were all generally successful examples of unified productions. Abe Burrows, whose biggest hits were *Can-Can* and *Silk Stockings,* is another significant director-librettist. Although they received no credit for any writing, both George S. Kaufman, director of *Guys and Dolls*, and Moss Hart, director of *My Fair Lady,* could call upon their experience as authors to add greater theatrical perspective to their work.

* The important part George Abbott has played in the careers of young writers for the musical stage has won him the title of "apprentice's sorcerer." Since 1941, he has been the director and frequently the author of the book of the first—or first successful—musicals by the following composers and lyricists: Hugh Martin and Ralph Blane (*Best Foot Forward*); Leonard Bernstein, Betty Comden, and Adolph Green (*On the Town*); Jule Styne (*High Button Shoes*); Frank Loesser (*Where's Charley?*); Richard Adler and Jerry Ross (*The Pajama Game*); Bob Merrill (*New Girl in Town*); Mary Rodgers and Marshall Barer (*Once Upon a Mattress*); and Jerry Bock and Sheldon Harnick (*Fiorello!*).

George Balanchine and Agnes de Mille were the first choreographers to stage entire productions. More recently, a greater emphasis has been placed on directors functioning in this dual capacity in order to create a greater homogeneity of style. Among the outstanding choreographer-directors are Jerome Robbins (*Bells Are Ringing, West Side Story, Gypsy*), Michael Kidd (*Li'l Abner, Destry Rides Again*), Bob Fosse (*Redhead*), and Gower Champion (*Bye Bye Birdie*).

The importance of a close relationship between story, song, and dance has helped bring about the decline of the once high-riding revue. George Lederer offered the first collection of disconnected songs and sketches in 1894. He called his entertainment *The Passing Show,* a title which was later appropriated by the Shubert brothers. Ziegfeld began his annual *Follies* in 1907, and other producers were quick to copy the yearly pattern. In the early Twenties, the *Greenwich Village Follies,* Raymond Hitchcock's *Hitchy-Koo* revues, and *George White's Scandals* were popular annual shows. They were soon joined by such other periodic pleasures as the *Music Box Revues, Earl Carroll Vanities,* and *The Grand Street Follies.*

Most of the revues of the Twenties failed to continue beyond their first year. Yet many optimistically affixed the year of their inception to create the impression that they were inaugurating an annual series: "Broncho Billy" Anderson's *Frivolities of 1920; Broadway Brevities of 1920; Snapshots of 1921; Spice of 1922;* Charles Dillingham's *Nifties of 1923;* the Shuberts' *Topics of 1923* and *Vogues of 1924;* Dillingham's *Puzzles of 1925; Bunk of 1926; Bad Habits of 1926; Bare Facts of 1926; Nic Nax of 1926; Padlocks of 1927;* etc., etc.

The sleek, sophisticated revues of Arthur Schwartz and Howard Dietz set the pattern for the early Thirties. After the Depression came the revues of social consciousness. The best of these was *Pins and Needles.* At the other extreme—and even more popular—was Olsen and Johnson's slapstick variety show, *Hellzapoppin.* The last successful year for revues was 1948, with *Make Mine Manhattan* (Richard Lewine-Arnold Horwitt), *Inside U.S.A.* (Schwartz-Dietz), and *Lend an Ear* (Charles Gaynor) all attracting large audiences. It was no coincidence that 1948 was also the year in which television started keeping people glued to their home screens. From then on, it became necessary for a musical to tell a coherent story in order to lure people away from the variety-type entertainment TV offered without charge. Thus, from an average of fourteen revues offered each season during the Twenties, seven during the Thirties, and six during the Forties, only three a season were shown during the Fifties. Indeed, the lone revue produced on Broadway during the season of 1958–1959 was the successful French import, *La Plume de Ma Tante.* The following season, of the four offered, the

4

only moderate success was the two-man British import, *At the Drop of a Hat*, with Michael Flanders and Donald Swann.

Off-Broadway revues, however, continue to provide a training ground for writers and performers. Ben Bagley's two *Shoestring Revues, The Billy Barnes Revue*, plus the night club revues of Julius Monk at the Upstairs at the Downstairs have helped develop new talent for the musical theatre. Because the revue is generally looked upon as being a step below book musicals, writers who succeed in creating scores and librettos for successful book shows seldom return to revues.

For the past three decades, the primary concern of the musical theatre has been in the strengthening of librettos and in the close integration of song and story. Good musical comedy songs accomplish this integration in three general ways: by creating the proper mood; by revealing character; and by advancing the plot. "Summertime," from *Porgy and Bess*, and "Oh, What a Beautiful Mornin'," from *Oklahoma!*, are used mainly for atmosphere. Billy Bigelow's "Soliloquy" in *Carousel* expresses his deep desires and fears. "The Rain in Spain" is performed in *My Fair Lady* at a climactic moment to provide a musical outlet essential to the story. But almost every show has at least one number, such as "Shipoopi" in *The Music Man* or "Brush Up Your Shakespeare" in *Kiss Me, Kate*, that is inserted solely as an applause-catching specialty, with little regard to its application to the story line. Frequently, too, shows dealing with musical or theatrical subjects avoid the awkwardness of having people break into song in the midst of a dramatic story by using the device of a show within a show; as in *The Cat and the Fiddle, Pal Joey,* and *Gypsy*.

In achieving a skillful blend of song and story, the modern musical theatre utilizes all available arts of stagecraft. No matter how well these arts are combined, however, the plots of musicals are still frequently variations of well-tested formulas. Even the daring *West Side Story* went back to Shakespeare's *Romeo and Juliet* for inspiration. The most persistent theme of all has been the Pygmalion legend, or its almost indistinguishable parallel, the Cinderella story. The process through which a drab young girl is transformed into a glamorous star or radiant beauty is a happily identifiable metamorphosis for audiences, one that has always had great appeal. Variations on this theme have included: *Mlle. Modiste* (1905), Parisian hat shop employee to prima donna; *The Firefly* (1912), Italian street singer to prima donna; *Irene* (1919), dress-shop employee to belle of the ball; *Sally* (1920), dishwasher to Ziegfeld star; *Peggy-Ann* (1926), drudge to dreamed-of adventuress; *Lady In the Dark* (1941), austere career woman to dreamed-of woman-of-the-world; *Annie Get Your Gun* (1946), hillbilly to world-famous sureshot; *Silk Stockings* (1955), stern communist to vivacious beauty; *Gypsy*

(1959), talentless vaudeville trouper to burlesque star. That *My Fair Lady* is, in Richard Maney's phrase, the classic Cinderella story is surely an important factor in its tremendous success.

To date, *Oklahoma!*, with 2,248 Broadway performances, holds the long-run record for musicals. Before *Oklahoma!*, only two musicals, *Pins and Needles* and *Hellzapoppin* had run over 800 performances; since *Oklahoma!*, there have been fifteen. The increasingly lengthy tenures of musicals in New York are due to a number of reasons. In the days of Victor Herbert and George M. Cohan, a Broadway run may have indicated a certain amount of prestige, but a show had to do well on the road in order to succeed financially. The depression of the early Thirties, plus the attraction of the movies, greatly reduced the number of touring companies. Subsequently, improved means of transportation enabled more people to travel to New York to see the original production. In recent years, high operating costs have made it necessary for shows to remain on Broadway longer in order to realize a profit.

Another contributing factor to the longevity of musicals is the impact of original-cast recordings. There is no doubt that hearing songs exactly the way they are performed in the theatre contributes to a desire to see the actual performance. Decca made the first original-cast album in 1943 when it recorded most of the *Oklahoma!* score. Since then, the major record companies have become competitive bidders for the recording rights to potential hit shows. Their eagerness is understandable; because of rapidly diminishing production costs, an original-cast LP can make a greater profit than that realized from ticket sales. In 1956, the Columbia Broadcasting System was the sole investor in *My Fair Lady*, thus ensuring that Columbia Records, a division of C.B.S., would get the recording rights. Their investment paid off; *Lady* has become the largest selling original-cast album of all time.

Although the term "musical comedy" is considered somewhat old-fashioned today, it is an apt designation. The commercial musical theatre is seldom concerned with really serious themes; despite the success of *West Side Story* and others, it is still primarily the theatre of pretty costumes, gay dances, and light, witty music and lyrics. In transforming *Pygmalion* into *My Fair Lady*, it was necessary to alter the rather cold ending to make it more palatable. *Liliom* was changed into *Carousel* only after an element of hopefulness had been added to soften the tragedy. Even titles give indication of the changes. The dour *Anna Christie* becomes a bright, expectant *New Girl in Town*, while *They Knew What They Wanted* takes on an entirely different spirit as *The Most Happy Fella*. (As Irving Kolodin once pointed out, the title is an inversion of one of Tony's lines in the original play in which he refers to himself as "the most *un*happy fella.")

In spite of this, there are constant howls that the American musical theatre is becoming too serious. The truth is that it has enough room for any worthwhile idea. Oscar Hammerstein II concisely summed up the situation when he wrote in *Variety:* "It is nonsense to say what a musical play should or should not be. It should be anything it wants to be, and if you don't like it you don't have to go to it. There is only one absolutely indispensable element that a musical play must have. It must have music. And there is only one thing that it has to be—it has to be good."

Victor Herbert.

8

CHAPTER TWO

Victor Herbert

THE EMERGENCE OF Victor Herbert as the first important composer of the American musical stage could not have been anticipated from his background. He was born in Dublin, educated in Germany, performed in symphony orchestras throughout Europe, and did not arrive in the United States until he was twenty-seven. Moreover, his coming to this country had nothing to do with writing musical comedies and operettas, he came here to play the cello in the orchestra of the Metropolitan Opera Company. His Broadway career did not begin until eight years later.

Born on February 1, 1859, Victor Herbert was the son of Edward and Fanny Lover Herbert. His father died when Victor was a child of two; and during his youth, he was strongly influenced by his maternal grandfather, Samuel Lover, the celebrated Irish artist-novelist-poet-composer.

After his mother's remarriage to a German physician, the boy was taken to live in Stuttgart. Although he was expected to follow in his stepfather's career, he was far more attracted to music than to medicine, and at fifteen began to study the cello. Herbert subsequently joined touring orchestras as a member of the string section and as a soloist. In Vienna, he played for a year in the orchestra of Johann Strauss's brother, Eduard, where he quickly acquired the difficult knack of conducting Viennese waltzes with the proper authority and lilt. During his five years with the Court Orchestra of Stuttgart, Herbert studied composition under Max Seifriz, a highly regarded conductor and composer. His first work, the *Suite for Cello and Orchestra,* was published at that time.

When Herbert was twenty-six, he met Therese Förster, a young soprano who had recently become a member of the Royal Opera at Stuttgart. They soon fell in love and made plans to marry—plans which were suddenly accelerated by an unusual stroke of good luck.

The Metropolitan Opera Company of New York, having completed its first season of German operas, was anxious to recruit new singers for its Wagnerian repertory. Frank Damrosch, one of the Metropolitan's scouts, journeyed to Stuttgart to audition a young tenor. The tenor failed to impress him, but while there Damrosch decided to listen to some other singers. Fraulein Förster pleased him so much that he promptly offered her a contract. Although she was elated with the offer, she insisted, with the blind confidence of youth, that her fiancé would also have to be hired. Damrosch was a bit skeptical, but when he heard Herbert play, he signed another contract. Therese Förster and Victor Herbert were married in Vienna, and spent their honeymoon on a steamer bound for New York.

Victor Herbert upon his arrival in New York at the age of 27.

Therese sang at the Metropolitan for only one season. From then on she was content to remain in the background as Victor Herbert's wife. His appearances as a soloist with Theodore Thomas's and Anton Seidl's orchestras were becoming important events in the musical life of New York, and he was rapidly being recognized as one of the country's leading cellists. In addition, he was winning a limited fame as a composer of concert music and as a conductor. However, such accomplishments gave him only partial satisfaction. Herbert was a warm, gregarious, fun-loving man who enjoyed all the popular amusements of the day—bands, parades, operettas, musical comedies—and he was extremely anxious to move to the top of this world. "Is it a crime to be popular?" he once asked. "I believe that which is not popular is not of much benefit to the world."

It was, therefore, natural that when he was offered the post of director of the 22nd New York National Guard Band (succeeding the famous Patrick Gilmore), he was delighted to accept. Such a positon would not only relieve him of the monotony of playing in an orchestra, but it would also give him time to compose and perform music that could win him wider popular acclaim than he could ever receive from opera and concert audiences.

Although Herbert enjoyed his work as bandmaster, he knew that only the theatre could provide him with the perfect outlet for his composing gifts. When he first began to give serious thought to working in the popular theatre, Herbert wanted to write for a kind of "folk theatre" he equated with the earthy entertainments of Harrigan and Hart. Though his Irish heritage made this ambition understandable, he soon realized that by training and temperament he was far better suited to follow the tradition of the middle European operetta.

According to Edward N. Waters, Herbert's biographer, the composer's first comic opera was *La Vivandière*, written in 1893 especially for Lillian Russell. Little is known about it, however, because it was never produced. The following year, Herbert wrote *Prince Ananias* for The Bostonians, a well-known touring company. They opened it in New York on November 20, 1894. The score for the new work was attractive, but it was hampered by an unusually dull and awkward libretto. Nevertheless, and in spite of a lukewarm reception, the operetta remained in the company's repertory for about two years.

Herbert's second production, *The Wizard of the Nile*, in 1895, began his frequent association with librettist Harry B. Smith and established him as one of the leading light opera composers in the country. Smith wrote the book as a vehicle for Frank Daniels, a popular comedian who had won fame for his performances in Charles Hoyt's musical farces. Herbert completed the delightful Near Eastern-flavored score within a month. In addition to the song "Star Light, Star Bright," the show is best remembered today for a recurring line, "Am I a wiz?" which soon became a popular slang expression.

Having supplied Daniels with a notable Broadway debut set in Egypt, Herbert and Smith created other musicals for him with equally exotic locales—India for *The Idol's Eye*, Afghanistan for *The Ameer*, Persia for *The Tattooed Man*. None of these repeated the triumph of *The Wizard of the Nile*, though *The Idol's Eye* did give Daniels a particularly clever number about the contented wife of "The Tattooed Man" of the circus.

> "Oh, why should I go abroad," she said,
> "To Germany, France or Rome?
>   When so fine a collection
>   Awaits my inspection
> In our happy little home."

In this exciting world of nerve-racking deadlines, frantic opening nights, and temperamental stars, Victor Herbert was able to find the stimulus for his most enduring compositions. He was a desperately hard worker; he loved the challenge that each new contract presented; and he enjoyed the money his work brought him.

Aside from the pleasure he found in composing, his favorite pastime was eating and drinking the best food and wine. Indeed, as his publisher, Isidore Witmark, once related, Herbert had an ingenious way of combining his work with his fondness for drink. In the season of 1899–1900, he composed the scores for four operettas almost simultaneously, while imbibing an appropriate wine for each one to get him in the proper mood. For *Cyrano de Bergerac*, which had a French locale, he drank claret and burgundy; for *The Singing Girl*, with its Austrian setting, Rhine wine and moselle; for the Afghan-flavored *Ameer*, some special "hard stuff"; for *The Viceroy*, an operetta laid in Venice, there was chianti. All these wines were kept on ice in a washtub in his studio because Herbert jumped from one score to another as it pleased him, rather than composing one at a time.

During his career, Victor Herbert helped establish the fame of three sopranos of unusual ability—Alice Nielsen, Fritzi Scheff, and Emma Trentini. The magic worked both ways. Herbert seemed to compose his best music when he worked with, and for, an outstanding singer. Even though *The Serenade*, Herbert's first truly distinguished score, was commissioned for The Bostonians in 1897, and was not created especially for Miss Nielsen, the leading role was given to her at the composer's insistence. Only twenty years old at the time, the soprano left the company the following year to form her own Alice Nielsen Comic Opera Company. Herbert and Smith then supplied her with a second substantial hit, *The Fortune Teller*, in which Eugene Cowles sang the comforting lullaby, "Gypsy Love Song"

THE FORTUNE TELLER *(1898). A dramatic moment during the operetta. Alice Nielsen, the star, is the one in the officer's uniform about to draw her sword.*

("Slumber on, my little gypsy sweetheart"). Miss Nielsen offered the amusing "Always Do as People Say You Should," and the spirit of comic-opera gypsies was tempestuously conveyed in "Romany Life."

Despite his heavy schedule of theatre work, soon after the opening of *The Fortune Teller* Herbert became musical director of the Pittsburgh Symphony Orchestra. That Leonard Bernstein can be both the conductor of the New York Philharmonic and also the composer of musical comedy scores is accepted today as proof of his great and varied talents. At the turn of the century, however, Herbert's dual occupation subjected him to a violent attack by Marc Blumenberg, editor of *The Musical Courier*. One particularly strong editorial boldly stated: ". . . this paper . . . long since declared not only that *The Fortune Teller* has no merit whatever, but that all of Victor Herbert's 'written-to-order' comic operas were pure and simple plagiarisms . . . Everything written by Herbert is copied; there is not one original strain in anything he has done . . . How Pittsburgh intelligence could ever select this clever bandmaster as its symphony director passes

13

comprehension, unless indeed the people there never really appreciated the true significance of the artistic movement a permanent symphony orchestra represents . . . The great symphony conductors are not drafted from the ranks of the composers of the shoddy American farce operas, alias leg shows, nor are they taken from the leaders of the parading military bands. . . ."

Herbert quickly sued *The Musical Courier* for libel. Expert testimony was offered on both sides as to what, if any, plagiarism had taken place. The trial was a sensation, and when all the bombast and rhetoric had spent itself, Herbert was awarded damages by the court.

After devoting about three years almost exclusively to the Pittsburgh Symphony, Herbert returned to Broadway in 1903. Fred Hamlin and Julian Mitchell, who had produced the highly successful *Wizard of Oz* by A. Baldwin Sloane and L. Frank Baum, commissioned him and Glen Mac-Donough to write a sequel. The new work was *Babes in Toyland*. Although it lacked the sturdiness of its predecessor's libretto, *Toyland* had a score of such appeal that it gave the play a lyricism the other production lacked. In fact, whenever it is revived today, the original score is always performed, whereas *The Wizard of Oz* inevitably substitutes the songs written for the 1939 movie version by Harold Arlen and E. Y. Harburg. Among the pieces

BABES IN TOYLAND *(1903). William Norris and Mabel Barrison lead the children of Toyland in singing "I Can't Do the Sum." (Setting by John Young.)*

IT HAPPENED IN NORDLAND (1904). *The American ambassadress to Nordland, Katherine Peepfogle, is deaf to the entreaties of her long-lost brother, Hubert. Marie Cahill and Lew Fields were the stars. (Setting by John Young.)*

that still give *Babes in Toyland* its continued charm are "March of the Toys," "Toyland," and the disarming "I Can't Do the Sum," which is performed to the accompaniment of chalk tapping on slates.

In 1950, Irving Berlin's *Call Me Madam* was concerned with the misadventures of a lady ambassador to the court of a mythical country called Lichtenburg; in 1904, Victor Herbert's *It Happened in Nordland* was concerned with the misadventures of a lady ambassador to the court of a mythical country called Nordland. But there the similarity ended. The Herbert work, written with Glen MacDonough, was a rather meandering though commercially successful vehicle for two popular entertainers, Marie Cahill (as Ambassador Katherine Peepfogle) and Lew Fields (as her long-lost brother, Hubert). Both Fields, who was appearing for the first time without Joe Weber, his regular partner, and Miss Cahill were continually adding lines and changing "business."

Herbert became particularly irritated with his female star, who went so far as to interpolate some of her own vaudeville numbers. The situation between star and composer became so strained that she refused to tour in the show. When *It Happened in Nordland* returned to New York, the part of the ambassadress was played by the equally undisciplined Blanche Ring, who quit after she too encountered difficulty when she insisted on adding special material. Finally, the role of Katherine Peepfogle was given to Pauline Frederick, a young actress in the company who subsequently won success in many dramatic roles on Broadway.

The score of *It Happened in Nordland* had many charming numbers, with "Absinthe Frappe" the biggest hit. "Al Fresco," originally a piano piece Herbert had written under the name of Frank Roland to test its popularity, was performed at the beginning of the second act to provide an appropriate musical setting for a gay carnival scene. Four years later, Herbert again wrote a score for a Lew Fields musical, *Old Dutch*, though it is mostly remembered today for the scene-stealing debut of a nine-year-old actress named Helen Hayes.

Writing sequels to long-running musicals and vehicles for popular entertainers was profitable, but Herbert was anxious to compose again for a truly gifted prima donna. Alice Nielsen had deserted comic opera for grand opera (only to return briefly in 1917 in Rudolf Friml's *Kitty Darlin'*), but producer Charles Dillingham had lured the vivacious, Viennese-born Fritzi Scheff from grand opera to comic opera. Although *Babette*, the first operetta Herbert composed for her, was a failure, the composer, in 1905, joined

OLD DUTCH *(1909). Though her part was small, this nine-year-old actress made an auspicious New York debut. As the critic of the New York Herald wrote: "Miss Helen Hayes, a wee miss, won the favor of the audience by a bit of acting that was refreshing."*

VICTOR HERBERT

librettist Henry Martyn Blossom, Jr., to create her greatest success, *Mlle. Modiste*. In story and dialogue, the musical was far more adult than anything Herbert had previously done.

"Kiss Me Again," Herbert's most universally popular piece, was introduced in *Mlle. Modiste*. At first, Miss Scheff did not want to sing it because she felt it was too low for her voice. Blossom and Dillingham agreed with the prima donna and recommended that Herbert drop it from the score. The composer, however, was adament, and the song remained in the show. "Kiss Me Again" was not originally sung as the sincere ballad it is accepted as today. Playing the role of Fifi, a stage-struck employee of a Paris hat shop, Fritzi Scheff offered it as part of a lengthy routine called "If I Were on the Stage." In it she attempted three different types of songs that might be suitable for her theatrical debut. As a country maid, she performed a gavotte, and as a French lady of history, a polonaise. Then, to introduce the third song, she sang:

> But best of all the parts I'd play,
> If I would only have my way,
> Would be a strong romantic role;
> Emotional and full of soul.

MLLE. MODISTE *(1905). True love conquers in the final scene at the charity bazaar. Fifi (Fritzi Scheff) is at last welcomed into the family of her beloved, Capt. Etienne de Bouvray (Walter Percival), by his uncle, the Comte de St. Mar (William Pruette). Claude Gillingwater stands between Pruette and Miss Scheff. (Setting by Homer Emens.)*

THE RED MILL (1906). "Con" Kidder and "Kid" Conner kick up their heels with two local belles beside the Red Mill Inn, in Katwyk-aan-Zee, Holland. Fred Stone, Allene Crater (Mrs. Fred Stone), David Montgomery, and Ethel Johnson.

> And I believe for such a thing
> A dreamy sensuous waltz I'd sing . . .

and immediately glided into "Sweet summer breeze, whispering trees . . ."

Herbert wrote two other operettas for Fritzi Scheff, *The Prima Donna* and *The Duchess*, but neither matched the triumph of *Mlle. Modiste*.

Much as he might have liked to write exclusively for gifted singers, Herbert could never bring himself to refuse a potentially commercial success. Therefore, in 1906, he readily agreed to collaborate with Henry Blossom on *The Red Mill*, a musical tailored to fit the talents of comedians Dave Montgomery and Fred Stone. The team had scored a great success three years earlier as the Tin Woodman and the Scarecrow in *The Wizard of Oz*. Their new vehicle proved to be just as popular, even though the stars managed to turn the show into more of a rowdy variety act than a book musical. Its run of 274 performances was the longest of any Herbert work performed during his lifetime. (Compare this with *Oklahoma!'s* Broadway encampment of 2,248.)

The score, possibly Herbert's most deliberately commercial one, was as responsible as the stars for the show's great appeal. (Another factor that helped *The Red Mill* succeed was that it had the first moving electric sign ever erected on Broadway.) Included in its succession of attractive melodies were the delicate "Moonbeams"; the piquant hymn to self-satisfaction, "When You're Pretty and the World Is Fair" ("Why be bothered by a thought or care?"); the strutting march, "Every Day Is Ladies' Day with Me"; and "In Old New York," a rollicking paean to the city where "the peach crop's always fine."

Like *The Fortune Teller* and *Mlle. Modiste, Naughty Marietta* was created for a particular prima donna. This was the diminutive Emma Trentini who, with her rotund leading man, Orville Harrold, had been one of the featured singers of Oscar Hammerstein's Manhattan Opera Company. Mounting debts had forced the colorful Hammerstein to return to the world of lighter entertainment and in 1910 he produced *Naughty Marietta* with all the care that he customarily lavished on grand opera.

Herbert's score was equal to the high standards of performance and production. It captured the flavor of old New Orleans so fully that Earl Derr Biggers, then a critic for the Boston *Traveler*, was inspired to write: "The warmth of 'Little Paris' must have been in Mr. Herbert's very blood when he did the score of this piece. Pirates, belles, knights resplendent in haberdashery, roses, convent walls must have danced before his eyes. (Is it proper for a convent wall to dance?) No matter. Romance was in the soul of Mr. Herbert."

NAUGHTY MARIETTA *(1910). Orville Harrold, as Capt. Richard Warrington, and Emma Trentini, as Marietta d'Altena, indulge in some coquettish finger holding.*

The romance in Mr. Herbert's soul has proven to be extremely durable. The buoyant coloratura classic "Italian Street Song" ("Zing, zing, zi-zi-zi-zi-zi-zi ZING BOOM AY!"); the sweeping confession, "I'm Falling in Love with Someone"; the magnolia-drenched " 'Neath the Southern Moon"; the heroic "Tramp, Tramp, Tramp"; the intense, expansive "Ah, Sweet Mystery of Life" —all these were part of a score that, along with Sigmund Romberg's *The Desert Song*, has epitomized the word "operetta" to more people than any other American work.

Soon after the première of *Naughty Marietta*, a young actress named Christie MacDonald won acclaim in *The Spring Maid*, written by Heinrich Reinhardt and the Smith brothers, Harry Bache and Robert Bache. Just three years later, the brothers and Fred De Gresac (a young woman whose real first name was Frederique) collaborated with Victor Herbert to create the delightful *Sweethearts* for Miss MacDonald.

The new work was one of those throughout the history of the musical stage that takes place in a mythical kingdom (in this case, Zilania). Many of the songs are fondly remembered today—the fervent, but impractical title piece, "Sweethearts" ("can live on love alone"), "Game of Love," "Angelus" (developed from the ringing of the actual Angelus), and the bouncy tale of a foiled elopement, "Jeannette and Her Little Wooden Shoes":

SWEETHEARTS *(1913). The ardent Prinz Franz of Zilania (Thomas Conkey) woos the demure Sylvia (Christie Mac-Donald) not knowing that she is really a princess.*

Clip-clop-clop,
Clip-clop-clop,
Over the tiles—
　　Her feet
　　　　were petite,
But you heard her for miles.*

With a modernized book, *Sweethearts* was successfully revived on Broadway in 1947 with Bobby Clark as the star.

Sweethearts was also important in establishing the authority of the American Society of Composers, Authors and Publishers (ASCAP). Herbert, along with composers Silvio Hein, Gustave Kerker, Raymond Hubbell, and Louis Hirsch, librettist Glen MacDonough, publishers George Maxwell and Jay Witmark, and attorney Nathan Burkan, had organized the society in 1914 to ensure that its members would receive whatever royalties were due from public performances of their music. The Society's first test case came the following year when Herbert brought suit against Shanley's Restaurant because its orchestra had played the song "Sweethearts" without authorization. After hearing both sides, Judge Learned Hand ruled against the composer. Herbert appealed to the Circuit Court of Appeals, where the verdict again went against him. Finally the U.S. Supreme Court ruled in favor of Herbert's position, in a decision written by Justice Oliver Wendell Holmes. The power of ASCAP was at last recognized!

The rest of Victor Herbert's career never achieved the heights he reached in his earlier works. Between *The Madcap Duchess* (1913) and the posthumously produced *The Dream Girl* eleven years later, the composer wrote twelve complete scores, plus many songs interpolated in book musicals and revues. Though some of the shows attained respectable runs, they are chiefly remembered because of one or two arias from each—"I Might Be Your Once-in-a-While" from *Angel Face*, "When You're Away" from *The Only Girl*, "Neapolitan Love Song" from *The Princess Pat*, "Thine Alone" and the incongruously titled "Free Trade and a Misty Moon" from *Eileen*, and "A Kiss in the Dark" from *Orange Blossoms*.

Herbert died of a heart attack on May 24, 1924, at the age of sixty-five. None of his contemporaries, and few who succeeded him, achieved as complete a mastery of the art of composing music for the theatre. When he began to compose for the Broadway stage, the most accomplished writers were John Philip Sousa, Reginald DeKoven, and Gustave Kerker. Herbert was unquestionably their superior in melodic inspiration and versatility, yet the musical theater that he represented was not really any more ad-

* From *Sweethearts* (Music by Victor Herbert, Lyrics by Robert B. Smith). Copyright 1913, 1940 by G. Schirmer. Reprinted by permission.

On April 16, 1916, some members of the recently formed American Society of Composers, Authors, and Publishers took part in an Actors's Fund Benefit at the Century Theatre in New York City. Seated at the piano is Oscar Hammerstein I, producer of Naughty Marietta. Standing behind him are Jerome Kern, Louis A. Hirsch, A. Baldwin Sloane, Rudolf Friml, Alfred Robyn, Gustave Kerker, Hugo Felix, John Philip Sousa, Leslie Stuart, Raymond Hubbell, John Golden, Silvio Hein, and Irving Berlin.

Seven years later, a similar group met for a similar purpose. Standing behind Victor Herbert are Gustave Kerker, Raymond Hubbell, Harry Tierney, Louis A. Hirsch, Rudolf Friml, Robert Hood Bowers, Silvio Hein, A. Baldwin Sloane, and Irving Berlin.

vanced than theirs. His chief historical impact was that during the first two decades of the century he stood alone in raising the standards of theatre music and orchestrations. No matter how pressed he was, Herbert always turned out work that revealed great care in both composition and in the way in which the theatre orchestra might best enhance the effectiveness of a score. "Some composers think in terms of the piano," he once said, "but I pay little attention to it. I consider all the resources of orchestra and voice given me to work with. If I did not work out my own orchestrations, it would be as if a painter conceived the idea of a picture and then had someone else paint it."

Victor Herbert was part of the Old World school of sentimental ballads, swirling waltzes, and spirited marches. Within this traditional form, however, he created a richly melodious musical theatre that was so well attuned to the New World that he became the dominant composer of the early days of the American musical theatre.

George M. Cohan.

CHAPTER THREE

George M. Cohan

Victor Herbert and George M. Cohan were the two most important creative figures of the American musical stage during the first decade of the twentieth century. Apart from this, and the coincidence that both were of Irish descent, each man epitomized an entirely disparate form of musical theatre. Herbert, the thoroughly trained musician, sought to perpetuate the traditions of the Viennese operetta; Cohan, the untrained song-and-dance man, tried to break away from anything that suggested the Old World. For Herbert, the Broadway stage was something of a step downward from the elevated world of opera and the concert hall; for Cohan, it was a definite step upward from the world of vaudeville of which he had been a part since birth. Herbert felt that the music and the orchestrations and the singers were the most important elements, but Cohan, who created most of his tunes from four chords he could play on only the black keys of a piano, believed that the essential ingredient of a musical show was "Speed! Speed! And lots of it! That's the idea of the thing. Perpetual motion!"

In a larger sense, both men were symbols of the changes taking place in the age in which they lived. The portly, elegant, mustachioed Victor Herbert was a genuine Victorian figure whose carriage-trade entertainments kept alive the spirit of an earlier day which many people were reluctant to give up, whereas the brash, fast-talking George M. Cohan spoke and sang directly to a new world and to a new century. "Never was a plant more indigenous to a particular part of the earth than was George M. Cohan to the United States of his day," Oscar Hammerstein II once wrote in the New York *Times*. "The whole nation was confident of its superiority, its moral virtue, its happy isolation from the intrigues of the 'old country,' from which many of our fathers and grandfathers had migrated."

While these attitudes shone through most of Cohan's works, the character he himself usually portrayed was not a loud-mouthed braggart. Compared to the exaggerated antics of some of the comedians for whom Victor Herbert wrote—Frank Daniels (with his trick eyebrows), Francis Wilson, Montgomery and Stone—Cohan's characterizations were models of subtlety, frequently in contrast to the razzle-dazzle of his own entertainments. Strutting, prancing, talking a song out of the corner of his mouth in a deep nasal twang, he was the personification of the debonair man of affairs with whom audiences were happy to identify themselves.

As Cohan was the star-composer-lyricist-librettist-director-producer of most of his shows, the public image of the man was taken from his stage roles. And Cohan was delighted to encourage the impression that he was indeed the living incarnation of George Washington, Jr., The Yankee Doodle Boy, The Yankee Prince, The Little Millionaire, The Man Who Owns Broadway, and The Song and Dance Man. Conversely, many of Cohan's stage characters were based on actual people he had met or read about. In *The Governor's Son* and *Running for Office,* Cohan depicted Tammany politicians he became acquainted with at the chowder outings of Big Tim Sullivan, one of the local bosses. For his first hit, *Little Johnny Jones,* he modeled the title part to fit Tod Sloan, a famous American jockey, and for the other main character, "The Unknown," he took as his inspiration the personality of Big Tom Foley, a former New York sheriff. Kid Burns of *Forty-Five Minutes from Broadway* was copied directly from an ex-prizefighter whose name was really Kid Burns.

In his song, "The Yankee Doodle Boy," Cohan said that he was "born on the Fourth of July." This started a myth that has persisted down to today. Actually, it was on the third of July, 1878 (verified by Ward Morehouse, Cohan's biographer), that George Michael Cohan was born in Providence, Rhode Island. His parents, Jeremiah (known as "Jerry") and Helen (known as "Nellie") were vaudeville performers; Georgie first appeared in front of the footlights as an infant, when he was carried on stage during a scene in one of his father's skits, *The Two Dans.* At eight, he played the violin in the pit orchestra; the following year he spoke his first lines on the stage. He later starred in *Peck's Bad Boy,* a part for which the pugnacious youth was exceptionally well qualified. Soon he began to write material for his

The Four Cohans—Jerry, Nellie, Josie, and George.

family's act, The Four Cohans, which consisted of himself, his parents, and his sister Josephine.

Cohan's first song was published when he was sixteen. It was called "Why Did Nellie Leave Her Home?" (the girl was named after his mother), but the pleasures of its publication were greatly lessened when the young composer discovered that another writer, Walter Ford, had been called in to rewrite the lyrics. From then on, however, he wrote all of his own music and words. Some of his early successes were "Hot Tamale Alley" (a favorite of vaudeville star, May Irwin), "Venus, My Shining Love," and "I Guess I'll Have to Telegraph My Baby" ("I need the money bad, 'deed I do").

As a vaudeville act, The Four Cohans had become one of the nation's leading attractions by the turn of the century. In addition to writing all their material, George was also the business manager. He was able to demand the unusually high sum of $1,000 per week for the act in addition to specifying billing, routes, and lengths of engagements. But the uncertainties and discomforts of trouping all over the country made Cohan long for the prestige of appearing on Broadway, not as part of a variety program, but in his own musical comedy. To gain this end, he made a deal with Louis Behman of the Hyde and Behman vaudeville circuit, to have The Four Cohans tour for one season, after which they would star in a musical comedy on Broadway to be produced by Behman. Cohan had already written his Broadway script, based on his own vaudeville sketch, *The Governor's Son.* So it was that the Four Cohans (with the addition of George's new wife, Ethel Levey) toured the country, and the following season, on February 25, 1901, New Yorkers saw the first musical written and directed by George M. Cohan.

27

The Governor's Son had a less-than-brilliant debut. The company, unaccustomed to a New York first-night audience, showed signs of nervousness. The pacing lacked spirit and spark. To make things worse, Cohan sprained his ankle in the first scene and had to limp through the rest of the performance. In spite of the discouraging critical verdict, the twenty-two-year-old author would not accept defeat. He closed the show after a month and took it on the road for a profitable tour. The following year, Cohan tried Broadway again with *Running for Office*, another expanded vaudeville sketch. Again he found New York audiences cool to his efforts.

This show also did well on the road, but it meant little to Cohan; Broadway, as he said, was "the only bell I wanted to ring." So determined was he to win recognition in the legitimate theatre that he formed a partnership in order to have some one to handle the business end while he devoted his time to improving his writing. Through a mutual friend, he met Sam H. Harris, a one-time manager of boxer Terry McGovern, who had had some experience producing melodramas on the Bowery with Al Woods and Paddy Sullivan. After a Sunday ride on a ferryboat, Cohan and Harris shook hands on a business partnership that was to last for fifteen years. (They were also related through marriage. Following his divorce from Ethel Levey in 1907, Cohan married Agnes Nolan, a dancer; two years later, Harris married her sister, Alice.)

Cohan's first Broadway success came in 1904; *Little Johnny Jones* followed the pattern of his first two musicals by opening to generally unfavorable reviews and an apathetic public. The company beat a fast retreat to the road. With Harris now taking care of the business details, however, Cohan could do considerable rewriting while the show was touring. When he bravely brought it back to New York the same season, it suddenly caught on and ran for a respectable three and a half months.

The naïve, patriotic sentimentality of *Little Johnny Jones*, combined with its headlong pace, caught the spirit of a country just beginning to emerge as a world power. Cohan's story of an American jockey wrongly accused of throwing a race in England served as a perfect vehicle for him to project his magnetic personality and to express such honest, direct emotions as the exultant "Yankee Doodle Boy" and "Give My Regards to Broadway." The tunes were meant to be whistled; the lyrics came from the heart. New York, as well as the entire country, soon responded to the electricity of George M. Cohan.

Everything that Cohan had written before 1906 had featured only himself, his family, and the American flag. It was, therefore, an irresistible challenge when producer A. L. (Abraham Lincoln) Erlanger approached him with the idea of writing a vehicle for Fay Templeton, a popular singer and comedienne who had won fame at the Weber and Fields Music Hall.

LITTLE JOHNNY JONES (1904)
Johnny Jones, an American
jockey in England, is slightly
taken aback by the antics of
his girl friend, Goldie Gates.
George M. Cohan, Donald
Brian, and Ethel Levey.

"Think you could write a play without a flag?" Erlanger asked Cohan. Cohan's reply was typically flippant: "I could write a play without anything but a pencil."

Cohan and his pencil created *Forty-Five Minutes from Broadway*, an even bigger hit than *Little Johnny Jones*. Opening on January 1, 1906 (one week after Victor Herbert's *Mlle. Modiste*), it was a well-constructed amalgam of melodrama and songs, among which were "Mary's a Grand Old Name" and "So Long, Mary." The title number, an amusing piece extolling the virtues of country life in New Rochelle, called the natives "Reubens" and noted their "whiskers like hay." These aspersions caused the local Chamber of Commerce to issue a proclamation urging the townspeople to boycott the show, thus giving Cohan some gratuitous publicity. Although Miss Templeton was the star, a young actor named Victor Moore, who had never appeared in a musical comedy before, gave an equally impressive performance as the "square-sporting man," Kid Burns. (When *Forty-Five Minutes from Broadway* was revived in 1912, Cohan himself took the part.)

With *George Washington, Jr.*, Cohan returned to his family and the flag. In spite of its preposterous story which dealt with a rich young man so incensed over his father's Anglomania that he adopted the name of the father of his country, the show succeeded chiefly because of the great

29

FORTY-FIVE MINUTES FROM BROADWAY *(1906). The final scene in the play in which Mary (Fay Templeton) proves her love for Kid Burns (Victor Moore) by tearing up the will that would have made her rich.*

appeal of Cohan and his songs. "I was born in Virgin-YUH! That's the state sure to win YUH!," sang Ethel Levey to the second balcony. With his head cocked to one side, Cohan delivered the irresistible "You're a Grand Old Flag." (Ironically, the song was originally called "You're a Grand Old Rag," but the protests of patriotic organizations forced the Yankee Doodle Boy to substitute "flag" for the affectionate term "rag.")

The originality and freshness soon ran out of George M. Cohan's musicals, even though they still found a wide audience. In 1907, Cohan offered a revised version of *Running for Office* called *The Honeymooners,* and he wrote *The Talk of New York* so that Victor Moore might again portray the popular character of Kid Burns. (The song hits were "When We Are M-A-Double R-I-E-D" and "When a Fellow's on the Level with a Girl That's on the Square.") *Fifty Miles from Boston* in 1908 (in which "Harrigan" was first sung) merely put the familiar Cohan characters into a new New

GEORGE WASHINGTON, JR. *(1906). George M. Cohan, in the title role, spurns the hand of his father, played by Jerry Cohan. (Setting by John Young.)*

THE LITTLE MILLIONAIRE *(1911). George M. Cohan makes an emphatic point to George Parsons. Note size of Cohan's heels.*

HELLO, BROADWAY! (1914). William Collier and George M. Cohan sing "Two Dandy Darkies" in Cohan's first revue.

BROWN BROS.

Rochelle setting—this time North Brookfield, Massachusetts, where the author spent his summers.*

Josie Cohan, who had left the act before *Little Johnny Jones*, was re-united with her family for *The Yankee Prince* in 1908, an occasion that inspired the star to bill himself as "George M. Cohan and his Royal Family." The customary chauvinism of Cohan's plots was here expanded to include a firm stand against the then-current practice of rich American families marrying off their daughters to titled foreigners. Cohan's feelings on the sub-ject were expressed in the song, "I'm to Marry a Nobleman" ("Quite a dutiful girl am I, Going to marry an earl am I"). Two and one-half years later Jerry and Nellie Cohan made their final appearances on the stage. This was in George's *The Little Millionaire*.

The trend toward revues accelerated in the mid-1910's. In an attempt to keep up with the change, Cohan presented *Hello, Broadway!*, "A Musical Crazy Quilt Patched and Threaded Together with Words and Music and Staged by George M. Cohan." There were also two editions of *The Cohan Revue*. Irving Berlin contributed half the score to the second one, which was described by its baseball-loving author as "A Hit and Run Play Batted out by George M. Cohan." These shows presented broad travesties on current theatrical attractions very much in the spirit of the old Weber and Fields burlesques. They always had at least one character who visited various places and entertainments to give them some semblance of a theme. In *Hello, Broad-way!*, for example, Cohan (co-starring with William Collier) played "George Babbit, the Millionaire Kid," whose tour of New York took him to see such attractions as Louise Dresser as "Patsy Pygmalion, a Flower Girl" in a lam-poon of the latest Bernard Shaw comedy, and Peggy Wood impersonating Elsie Ferguson in the dramatic play, *Outcast*. Miss Wood recalls that she was also in the finale, "draped in a costume of white satin decorated with red beads embroidered in stripes, a blue bodice with silver stars, and a spiked crown. I leave it to you what I was as."

Even though younger musical talents, such as Jerome Kern and Irving Berlin, were soon surpassing Cohan in the freshness, skill, and variety of their work, Cohan continued to be active in all phases of the theatre. Yet his most famous World War I song, "Over There," had nothing to do with show business. Skillfully built on the repetition of three bugle call notes and catchy enough to be whistled even after being heard but once, the song became the most popular musical expression of the war. Cohan later wrote

---

* It was during the tryout of *Fifty Miles from Boston* that Donald Brian, the leading man, received an offer to co-star in another musical then in rehearsal. Cohan agreed to release him from his contract and, as Prince Danilo in Lehár's *The Merry Widow*, the young tenor became one of the first matinee idols of the musical theatre.

I'D RATHER BE RIGHT (1937)
*George M. Cohan, as Franklin
D. Roosevelt, delivers a radio
speech in front of a portable
fireplace.*

PHOTO BY ALFREDO VALENTE

34

a sequel to it which enjoyed a brief vogue. It was called "When You Come Back, and You Will Come Back" ("There's a whole world waiting for you").

One of Cohan's great skills was that of play doctor. In 1919, when an old-fashioned cloak-and-dagger operetta called *The Royal Vagabond* was floundering during its out-of-town tryout, Cohan rewrote and restaged it, and turned it into a hit as a "Cohanized Opera Comique." During the run of this show, the famous strike of Actors' Equity was called to compel producers to recognize the recently formed union. Even though Cohan was both an actor and a producer, his loyalties were entirely on the side of management, and he did everything he could to crush the eventually victorious union. For the rest of his career, Cohan steadfastly refused to join Equity and always had to receive special permission to perform.

The irony of this dispute is that throughout the rest of his life Cohan won far greater fame as an actor than as a writer or producer. Indeed, his two most distinguished performances, Nat Miller in Eugene O'Neill's *Ah, Wilderness!* (1934), and President Roosevelt in *I'd Rather Be Right* (1937), were in plays written and produced by others. Although Cohan had already presented two musicals not written by himself (*Mary* and *The O'Brien Girl*, both by Louis Hirsch, Otto Harbach, and Frank Mandel), his impersonation of F.D.R. was his only appearance in a musical created by other talents. It was no secret that while he was happy to be reunited with the producer, Sam Harris, he felt uncomfortable singing the songs Rodgers and Hart had written for him.

George M. Cohan died on November 4, 1942, at the age of sixty-four. As a creative force in the molding of the American musical theatre, however, his influence had ended many years before. His entire appeal as a writer was based on his youthful verve, his breeziness, and his popular flag waving. No matter what he wrote during his later life (his last musical, *Billie*, was produced in 1928), Cohan never progressed beyond the simple entertainments he had created early in the first decade of the century.

Victor Herbert and George M. Cohan were separate and distinct, yet typical, products of their time. They set the pattern for the two different kinds of musicals that were to flourish in the Twenties, the romantic operettas and the fast-moving musical comedies. Even today, we still see their influence at work. *My Fair Lady* may display a dramatic and musical cohesion undreamed of by Herbert, but it does follow in the stunningly theatrical tradition that he represented. And surely, the pace of a George Abbott show or the atmosphere and characters in *The Music Man* prove the lasting appeal of the kind of theatre that first burst upon the scene in the dynamic, sentimental, corny musicals created by George M. Cohan.

Rudolf Friml.

PHOTO BY JOHN ALFRED PIVER. COURTESY G. SCHIRMER, INC.

CHAPTER FOUR

Rudolf Friml

Despite the movement toward a genuinely native musical theatre
that George M. Cohan started, there has always been a large audience
for the sentimental and romantic operettas that are more a part of the Old
World than the New. Victor Herbert's mantle as the leading composer of
operetta in America fell on the shoulders of Rudolf Friml and Sigmund Romberg. Both Friml and Romberg were of European birth, both were thoroughly
schooled in classical music, and both settled in New York in the early 1900's.
Friml, the older, had his last success in 1928 with *The Three Musketeers;*
Romberg, as if to confuse those who like theatrical trends to be neatly
defined, had one of his greatest hits, *Up in Central Park*, as late as 1945.
But the period during which both men scored their greatest triumphs was
roughly from the outbreak of the First World War to the Wall Street Crash.
Between them, Friml and Romberg perpetuated a musical theatre that was
colorful, nostalgic, and melodious—surely as soothing to the tired businessman as a leg show.

Rudolf Friml won fame far quicker than did Sigmund Romberg, although only a year separated their initial contributions to the theatre. In
1912, Friml was suddenly called upon to substitute for Victor Herbert as
composer of *The Firefly*—a task for which he seemed to have had little train-

ing or inclination. He was born in Prague, Bohemia (now Czechoslovakia), on December 7, 1879. At ten, he composed a barcarolle. Four years later, he enrolled in the Prague Conservatory of Music, where he studied composition under Antonin Dvorák. He was such an excellent student that he completed a six-year course in three years. After graduation, Friml went on a concert tour of Europe with a fellow student, the violinist Jan Kubelik; in 1901, they gave their first recital in the United States. Three years later, Friml performed his own composition, the *Piano Concerto in B-Major*, at Carnegie Hall, with Walter Damrosch conducting the New York Symphony. The response to his work was so favorable and his future seemed so assured that the young composer decided to remain in the United States.

In March, 1912, a newspaper item announced that Emma Trentini, then starring in *Naughty Marietta*, would next appear in a new work by Victor Herbert and librettist Otto Abels Hauerbach (since changed to "Harbach"), under the sponsorship of Oscar Hammerstein's son, Arthur. But these plans collapsed the following month. At a special performance of *Naughty Marietta* conducted by Herbert himself, Miss Trentini publicly insulted the composer by refusing to sing an encore of his "Italian Street Song," despite the demands of the audience. Herbert, in a rage, stormed from the orchestra pit, handed the baton to William Axt, the regular conductor, and refused to have anything further to do with the temperamental actress or her next vehicle.

A near-frantic search was then begun to find a suitable replacement for Herbert to compose the score of the forthcoming musical. Because none of the prominent song writers of the day could match Herbert's skill at writing operetta, Hammerstein felt that an unknown composer, one with a thorough background in the classics, would be best suited to take over the assignment. Friml, who had not achieved the stature he had hoped for in the world of concert music, had become interested in composing for the stage. When he heard about the search for someone to do the *Firefly* score, he felt that this might be his big chance. At the urging of Rudolph Schirmer, his publisher, and also of Max Dreyfus of Harms, Inc., Arthur Hammerstein agreed to let the thirty-three-year-old composer take over the assignment. Friml completed the score for *The Firefly* within a month, Signorina Trentini had a second hit in a row, and from then until 1934, the serious, classics-trained composer and pianist devoted himself almost exclusively to the world of Broadway musicals.

The story of *The Firefly* was constructed along familiar Cinderella lines: an Italian street singer disguises herself as a cabin boy to be near the yachtsman she loves, and somehow ends up a prima donna. Though the plot was serviceable, the music and the singing were unquestionably the chief attractions. Critic H. T. Parker, writing in the Boston *Transcript*, observed:

THE FIREFLY (*1912*). *A scene in the first act in which Emma Trentini (supposedly disguised as a cabin boy) exchanges harsh words with Audrey Maple. Looking on are Roy Atwell, Katherine Stewart, Ruby Norton, and Craig Campbell.*

"Mr. Friml writes for an orchestra like a musician, setting it to warm, songful, rhythmic and well-colored accompaniments and not like a Broadway jingler picking out his 'toons' with one finger on the piano and leaving the rest to an assistant and the drum sticks."

Among the best of Friml's melodies are "Giannina Mia" (another Italian street song for the diva), "Love Is Like a Firefly," "When a Maid Comes Knocking at Your Heart," and the swooping waltz, "Sympathy." ("The Donkey Serenade," without which no revival of *The Firefly* would dare be presented, was created for the 1937 film version of the operetta from a piano piece originally called "Chanson.") It should be noted, incidentally, that Emma Trentini's relationship with Rudolf Friml was far more amicable than it had been with Victor Herbert. When Friml's wife divorced him in 1915, she named the singer as corespondent.

With his first attempts for the theatre an immediate success, Friml gladly signed a contract to create additional scores for Arthur Hammerstein. His next three, *High Jinks, Katinka,* and *You're In Love,* were notable hits during the mid-1910's. *High Jinks* (the title referred to a perfume which was sprayed on the audience) contained the waltz "Love's Own Kiss," the coquettish postponement of marriage "Not Now But Later," and the insinuating piece of nonsense:

SOMETIME *(1918). Ed Wynn, as Loney Bright, is slightly dazed by the charms of Argentine dancer Mildred LeGue.*

Something seems tingle—
              ingle—
                    ingle—
                          ingle—
                                ingle-ing

So queer,
Here in your ear,
Nearer and near . . .*

The quasi-oriental "Allah's Holiday" came from *Katinka,* as did "Rackety-Coo" (which had a flock of trained pigeons accompanying the singing), and the inevitable grandiose waltz (with a particularly grandiose title), "'Tis the End, So Farewell." *You're in Love,* in 1917, had the distinction of being the first Broadway musical to employ a young Columbia University graduate, Oscar Hammerstein II, here serving as an assistant stage manager for his uncle's production.

Broadway continued to provide Friml with commercial successes, though many of his assignments during the late 1910's and early 1920's were

* From *High Jinks* (Music by Rudolf Friml, Lyrics by Otto Harbach). Copyright 1913, 1941 by G. Schirmer. Reprinted by permission.

for inferior works. Moreover, their post-war stories and settings found the composer straining to create rhythms and melodies that were contrary to his natural musical inclination. Four of his shows achieved respectable runs during this period—*Sometime* (sometimes written *Some Time*) starring Ed Wynn, with Francine Larrimore and Mae West; *Tumble In,* described as "A Comic Rhapsody in Two Raps and Four Taps"; *The Little Whopper,* featuring Vivienne Segal and David Torrence; and *The Blue Kitten,* with Joseph Cawthorn.

Most of these shows were written for Arthur Hammerstein, whose love of spectacular stage effects led to the production of Rudolf Friml's greatest success. Early in 1924, someone told the producer about an ice carnival held every year in Quebec, the highlight of which was the melting of a huge ice palace. This struck him as an excitingly original scene for the theatre, even though he had no idea how it could be accomplished on a stage. He quickly sent Otto Harbach, and his nephew, Oscar, to Canada to do research on the project. When they arrived they found that no one had ever heard of such a celebration. Even this news did not discourage the elder Hammerstein. So determined was he to have his next musical with a Canadian locale that he told the writers to forget about the ice carnival and the ice palace and to make up their own story. He then hired Friml and Herbert Stothart to compose the score, signed Mary Ellis, Dennis King, and William Kent for the leads, and, in September, 1924, unveiled one of the decade's most enduring musicals, *Rose-Marie*.

ROSE-MARIE *(1924). The ladies of the ensemble as they performed the "Totem Tom-Tom" dance. "One of the most effective chorus numbers we have ever seen," wrote Robert Benchley in* Life. *(Costumes by Charles LeMaire.)*

CULVER PICTURES, INC.

ROSE-MARIE *(1924). According to Arthur Hornblow of* Theatre Magazine, *"Mary Ellis establishes herself as the peer of any musical show star in this country." This is the way she looked in the wedding scene. (Costume by Charles LeMaire.)*

42

In addition to being the first (and only) stage musical to have the Canadian Rockies as a setting, *Rose-Marie* was a pioneering effort in its use of a murder as an important part of the story and in its attempts to integrate the music with the plot. In fact, instead of listing the individual songs, the printed program carried the following message: "The musical numbers of this play are such an integral part of the action that we do not think we should list them as separate episodes. The songs which stand out, independent of their dramatic association, are 'Rose-Marie,' 'Indian Love Call,' 'Totem Tom-Tom,' and 'Why Shouldn't We?' in the first act, and 'The Door of My Dreams' in the second act." The need for such a note may seem pretentious and misleading today as the play did contain many specialty numbers. Nevertheless, there was such an undeniably conscientious attempt to fit songs intelligently within the framework of a plot that Arthur Hornblow of *Theatre Magazine* considered it "head, shoulders, and waist above the customary dribble about Prohibition and Brooklyn."

A year after appearing in *Rose-Marie*, Dennis King starred in another outstanding Friml operetta, *The Vagabond King*. Faced with the competi-

THE VAGABOND KING *(1925).* *Dennis King, as Francois Villon, about to lead the "rabble of low degree." (Costume by James Reynolds.)*

THE THREE MUSKETEERS (1928). *Athos (Douglass Dumbrille), Aramis (Joseph Macaulay), and Porthos (Detmar Poppen) cross swords with the dashing D'Artagnan (Dennis King). Mr. King, according to Percy Hammond, had "the voice of a canary, the grace of a swallow, and the valor of an eagle." (Costumes by John Harkrider; setting by Joseph Urban.)*

tion of *No, No, Nanette, Dearest Enemy,* and *Sunny* all opening within the same seven-day period, *The Vagabond King* was still capable of achieving an impressive run of over 500 performances. Adapted by Brian Hooker and W. H. Post from Justin McCarthy's *If I Were King,* the story told a fanciful tale of how poet François Villon became king of France for a day. Its melodies, rich in emotion and spirit, included "Only a Rose" ("I gi-i-ve you"), "Waltz Huguette," "Some Day," and the earthy, stirring call to arms, "The Song of the Vagabonds":

> Onward! Onward! Swords against the foe!
> Forward! Forward! The lily banners go!*

Friml's last success, *The Three Musketeers,* was presented by Florenz Ziegfeld in 1928. For the third time, Dennis King was the dashing hero of a Friml operetta, this time appearing as D'Artagnan opposite Vivienne Segal as Lady Constance. The production's extreme length (its opening-night performance continued past midnight) prompted Alexander Woollcott's famous comment, "I did greatly enjoy the first few years of Act I." Apparently this did not disturb greedier playgoers who kept the operetta running almost a year.

* Copyright © 1925 by Famous Music Corporation. Copyright renewed 1952 and assigned to Famous Music Corporation.

Although Friml "poured melody out of his sleeve" (in Otto Harbach's phrase), after the Twenties he seemed unable either to keep up with musical and theatrical changes, or to create anything in his accustomed style that could attract the wide and loyal following he once had. There was little appeal in either *Luana* or *Music Hath Charms;* the quickly accelerating changes within the world of musical comedy during the early Thirties had made it imperative for a new work to offer more than soaring, melodic arias. Friml was aware of the change, yet he realized that the modern sophisticated musicals born of the Depression years were not for him. "When I write music for the theatre," he once told an interviewer in the mid-Thirties, "I like books with charm to them. And charm suggests the old things—the finest things that were done long ago. I like a full-bodied libretto with luscious melody, rousing choruses, and romantic passions."

Rudolf Friml was probably the least assimilated composer of the American musical theatre. His European background, his classical training, and his basically Old World outlook combined to give most of his scores—even his earliest ones—a fundamentally old-fashioned quality. That they continue to have great appeal, however, there is no doubt. Though most of the musical comedies of the Twenties and Thirties can no longer be performed as originally written, the rich, emotional music of Rudolf Friml continues to provide occasions of melodic pleasure whenever his operettas are revived. Like Sigmund Romberg, he is a composer whose melodies are best appreciated when heard far from the rush of Broadway, preferably in open-air theatres on balmy, romantic summer evenings.

Sigmund Romberg.

CHAPTER FIVE

Sigmund Romberg

A<small>LTHOUGH BOTH</small> S<small>IGMUND</small> R<small>OMBERG AND</small> R<small>UDOLF</small> F<small>RIML</small> won fame through their series of operettas, the former was a far more prolific and versatile composer. His debut in the musical theatre may have been less auspicious, but he was able to maintain his position there for a much longer period. In fact, no other theatre composer has ever matched Romberg's output: from *The Whirl of the World* in 1914 to the posthumously produced *The Girl in Pink Tights* forty years later, he was the composer or co-composer of fifty-six musicals. These included operettas, musical comedies, spectacles, and revues, all in such profusion that their names are easily confused—*Maytime* and *May Wine, Blossom Time* and *Cherry Blossoms; The Whirl of the World* and *A World of Pleasure; Dancing Around* and *The Dancing Girl; The Magic Melody, Forbidden Melody,* and just plain *Melody.*

Sigmund Romberg was born in Nagy Kaniza, Hungary, on July 29, 1887. His first composition, "The Red Cross March," was written while he was still in elementary school. Although his early fondness for music greatly pleased his parents, they did not want him to become a musician, and so sent him off to Vienna to study engineering. There, away from the stern glances of his parents, he gave only part of his time to academic studies, putting much of his energy toward the study of composition and harmony under Victor Heuberger.

Romberg was interested in almost every kind of music, but became increasingly devoted to operettas. He spent many evenings at the local theatres, viewing the creations of Johann Strauss, Oscar Straus, Franz Lehár, and other prominent Viennese composers. In a vain attempt to dissuade him from following a musical career, Romberg's parents permitted him to take a trip to England and to the United States, hoping that this would give him sufficient time and "maturity" to become convinced of the wisdom of continuing his engineering studies. After two weeks in London, the twenty-two-year-old traveler sailed for New York. On his arrival, he immediately became caught up in the excitement and vitality of the city. Because the money his parents had given him was almost gone, Romberg took a job as a worker in a pencil factory at seven dollars a week. Soon he secured a more suitable position as a pianist in a small East Side café; later, he was hired by a larger restaurant. Determined to remain in New York, Romberg advised his parents that he would not return to Hungary and that he intended to become an American citizen.

He now had a new ambition—he wanted to compose popular songs. The ragtime craze, sparked by Irving Berlin's "Alexander's Ragtime Band," had made revolutionary changes in the kind of music performed in restaurants. As conductor of the orchestra at Bustanoby's, a popular eating place, Romberg was persuaded by music publisher Edward Marks to try to write a turkey trot in the style of a popular French tune, "Très Moutarde." Romberg deliberately copied its rhythm for his first two published songs, "Some Smoke" and "Leg of Mutton"—even adding alternate French titles, "De la Fumée" and "Le Gigot," to emphasize the relationship. They became instantly popular with the restaurant's patrons, as did another early effort, a waltz called "The Poem" ("Le Poème").

The first two numbers attracted the attention of J. J. Shubert, a steady customer at Bustanoby's. J. J. and his brother, Lee, were successful Broadway producers and theatre owners whose large organization turned out both dramatic and musical attractions with almost assembly-line precision. The brothers had built the Winter Garden Theatre as a showcase for a series of lavish musicals to be offered on a well-regulated time table—a different spectacle for the fall and spring, plus an annual revue called *The Passing Show* during the summer. Louis Achille Hirsch and Jean Schwartz had collaborated with librettist-sketchwriter-lyricist Harold Atteridge on most of the Winter Garden shows, and Hirsch was to be the composer for the next offering, *The Whirl of the World,* scheduled to open in January, 1914. But just as an argument between Victor Herbert and Emma Trentini had brought about Rudolf Friml's first Broadway score, so a disagreement between Hirsch and J. J. Shubert was responsible for winning Romberg his first assignment. However, the two commissions were completely dissimilar.

Shubert wanted Romberg to provide innocuous, pleasant tunes for his extravaganza. Never, under any circumstances, was the music to detract from the scenic splendor, the antics of the comedians, or the bevy of girls, girls, girls. Indeed, in a brochure heralding the pleasures of *The Whirl of the World,* the entertainment was enticingly described as "An Isle of Gorgeousness, Fun and Music, Entirely Surrounded by Girls. Wherever You Look—Just Girls. Whenever You Look—Just Girls." Although this advertisement named the leading members of the cast (Lillian Lorraine, Bernard Granville, Eugene and Willie Howard, Walter C. Kelly, Rozsika Dolly), there was no mention at all of the composer. Moreover, the critics paid scant attention to the music. So overcome by the isle of gorgeousness was Alan Dale of the *American* that he devoted part of his review to the mock warning: "Oh, mothers of lads, send your susceptible ones to *The Philanderer*—or, er, Forbes-Robertson, but keep them, aye, keep them from the Winter Garden!"

Romberg was young and ambitious, and though the score brought little fame or satisfaction, he became convinced that the best way for him to succeed was to accept Shubert's offer to become a staff composer. The work would be steady, he would be paid well, and he was confident that some day he would have the opportunity to show his talent.

With Atteridge as collaborator, the new cog in the Shubert theatrical wheel ground out a lengthy procession of songs for revues and spectacles, most of which have long been forgotten. But there were the occasionally compensating pleasures of working with talented performers. Marilyn Miller returned from the Lotus Club in London to make her Broadway debut singing Romberg's "Omar Khayyam" in *The Passing Show of 1914.* Al Jolson,

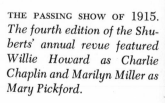

THE PASSING SHOW OF 1915. *The fourth edition of the Shuberts' annual revue featured Willie Howard as Charlie Chaplin and Marilyn Miller as Mary Pickford.*

CULVER PICTURES, INC.

THE BLUE PARADISE (1915). Ted Lorraine and Vivienne Segal seem to be powerless to keep Teddy Webb from choking on a loaf of bread.

who had first attracted notice in *Vera Violetta* in 1911, became a star in *Dancing Around*, though many of his specialty numbers were written by other composers.

Romberg also received assignments to add music to European importations. One of these was *The Blue Paradise*, produced in 1915. Based on a Viennese operetta for which Edmund Eysler had created the original score, it was a tender, nostalgic musical about a fleeting romance at an inn called The Blue Paradise. For the important scene in which the young girl must say a final goodbye to her lover, the composer wrote the touching waltz, "Auf Wiedersehn," which became his first successful song. (The words were by Herbert Reynolds, who had been the lyricist for Jerome Kern's first big hit, "They Didn't Believe Me," the previous year.)

The Blue Paradise was also responsible for beginning a notable theatrical career. After the leading soprano had proved unsatisfactory during the tryout, a search was made to find a suitable replacement. Because none of the professional singers auditioned seemed right for the part of the innocent and unspoiled heroine, the Shuberts decided to take a chance on an eighteen-year-old vocal student at the Curtis Institute of Music in Philadelphia. The girl was Vivienne Segal, who managed to give a memorable opening-night performance after only four days of rehearsing.

From *The Whirl of the World* to *The Passing Show of 1917*, Sigmund Romberg worked on fourteen musicals—all within twenty-six months! There was nothing about these entertainments to inspire a composer of Romberg's temperament; his melodies served the purpose for which they were written and little more. However, his next assignment, *Maytime*, made him optimistic that, at last, his hack-writing days would be over. Adapted by Rida Johnson Young from a Viennese operetta, it starred Peggy Wood and Charles Purcell in just the kind of sentimental, bittersweet romance that the composer loved, and for which he would create his most endearing music. Heralded in advertisements as "Fragrant as Flowers in May," *Maytime* was brimming full of melodic warmth, with the touching waltz "Will You Remember?" and the expressive "Road to Paradise" as its most lasting songs. The musical's immense popularity also made it unique in theatre history. Within a year after its August, 1917, première at the Shubert Theatre, a second New York company opened at the 44th Street Theatre almost directly opposite.

MAYTIME *(1917). Young Ottillie Van Zandt and Richard Wayne are a rich girl and a poor boy who have fallen in love. Peggy Wood played Ottillie and Charles Purcell was Richard. According to Miss Wood,* Maytime *was the show the boys all asked to see before they went overseas.*

The image of the new Romberg, however, could not replace the old. Shubert made him follow *Maytime* with such transient diversions as *Doing Our Bit* (with Ed Wynn, Frank Tinney, and the Duncan Sisters); *Over the Top* (the first New York musical to feature two youngsters from Nebraska, Fred and Adele Astaire); *Sinbad* (Romberg's third show for Al Jolson, but again full of interpolated numbers); and two more of the inevitable *Passing Shows* (these featuring the Astaires, Willie and Eugene Howard, Nita Naldi, Charles Winninger, and James Barton).

Enough, this time, was enough. Critics were beginning to look upon *Maytime* as an accident, and the name Sigmund Romberg was again becoming a synonym for Shubert hack. As soon as he had finished his assignment for *The Passing Show of 1919*, Romberg broke with the producers to form his own producing organization with Max R. Wilner. Although they had ambitious plans, neither of their productions, *The Magic Melody* and *Love Birds*, was successful. When the partnership was dissolved after only two years, the composer reluctantly went back to his former employers. (During this period of independence, Romberg also contributed eight songs to Lew Fields's *Poor Little Ritz Girl*, which had originally been intended as the sole product of a new song-writing team, Richard Rodgers and Lorenz Hart.)

Upon his return, Romberg was given an assignment that J. J. Shubert was sure would please him. Dorothy Donnelly had adapted *Blossom Time*

BLOSSOM TIME *(1921). Olga Cook (as Mitzi) listens as Bertram Peacock (as Franz Schubert) plays his "Song of Love."*

BROWN BROS.

from a Viennese operetta, *Das Dreimaderlhaus,* for which Heinrich Berté had rearranged well-known themes by Franz Schubert into appropriate vocal arias. Convinced that Romberg could do a better job of organizing the songs than Berté had done, Shubert wanted the composer to scrap the previous arrangements and to create his own. Although the idea of tampering with another composer's works did not appeal to Romberg, he was greatly in need of money and reluctantly accepted the commission.

The plot of *Blossom Time,* accurately described by Romberg's biographer, Elliott Arnold, as "the old *Cyrano de Bergerac* story played somewhat in reverse," was a fictitious piece about Franz Schubert's unrequited love for a girl named Mitzi. In spite of its high sugar content, the operetta became a favorite of both critics and public. Even the usually acerbic George S. Kaufman, then a reviewer for the *Times,* wrote of the "songs of passionate longing that illuminate *Blossom Time* like pictures in a Christmas book." Four road companies set out soon after it opened on September 29, 1921, thereby beginning the celebrated cross-country association of Schubert and Shubert.

Despite Romberg's preference for tender romances, the Shubert brothers' formula of musical creation could not be altered to suit one composer. The week after *Blossom Time* opened on Broadway, *Bombo,* another Romberg vehicle for Jolson, had its première. Indeed, it was not until three years had elapsed (and ten musicals had expired) that Shubert again

BOMBO *(1921). Romberg was the nominal composer of this Al Jolson hit, but other writers were called in to contribute such songs as "Toot Toot Tootsie," "April Showers," and "My Mammy."*

53

THE STUDENT PRINCE IN HEI-
DELBERG (1924). *Peeking out
from behind the roses are the
romantic duo, Prince Karl
(Howard Marsh) and Kathy
(Ilse Marvenga).*

offered the composer a score worthy of his ability. Billed as "A Stupendous
Musical Production," *The Student Prince in Heidelberg* was in the direct
line of *The Blue Paradise* and *Maytime,* as it told of the fleeting love affair
between Prince Karl (Howard Marsh) and a waitress named Kathy (Ilse
Marvenga) in the university city of Heidelberg. The story provided the com-
poser with inspiration for some of his most dulcet melodies and robust
rhythms — "Golden Days," "To the Inn We're Marching," "The Drinking
Song" (a great favorite with Prohibition audiences), "Deep in My Heart,
Dear," and "Serenade." With a total of 608 performances in New York,
The Student Prince had the longest run of any Romberg operetta.

It had taken almost eleven years, but Sigmund Romberg had finally
achieved the eminence of a composer who could choose his own assignments
—and producers. For Ziegfeld he did the successful *Louie the 14th* (referring to a waiter named Louie, played by Leon Errol, who was hired as the
fourteenth guest at a dinner party), and for the new producing team of
Laurence Schwab and Frank Mandel, he created the music for that exotic
saga of burning dunes and lofty tunes, *The Desert Song.* Originally known as
Lady Fair, this production marked the composer's first association with Otto
Harbach and Oscar Hammerstein II, who supplied the lyrics and collabo-

THE DESERT SONG (1926). *A moment of high drama in French Morocco, as Margot Bonvalet (Vivienne Segal) pleads with Gen. Birabeau (Edmund Elton) to spare the life of the Red Shadow (Robert Halliday). Also deeply concerned is the native girl, Azuri (Pearl Regay). (Costumes by Vyvyan Donner and Mark Mooring; setting by Woodman Thompson.)*

rated on the book with Mandel. Its cast was headed by Robert Halliday and Vivienne Segal (as in *The Blue Paradise*, she had been called in just before the opening to replace another actress), with Eddie Buzzell as the leading comic. The score, still a great favorite, contained the smoldering title song, the muscular "Riff Song," the ardent "One Alone," and the slightly out-of-place tribute to the Elinor-Glyn-Clara Bow influence, simply called "It."

The remarkable durability of *The Desert Song* has made most people forget that it received a mixed critical reception when it opened in 1926, and that a full month elapsed before it caught on with the public. The sheik plot was so old fashioned that Richard Watts, Jr., began his *Herald Tribune* review with: "The question of how simple-minded the book of a musical comedy can be was debated last night, and the verdict arrived at was 'no end.'" But the songs, combined with an enticing locale that has always conjured up an atmosphere of mystery and grand passion, still make *The Desert Song*

ROSALIE *(1928). Jack Donahue, George Gershwin, Sigmund Romberg, Marilyn Miller, and Florenz Ziegfeld backstage during a rehearsal.*

one of the small group of musicals that summer-theatre managers can always depend on to play to packed houses.

The Shubert brothers induced Romberg back to write for a few moderately popular attractions, and one, *My Maryland* (based on Clyde Fitch's *Barbara Frietchie*), that was a decided hit. With many producers now bidding for his services, the composer agreed to undertake two commissions at almost the same time: Schwab and Mandel signed him to compose the music for *The New Moon*, and Ziegfeld hired him for *Rosalie.*

Because of the problem created by writing two scores almost simultaneously, Romberg insisted that George Gershwin be called in to share the work on *Rosalie*. The results may have been musically anachronistic, but Marilyn Miller and Jack Donahue helped make the up-to-date operetta a huge success. (The story was particularly timely, inspired as it was by the recent well-publicized visit to New York of Queen Marie of Rumania and her daughter, Princess Ileana. Also, one of the leading characters was modeled after Lindbergh.)

The New Moon could have used all of Romberg's time. With a book written by Hammerstein, Mandel, and Schwab, the show was such a disaster when it opened in Philadelphia in December, 1927, that it was quickly withdrawn for repairs. The libretto was completely rewritten, an almost entirely new score was composed, and major replacements were made in the cast. What should have been titled *The New, New Moon* reopened eight months later in Cleveland. This time all went well, and it soon began a highly profitable New York engagement. Starring Robert Halliday and Evelyn Herbert, the musical was very much in the accepted tradition of Graustarkian operetta, even though its adventuresome tale was based on an actual historical occurrence. As for the performances, according to Robert Benchley, "We haven't seen such refayned acting since the days when the Mysterious Stranger with the white plume turned out to be Prince Boris in disguise. And *then* what merry-making at the inn there was! A toast, a toast to Prince Boris!"

The score of *The New Moon* contained more hits than any other Romberg musical—"One Kiss" (echoing Vincent Youmans' "No, No, Nanette"), "Wanting You," "Stouthearted Men," "Lover, Come Back to Me" (described by critic Percy Hammond as "A hot torch psalm"), and "Softly, As in a Morning Sunrise" (which has prompted some unromantic souls to question if there is any other kind).

In addition to many motion picture assignments in the 1930's, Romberg continued to compose for the theatre, though with lessened activity and success. The moderately popular *May Wine*, written with Frank Mandel and Oscar Hammerstein II, was somewhat daring because it dealt with psycho-

THE NEW MOON *(1928). Robert Halliday, Evelyn Herbert, and William O'Neal find happiness on a peaceful island after arriving on the good ship* New Moon. (*Costumes by Charles LeMaire.*)

analysis and because it also eliminated the customary chorus line. Nevertheless, the story was still so basically time-worn that George Jean Nathan dismissed it as "a musical mothball laid scenically in Vienna and critically in Cain's."

Like Friml, Romberg cared little about keeping up with musical trends. For a while, when it seemed that audiences no longer appreciated his type of musical theatre, he abandoned composing to form an orchestra. It toured successfully during the early Forties, giving concerts devoted to semiclassical music, with an emphasis on his own compositions.

Romberg returned to Broadway in 1945 with *Up in Central Park*. The previous year, producer Michael Todd had read a book about the corrupt political leader, Boss Tweed, and his gang. This gave him an idea for a musical of old New York that would contrast the machinations of Tweed and Tammany Hall with the simple pastoral pleasures of Central Park. When Todd approached Herbert and Dorothy Fields to write the book, they immediately thought of Romberg for the music. The opportunity to create another period score proved irresistible, and he readily agreed to compose the music, with Miss Fields supplying the lyrics. Their songs succeeded admirably in capturing the nostalgic, Currier and Ives atmosphere of the production, most

UP IN CENTRAL PARK *(1945). Helen Tamiris' "Skating Ballet" was in the manner of an animated Currier and Ives print. (Costumes by Grace Houston and Ernest Schraps; setting by Howard Bay.)*

notably in "The Big Back Yard," "Carousel in the Park," "April Snow," and "Close as Pages in a Book." The libretto may have been moldy, but wartime audiences found in the musical enough of the romantic charm of a bygone day to make it one of Romberg's longest-running hits.

The composer's last two theatrical ventures were also set in New York in the nineteenth century. Neither one, however, did well at the box office. *My Romance*, adapted from Edward Sheldon's play, *Romance*, was Romberg's first Shubert production in eighteen years. Other than making a star of Anne Jeffreys, however, it offered little that was noteworthy.

On November 10, 1951, at the age of sixty-four, Romberg died of a cerebral hemorrhage. The show he was working on at the time, *The Girl in Pink Tights*, was produced two and a half years later, with a score completed by Don Walker. Its historically accurate account of the first American musical comedy, *The Black Crook*, may have been fairly dull, but it did serve well enough to display the ample talents of Jeanmaire, the dynamic French dancer, making her first appearance in a Broadway musical.

Once when he was asked about musical trends, Sigmund Romberg replied, "I don't care what the form is. But a melody is still a melody. Nothing succeeds like a popular tune—a romantic tune. Romantic music will never die because deep at the roots of all people is the theme of love." Today, we might add to the Romberg observation that nothing succeeds like a Romberg operetta—particularly in the summertime. Whether they are presented in the open or under a tent; whether with amateurs, semiprofessionals, or all-Equity casts, the hardiest, most perennial summer-theatre attractions are the melodious, old-fashioned, but enduring works overflowing with sentiment, charm, and romance. Indeed, as the Jerry Bock–Sheldon Harnick song, "Summer Is," so delightfully tells us:

> Winter is gloves and homburg,
> Winter is cold cement;
> Summer is Sigmund Romberg
> In a music tent.*

* Reprinted by permission of Valando Music Corp.

Jerome Kern.

PHOTO BY ALFREDO VALENTE

CHAPTER SIX

Jerome Kern

FRANZ LEHAR's *The Merry Widow* swirled into New York at the New Amsterdam Theatre on October 21, 1907. Not only did it become the supreme musical attraction of the period, but it also inaugurated Broadway's greatest influx of European-originated or European-inspired operettas. Thereafter, for almost a decade, anything that had been shown on the banks of the Thames, the Seine, or, even better, the Danube, was imported by hopeful producers anxious to duplicate the success of the Lehár work. Of course, American writers were also creating musical entertainments. But apart from the George M. Cohan shows and the elaborate Ziegfeld and Shubert revues, the strains of the waltz heard in the Kingdom of Graustark set the musical pattern on Broadway for at least ten years.

This pattern may be detected merely from the titles of some of the leading importations. After *The Merry Widow* came *The Gay Hussars* by Emmerich Kalman, followed by Oscar Straus's *The Chocolate Soldier* and Lehár's *The Count of Luxembourg*. Female royalty of the day included *The Dollar Princess, The Slim Princess, The Balkan Princess*, and *The Merry Countess* (which was just another name for Johann Strauss's *Die Fledermaus*). Ladies of less noble birth were ardently serenaded in *The Spring Maid, The Pink Lady, The Quaker Girl, The Doll Girl*, and even *The Peasant*

Girl. Broadway also had a *Sunshine Girl* by Paul Rubens and a *Midnight Girl* by Jean Briquet, while *The Girl from Montmartre, The Maid of Athens,* and *The Girl from Brazil* used titles designed to emphasize the exotic nature of their respective locales.

Although such a grand parade of grand operettas did occasionally provide evenings that were entertaining, these productions usually proved to be just too heavy, in their original form, for American audiences. It was often necessary to call in an American composer—or, at least, one familiar with American audiences—to provide some light, bright tunes to make them more palatable. The man most often chosen for this musical grafting was a young, studious-looking song-writer named Jerome Kern. Kern had the knack of injecting a new lilt into the most soporific operettas; frequently, his would be the only songs in the scores to achieve any kind of popularity with sheet-music and record buyers.

These assignments gave Kern steady work for over ten years. Yet he was well aware that there was something wrong with a musical theatre that made such interpolations necessary, and he was determined that some day he would do what he could to rid the stage of patchwork scores and the artificial extravaganzas for which they were assembled. The Princess Theatre musicals in the mid-1910's gave him his long-desired opportunity. They were fresh, intimate, well-integrated shows, full of youth and melody, and they served better than anything else to establish Kern's reputation as a composer.

Perhaps more important than their popular acceptance, Kern's songs and musicals had an incalculable influence on future theatre composers. In 1914, a sixteen-year-old boy named George Gershwin attended his aunt's wedding at the Grand Central Hotel. After listening to the orchestra play Kern's "You're Here and I'm Here" from *The Laughing Husband,* he became so impressed with the number that he resolved to try to emulate the composer's invigorating style. Two years later, Richard Rodgers, then fourteen, saw Jerome Kern's musical, *Very Good Eddie,* at least a dozen times at the Standard Theatre at Broadway and 90th Street in order to absorb what he could of its sparkling and original music.

Years later, in recalling those days, Rodgers wrote in the New York *Times:* "Kern was typical of what was, and still is, good in our general maturity in this country in that he had his musical roots in the fertile middle European and English school of operetta writing, and amalgamated it with everything that was fresh in the American scene to give us something wonderfully new and clear in music writing."

Jerome David Kern was born in New York, on January 27, 1885. His father, Henry Kern, owned the street sprinkling concession in Manhattan; his mother, Fanny, was a gifted pianist and Jerome's first teacher. Soon after his son was born, the elder Kern sold his business to open a merchandising store in Newark, New Jersey, where "Romie" Kern attended grammar and high school. Because of his interest in music, he soon became proficient at the organ, and also composed songs for the school plays. In spite of this interest, however, his father insisted that he go into the family business. One of his first assignments was to buy two pianos from a dealer in New York. The man proved to be so persuasive that the seventeen-year-old buyer was talked into purchasing *two hundred* pianos. This experience convinced Kern's enraged father that his son was no businessman (though he eventually sold all two hundred at a profit) and he gave in to his wife's and his son's entreaties: Jerome could go to music school.

At the New York College of Music, Kern studied piano and harmony for about a year. He then persuaded his father to let him go to Europe for further studies in theory and composition. After spending some time on the Continent, he went to London, where he was able to secure a song-writing job with producer Charles Frohman. The task was rather menial, but it was good experience. In those days, English audiences always arrived fashionably late to the theatre; to accommodate this custom, unrelated songs were usually interpolated at the start of the shows to fill in the time while people were being seated. Kern created many such numbers, few of which received any notice.

Kern returned to New York in the fall of 1904 determined to find a place in the world of musical comedy. His work in London, unimportant though it was, had convinced him that only in the theatre could he write the kind of music for which he was best suited and which gave him the greatest personal satisfaction. With this goal in mind, he planned his career with considerable foresight. Following a brief period as a song-plugger for the Lyceum Publishing Company (which had published his first piece, "At the Casino," even before he entered the New York College of Music), he was hired by Max Dreyfus of T. B. Harms as a salesman. Since Harms was a leading publisher of theatre scores, this enabled Kern to become friendly with many of the people associated with the musical theatre. He quickly convinced them of his talents as a pianist, and whenever the need arose for someone to serve as a rehearsal pianist, it was Jerome Kern who was most frequently in demand. Once hired, he would take every opportunity he could —usually during the lunch period or during rehearsal breaks—to play his own compositions. These tunes often sounded much fresher than anything in the original score—particularly after weeks of rehearsing the same numbers— and presently a song or two by Jerome Kern would be added to the production.

Kern's first important assignment came in 1904 when he revised the score of an English show, *Mr. Wix of Wickham,* to fit the special talents of Julian Eltinge, the celebrated female impersonator, who was making his first appearance in a musical comedy. The composer's efforts won the critical approbation of the *American's* Alan Dale, who wrote: "Its music by Jerome D. Kern towers in such an Eiffel way above the hurdy-gurdy, penny-in-the-slot primitive accompaniment to the musical show that criticism is disarmed."

The next year, Kern had his first song hit, "How'd You Like to Spoon with Me?", set to a lyric by Edward Laska. Included in another English importation, *The Earl and the Girl*, the fetching invitation was posed by a bevy of six young ladies, all dressed in organdy, who sat on flower-bedecked swings that swung out over the audience.

Between *The Earl and the Girl* in 1905 and *The Red Petticoat*, Kern's first complete score five years later, the composer had songs interpolated in *The Catch of the Season*, *The Rich Mr. Hoggenheimer*, *The Dairy Maids*, *Fascinating Flora*, *Fluffy Ruffles*, *The Dollar Princess*, *The Gay Hussars*, *The Kiss Waltz*, and at least a dozen others. He was also co-composer of *The King of Cadonia* and *La Belle Paree*. The latter ("A Cook's Tour through Vaudeville with a Parisian Landscape"), was part of the program offered as the initial attraction of the Winter Garden Theatre. Making his Broadway debut in the show was Al Jolson, who played Erastus Sparkle, "a colored aristocrat of San Juan Hill, cutting a wide swath in Paris." *La Belle Paree* was one of the few productions Kern was associated with at the time that did not owe its origin to a work created in Europe.

The Red Petticoat was another all-American product. Adapted by Rida Johnson Young from her play *Next!*, the musical dealt with the adventures of a lady barber, Sophie Brush (played by Helen Lowell), in the silver-

LA BELLE PAREE *(1911). This "Jumble of Jollity" was the featured attraction of the first program at the Winter Garden. Among the identifiable members of the cast are Kitty Gordon (fourth from left), Mitzi Hajos (sixth from left), and Stella Mayhew and Al Jolson (seventh and eighth from right). It was Jolson's first appearance in a Broadway show.*

THE GIRL FROM UTAH *(1914). Joseph Cawthorn, Julia Sanderson, and Donald Brian.*

mining town of Lost River, Nevada. The lode was not a rich one, for the musical only ran for two months, but it did have the distinction of being the first musical comedy western.

Even after *The Red Petticoat,* Kern continued to supply additional songs for imported shows. Such an assignment was the somewhat misleadingly titled *The Girl from Utah,* an English musical with an English setting about a girl *from* Utah. Although the show had been a hit in London, producer Charles Frohman left nothing to chance. He hired Donald Brian, Julia Sanderson, and Joseph Cawthorn for the leads and commissioned Jerome Kern and Harry B. Smith to provide at least five new numbers. One of the additional songs, the soft, lovely "They Didn't Believe Me," was a contribution of Kern and M. E. (Michael Elder) Rourke, who had just begun to write lyrics under the pen name of Herbert Reynolds. As sung by Miss Sanderson and Mr. Brian, it not only became the outstanding song in the show, but it established Jerome Kern as one of the leading musical talents in the theatre.

His next endeavor, *90 in the Shade,* was a quick failure. Nevertheless, it served to begin his association with a young English librettist, Guy Regi-

65

nald Bolton. About this time (1915), F. Ray Comstock was having difficulties in presenting suitable attractions at his 299-seat Princess Theatre. He mentioned his problem to Elisabeth Marbury, a well-known literary agent, who came up with an idea: why not put on a series of musicals? "Everyone seems to be reforming the drama," she told him. "Various societies are doing their best to elevate it. It seems to me that now is the time for someone to do the same thing for musical comedy." Comstock agreed to give the plan a trial. He also made Bessie Marbury his co-producer and, at her suggestion, hired Guy Bolton and Jerome Kern to supply the librettos and the music.

The Princess Theatre musicals gave the thirty-year-old composer the chance he had been waiting for. The new shows would have modern stories dealing with people caught in comic but believable situations, uncluttered by massed choruses or spectacular scenery. The casts would be limited to about thirty, the orchestra would consist of eleven pieces, and there would be only two sets in each production. But most important to Kern was that he could at last create songs that would be introduced logically and meaningfully into the action of the play without the usual lengthy and obvious song cues.

The project was undeniably risky. Broadway audiences seemed to be satisfied with the elaborate costume musicals that were still the biggest drawing card in the musical theatre. Also, many theatre people doubted that such an adventurous scheme could attract customers to the tiny playhouse. Indeed, the first of the Princess Theatre series, *Nobody Home,* was a compromise between new and old. It was based on Paul Rubens' English musical, *Mr. Popple of Ippleton,* and even contained a few interpolated songs. However, Kern and Bolton (aided by at least three other lyricists) managed to turn it into what the ads called "a zippy, fox trotty musical treat," and its run of four months was decidedly encouraging. (It later toured with Fanny Brice succeeding Adele Rowland in the leading feminine role.)

By December, 1915, when they offered the second attraction, *Very Good Eddie,* Kern and his associates had perfected the new technique to such a degree that the show was an instant hit. The original libretto by Philip Bartholomae and Guy Bolton may not have been marked by any literary distinction, but it told a credible, human story about two average honeymooning couples and the comic situations that arise when they become separated on a Hudson River steamboat. As Bolton wrote in his book *Bring on the Girls!:* "It was the first of its kind to rely on situation and character laughs instead of using clowning and Weberfieldian cross-talk with which the large-scale musical filled in between the romantic scenes."*

---

* From *Bring on the Girls!* by P. G. Wodehouse and Guy Bolton. New York: Simon and Schuster, Inc.

VERY GOOD EDDIE *(1915).*
Eddie (Ernest Truex) finds
himself in the embarrassing
situation of going on a honey-
moon with another man's
bride. The equally embar-
rassed lady is Alive Dovey.

In addition, *Very Good Eddie* had a particularly winning score which included "Some Sort of Somebody" (the lyric was by Elsie Janis, who had previously introduced it in *Miss Information*); Ernest Truex's "Thirteen Collar," and the plaintive "Babes in the Wood." The show played one year in New York (it moved to a larger theatre after five months at the Princess), and then toured for another year.

At the opening night of *Very Good Eddie*, Kern met an old friend, P. G. (Pelham Granville) Wodehouse, with whom he had once collaborated on some songs for a London musical, *The Beauty of Bath*. Kern introduced Bolton to Wodehouse, the three had supper together, and before the evening ended they had agreed to form a partnership with Bolton and Wodehouse collaborating on the librettos and Wodehouse writing the lyrics to Kern's compositions.

The new team lost little time. During 1917, Bolton, Wodehouse, and Kern collaborated on four musicals—*Have a Heart, Oh, Boy!, Leave It to Jane,* and *Miss 1917* (an unsuccessful revue with music also by Victor Herbert). *Have a Heart* was originally intended to follow *Very Good Eddie* at the Princess. Unknown to Kern and Bolton, however, Wodehouse had already promised the musical to Col. Henry W. Savage, the producer of

67

OH BOY! *(1917). Tom Powers and Marie Carroll are the ones in the center being joined in matrimony by a justice of the peace. To their left are Hal Forde and Anna Wheaton. Edna May Oliver is second from the right. Justine Johnstone (far left) and Marion Davies (third from left) were recent graduates of the Ziegfeld Follies.*

The Merry Widow. Billed as "An Up-to-Date Musical Comedy," *Have a Heart* had some attractive melodies ("And I Am All Alone," "The Road That Lies Before"), and an amusing title song which revealed the deep concern felt by a remarkably solicitous department-store owner for the welfare of his employees.

Kern and Bolton (plus Wodehouse) returned to the Princess Theatre shortly thereafter for their greatest triumph, *Oh, Boy!* According to Bolton's claim at the time, the musical was one in which "every song and lyric contributed to the action. The humor was based on situation, not interjected by the comedians." Recruited for its cast were Marion Davies and Justine Johnstone, two of Ziegfeld's most celebrated showgirls, who had small but decorative roles in support of the principals, Anna Wheaton, Tom Powers, Marie Carroll, Hal Forde, and Edna May Oliver. The sprightly "Till the Clouds Roll By" was the most popular song.

Although it was not presented at the Princess Theatre, *Leave It to Jane* was created for the Princess Theatre management, and everyone concerned made sure that it adhered to the prescribed rules of integration and intimacy. As one of the earliest musicals to use a college campus for a setting, it gave the composer and lyricist the opportunity to write songs dealing with such historical and literary subjects as "Sir Galahad," "Cleopatterer," and the legend of the Lorelei in the willowy "Siren's Song." More modern sentiments were expressed in the go-getter's anthem, "Just You Watch My Step," while the entire company energetically joined in the advice to leave it to Jane, Jane, Jane. The show was so coherent and logical in its libretto, lyrics, and music that Alan Dale was moved to comment in the New York *American*: "No more are we asked to laugh at the bottle-nosed comedian as he falls down stairs; no longer is the heroine a lovely princess masquerading as the serving maid, and no more is the scene Ruritania or Monte Carlo. Today is rationally American, and the musical show has taken on a new lease of life."

The second and last musical by Bolton, Wodehouse, and Kern to play the Princess was the exclamatory successor to *Oh, Boy!*, called *Oh, Lady! Lady!!* The plot of the new work was concerned with pre- and post-marital complications on Long Island and in Greenwich Village, and its cohesion between song and story was equal to that achieved in its predecessor. Seldom before had Kern's music or Wodehouse's lyrics been more delectable. In "Before I Met You," both Vivienne Segal and Carl Randall, in the leading

COURTESY HELEN RICH

LEAVE IT TO JANE (1917). *Posing on the campus of good old Atwater College are Arlene Chase, Oscar Shaw, Helen Rich, Olin Howland, Tess Mayer, and Ruloff Cuttin.*

OH, LADY! LADY!! *(1918). The happy newlyweds, Mollie (Vivienne Segal) and Willoughby French (Carl Randall). (Setting by Clifford Pember.)*

roles, admitted to previous loves—she had had a crush on John Drew when she was nine and he had been enamored of Lillian Russell when he was fourteen. "Not Yet" was an amusingly coquettish postponement of marriage, and in "Greenwich Village" Broadway had its first musical description of New York's Latin Quarter.

One song sung by Miss Segal during the tryout was dropped from the score before the New York première. It was a torch ballad in which the singer, after dreaming of her ideal man in the verse, then admitted:

> Along came Bill
> Who's quite the opposite
> Of all the men
> In story books.
> In grace and looks
> I know that Apollo
> Would beat him all hollow . . .*

This lyric, however, did not accurately describe the talented and handsome Carl Randall (who played the part of Willoughby French). Therefore, another song, "Do Look at Him," in which Bill did live up to the man of Miss

* Copyright © 1918 by T. B. Harms Company, New York. Copyright renewed.

70

Morris Gest (coproducer of Leave It to Jane), *P. G. Wodehouse, Guy Bolton, F. Ray Comstock, and Jerome Kern.*

Segal's dreams, had to be substituted. Three years later, attempts were made to fit "Bill" into *Sally,* but Marilyn Miller's voice was too small to make it effective. In fact, it was not until 1927, when a tearful lament was needed for Helen Morgan in a cabaret scene in *Show Boat,* that the song was revived (and revised) and at last heard on a New York stage.

The Princess Theatre shows of Guy Bolton, P. G. Wodehouse, and Jerome Kern were the first real advancements in the development of a truly native musical theatre—despite the fact that two of the members of the trio were born in England! Not only did their musicals point up the foolishness of many of the contemporary extravaganzas and operettas, but they also made the formulas of George M. Cohan seem crude and obvious. Today, this "integration" might appear somewhat awkward to modern audiences, but it is important to point out that all the Princess Theatre musicals were conscientious efforts to break away from the conventions of the theatre at that time and to establish a genuinely new form of musical comedy. Kern said, "It is my opinion that the musical numbers should carry the action of the play and should be representative of the personalities of the characters who sing them. Songs must be suited to the action and the mood of the play." That view was expressed in 1917.*

* Two more Princess Theatre shows followed *Oh, Lady! Lady!!,* though neither *Oh, My Dear* by Bolton, Wodehouse, and Louis Hirsch, nor *Toot-Sweet* by Richard A. Whiting and Leo Egan was successful. The theatre itself attracted little notice until twenty years later when the International Ladies Garment Workers Union bought it, renamed it the Labor Stage, and presented a modest revue of its own titled *Pins and Needles.*

Jerome Kern was undeniably sincere in his aims for the musical comedy theatre, but he had little opportunity to put them into practice when he again began to write for the regular Broadway stage. His successes at the Princess had given him prestige equal to any other theatre composer, yet when Henry Savage, or Charles Dillingham, or Florenz Ziegfeld wanted him for a lavish new production he found that they cared little for his theories of how musicals should be constructed. They wanted love songs, specialty songs, chorus songs, and, above all, hit songs, and whether a song fitted a situation in a story meant little to them. Kern had no other choice than to go along with what they wanted—if he wanted to stay active in the Broadway theatre. Therefore, it was not until he wrote *Show Boat* in 1927 that the composer again contributed anything notable to the form of musical comedy. His biggest hits of the first half of the Twenties were two conventionally ornate star vehicles with almost indistinguishable titles, *Sally* (1920) and *Sunny* (1925).

Ziegfeld planned *Sally* with meticulous care. It was to be the first starring appearance in a book musical of the delightful Marilyn (then spelled "Marilynn") Miller. To give her the strongest possible support, the producer

SALLY *(1920). Walter Catlett obviously feels he can make a glamorous star of Marilyn Miller, the poor dishwasher of the Alley Inn. Mary Hay, however, seems momentarily distracted. (Setting by Joseph Urban.)*

signed two expert comedians, Leon Errol and Walter Catlett, for important roles. Originally, it was to have been another Bolton, Wodehouse, and Kern collaboration, but as Wodehouse was in England writing a novel, most of the lyrics were written by another English-born writer, Clifford Grey. The book, a durable Cinderella fable about a poor slavey who becomes a *Ziegfeld Follies* star, was patterned along lines similar to a recent hit called *Irene*. (Indeed, *Sally* was also related to two other shows that followed it: *Mary* and the all-inclusive *Sally, Irene and Mary*.)

Though the eminent Victor Herbert was called upon to provide a "Butterfly Ballet" for the finale, it was Jerome Kern whom Alexander Woollcott was now referring to as "that fount of melody." Three of Kern's songs for *Sally* were originally intended for two unproduced musicals—from *The Little Thing*, he took "The Church 'round the Corner" (lyric by Wodehouse), and from *Brewster's Millions*, he added the airy "Whip-poor-will" and the poignant "Look for the Silver Lining" (both lyrics by George Gard "Bud" DeSylva). The New York run of *Sally* was 570 performances, just two less than the initial run of *Show Boat*.

Sunny, which opened five years after *Sally*, made every effort to capitalize on the fame of its predecessor. Produced by Charles Dillingham, its "box-office" cast was headed by Marilyn Miller (again in the title role), Jack

SUNNY *(1925). The "particularly luminous beauty of Marilyn Miller" (to use the* Times's *phrase) is here displayed in a circus costume designed by James Reynolds.*

BROWN BROS.

73

Donahue, Clifton Webb, Mary Hay (who had also been in *Sally*), Joseph Cawthorn, Cliff "Ukulele Ike" Edwards (succeeded during most of the run by Borrah Minevitch), Pert Kelton, and George Olsen and his Orchestra. It also marked the first association between Jerome Kern and the team of Otto Harbach and Oscar Hammerstein II. As in *Sally*, there was little attempt to tell a coherent tale in dialogue and songs ("Our job was to tell a story with a cast that had been assembled as if for a revue," recalls Hammerstein). But the performances were excellent, the James Reynolds settings and costumes were sumptuous, and the songs, especially the still-popular "Who?," were whistled and hummed as soon as they were heard. Among them were the title number (with its nonconformist advice, "Never comb your hair, Suuuunny!"); the consoling duet, "Two Little Bluebirds"; "D'Ye Love Me?"; and the joyfully expectant "When We Get Our Divorce."

Secure in his fame and prestige, Kern was anxious to try something more daring than the frothy entertainments he was regularly called upon to turn

SHOW BOAT *(1927). The dramatic scene in which Julie, the mulatto entertainer of the "Cotton Blossom," faints after her white husband, Steve Baker, has sucked the blood from one of her fingers. Francis X. Mahoney as Rubber Face, Charles Ellis as Steve, Helen Morgan as Julie, Norma Terris as Magnolia, Eve Puck as Ellie, Charles Winninger as Cap'n Andy, and Edna May Oliver as Parthy. (Costumes by John Harkrider; setting by Joseph Urban.)*

BROWN BROS.

out. The breezy intimacy of the Princess shows had given way to opulent star-studded attractions, as inane in their way as the turgid operettas for which he had once supplied additional songs. Both Kern and Hammerstein discussed the matter often, and they finally agreed to undertake an adult musical together if either one ever found a good enough story.

Relaxing one evening, Kern began to read a new novel by Edna Ferber called *Show Boat*. Even before he had finished it, he knew that here, at last, was the perfect work to transform into a musical. Not only did it have a great title, but it also had a romantic yet credible story, colorful characters, and nostalgic locales. Hammerstein, also excited about its possibilities, promptly agreed to do the adaptation and the lyrics.

Many "old pros" in the theatre thought the scheme was impractical. *Show Boat* shattered too many musical comedy conventions and taboos. It dealt with two unhappy marriages. It showed the harsh life of southern Negroes. Part of its dramatic conflict resulted from the delicate subject of miscegenation. The biggest surprise of the year came when Florenz Ziegfeld agreed to produce it. Perhaps the Great Glorifier had some notion about glorifying the American Negro, but he soon realized that in this production the authors would need a free hand in most artistic matters.

Show Boat broke with tradition right from the start. In the first scene on the Natchez levee, there were no rows of leggy young ladies all chirping in unison about how it feels just dandy to be with Cap'n Andy. The writers took the bold step of opening the play with a group of colored dock workers lamenting the drudgery of lifting the back-breaking bales of cotton. When

CULVER PICTURES, INC.

SHOW BOAT *(1927). Cap'n Andy quiets the crowd during a performance of* The Parson's Bride, *after a backwoodsman, in the box directly above his head, has threatened to shoot the villain in the play. Charles Winninger as Cap'n Andy. (Costumes by John Harkrider; setting by Joseph Urban.)*

75

the ladies of the town arrived with their beaux to welcome the showboat troupe, both whites and Negroes sang about the "cotton blossom"—the towns-people referring to the name of the ship and the stevedores still concerned only with the weight of the cotton bales. Other numbers were equally valid with regard to character and to mood. "Make Believe"—which came right after the self-doubting "Where's the Mate for Me?", sung by the gambler, Gaylord Ravenal—was a sentiment both Ravenal and Magnolia Hawks could express naturally upon first meeting. Later, the expansive, "You Are Love" revealed their more mature emotions. To provide a unifying theme for the somewhat sprawling plot, "Ol' Man River" was sung by a Negro dock worker to convey the hopelessness he felt in contrast to the might and indifference of the Mississippi River.

For the tragic mulatto, Julie LaVerne, there were two songs to reveal her deep attachment to her worthless man—"Can't Help Lovin' Dat Man" and "Bill," the song that had been discarded from *Oh, Lady! Lady!!* Ravenal's "Till Good Luck Comes My Way" was a swaggering piece in which Kern skillfully repeated four bars from "Make Believe" in order to point up Magnolia's hold on the outwardly indifferent gambler. The comic dancers, Frank and Ellie, had an amusing duet in "I Might Fall Back on You," and Ellie, as a solo, did the mocking lament, "Life upon the Wicked Stage."

Ziegfeld wanted to make *Show Boat* the initial attraction at his newly constructed Ziegfeld Theatre, with Elizabeth Hines, Guy Robertson, and Paul Robeson signed for the leading parts. Production delays, however, forced him to substitute *Rio Rita* (score by Harry Tierney and Joseph McCarthy) as the Ziegfeld Theatre's first tenant in February, 1927.*

Heralded as "An All-American Musical Comedy," *Show Boat* began its tryout tour in Washington, D. C., with a cast headed by Charles Winninger (Cap'n Andy), Norma Terris (Magnolia), Howard Marsh (Ravenal), Jules Bledsoe (Joe), Helen Morgan (Julie), and the team of Sammy White and Eva Puck as Frank and Ellie. At its first public performance, the show ran an hour and a half overtime. This caused the deletion of seven songs, including "Mis'ry's Comin' 'Round," parts of which still remain in the score as back-ground themes. "Why Do I Love You?," the third major love duet, was added in Philadelphia.

Show Boat arrived at the Ziegfeld Theatre on December 27, 1927, pre-ceded by the largest advance ticket sale up to that time. It became such a sub-stantial hit that, within a year after its opening, the producer made plans to assemble another company to run concurrently in New York, with Raymond Hitchcock as Cap'n Andy, Libby Holman as Julie, and Paul Robeson as Joe.

* The producer's cancellation of the *Show Boat* contracts provoked a $55,000 law suit by Miss Hines. She later settled for $12,000.

These plans, however, never materialized. At the completion of its run, *Show Boat* toured for seven months with its original cast, except that Miss Terris was succeeded by her understudy, Irene Dunne.

Ziegfeld revived the musical only three years after its first New York engagement. Apart from the replacements of Dennis King for Howard Marsh and Paul Robeson for Jules Bledsoe, the featured performers were the same as in the original company. A second major revival in 1946 ran for a year at the Ziegfeld Theatre. Its cast was headed by Ralph Dumke, Jan Clayton, Carol Bruce, Kenneth Spencer, and Buddy Ebsen.

Of all his musicals, *Show Boat* is undeniably Jerome Kern's most impressive work. It remains as warm and colorful to today's audiences as it was to those of thirty years ago. Its magnificent score is such an essential part of the story that even the time-worn sequences still have the power to move audiences. By at least attempting to deal with the serious aspects of society, Kern and Hammerstein broadened the scope of subject matter and treatment in the musical theatre and thus laid the foundation for *Porgy and Bess, South Pacific*, and other serious musical plays. In his review of *Show Boat* in *McCalls*, Stark Young accurately predicted: "Some of its best numbers are so successful in their combination of the theatrical elements, music, acting, scene, as to suggest openings for the development not of mere musical comedy, but of popular opera."

The great success scored by Helen Morgan in *Show Boat* prompted Kern and Hammerstein to write a musical specifically for her, *Sweet Adeline*, which was frankly designed to capitalize on the singer's great popularity. Nevertheless, with a score that included such pieces as "Why Was I Born?" and "Don't Ever Leave Me," the authors made effective use of music to enhance the sweet, delicate, turn-of-the-century atmosphere of the story.

During the early Thirties, the musical theatre offered many sophisticated and satirical works that reflected the mood of a country going through a depression. This was not the theatre of Jerome Kern. In his musicals he tried to capture a quality of timelessness that would have no relation either to the artificial operettas of the past or to the glossy smartness of most contemporary productions. Particularly with *The Cat and the Fiddle* (written with Otto Harbach) and *Music in the Air* (written with Oscar Hammerstein), Kern shut out the world around him and replaced it with a very personal theatrical world of his own. Both of these musicals were set in modern Europe (but contained no political implications), both were concerned with backstage romances, and both depended completely on music to tell their stories. Each work even avoided a conventional designation—*The Cat and the Fiddle* was billed as "A Musical Love Story," while *Music in the Air* was "A Musical Adventure."

THE CAT AND THE FIDDLE
*(1931). Georges Metaxa and
Bettina Hall are serenaded by
George Meader singing "The
Night Was Made for Love."
(Setting by Henry Dreyfuss.)*

MUSIC IN THE AIR *(1932) Oscar
Hammerstein II and Jerome
Kern photographed in the
orchestra pit of the Alvin
Theatre during a rehearsal.*

"Broadway has not heard lovelier music in all its life," was the glowing verdict of the *American's* critic, Gilbert Gabriel, in his review of *The Cat and the Fiddle*. As for the spell cast by *Music in the Air*, it was potent enough to have Alexander Woollcott hail it as "that endearing refuge, that gracious shelter from a troubled world . . . so drenched in melody that it is an unfailing delight." Both productions—particularly *The Cat and the Fiddle*—were burdened by a stodgy plot, but the songs and the adroit way in which they contributed to the action brought a quality of lyricism to the Broadway theatre that no other musical of the period could match. Among the melodies of *The Cat and the Fiddle* were "The Night Was Made for Love," "She Didn't Say, 'Yes,'" "Try to Forget," "One Moment Alone," and "I Watch the Love Parade." From *Music in the Air* have come "I've Told Every Little Star," "And Love Was Born," "The Song Is You," and "In Egern on the Tegern See."

Although Kern and Harbach's *Roberta* attempted to follow the pattern of *The Cat and the Fiddle* and *Music in the Air*, it was far too dependent on

PHOTO BY VANDAMM

MUSIC IN THE AIR (1932). *Following their adventures in the sophisticated theatrical world of Munich, Karl and Sieglinde return to their simple life in Edendorf, in the Bavarian mountains. Reinald Werrenrath as Cornelius, Al Shean as Dr. Lessing, Mary McQuade as Tila, Katherine Carrington as Sieglinde, and Walter Slezak as Karl. (Costumes by John Harkrider; setting by Joseph Urban.)*

79

ROBERTA (1933). *Bob Hope has difficulty tearing Ray Middleton away from Lyda Roberti and Sydney Greenstreet. (Costumes by Kiviette; setting by Clark Robinson.)*

the stock formulas of musical comedy. The show was a commercial success, however, partly due to its now famous cast (Tamara, Ray Middleton, Bob Hope, Sydney Greenstreet, Fay Templeton, and George Murphy, plus Fred MacMurray as a member of a vocal and instrumental group known as the California Collegians), and partly due to its many attractive Jerome Kern melodies. One of them, "Smoke Gets in Your Eyes," ranks among the composer's most inspired creations, but some found its beauties hard to detect upon first hearing. In his review in the *World-Telegram*, critic Robert Garland complained: "There's no tune you can whistle when you leave the theatre. I tried to pucker on the one about smoke getting in your eyes, but it turned out to be 'The Last Roundup' before I reached the sidewalk."

From 1934 on, Jerome Kern made his permanent home in California, where he composed many songs for the films. He returned to New York twice for theatre assignments. In 1939, he collaborated with Oscar Hammerstein

II on *Very Warm for May,* a commercial failure in spite of a frequently witty book and a score that contained the classic "All the Things You Are."

Six years later Kern returned to New York. He planned to produce a revival of *Show Boat* with Hammerstein, and he was also preparing a score for a musical sponsored by Rodgers and Hammerstein based on the life of Annie Oakley. A few days after his arrival in the city he suffered a fatal heart attack. He died on November 11, 1945, at the age of sixty.

Jerome Kern was the first real pioneer in the creation of a genuinely native musical theatre, the "daddy of modern musical comedy music," as Arthur Schwartz once called him. Apart from his unrivaled gifts as a melodist, he was a brilliant creator of purely functional theatrical music. It was in the application of this ability that he had such a profound influence on the structure of the American musical stage. Frequently dogmatic about the manner in which his songs were to be performed, he was nonetheless the first major composer to become actively interested in raising the level of musical comedy librettos and lyrics. From the Princess Theatre shows, through *Show Boat, The Cat and the Fiddle,* and *Music in the Air,* Kern was a leader in establishing the pattern for the modern musical theatre.

The durability of Kern's music was dramatically affirmed in March, 1960, when it was announced that about a dozen of some seventy-five recently discovered Jerome Kern songs would be used in a forthcoming Broadway production. Apart from any other merits it might possess, such a work will again emphasize one of Kern's most distinguishing traits: throughout all the fads and fashions in music, Kern never varied from his own individual style. Without catering to popular taste, he created a very personal musical expression that was both timeless and modern.

Irving Berlin.

CHAPTER SEVEN

Irving Berlin

BOTH TIN PAN ALLEY and the Broadway musical theatre are ostensibly concerned with popular music, but the attitudes and approaches of song-writers in both localities are almost entirely different. Tin Pan Alley writers are only interested in creating hit songs with the widest possible appeal to the record and sheet-music buying public. Composers and lyricists for the theatre, however, are interested in the finer points; how songs fit characters and situations in a story, and how they are sung and performed. That many show tunes become individual hits is proof of their power to surmount the many theatrical elements—settings, costumes, dancing, singing, plot—that are also vying for the audience's attention.

Geographically, Tin Pan Alley is just around the corner from Broadway, but only a few writers have successfully turned that corner. The prolific Walter Donaldson wrote two scores in the Twenties, *Sweetheart Time* and *Whoopee,* and more recently, Bob Merrill, "Doggie In the Window's" master, has been setting dramas of Eugene O'Neill to music. Conversely, theatre writers occasionally do well in the pop-song market place. Such hits as Kern and Hammerstein's "The Last Time I Saw Paris," and Rodgers and Hart's "Blue Moon" achieved popularity without having first been heard in a play or a movie.

Irving Berlin is unique among his colleagues. He has lived and thrived in both worlds. Some of his most enduring songs were first heard across the footlights, but just as many were composed with no other purpose than to strike a responsive chord in as many people as possible. Not only has Berlin thrived, he has been a leader in both areas. A creator of music and lyrics for over half a century, he has written songs that have become so much a part of our lives that it is a bit difficult to think of him as once having been the most daring and influential innovator in the field of popular music.

Berlin popularized ragtime with "Alexander's Ragtime Band," thereby starting the dance craze and paving the way for the popular acceptance of jazz. He introduced ragtime into the theatre with *Watch Your Step,* and later wrote the music for four *Music Box Revues,* probably the most tasteful, melodious series ever offered. In the Thirties, he kept up with the times by contributing to the politically satirical musicals born of the depression years. Then, in 1946, after forty years as a song-writer, Berlin was able to achieve his greatest theatrical success, *Annie Get Your Gun.*

As a creator of popular songs, Irving Berlin has the wonderful ability to communicate his own emotions in words and music. Frequently working with a title idea or an accidental phrase, he has developed many of his most famous songs from everyday expressions that are instantly understood and appreciated. Four of his ballads, "All Alone," "What'll I Do," "Always," and "Remember," which were inspired by events in his own life, are considered today as the apotheosis of the romantic waltz. Yet each one begins with an almost conversational phrase ("All alone, I'm so all alone . . ."; "What'll I do . . ."; "I'll be loving you, always . . ."; "Remember the night . . .") and then goes on to unexpected musical and lyrical ideas. Berlin himself has said, "There's no such thing as a new melody. Our work is to connect the old phrases in a new way, so that they will sound like a new tune. Do you know that the public, when it hears a new song, anticipates the next line? Well, the writers who do *not* give them something they are expecting are those who are successful."

Famous for the apparent simplicity of many of his songs, Berlin has also created melodies and lyrics of remarkable ingenuity. Of these, "Lazy," composed in 1924, is a notable example. Its melodic line, which switches every four or eight bars without repeating a previous musical phrase, is so artfully constructed that the singer is made to sound as if he is actually getting lazier and lazier. Moreover, it mated to a lyric abounding in such intricate rhyming as:

> I wanna peep through the deep
> Tangled wildwood
> Counting sheep till I sleep
> Like a child would.

With a great big valise-full
Of books to read where it's peaceful,
While I'm killing time
Being lazy.*

Irving Berlin was born in the little Russian town of Temun (he himself is not sure of the exact spelling) on May 11, 1888, the youngest of eight children of Cantor Moses and Leah Baline. His real first name is Israel. At the age of two, he was taken by his family to the United States in their escape from the anti-Semitic raids of the Cossacks. Along with many other immigrant families, the Balines went to live on the lower East Side of New York. As Berlin recalls, "There were ten of us in four rooms, and in the summer some of us slept on the fire escape or on the roof. I was a boy with poor parents, but I didn't starve; I wasn't cold or hungry. There was always bread and butter and hot tea. I guess I never felt poverty because I'd never known anything else."

Irving was eight when his father died. Just six years later, to avoid being a burden to his mother, he ran away from home. To a runaway boy, the Bowery was the only place to go. There Berlin earned pennies by favoring saloon patrons with his vocal renditions of the tearful ballads of the day. One evening he discovered an abandoned upright piano in the back room of a saloon, and he would return there night after night to try to pick out tunes on the worn keyboard. This was as far as his musical education ever went; he still can play only in the key of F sharp.

In the early years of the century, it was not particularly difficult to get a part in the chorus of a touring musical show. Berlin was only fourteen when he was seen briefly in Edward E. Rice's production, *The Show Girl.* The show eventually reached Broadway, but Berlin was left stranded in Binghamton.

Despite reverses, Berlin became convinced that his future lay in the field of music. He next got a job as a song plugger for Harry Von Tilzer, a leading composer and publisher. One of Von Tilzer's songs was then being introduced by Buster Keaton and his family at Tony Pastor's Music Hall. Berlin's job was simple. After the song was sung, he would rise from his seat in the balcony—as if spontaneously inspired—to reprise the refrain of the song. For this he received five dollars a week.

Berlin soon acquired a steadier position as a singing waiter at the fashionably named Pelham Café in Chinatown. It was while working there that the young minstrel wrote his first lyric. The song was "Marie from Sunny Italy," and the music was created by "Nick" Nicholson, the pianist at the café. It came to be written because Nicholson and the proprietor, Mike Salter, became irritated when they discovered that two waiters at a rival tavern had already

* Copyright 1924 Irving Berlin. Copyright renewed. Reprinted by permission of Irving Berlin Music Corporation.

written a song and had had it published. As Berlin was already known for his parodies of popular songs, Nicholson asked him to write the words for the new piece. They even found a publisher, Joseph W. Stern and Company (which later published Romberg's first compositions), but all "Marie from Sunny Italy" ever netted the neophyte lyricist was thirty-seven cents. The song, however, started both a career and a new name: "I. Berlin" was the way he was credited on the sheet music.

Undaunted by the meager returns from his first effort, Berlin tried writing other songs, this time creating both the words and the music. His initial attempts resulted in "The Best of Friends Must Part," "Queenie, My Own," and "Dorando." The last song (an Italian dialect number about a famous marathon runner) was the one that really started Berlin's career as a full-time song-writer. It had been commissioned by a vaudeville performer who never returned to claim it and to pay the promised ten dollars. Unwilling to let his

Irving Berlin working for Ted Snyder as a $25 a week composer.

efforts go unrewarded, young Berlin bravely took the manuscript to Ted Snyder, a composer and publisher. To Berlin's surprise, Snyder liked the lyric so much that he offered twenty-five dollars for both the words and the music. There was just one difficulty—Berlin had written only the words. Putting on a bold front, he nervously improvised a hesitant melody while an arranger took down the notes. Fortunately, he got away with the ruse and the song was published. It did fairly well. Even more successful was "Sadie Salome, Go Home," an operatic parody, which prompted Snyder to hire Berlin as a staff lyricist at twenty-five dollars a week, plus royalties. As Alexander Woollcott, Berlin's biographer, wrote, "He had turned a corner and found himself in Tin Pan Alley."

Berlin worked hard, even painfully, on his songs. His ambition was to write the music as well as the words, and in order to show Snyder that he could do both, the young man would return to the office every morning at two and work until dawn. He turned out songs in such profusion—with an impressive amount of hits—that Snyder took him in as a partner. The two men also appeared together in a revue, *Up and Down Broadway*, in which they were attired as tennis playing men-about-town and sang a medley of their creations.

In 1911, Berlin, as a successful music publisher and writer of more than fifty songs, was elected to membership in the exclusive theatrical club, The Friars. The club was then preparing its first annual *Friars' Frolics* revue. Berlin was going to appear in it with his idol, George M. Cohan, and he was anxious to introduce a new song in honor of the occasion. He had already published a song called "Alexander and his Clarinet"; although it did not do very well, Berlin felt that the lyric could still be salvaged if combined with a stronger melody. He tried it out with an untitled instrumental piece he had composed, and found that with certain changes in the words it not only could be made to fit but that it also had a particularly infectious quality. He called it "Alexander's Ragtime Band." Encouraged by its reception in the *Friars' Frolics*, Berlin submitted it to the management of the *Folies Bergère*, a vaudeville show, who promptly rejected it. "Alexander" finally found a home on Broadway—if only temporarily—as part of the musical accompaniment at the Columbia Burlesque House.

The first real response to "Alexander's Ragtime Band" came when it was trumpeted out by the dynamic Emma Carus during a vaudeville engagement in Chicago. Audiences quickly responded to the compelling invitation to "Come on an' hear! Come on an' hear!" and before long the entire nation was singing it and dancing to it. Technically, except in a few places, the song is not authentic ragtime. But Berlin, who had tried to popularize the "ragged meter" before, felt that it would be uncommercial at the time and so used a melody that combined a march rhythm, simulated bugle calls, and a deliberately borrowed line from Stephen Foster's "Old Folks at Home." To the public, however, the song was different enough and exciting enough to be accepted as something brand new. Tin Pan Alley had safely broken with the past, ragtime ballroom dancing (with its menagerie of Turkey Trots, Bunny Hugs, and Grizzly Bears) became the latest dance craze, and at twenty-three, Irving Berlin was the most successful song-writer in the United States.

Just as Berlin was beginning to enjoy his sudden eminence, his young bride, the former Dorothy Goetz (sister of song-writer and producer E. Ray Goetz) died after contracting typhoid fever on their wedding trip to Cuba. This tragedy inspired his first real ballad, "When I Lost You," a marked departure from the earlier comic dialect numbers he had written to cover his lack of grammatical assurance.

Although many of Berlin's early creations had been added to musical comedies and revues, it was not until 1914 that he was given the opportunity to compose an entire score. At the urging of producer Charles Dillingham, Berlin wrote the songs for *Watch Your Step,* "A Syncopated Musical Show" designed specifically to show off the dancing skills of Vernon and Irene Castle. The program credited "plot, if any" to the ubiquitous Harry B. Smith, though the show was basically a revue. Smith, who had served as lyricist for many of the theatre's greatest composers, admired Berlin's facility with rhymes, particularly one in the song of the matinee idol, "They Always Follow Me Around":

> The matinee I play on Wednesday
> Is what I've nicknamed my old hen's day.*

The number that has remained the most popular is "Play a Simple Melody," in which a counter melody is ingeniously used to comment musically and verbally on the old-fashioned sentiments of the main theme. But there was such a native vitality and freshness about the entire score that the anonymous critic of *Theatre Magazine* summed up his appraisal of the music by stating unequivocally, if ungeographically, "Berlin is now a part of America."

Other musicals followed in rapid succession. Among them were *Stop! Look! Listen!*, *The Century Girl* (with songs also by Victor Herbert), and *Dance and Grow Thin,* one of the then-fashionable midnight revues that entertained theatregoing insomniacs.

During the First World War, Sgt. Irving Berlin received a special commission to write the songs for *Yip, Yip, Yaphank,* "A Musical 'Mess' Cooked Up by the Boys of Camp Upton." George M. Cohan may have conveyed the spirit of aggressive patriotism in his rousing "Over There," but it was Berlin who caught the more human emotions of the lowly soldier in such poignant pieces

* Copyright © 1914 Irving Berlin. Copyright renewed. Reprinted by permission of Irving Berlin Music Corporation.

WATCH YOUR STEP (1914).
*The Castle Walk as performed
by Vernon and Irene Castle.*

BROWN BROS.

as "Oh, How I Hate to Get Up In the Morning" and "Kitchen Police," the later with its mocking, mournful lines:

> Against my wishes
> I wash the dishes
> To make
>   this
>   wide
>   world
> Safe for democracy*

The highlight of the minstrel show that opened the first act of *Yip, Yip, Yaphank* was the joyous cakewalk, "Mandy." Berlin used the number in the *Ziegfeld Follies* the following year. In the new production, it became the first act finale, and it brought down the curtain on a strutting spectacle featuring Van and Schenck, Marilyn Miller as the famous minstrel, George Primrose, and Ray Dooley as Mandy.†

* Copyright 1918 Irving Berlin. Copyright renewed. Reprinted by permission of Irving Berlin Music Corporation.

† Another song first intended for *Yip, Yip, Yaphank* was never used because its author felt that it was too full of patriotic zeal to fit comfortably into the revue's lighthearted format. This was "God Bless America," which remained unpublished until twenty years later when it was introduced by Kate Smith at an Armistice Day celebration.

The *Follies of 1919* contained other delightful Irving Berlin songs—"A Pretty Girl Is like a Melody" (which became the unofficial theme song of *all* the *Follies*); "You'd Be Surprised" (a wide-eyed piece of suggestiveness sung by Eddie Cantor); and an anti-Prohibition Bert Williams specialty, "You Cannot Make Your Shimmy Shake on Tea," co-authored with Rennold Wolf.

When he was still in uniform, Berlin once made a casual suggestion to Sam Harris that led to one of his most ambitious and successful ventures. Meeting the Broadway producer at the Friars Club one day, he remarked, "Sam, if you ever build a theatre just for musicals, why not call it the Music Box?" Several weeks later, Harris telephoned Berlin. "Remember that Music Box idea of yours? Well, I've just bought a piece of land on the Astor property on West 45th Street. You can have your Music Box whenever you want it."

In association with film producer Joseph Schenck, Harris and Berlin built the intimate, elegantly appointed Music Box as the only theatre ever intended to display the musical creations of just one composer in a series of annual revues. The *Music Box Revues* were as lavish as anything Ziegfeld

COURTESY IRVING BERLIN

MUSIC BOX REVUE OF 1921. *Irving Berlin as he appeared in the next-to-closing spot with the young ladies known as the Eight Notes. The eighth note (extreme right) is Miriam Hopkins.*

put on, but they showed decidedly more imagination in stagecraft and in settings. Writing of the second edition, Alexander Woollcott once commented that for a while it looked as if none of the players "would be permitted to resort to any such routine and hackneyed entrance as merely walking on the stage. No, they emerge from tree trunks and bird cages, spring up out of trap doors and lightly swing down from high trapezes. When this is not possible they walk groggily down interminable staircases of black velvet, managing the perilous descent as nonchalantly as possible under the circumstances of having to carry with them gowns of silver sequins weighing about a ton each."

In addition to their technical innovations, the *Music Box Revues* were so distinguished by the quality of their humor and their music that people eagerly parted with the unusually high price of $5.50 per ticket in order to experience the myriad pleasures of sight and sound (and in two editions, even smell) that were assembled under the guidance of director Hassard Short.

At a cost of $947,000 for the theatre (including the land) and almost $188,000 for the first *Music Box Revue*, both were officially opened on September 22, 1921. Customers came to see the theatre and the revue in such numbers that construction and production expenses were paid back before a year had gone by. Among the musical attractions of this edition were the Brox Sisters tearing through the masterful rag, "Everybody Step"; Sam Bernard commenting wryly on dance-floor gyrations in "They Call It Dancing" ("A man can squeeze all the she's/With his arms and his knees"*); and Paul Frawley and Wilda Bennett singing the graceful theme song, "Say It with Music." Unlike "A Pretty Girl Is like a Melody," which developed into the anthem of the *Ziegfeld Follies* almost accidentally, "Say It with Music" was composed especially to be the official song of all the *Music Box Revues.* However, this "molten masterpiece" (in Percy Hammond's phrase) was completed long before the theatre itself was finished, and Berlin, still the irrepressible song-plugger, could not wait until the première to hear it played by an orchestra. One night he gave the manuscript to the band leader at the Sixty Club to play just once. But the customers kept demanding it again and again, and "Say It with Music" was whistled and sung by New Yorkers for months before its official introduction.

Other *Music Box Revues* were also filled with musical riches. The lilting jewel, "Lady of the Evening," was in the second edition, in which it was sung by John Steel who stood alone on the stage in front of a simple rooftop background. In the same show, Grace La Rue, wearing a dress with a hoop skirt that filled almost the entire stage, yearned tenderly for "those dear old Crinoline Days," while Charlotte Greenwood revealed the plight of a long-legged girl in "I'm Looking for a Daddy Long Legs." The first-act finale,

* Copyright © 1921 Irving Berlin. Copyright renewed. Reprinted by permission of Irving Berlin Music Corporation.

MUSIC BOX REVUE OF 1924. *Bobby Clark and Fanny Brice in the sketch, "Adam and Eve," by Bert Kalmar and Harry Ruby. Note Miss Brice's snake headdress. (Costumes by James Reynolds.)*

depicting Satan's Palace, had the McCarthy Sisters leading the cast through the fiery "Pack Up Your Sins and Go to the Devil."

The third *Music Box Revue* added Grace Moore to the roster to sing "An Orange Grove in California" with John Steel, against a setting of orange trees which sprayed the audience with orange-scented perfume. "What'll I Do?," also sung by Miss Moore and Mr. Steel, was added during the run of the show. "Learn to Do the Strut," led by the Brox Sisters, had the full company dancing on a raised stage that was slanted down to the footlights. The 1923 *Music Box Revue* was also responsible for the professional acting debut of Robert Benchley, then the drama critic for the old *Life*. Benchley had appeared with a number of other literary celebrities in an amateur revue called *No, Sirree!* at the Hotel Algonquin. His routine was a parody of all the dull treasurers' reports he had ever heard, and it was so funny that Berlin and Harris, who were at the performance, asked him to do the act in their next revue. Because he did not feel that a drama critic should also be a professional entertainer, Benchley demanded what he considered the outlandish fee of $500 a week. When Harris agreed to the figure, the humorist reluctantly gave in. His bumbling "Treasurer's Report" has since become a classic.

"All Alone" was interpolated briefly in the fourth and final *Music Box Revue*. Grace Moore and Oscar Shaw sang it to each other via illuminated telephones as they stood on opposite sides of a bare, darkened stage. Others present were Fanny Brice to wail the song of the immigrant, "Don't Send Me Back to Petrograd," and to confess, with appropriate relish, "I Want to Be a

Ballet Dancer"; Clark and McCullough to tell the sibilant tale of "A Couple of Senseless Censors"; and Grace Moore to sing the romantic "Tell Her in the Springtime," accompanied by more perfume spraying.

Although they were still popular, four *Music Box Revues* were apparently the limit for the series. Ideas no longer seemed quite so fresh or daring, even with John Murray Anderson of the *Greenwich Village Follies* succeeding Hassard Short as director of the last edition. (It was an even exchange, as Short then replaced Anderson for the 1925 *Follies*.) Berlin, convinced that he needed a change, agreed to supply the songs for the Marx Brothers' *The Cocoanuts*, one of his lesser efforts.

Grace Moore once wrote that whenever she sang a romantic ballad in one of the *Music Box Revues* she always felt as if she were a singing telegram. For it was about that time that Irving Berlin had met and fallen in love with Ellin Mackay, daughter of the socially prominent president of Postal Tele-

ZIEGFELD FOLLIES OF 1927. *Backstage shot of Eddie Cantor, Florenz Ziegfeld, Irving Berlin, and dance director Sammy Lee surrounded by the ladies of the chorus.*

graph, Clarence Mackay. In spite of the opposition of Ellin's father, she and Berlin were married after one of the most widely reported courtships of the Twenties. Some of Berlin's most tender songs, notably "Remember" and "Always," were inspired by his personal emotions.

In the early Thirties, the elaborate revues and musical comedies were rapidly becoming out of date; the unhappy state of the United States had provoked a deeper social awareness in the theatre of Broadway, even in its most customarily frivolous branch. Not that musicals could not and should not be lighthearted and entertaining, but the song-and-dance entertainments, just as every other aspect of American life, reflected the times. The Gershwin brothers with Morrie Ryskind and George S. Kaufman had inaugurated the era of adult, satirical musicals when they wrote *Strike Up the Band* and *Of Thee I Sing*. Berlin, along with librettist Moss Hart, was quick to move along in the new direction with *Face the Music* in 1932 and *As Thousands Cheer* in 1933.

Both Berlin shows were daring. *Face the Music* dealt with the general theme of the depression and the specific theme of police and political corruption. It also managed to aim some of its darts at the more vulgar and elaborate forms of musical shows. Although Irving Berlin is not generally thought of as a lyricist in the socially conscious vein of E. Y. Harburg or Harold Rome, he easily adapted himself to the demands of the script. However, while his

FACE THE MUSIC *(1932). Mary Boland, as Mrs. Martin Van Buren Meshbesher, is perched atop the elephant for the grand finale. (Costumes by Kiviette; setting by Albert Johnson.)*

AS THOUSANDS CHEER *(1933).*
Marilyn Miller, Clifton Webb,
and Helen Broderick about to
stroll down Fifth Avenue in
the Easter Parade of 1883.
(Costumes by Irene Sharaff.)

PHOTO BY VANDAMM

lyrics contained topical references and comments, he never forgot that he
was still writing songs for a gay musical comedy. Thus we find him either
cheerfully optimistic about the economic situation in "Let's Have Another
Cup o' Coffee," or bravely indifferent in "I Say It's Spinach" ("And the hell
with it"), or completely in a melodious world of his own in "Soft Lights and
Sweet Music."

As Thousands Cheer had a strikingly original format: the entire revue
was created out of sections of a daily newspaper, with individual scenes depicting news events, the funnies, the lonelyhearts column, the society page,
and other features. Real names of famous people were used, so that in one
evening an audience might see Prince Mdivani (Clifton Webb) wooing Barbara Hutton (Marilyn Miller) with "How's chances, for one of those
glances . . ."; or Aimee Semple MacPherson (Helen Broderick) trying to get
Mahatma Gandhi (Mr. Webb) to end his hunger strike; or John D. Rockefeller (Mr. Webb) going after his children with a carving knife after they
have made him a present of Rockefeller Center on his ninety-fourth birthday;
or Josephine Baker (Ethel Waters) admitting that, in spite of her fancy
French chateau, she still had "Harlem on My Mind."

Miss Waters made even more lasting impressions with her interpretations of two other headlines. "HEAT WAVE HITS NEW YORK" offered her as a highly animated weather report, relating the sizzling tale of the lady from Martinique who started the heat wave by making her seat wave; "UNKNOWN NEGRO LYNCHED BY FRENZIED MOB" showed her as the man's widow who wonders aloud as she sets the table how she will be able to tell her children that their father "ain't comin' home no more." Before the show opened in Philadelphia to begin its tryout tour, there were many who felt that such a threnody had no place in a lavish revue. Both Berlin and producer Sam Harris were adamant; the number stayed in and became one of the most moving pieces ever sung by Ethel Waters. "If one song can tell the whole tragic history of a race," she wrote in her autobiography, *His Eye Is on the Sparrow*, " 'Supper Time' was that song."*

* From *His Eye Is On the Sparrow* by Ethel Waters and Charles Samuels. Garden City, N.Y.: Doubleday & Company, 1951.

PHOTO BY VANDAMM

AS THOUSANDS CHEER (1933). *Ethel Waters sings "Supper Time."*

LOUISIANA PURCHASE *(1940).* *Victor Moore as the investigating Sen. Oliver P. Loganberry looks the other way as a disguised political boss (William Gaxton) sets the table for his rendezvous with Vera Zorina. Critic John Anderson uncompromisingly labeled Mr. Moore "the most endearing comedian of our stage." (Costumes and setting by Tom Lee.)*

PHOTO BY FRED FEHL

For the first-act finale, Berlin went back to a tune he had composed sixteen years before under the title, "Smile and Show Your Dimple." The scene in *As Thousands Cheer* was the rotogravure section showing an old-fashioned Easter Parade on Fifth Avenue. And leading the grand parade was the debonair Clifton Webb serenading the lovely Marilyn Miller with the old melody set to a new lyric, "In your Easter bonnet. . . ."

Eight years later (after writing three film scores for Fred Astaire and Ginger Rogers), Irving Berlin returned to Broadway—and another musical about politics. Unfortunately, the satire of *Louisiana Purchase* was not very barbed, even though the show dealt with such a likely subject as the attempts of a Huey Long-type boss (William Gaxton) to blackmail an investigating senator (Victor Moore) by getting him involved with three attractive ladies (Vera Zorina, Carol Bruce, and Irene Bordoni). Berlin's output was up to his best—two appealing ballads, "It's a Lovely Day Tomorrow" and "You're Lonely and I'm Lonely"; Moore's plaintive "What Chance Have I?"; the spiritual-derived "Lord Done Fixed Up My Soul"; and the amorously tenacious "You Can't Brush Me Off."

Except for the brilliant World War II all-soldier show, *This Is the Army* (with the composer back in uniform to bleat again, "Oh, How I Hate to Get Up in the Morning"), a number of years elapsed before Berlin wrote his next show. During that time, the musical theatre, like almost everything else in the world, was going through important changes. The emergence of Rodgers and Hammerstein had placed greater emphasis on the book value of musicals, and

97

THIS IS THE ARMY (1942). *Irving Berlin, once again in his World War I uniform is about to break out into "Oh, How I Hate to Get Up in the Morning."*

composers were forced to become more concerned with the way their songs were integrated with the librettos.

Annie Get Your Gun presented a challenge to Irving Berlin for two reasons: it was being produced by Rodgers and Hammerstein themselves, and he had been asked to take over the assignment only after the death of Jerome Kern, the original composer. When he was first approached in the fall of 1945, Berlin frankly admitted to Hammerstein that he just did not think he was capable of such a task. Hammerstein's insistence that he was the only one who could do the score made the composer reconsider, and he agreed to go away to Atlantic City for a week to think over the proposition. Not only did he think, he worked, composing songs such as "Doin' What Comes Natur'lly," "There's No Business like Show Business," and "They Say It's Wonderful."

PHOTO BY FRED FEHL

ANNIE GET YOUR GUN *(1946). Wrote Wolcott Gibbs: "Ethel Merman, whose voice might easily have tumbled the walls of Jericho, has some songs that will probably do the same thing for the Imperial Theatre." Here she is seen trumpeting "You Can't Get a Man with a Gun." (Costume by Lucinda Ballard.)*

Still uncertain, Berlin returned to New York. He told Rodgers and Hammerstein that he had written a few songs and wanted to audition for them. Once the songs were heard, of course, Berlin easily demonstrated to the producers' satisfaction—if not to his own—that he was still a master at writing musical comedy numbers. Moreover, these were songs that fitted logically into the story and perfectly suited the characters for whom they were intended. Berlin was also able to create something of a new stage personality for Ethel Merman, the star of the show. Before she played Annie, Miss Merman had always had to have some comic angle injected into her love songs, because composers and lyricists felt that the usual Merman characterization of a brassy but bighearted dame would not be believable in a sincere romantic expression. Berlin gave her such straight ballads as "They Say It's Wonderful" and "I Got Lost in His Arms" to help reveal the genuine warmth and femininity of the character. Even the exuberant pieces, "You Can't Get a Man with a Gun," "Doin' What Comes Natur'lly," and "I Got the Sun in the Morning," were still part of the personality of the determined but

COURTESY IRVING BERLIN

womanly sharpshooter. As Merman herself admits, "Irving Berlin made a lady out of me."

Although *Annie Get Your Gun* produced the unofficial anthem of the theatre, "There's No Business like Show Business," the song was almost thrown out of the score because Berlin mistakenly thought Rodgers did not like it. While he himself continually has such doubts about his work, Berlin is convinced that the opinion of the public is never wrong. As Howard Dietz has written, "He does not care to be considered witty or brilliant or artistic. He wants to be a hit." Surely, the musical's Broadway run of 1,147 performances gave Berlin exactly what he wanted, and was more responsible than anything else for wiping out the feeling of uncertainty that he felt when he first undertook the assignment. (Once, when a friend described *Annie Get Your Gun* as old-fashioned, Berlin replied, "Yes, a good old-fashioned smash!")

Three years after *Annie Get Your Gun*, Berlin had a fair success in *Miss Liberty*, on which he collaborated with Robert E. Sherwood (book) and Moss

ANNIE GET YOUR GUN (1946). The final tableau. Ray Middleton as Frank Butler and Ethel Merman as Annie Oakley are in the center, flanked by William O'Neal as Buffalo Bill and George Lipton as Pawnee Bill. (Costumes by Lucinda Ballard; setting by Jo Mielziner)

Hart (direction). The tale of the search for the model who posed for the Statue of Liberty is best remembered for the composer's moving musical setting to Emma Lazarus' poem, "Give Me Your Tired, Your Poor" (which is inscribed on the base of the statue), and the sight of the seventy-one-year-old Ethel Griffies kicking up her heels and croaking "Only for Americans."

Call Me Madam, another vehicle for Ethel Merman, brought Irving Berlin back to Broadway in 1950. Inspired by the appointment of Washington party-giver Perle Mesta as President Truman's ambassador to Luxembourg, Howard Lindsay and Russel Crouse created a harmless spoof that offended no one. Even Harry Truman, in the person of former musical comedy juvenile Irving Fisher, nightly took a curtain call with Miss Merman. The song that has lingered the longest from the score is "You're Just in Love," with its down-to-earth counter melody commenting sympathetically on the starry-eyed emotions of the main theme. "They Like Ike," a relatively nonpartisan specialty number, soon became both a campaign song and a much-chanted slogan merely by changing the pronoun to the first person.

Irving Berlin has been called the "Last of the Troubadours." It is an accurate title. The troubadours of the Middle Ages may not have been trained

CALL ME MADAM *(1950) Backstage shot of Raoul Pène DuBois (settings and costumes), Leland Hayward (producer), Jerome Robbins (choreographer), Howard Lindsay (co-librettist), Russel Crouse (colibrettist), Ethel Merman, Paul Lukas, Irving Berlin, and, kneeling, George Abbott (director).*

musicians, but they did have the rare faculty of being able to communicate their sentiments and their songs to vast numbers of people. Possibly no other song-writer in history has had this gift to such an extent as Irving Berlin. Whether he is writing about a soldier who hates to get up in the morning, a lonely lover who waits by the telephone, the thrills of taking a bow on the stage, the simple joys of getting out on a dance floor, or any of the hundreds of other human emotions, and thoughts, and experiences he has written about, Irving Berlin knows how to express feelings in such a way that they are universally shared.

Jerome Kern's succinct tribute to Berlin's ability to embody a nation's music is justly famous: "Irving Berlin has no *place* in American music. He *is* American music," was the way he once ended a letter to Alexander Woollcott, when Woollcott was preparing a biography of the composer. Preceeding this, Kern summed up beautifully the ways in which Berlin's music epitomized the average American: "Both the typical Yankee and the Berlin tune have humor, originality, pace, and popularity; both are wide-awake, and both are sometimes a little loud—but what might unsympathetically be mistake for brass, is really gold . . . He doesn't attempt to stuff the public's ears with pseudo-original, ultra modernism, but he honestly absorbs the vibrations emanating from the people, manners and life of his time, and in turn, gives these impressions back to the world—simplified—clarified—glorified."

George Gershwin.

CHAPTER EIGHT

George Gershwin

THE DEATH OF George Gershwin on July 11, 1937, was a stunning, almost unbelievable event. At the age of thirty-eight, at the height of his creative powers, he died in Hollywood of a brain tumor—a tragedy made all the sadder by the lingering doubts of many that if a certain brain specialist had been located in time, Gershwin's life might have been saved. The consolation that he is kept alive through the continuous performing of his music is always tempered by speculation as to what he might have gone on to achieve. Oscar Levant wrote in *A Smattering of Ignorance:* "No quantity of music could compensate for the loss of his corporeal presence, the cessation of his creative being—especially when we could have had both."* Vernon Duke, in his autobiography, *Passport to Paris,* echoed the sentiment: "Death can be kind and it can be just; but it had no business taking our George, who was in the full flower of his fine youth and who was unquestionably doing his best work."†

The frustration that many felt was understandable. For, in many ways, Gershwin represented the exciting, daring, adventuresome spirit of American

* From *A Smattering of Ignorance* by Oscar Levant. Garden City, N. Y.: Doubleday and Company.
† *From* Passport to Paris *by Vernon Duke. Boston: Little, Brown and Company.*

youth itself. Not only did he capture the pulse of the people, but, as Arthur Schwartz has commented, "he quickened it." To his friends and co-composers, he was an acknowledged leader—warm, understanding, and just as eager to praise someone else's music as he was to delight in his own. Indeed, this feeling about his own music, which led many to think of him as conceited, was nothing more than an almost detached and honest appreciation of his own worth, and he showed equal enthusiasm for the songs of Irving Berlin, Jerome Kern, and others. It was Gershwin who helped Vincent Youmans get his first assignment on Broadway, and composers such as Arthur Schwartz, Vernon Duke, and Harold Arlen have attested to Gershwin's encouragement and help. The people who knew George Gershwin only through his music felt his death almost as keenly as did his friends. Even though his audience may not have been fully conscious of it, the personality of Gershwin and of his music was the same. According to Arlen, "He bubbled just as much as his music does. That is why I believe that anyone who knows George's work, knows George. The humor, the satire, the playfulness of most of his melodic phrases were the natural expression of the man."

In a literal sense, Gershwin and his songs were seldom parted during the composer's life. He was an expert pianist with an almost-compulsive urge to play his own music. People gave parties for him because they knew he would be delighted to spend the entire evening entertaining them at the piano. Frequently, Gershwin became so excited about a new score that he would play the songs in public well in advance of the première of the show for which they were intended. "George's music gets around so much before an opening," George S. Kaufman once remarked dryly, "that the first night audience thinks it's at a revival."

Gershwin had the remarkable ability of projecting his own magnetism through the bright, athletic rhythms of his songs. He was also the first—and, at this writing, the only—song-writer who started out in Tin Pan Alley ever to be accepted with equal honors as a composer of concert and opera music. Herbert, Friml, Duke, Weill, and Bernstein all came to Broadway after years of training and experience as "classical" musicians and composers; Gershwin's apprenticeship as a "classical" musician and composer was spent as a song-plugger, vaudeville accompanist, rehearsal pianist, and the creator of the music for *George White's Scandals.* Today, his greatness rests not only on his succession of outstanding show tunes, but also on such works as the *Rhapsody in Blue,* the *Piano Concerto in F, An American in Paris,* and *Porgy and Bess.* None of the other composers discussed in this book—no matter what their backgrounds—ever mastered as many forms of musical expression as did George Gershwin. And he did it in less than twenty years.

Gershwin was born in Brooklyn, on September 26, 1898. His parents were Morris and Rose Gershvin, who later substituted the more Americanized *w* for the *v*. George was the second of four children; his older brother, Ira, was born on December 6, 1896. Their father was constantly becoming involved in a variety of business activities (turkish baths, bakeries, restaurants, etc.) that required the family to move from one neighborhood to another almost yearly. While they were living on the lower East Side of Manhattan, Mrs. Gershwin bought a piano. She wanted Ira to take lessons, but when George showed the greater musical aptitude, he was substituted for his reluctant brother. George's first important teacher was Charles Hambitzer, who later brought him to Edward Kilenyi for instructions in theory.

Music quickly became Gershwin's life. He left the High School of Commerce to take a job as a pianist for the Jerome H. Remick Music Publishing Company; at fifteen, he was the youngest pounder in Tin Pan Alley. His first attempts at composing, "Since I Found You," and "Ragging the Traumerei," went unpublished, although he did manage to sell his third effort to publisher Harry Von Tilzer for five dollars. Murray Roth's lyric was almost self-contained in the title—"When You Want 'Em, You Can't Have 'Em; When You Have 'Em, You Don't Want 'Em." It referred, of course, to the eternal problem of men—women.

At the beginning of Gershwin's career, his two idols were Irving Berlin and Jerome Kern. ("Many things I wrote at this period sounded as though Kern had written them himself," he later admitted.) He not only admired Kern's songs, he also admired Kern's success in getting his early works interpolated in musicals. Trying to emulate this success, Gershwin quit his job at Remick's to become a vaudeville accompanist. Then when he heard of an opening for a rehearsal pianist for a musical (with a score provided by both Jerome Kern and Victor Herbert), he applied for the job and was hired. Though the show itself, *Miss 1917*, lasted only forty-eight performances, the job proved to be an important step in the fledgling composer's career. The revue was housed at the Century Theatre, where, as a possible impetus to business, a series of Sunday evening variety "concerts" was presented. Gershwin, who had been hired to play at these performances, persuaded Vivienne Segal to introduce two of his songs, "You-oo Just You," a romantic ballad of Old Dixie, and "There's More to the Kiss Than the X-X-X," which made use of the simulated sounds of a kiss as part of the lyric. Someone brought the songs to the attention of publisher Max Dreyfus who thought so highly of them that he engaged Gershwin, not as a lowly song plugger or salesman, but as a regular staff composer.

In 1918, George and Ira wrote their first professional song together, "The Real American Folk Song" ("Is a rag—a mental jag"). Nora Bayes sang it in *Ladies First*. The same year, Dreyfus recommended George Gershwin to a producer who was planning a revue starring Joe Cook. The show was called *Half-Past Eight,* with Gershwin contributing five songs. The attraction turned out to be so poor that it never got any closer to New York than Syracuse.

A more significant advancement occurred a few months later. Alex A. Aarons, a musician and incipient producer, had become fascinated by the many original touches Gershwin put into his music. Soon the two men began making plans for the show that was to mark their mutual debuts on Broadway, *La La Lucille* ("The New Up-to-the-Minute Musical Comedy of Class and Distinction"). Though it was initially presented by Alex's father, Alfred E. Aarons, within a few weeks the names of Alex A. Aarons and George B. Seitz appeared on the program as co-sponsors.

La La Lucille, a moderately amusing bedroom farce, served well enough as a showcase for the talents of the twenty-year-old composer, and it had a

LA LA LUCILLE *(1919). The first Broadway musical for which Gershwin wrote the entire score. The scene below shows Marjorie Bentley surrounded by four dapper gentlemen of the chorus.*

CULVER PICTURES, INC.

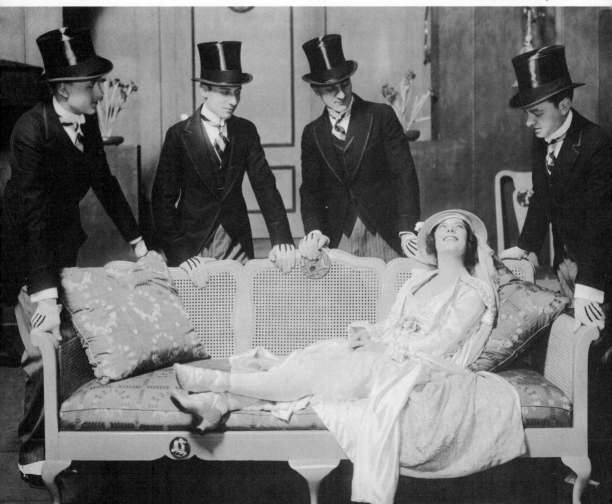

respectable run. Appraising its score, Heywood Broun wrote in the *Tribune:* "The music is spirited rather than melodious. 'Tee-Oodle-Um-Bum-Bo' was the song most appreciated by the first-night audience. This may furnish some clue to the nature of the lyrics." "Personally," countered Alan Dale of the *American,* "I prefer 'Tee-Oodle-Um-Bum-Bo' to bed, bath, or plot. In the favorite parlance of the theatre, it has 'ginger.' "

The "ginger" of "Tee-Oodle-Um-Bum-Bo" was rather bland compared to the ingredients found in "Swanee," Gershwin's first really big hit, which he wrote with Irving Caesar. "At that time," Caesar recalls, "there was a raging one-step sensation, 'Hindustan.' I said to George that we ought to write a one-step and give it an American flavor." The two men discussed the idea at dinner, took a bus ride up to Gershwin's home on Washington Heights, and completed the entire song in about fifteen minutes. "Swanee" attracted little notice when it was first introduced in 1919 in a revue at the newly constructed Capitol Theatre at Broadway and 50th Street. However, Al Jolson, who was then starring in *Sinbad* at the Winter Garden across the street, liked it so much that he reintroduced it in his own show. There was no doubt that Jolson's spirited delivery made the difference; before long, "Swanee" became the biggest hit in the country.

The composer's reputation as a result of "Swanee" made it easy for him to convince George White that he should be given the commission to supply songs for the next edition of the *George White's Scandals.* White had begun his series of annual revues the previous year; they were youthful, fast-moving affairs, and the driving excitement of Gershwin's songs made him well-suited to provide the proper kind of music. While his output covered five successive editions, from 1920 to 1924, few of these songs are known today. Only the gracefully flowing "Drifting Along with the Tide" and the pseudo-tropical "South Sea Isles" have survived the first two editions—and even they are rarely performed. However, the 1922 *Scandals* did have the remarkably constructed "Stairway to Paradise" (revised from an earlier song, "New Step Every Day") for an elaborate first-act finale in which the entire company joined in the ascent. Otherwise, there were such undistinguished items as "I Found a Four-Leaf Clover" ("And the next day I found you") and "Cinderelatives," a serenade to the rags-to-riches heroines of such recent Broadway musicals as *Irene, Sally, The Love Nest, The O'Brien Girl,* and *Good Morning Dearie.*

The most unusual item of the 1922 *Scandals* was a twenty-minute "jazz opera" by Gershwin and B. G. DeSylva called *Blue Monday.* While it was a tentative step in the direction that the composer was later to follow in *Porgy and Bess,* it proved so out of place in its Scandalous surroundings that it was cut from the show after the opening-night performance. As in Gershwin's later folk opera, the work dealt with the theme of infidelity among Negroes, although in the custom of the day, white members of the cast appeared in blackface.

The critics were a little confused by *Blue Monday*. Kenneth Macgowan of the *Globe* called it "a very painful and long-drawn incident, a sort of rag-time opera, that drags the tedious 'Mammy' motif to unbearable lengths"; Charles Pike Sawyer of the *Post* was of the opinion that, "from an artistic point of view, it was the best number in the show"; the unspecified critic of the *Telegram* (who must have been at a different theatre) referred to it as "a delicious bit of musical fun"; Charles Darnton of the *Evening World* hit the hardest with "the most dismal, stupid, and incredible blackface sketch that has probably ever been perpetrated"; while the *Sun's* Stephen Rathbun summed up his verdict with "It's not successful from any angle—comedy, burlesque, opera or tragedy."

Admittedly, Gershwin had much to learn before he could master the operatic form. Yet, in spite of its apparent defects, *Blue Monday* (later re-titled *135th Street*) did have some moving themes. Of these, "Blue Monday Blues" still remains a haunting, expressive piece that conveys so well the feeling of frustration and hopelessness on a day when everything goes wrong.

The year 1924 was a memorable one for Gershwin; he began his career as a composer and performer of concert music, and he wrote his first Broadway musical comedy in collaboration with his brother, Ira. The first important event took place at Aeolian Hall in February. Paul Whiteman, who had been featured with his orchestra in the *Scandals of 1922*, was one of the few who had always had a fondness for *Blue Monday*. While working on the show, Whiteman told Gershwin about an idea he had for a concert devoted to American music. Would George be able to contribute a serious composition for the occasion? The result was the *Rhapsody in Blue*, which Gershwin himself performed with Whiteman's augmented "Palais Royal Orchestra." The enthusiastic reception to the *Rhapsody* (which had been given the choice "next-to-closing" spot on the program) presaged the eminence Gershwin would later attain as both a "serious" composer and performer.

Lady, Be Good!, which opened in December, was Gershwin's second major musical event of the year. Not only was it the first success on which he and Ira collaborated (*A Dangerous Maid* had failed on the road in 1921), but it also inaugurated a series of seven musicals they were to write for a producing firm Alex Aarons had recently organized with a former actor, Vinton Freedley. Excluding the unsuccessful *Tell Me More!* which was produced by Aarons alone, the seven productions were: *Lady, Be Good!* (Fred and Adele Astaire); *Tip-Toes* (Queenie Smith, Allen Kearns, Jeanette MacDonald); *Oh, Kay!* (Gertrude Lawrence, Oscar Shaw, Victor Moore); *Funny Face* (the Astaires, Victor Moore); *Treasure Girl* (Gertrude Lawrence, Clifton Webb); *Girl Crazy* (Willie Howard, Ginger Rogers, Ethel

LADY, BE GOOD! *(1924). Adele and Fred Astaire perform their famous run-around step to "Swiss Miss."*

BROWN BROS.

Merman); and *Pardon My English* (Jack Pearl, Lyda Roberti). Of these, only *Treasure Girl* and *Pardon My English* were failures. Indeed, the last production was such a fiasco that it was one of the direct causes of the termination of the ten-year Aarons and Freedley partnership.

At first, it was the producers' intention to have these shows follow the bright, witty pattern of the old Princess Theatre attractions, only, according to Guy Bolton, on a larger scale. (Bolton was co-librettist on four of the musicals, and was joined on *Oh, Kay!* by his Princess Theatre collaborator, P. G. Wodehouse.) Despite these intentions, the shows soon became star vehicles rather than closely coordinated book-and-music shows. But in choosing a composer like Gershwin, Aarons and Freedley were motivated by the same considerations that had prompted F. Ray Comstock and Elisabeth Marbury to choose Jerome Kern—he was the freshest, most original composer of theatre music on Broadway. Though he was again following in the pat-

111

TIP-TOES *(1925). The distracted lady about to have her
pocket picked is Jeanette Mac-
Donald. The pranksters are
Allen Kearns and Robert Halliday.*

tern of his first idol, Kern, Gershwin could no longer be accused of imitating
him. His own sparkling music had already established its individuality; the
Aarons-Freedley succession of hits merely provided him with greater opportunities to develop his skills. For although these shows pioneered no new
theatrical ground, they did feature a number of outstanding performers who
inspired the composer to produce some of his most enduring music.

Lady, Be Good! gave Fred and Adele Astaire their second Broadway
triumph. They had just returned from England where they had captivated
audiences in Alex Aarons' production of *Stop Flirting* (called *For Goodness
Sake* in New York). With the Gershwins' help they scored an even greater
success in the new musical. *Lady, Be Good!* had a whole hopper of engaging
tunes—the wistful "So Am I"; "Fascinating Rhythm"; the lonely, lighthearted
plea, "Oh, Lady, Be Good!"; and the ragtime lament of the ardent suitor,
" 'The Half Of It, Dearie' Blues."

One of the scenes early in the first act of *Lady, Be Good!* has always been
considered as something of a classic in the field of pure mid-Twenties musical
comedy. As the curtain rises, Fred and Adele, as brother and sister, have

just been evicted from their apartment. Surrounded by their furniture, they try to cheer each other up by arranging the tables and chairs as if they were in their own home. Adele even hangs up a GOD BLESS OUR HOME sign on the nearest lamppost. When it begins to rain, Fred and Adele duck under a huge umbrella and break out into a consoling song-and-dance duet, "Hang On to Me."

"The Man I Love," one of the composer's most popular songs, had been intended for *Lady, Be Good!*, but it was dropped before the show reached New York. It fared no better three years later, when it was added to the first version of *Strike Up the Band;* then the musical itself closed on the road. The following year, after an attempt to fit "The Man I Love" into *Rosalie*, the song was dropped again. That it was never sung on Broadway did not disturb Gershwin. "The song is not a production number," he once explained. "It allows little or no action while it is being sung. It lacks a soothing, seducing rhythm; instead, it has a certain slow lilt that disturbs the audience instead of lulling it into acceptance. Then, too, there is the melody, which is not easy to catch; it presents too many chromatic pitfalls." Pitfalls or not, "The Man I Love" did manage to succeed on its own, unaided by a theatrical presentation.

Tell Me More!, which opened in April, 1925, was unsuccessful. But it did have one distinction: during its tryout tour it was known as *My Fair Lady*. This was also the name of one of the songs, with the musical derivation of its title line stemming from "London Bridge Is Falling Down."

The same year, Aarons and Freedley offered a more profitable Gershwin attraction called *Tip-Toes*. "Looking For a Boy," "Sweet and Low-Down" (sung to the accompaniment of a group of kazoo trumpets), and "That Certain Feeling" were some of its musical pleasures. In his book *Lyrics on Several Occasions*, Ira Gershwin claims that *Tip-Toes* had the first score in which he noticed any development in his skills as a lyricist. He was particularly pleased with "These Charming People," which he felt was at last equal to the kind of witty lyrics that P. G. Wodehouse had created for the Princess Theatre shows.

The gay, modern pattern of musical comedy was scrupulously adhered to in a tale of rum-running and Long Island society called *Oh, Kay!* For their star, Aarons and Freedley were able to secure Gertrude Lawrence, then very much in demand as a result of her success in the imported *Charlot's Revues*. Her reason for choosing *Oh, Kay!* as her first American musical was simple: "George Gershwin was writing the music especially for me."

After its première on November 8, 1926, the score of the Gershwin-Gershwin-Bolton-Wodehouse musical prompted critic Percy Hammond to dub the composer as the "premier music-master," and to reveal how "all of us simply floated away on the canoodling notes of 'Maybe,' and were brought

OH, KAY! *(1926). Gertrude Lawrence, of whom Bide Dudley wrote: "Here is an artiste from bob to toe."*

back to Broadway by such flesh and bony anthems as 'Fidgety Feet' and 'Clap Yo' Hands.'" As for "Someone to Watch Over Me," Hammond testified that Gershwin had "wrung the withers of even the most hard-hearted of those present."

After creating another sensation in England in *Lady, Be Good!*, the Astaires returned to Broadway in *Funny Face*. Although its book was initially to have been the product of Fred Thompson and Robert Benchley, the humorist withdrew during its hectic out-of-town tryout and was succeeded by Paul Gerard Smith. Almost to everyone's surprise, when the show opened in November, 1927, at the newly built Alvin Theatre ("Al" for Alex Aarons, "vin" for Vinton Freedley), it turned out to be an unqualified smash. The combination of the singing and the dancing of Fred and Adele and the songs of George and Ira again proved irresistible, particularly in such numbers as "He Loves and She Loves," "High Hat," "My One and Only," "Funny Face" (a forerunner of Rodgers and Hart's "My Funny Valentine" as a paean to physical plainness), and the brilliant compilation of conversational cliches, "The Babbitt and the Bromide," during which the Astaires performed their celebrated "run-around" dance.

Apparently, neither the presence of Gertrude Lawrence nor the Gershwin songs could help *Treasure Girl*. It lasted only two months, in spite of a score that included "I've Got a Crush on You," "Where's the Boy?," "Oh, So Nice," "Feeling I'm Falling," and "I Don't Think I'll Fall in Love Today" (which dared to rhyme the seven syllable word "incompatibility" with "A B C").

Aarons and Freedley and the Gershwin brothers came back successfully in 1930 with *Girl Crazy*. Perhaps its simple-minded story was already old-fashioned (the Gershwins' *Strike Up the Band* had opened earlier that year), but there were enough other attractions to compensate for the book. In a part originally intended for Bert Lahr, Willie Howard gave an immensely comic performance as a New York taxi driver who takes a fare to Custerville, Arizona, and ends up as the sheriff. The leading female character was played by a nineteen-year-old dancer named Ginger Rogers, who had already attracted notice in *Top Speed* and in the film *Young Man of Manhattan*. She was given the romantic songs ("But Not for Me" and "Embraceable You") which were suitable for her small but attractive voice. The more raucous, direct numbers, however, needed someone who could really belt them out. Freedley found the girl he wanted at the Brooklyn Paramount where, for the first time, Ethel Zimmerman from Astoria, Long Island, was singing professionally as Ethel Merman. At the opening night of *Girl Crazy* it was she who scored the greatest personal triumph with her delivery of "Sam and Delilah," Boy! What Love Has Done to Me!", and "I Got Rhythm." During the last number, as *Newsweek* magazine once noted, Miss Merman made history by holding one note for the full second chorus in defiance of the second law of thermodynamics, i.e., all forces must eventually come to rest.

But for a world going through the Depression, the completely meaningless, anything-for-a-laugh musical was rapidly losing its flavor and, beginning with *Strike Up the Band,* the Gershwin brothers and their collaborators were

FUNNY FACE (1927). *The ladies Fred Astaire is pointing to are Betty Compton, Adele Astaire, and Gertrude McDonald.*

115

STRIKE UP THE BAND *(1930).*
*Paul McCullough and Bobby
Clark.*

GIRL CRAZY *(1930). Ethel Merman as Kate Fothergill. Miss
Merman, according to* Time
Magazine, *"approaches sex in
song with the cold fury of a
philosopher. She aims at a
point slightly above the en-
trails, but she knocks you out
just the same."*

OF THEE I SING (1931). Lyricist Ira Gershwin, composer George Gershwin, colibrettists George S. Kaufman and Morrie Ryskind.

in the forefront of the change. *Strike Up the Band* was originally to have been presented in 1927, but the anti-war sentiments of the George S. Kaufman book were so uncompromising—even to the ending in which the United States is seen preparing for war with the Soviet Union—that it folded on the road. Morrie Ryskind's revised script three years later blunted the edge somewhat by having the action take place in a dream, changing the enemy to Switzerland, and giving the leads to two zany comics, Bobby Clark and Paul McCullough. Nevertheless, *Strike Up the Band* was a bold innovation in the musical theatre, capable of inspiring William Bolitho to comment in the *World:* "I don't remember ever before in a musical comedy having noticed or understood what it was all about. Here all is not only clear but really startling. Of all things in the world, here is a bitter, rather good satirical attack on war, genuine propaganda at times, sung and danced on Broadway to standing room only."

"I've Got a Crush on You" was salvaged from the unsuccessful *Treasure Girl*, while others in the amorous spirit were the mellifluous "Soon" and the bashful lover's stammering proposal, "I Mean to Say." Most of the numbers, however, were used to fill a more important need—commenting satirically upon developments in the plot and upon the characters. "The Unofficial Spokesman," inspired by the career of President Wilson's adviser, Colonel House, gave advice on how to reach the top in politics (keep your mouth shut), and "A Typical Self-Made Man" detailed the steps that must be taken for the go-getter in business. The mocking title song (which, ironically, has since become accepted as a sincerely patriotic march) set the tone of the entire show both in words and music.

Strike Up the Band was a satirical musical comedy. *Of Thee I Sing* was more in the style of a Gilbert and Sullivan satirical comic opera. Produced by Sam H. Harris, it united for the first time the comedy team of William Gaxton and Victor Moore as the immortal John P. Wintergreen and Alexander Throttlebottom, candidates, respectively, for President and Vice President of the United States. The script by Kaufman (he also directed) and Ryskind was careful to aim its darts not at individuals but at various aspects of society— political conventions, the Congress, the Supreme Court, bathing beauty contests, even motherhood. Yet, it was all done so artfully and entertainingly that there was never a hint of viciousness or of preaching.

In 1931, *Of Thee I Sing* received the Pulitzer Prize for drama. Although this was the first time that the writers of a musical comedy were so honored, the judges refused to include the name of George Gershwin in its citation on the strict technicality that he had not contributed to the actual story. The

OF THEE I SING *(1931). The final scene in the musical. The proud parents of twins are President John P. Wintergreen (William Gaxton) and Mary Turner Wintergreen (Lois Moran). Vice President Alexander Throttlebottom (Victor Moore) beams approvingly at the far left. (Setting by Jo Mielziner.)*

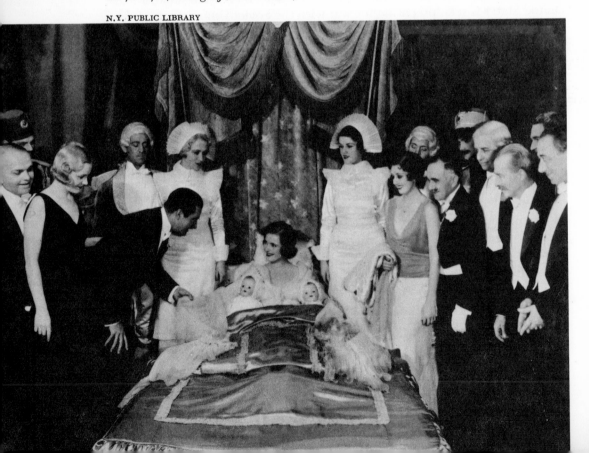

fact was, of course, that the entire production was built on the music, either in its satirical commentary or in its dramatic use to propel and develop the action of the play.

The proper mood is set immediately. When the curtain rises the stage is full of a group of noisy campaigners and voters marching up and down and singing the stirring "Wintergreen for President" while waving banners with such slogans as "TURN THE REFORMERS OUT," "VOTE FOR PROSPERITY AND SEE WHAT YOU GET,' and "WINTERGREEN—THE FLAVOR LASTS." The music itself, Oscar Levant once observed, contains "an actual feeling of social comment," particularly with the intermingling of various airs including "Tammany," "The Sidewalks of New York," and "Hail, Hail, the Gang's All Here."

The song, "Of Thee I Sing," in which the word "baby" is irreverently added to the familiar line from "America," is another example of the deftness of the Gershwin brothers' touch. But, more than consisting of mere touches, the music for *Of Thee I Sing* was employed throughout in what was unquestionably the most closely integrated manner of any Broadway show to that time. Almost all of the Atlantic City bathing-beauty pageant episode was set to music, carrying the action from the selection of Diana Devereaux as queen to the conclusion, in which Wintergreen refuses to marry her because she cannot bake corn muffins. The last scenes of the play, with their profusion of political, judicial, diplomatic, amorous, and natal complications, were sung in a series of arias, choruses, and recitatives. Indeed, almost everything about *Of Thee I Sing* was created with a skill that has rarely been equaled in the musical comedy theatre.

Sequels seldom succeed. In 1933, *Let 'Em Eat Cake*, the successor to *Of Thee I Sing*, adhered faithfully to the rule. With the same producer, librettists, director, and stars, the new work was more astringent, more cutting than the first. An almost grim mood penetrated its discordant, contrapuntal score. Indeed, even the single love song "Mine" used a chorus to interject a sarcastic commentary during Wintergreen's serenading of Mary Turner. In spite of its failure at the box office, however, Gershwin still felt that *Let 'Em Eat Cake* was his best work to that date, calling it "the composer's claim to legitimacy."

LET 'EM EAT CAKE *(1933). John P. Wintergreen (William Gaxton) establishes a dictatorship of the proletariat and sings "Let 'Em Eat Cake" as the first act finale. Joining him on the White House portico are the faithful Mary (Lois Moran) and Alexander Throttlebottom (Victor Moore). (Setting by Albert Johnson.)*

Ever since a particularly trying day in 1926 when nothing seemed to go right at a rehearsal of *Oh, Kay!*, George Gershwin's ambition had been to compose an opera based on DuBose Heyward's short novel, *Porgy*. After returning home that day, he picked up the book hoping that it would lull him to sleep. He read it straight through, however, and became so excited about its possibilities for the theatre that, at four in the morning, he scribbled a letter to Heyward expressing his interest in transforming the novel into an opera. To his surprise, Gershwin soon learned that Dorothy Heyward, the author's wife, had already begun to dramatize his story of the lame beggar of Catfish Row. But this did not really matter; Gershwin, with a remarkable cool personal insight, knew that it would take him years of study before he would have sufficient command of his medium to undertake such an ambitious project. DuBose Heyward collaborated with his wife on the play, the Theatre Guild produced it in 1927, and *Porgy* became one of the dramatic hits of the Broadway season.

Its success only fortified Gershwin's conviction that he must, someday, create an opera out of *Porgy*. In fact, the composer made no secret of this conviction even when the play opened. Critic Gilbert Gabriel of the *Sun*, who was one of the few who did not like the play, prophetically summed up his observations with: "It seems all bits, and nothing but. Or else nothing but the beginnings of the opera George Gershwin hopes to make of it."

In 1932, the Gershwin-Heyward correspondence began again. Although the composer was still interested in *Porgy*, he advised Heyward that there would have to be further delays because of his commitments to write the music for *Pardon My English* and *Let 'Em Eat Cake*. Heyward was particularly disappointed by this news; he had hoped that Gershwin's proposed operatic version of *Porgy* would bring a reverse in the financial difficulties he was having at the time. The Theatre Guild had already approached him with the tempting idea of letting Jerome Kern and Oscar Hammerstein II make a musical of the story with Al Jolson in the title role. Heyward, however, agreed to wait for Gershwin when the composer gave his assurance that he would definitely begin the opera once *Let 'Em Eat Cake* had opened on Broadway. Five days after the première, contracts were signed with the Theatre Guild; shortly thereafter, the actual writing of *Porgy and Bess* was begun.

Most of the collaboration between November, 1933, and July of the following year was done by mail, as Heyward preferred writing in the South and Gershwin was kept in New York by a radio contract. Their postal teamwork was arranged so that scenes and lyrics would be written first, and then mailed north to Gershwin to supply the appropriate music. A few months after the project had started, Ira Gershwin joined the collaboration as colyricist and general liaison man. (Heyward once wrote how, upon receiving

PORGY AND BESS (1935). *The citizens of Catfish Row are about to go off on a picnic on Kittiwah Island. Sportin' Life (John W. Bubbles) stands on a table at the left; Porgy (Todd Duncan) and Bess (Anne Brown) are seated on the steps at the right. (Setting by Sergei Soudekine.)*

the scenes, "the brothers Gershwin, after their extraordinary fashion, would get at the piano, pound, wrangle, swear, burst into weird snatches of song, and eventually emerge with a polished lyric.")

Including visits to Charleston, South Carolina, where the Heywards lived, Gershwin worked on the score for eleven months. Nine more were devoted to orchestrations. During its creation, the opera was called *Porgy*, but to avoid confusion with the original play—and to give it a more "operatic" flavor—the name was changed to *Porgy and Bess*. Rouben Mamoulian (who had also directed the nonoperatic *Porgy*) staged the new work, and the cast, consisting mostly of unknown singers and actors, was headed by Todd Duncan (Porgy), Anne Brown (Bess), and John W. Bubbles (Sportin' Life). Alexander Smallens conducted the forty-two-piece orchestra. Billed as "An American Folk-Opera," *Porgy and Bess* opened at the Alvin Theatre on October 10, 1935.

Convinced that *Porgy and Bess* was worthy of both dramatic and musical appraisal, the larger daily newspapers sent both drama and music critics to the première, and then ran their reviews in adjoining columns. There were wide differences of opinion within both groups, although, in general, the drama reviewers liked it better than the music critics. Burns Mantle (*News*) gave it his highest rating of four stars; Brooks Atkinson (*Times*) wrote: "The story gained by its musical investiture"; John Mason Brown (*Post*): "A memorable production"; Robert Garland (*World-Telegram*): "A modern masterpiece." There were also varying degrees of approval from Richard Watts, Jr., (*Herald Tribune*), Gilbert Gabriel (*American*), and Walter Winchell (*Mirror*). Among those who disapproved were John Anderson of the *Journal,* who felt that it was too long; George Jean Nathan of *Life* ("indeterminate, wobbly, and frequently dull"); Stark Young of the *New Republic* ("curiously monotonous"), and Joseph Wood Krutch of *The Nation* ("I never felt myself profoundly interested or deeply moved").

The music critics seemed to have had some difficulty in trying to determine what *Porgy and Bess* really was. Samuel Chotzinoff (*Post*) called it a "hybrid"; Robert A. Simon (*The New Yorker*): "forceful and often brilliant"; Leonard Liebling (*American*): "the first authentic American opera"; Winthrop Sargeant: "no advance in American operatic composition"; Pitts San-

PORGY AND BESS (1935). *The picnic at Kittiwah Island. John W. Bubbles, as Sportin' Life, sings "It Ain't Necessarily So." (Setting by Sergei Soudekine.)*

born (*World-Telegram*): "an unquestionable advance in Gershwin's art"; Paul Rosenfeld: "the score sustains no mood"; Marcia Davenport (*Stage*): "qualities of conviction and genuineness and importance"; Virgil Thomson (*Modern Music*): "falsely conceived and rather clumsily executed, but it is an important work"; Olin Downes (*Times*): "much to recommend it even though it does not utilize all the resources of the operatic composer."

Whether *Porgy and Bess* is really an opera is still being debated; that it is surely one of the most fully realized musical plays of the American theatre there is no doubt. By combining elements of the Broadway stage that he knew so well with the more challenging features of opera with which he was less familiar, Gershwin created a theatrical and musical entity that, more than twenty-five years later, still stands as a drama of towering emotional power and vitality. More than any other work, it is the one that is most universally accepted as a truly American form of opera.

Although its initial production lasted a bare 124 performances in New York (remarkable for a new opera, but a flop according to Broadway standards), the subsequent major revivals of *Porgy and Bess* in 1942 (Cheryl Crawford production) and in 1953 (as part of the Blevins Davis–Robert Breen international tour) have now raised the total number of its Broadway performances to 715.

What would George Gershwin have accomplished had he not died in 1937? His entire career had been the most steady, step-by-step advance of any theatre composer. There was some overlapping, but it is remarkable that his rise was so chronologically systematic—from revues (1920–1924), to musical comedies (1924–1930), to satirical comic operas (1931–1933), to an American folk-opera (1935). This continual striving after new means of expression certainly would have continued. In their book *The Gershwin Years*, Edward Jablonski and Lawrence D. Stewart reveal that before he died, the composer was planning a film ballet for George Balanchine, a symphony, and a concert tour of Europe. For the theatre he was considering three proposals: a musical cavalcade of American history for the Theatre Guild; a musical about the writing of a musical, with a book by George S. Kaufman and Moss Hart; and an opera with a libretto by Lynn Riggs. Nor had he forgotten DuBose Heyward. According to Frank Durham, the novelist's biographer, Gershwin wrote to his *Porgy and Bess* collaborator just six months before his death to discuss the possibilities of adapting Heyward's book *Star-Spangled Virgin* for the musical stage.

No matter what Gershwin would have chosen to do, however, this much is certain: it would have revealed yet another facet of the endlessly searching and inquisitive nature that distinguished both the man and the musician.

Vincent Youmans.

CHAPTER NINE

Vincent Youmans

THE 1920'S ARE probably the most fondly remembered decade of musical comedy. World War I brought the country back to "normalcy," an awkward word but one well suited to describe the uneasy prosperity that prevailed. People were spending money like water in those Prohibition days, and Broadway was perhaps the wettest street in the land. Hardly a season went by without at least forty new book musicals and revues, and three seasons had as many as fifty. Mere numbers, of course, prove little about the quality of the productions, and it must be admitted that the plots assembled for the book musicals were generally without merit.

Indeed, if ever a period of musical comedy belonged to its composers and lyricists, it was the decade between 1920 and 1930. The war had succeeded in doing what Cohan, and later Kern and Berlin, had been trying to do since the turn of the century—it cut to a minimum the influx of European operettas, thus enabling the works of a rising generation of American writers to be heard. "Back in those days," Douglas Watt once wrote in *The New Yorker,* "a sense of gaiety predominated among songwriters, but there was also a sense of pride—pride in the stimulating little island called Manhattan, pride in breaking away from European-influenced operettas, and, most of all, pride in their own audacity, for almost all of them were young men."

The twenty-year-old George Gershwin had led the way in 1919 with *La La Lucille*. Oscar Hammerstein II was twenty-four when he wrote the book and lyrics for his first musical, *Always You*, the following year. A few months later, Richard Rodgers, then all of eighteen, and Lorenz Hart, then twenty-five, were represented by their first show, *Poor Little Ritz Girl*. When he was twenty-one, Vincent Youmans composed the music for his initial entry, *Two Little Girls in Blue*, with lyrics by the twenty-four-year-old Ira Gershwin. Cole Porter, though he had written two scores before the Twenties, came back from Europe at the age of thirty-one to do *The Greenwich Village Follies of 1924*. The same year, Howard Dietz was twenty-eight when he wrote the words to Jerome Kern's music for *Dear Sir*; two years later, his future partner, Arthur Schwartz, contributed his first numbers to *The Grand Street Follies* when he was twenty-five.

Of all the young composers, however, none was more the product of, or is more directly associated with, the Broadway musical theatre of the 1920's than Vincent Youmans. All his successful stage productions were presented during that period, including three, *Wildflower*, *No, No, Nanette*, and *Hit the Deck*, that were among the biggest hits of the decade.

Youmans' career has always been somewhat overshadowed by that of the more prolific George Gershwin. Indeed, there are several striking, if superficial, parallels in their lives and works. Youmans was born on September 27, 1898, just one day after Gershwin. Both worked for Max Dreyfus when they were young, and both were given their first Broadway assignments by Alex Aarons. The Youmans show, *Two Little Girls in Blue*, even had a book written by Fred Jackson, the author of Gershwin's *La La Lucille*, and the lyricist was George's brother, Ira. Toward the end of the 1920's, Gershwin and Youmans attempted to broaden the scope of the musical theatre, though only Gershwin was able to succeed in his more adventuresome undertakings. And, of course, the tragedy of the two composers is that their careers came to an end when they were both young—Gershwin died at thirty-eight and Youmans was forced into retirement because of tuberculosis when he was thirty-five.

The personalities of the men, however, were entirely different. Gershwin was gregarious, warmhearted, pulsating with his own vibrant excitement with life; Youmans was a genuinely shy person whose constant illnesses were partly responsible for making him seem cold and aloof. In their careers, Gershwin was surely the more fortunate of the two in having such a close working arrangement with his brother; Youmans seldom was able to find a lyricist worthy of his music, and, in fact, seldom worked with the same one twice. But perhaps the most unfortunate aspect of Youmans' life was that he had to stop working when he was so young; Gershwin, at least, was spared the mental and physical strain of a prolonged invalidism.

Vincent Millie Youmans (he was the third in his family with that name) was born in New York. His father was a prosperous maker of men's hats, and his mother, Lucy (Gibson) Youmans, came from a socially prominent family. At the age of four, young Vincent could play chords on the piano; soon afterward, encouraged by his mother, he began to take lessons. Although he first wanted to become an engineer, he took his father's advice and got a job with a Wall Street brokerage firm. After enlisting in the Navy at the outbreak of the war, Youmans was assigned to the Great Lakes Naval Training Station, where he began to compose songs and produce shows for his fellow servicemen.

This experience changed his mind about his future career; upon his return to civilian life, he was determined to become a song-writer. To achieve this aim, he followed the familiar path of song-plugger (for Max Dreyfus) and rehearsal pianist (mostly for Victor Herbert operettas). In 1920, inspired by the motion picture *The Country Cousin*, Youmans wrote his first published song and gave it the same title. Alfred Bryan, the veteran lyricist, wrote the words.

Youmans and Gershwin first met and became good friends when they were both working for Harms. Gershwin, highly appreciative of Youmans' talent, played a number of his friend's songs to convince producer Alex Aarons that he should hire Youmans for his next musical, *Two Little Girls in Blue*. Aarons was impressed, and Youmans got the job as co-composer with Paul Lannin, with lyrics supplied by Ira Gershwin (then modestly known by the pseudonym Arthur Francis).

TWO LITTLE GIRLS IN BLUE *(1921). Madeline and Marion Fairbanks (as Dolly and Polly Sartoris) have many shipboard adventures on their way to India to claim an inheritance. It was the first Broadway musical for both Vincent Youmans and Ira Gershwin.*

Just before rehearsals began, Aarons sold the musical to A. L. Erlanger for $100,000. The composer and lyricist were retained but Ned Wayburn, Erlanger's director, warned Youmans and Ira Gershwin to stay away from rehearsals lest the producer become panicky over their youthful appearances. Erlanger really had no cause to worry. *Two Little Girls in Blue*, which opened in May, 1921, had a respectable run of 135 performances and produced three songs ("Who's Who with You," "Dolly," and "Oh, Me! Oh, My!") that sold a good many reams of sheet music.

Youmans' second musical, *Wildflower*, was one of the biggest successes of the Twenties. Responsible for its plot and lyrics were Otto Harbach and Oscar Hammerstein II, who had been brought together in 1920 by producer Arthur Hammerstein. Harbach, the older of the two, had already written such hits as *The Three Twins, Madame Sherry,* and *The Firefly,* and the producer felt that he would be of great help to his young nephew, then beginning to write for the theatre. The year that they met, Harbach and Hammerstein

WILDFLOWER *(1923). Edith Day as the strong-willed Nina Benedetto, who can inherit her grandfather's millions only by keeping her temper under control for six months. (Costume by Charles LeMaire; setting by Frank E. Gates and E. A. Morange.)*

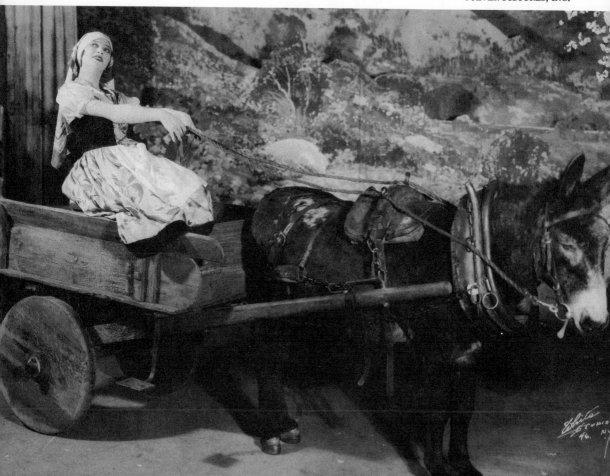

NO, NO, NANETTE (1925).
*Louise Groody & Charles
Winninger sing "I Want to
Be Happy."*

collaborated on the successful *Tickle Me* (for Frank Tinney) and the un-successful *Jimmie*, both with music by Herbert Stothart. In 1924, the trio of Harbach, Hammerstein, and Stothart—augmented by Vincent Youmans—was reunited by Arthur Hammerstein for *Wildflower*.

Wildflower gave Edith Day her biggest success since Harry Tierney's and Joseph McCarthy's *Irene*. The score contained many delightful numbers, among them the ever-recurrent "Bambalina," which told of an eccentric old fiddler at a country fair who liked to stop playing in the middle of a number just to embarrass the dancers. The critics were far from happy about the story. The *News's* Burns Mantle dismissed it as "one of those 'here come the girls and boys now' operettas," though Robert Benchley of *Life*, while conceding that the book was weak, concluded his review on a philosophical note: "If you're going in for books, you might as well stay home and tell stories every evening."

In spite of its shorter Broadway run, *No, No, Nanette* had a far more impressive history than *Wildflower*. Indeed, if we consider its worldwide reception and its numerous touring companies, *No, No, Nanette* was probably the biggest international hit of any of the conventional musical comedies of the decade. Without being pioneering or even particularly original, it was nonetheless a skillful combination of many of the stock farce elements then so common in musical comedy—the philandering husband, the domineering wife, the innocent ingenue, and the amorous complications resulting from mistaken identity.

At first, *No, No, Nanette* showed all the symptoms of pre-Broadway egg-laying. Immediately following the coolly received opening performance in Detroit, in April, 1924, producer H. H. Frazee made some drastic changes: he took over as director, made librettists Frank Mandel and Otto Harbach rewrite the script, and threw out five songs. After frantic effort, Youmans and lyricist Irving Caesar produced four new numbers, including two, "I Want to Be Happy" and "Tea for Two," that became the most durable songs in the score.

Frazee continued making changes even after the show opened in Chicago. In June, he replaced almost all of the original leads, with the two most important roles, the negatively admonished heroine and the playboy husband, taken over by Louise Groody and Charles Winninger. The musical quickly became such a hit that the producer kept it in Chicago for almost a year. Even before this company was to arrive in New York, Frazee took the unprecedented step of sending out three other companies to tour the United States, and of allowing the musical to be presented in London and other foreign localities. When, on September 16, 1925, *No, No, Nanette* at last opened in New York at the Globe Theatre (now the Lunt-Fontanne), it settled down to a respectable run of 321 performances. (Youmans always maintained that it could have run much longer if it had not toured so extensively both before and during the Broadway engagement.)

The music and lyrics of *No, No, Nanette* are full of the irresistibly buoyant spirit of the Twenties. Indeed, the words occasionally seem to be unconsciously parodying the entire era. When the curtain rises on the first scene (the reception room in the home of wealthy Jimmy Smith), a covey of boys and girls are seen as they arrive to call on Nanette, Jimmy's ward. While waiting for her, they prance merrily down to the footlights to reveal gleefully in song that they are all "flippant and fly and free," and that they only have time for "petting parties with the smarties." Much of the period flavor is also captured in "You Can Dance with Any Girl at All," "Too Many Rings around Rosie" ("Will never get Rosie a ring!"), and the sparkling title song (whose melody Youmans appropriated from his own "My Boy and I," heard briefly in *Mary Jane McKane*).*

By 1927, although his output was limited by ill health, Youmans had become recognized as one of the leading composers of the theatre. Yet he was seldom satisfied with the way his songs were sung or performed. His first seven scores had been created with at least nine lyricists for six different producers, and his relationship was not close with any of them. He knew that he would always have to depend on others for lyrics, but there was nothing to

* Two years after *No, No, Nanette* opened in New York, producer Frazee presented an alliterative sequel, *Yes, Yes, Yvette,* with lyrics by Caesar and music by Phil Charig and Ben Jerome. Despite its affirmative title, however, the show was a quick failure.

HIT THE DECK *(1927). "Bilge" Smith (Charles King) surrounded by the admiring ladies of the ensemble. (Costumes by Mark Mooring; setting by Ward and Harvey.)*

BROWN BROS.

prevent him from becoming his own producer. Therefore, at twenty-eight, Youmans formed a partnership with Lew Fields (who withdrew shortly after the opening) to present *Hit the Deck*, "A Nautical Musical Comedy" written by Fields's son, Herbert. "For the first time in my life," Youmans said at that time, "I am able to select my own singers and my own cast to interpret my music and to play the parts as I would like to have them played. For the past six or seven years, I have been completely at the mercy of the managers and of the actors."

Hit the Deck, with a cast headed by Louise Groody, Charles King, and Stella Mayhew, became Youmans' third big hit of the Twenties. To critic Percy Hammond, though he allowed that it did contain a "few fleshly jots and titles," the show was "clean, pretty, bright, and happy," with "quantities of jolly dancing, three good songs, and romance teeming with badinage and bon mots." Its story was also considered stronger than most musical comedies

131

RAINBOW *(1928). Libby Holman, as Lotta, about to sing the torch song, "I Want a Man."
(Costume by Charles LeMaire.)*

132

of the day as it was based on a popular play, *Shore Leave*, which had been shown on Broadway five years before.

Two of the "three good songs" mentioned by Hammond were undoubtably "Sometimes I'm Happy" and "Hallelujah!" Coincidentally, both had melodies that were not specifically created for *Hit the Deck*. "Hallelujah!", the first song Youmans had ever written, was composed during the First World War at Great Lakes. Somewhat timidly, he showed the manuscript to "Red" Carney, the bandmaster of his group, who liked the piece very much. According to Youmans, Carney was the first man ever to encourage him to become a composer, though, paradoxically, he never played the number.

"Sometimes I'm Happy" had been known as "Come on and Pet Me" when Oscar Hammerstein II and William Cary Duncan first put words to it for the 1923 musical *Mary Jane McKane*. However, it was cut before the show reached New York. In 1925, with a new lyric by Irving Caesar and Clifford Grey, "Sometimes I'm Happy" was added to the score of *A Night Out*. This time it was the show itself that did not reach New York. Youmans had faith that the song would eventually become a hit, and he made sure that a suitable place was found for it in *Hit the Deck*.

Vincent Youmans never again had a theatrical hit for which he composed the entire score. Because of failing health, he agreed to relinquish his producing activities temporarily to write the songs for Philip Goodman's production of *Rainbow*. The prospects of the show were decidedly favorable: the libretto, by Laurence Stallings and Oscar Hammerstein II, was an especially strong one, and Hammerstein's lyrics and Youmans' music were combined into a surging, dramatic score. Set in 1849 during the California gold rush, the story told of a young scout at Fort Independence, Missouri, who kills an officer in self-defense, joins a wagon train heading West, and eventually wins both a pardon and the colonel's daughter. With its realistic situations, lusty dialogue, three-dimensional characters, and intelligent use of music, *Rainbow* was in the grand tradition of *Show Boat*, with which it was favorably compared.

Unfortunately, when presented on the stage, the production lacked pace, and almost everything went wrong with it during its première on November 21, 1928. The first-act curtain didn't fall until ten minutes to eleven, a mule misbehaved on stage, the backdrops twitched and shook throughout the entire evening, and, as Gilbert Gabriel wrote, "One intermission was so long and lapsy that the orchestra played everything but 'Dixie' to fill it up." Moreover, as a result of a disagreement between Youmans and the producer, the single love duet, "Who Am I That You Should Care for Me?" (lyric by Gus Kahn), had been removed during the tryout, leaving the score with stirring marches, torch songs, comic numbers, but not one real ballad. Most of the critics, fortunately, overlooked its faults to comment enthusiastically about the daring and originality of the work. The cast included Allan Prior, Charles Ruggles, Louise Brown, Mae Barnes, and the torrid Libby Holman, who achieved her first notice on Broadway by intoning the languorous "I Want A Man." The show never recovered from its opening-night problems, and lasted only thirty performances.

After his disappointment with *Rainbow*, Youmans again tried to be his own producer. He bought the Cosmopolitan Theatre at Columbus Circle, renamed it the "Youmans Cosmopolitan," and set about preparing *Great Day!*, with "Characters and locale of the story conceived by Vincent Youmans." But nothing went the way he wanted it. During the four months of tryouts before its October, 1929, opening in New York, writers, directors, actors, and even the costume designer quit or were fired. Moreover, of its ten original songs, only "Happy Because I'm in Love," "More Than You Know," "Without a Song," and "Great Day" were in the show by the time it had its Broadway première. (Among the casualties was Harold Arlen, who played the part of the piano player in the scene in the Hot Ace Dance Hall, and sang a song called "Doo-Dah-Dey.") *Great Day!* lasted six performances longer than *Rainbow*.

Youmans' misfortunes continued. In 1930, Ziegfeld wanted him for a production that appeared to be a certain hit: the combined talents of Marilyn Miller and Fred and Adele Astaire in a story based on an idea by Noël Coward. The show was called *Smiles*, though few were seen during either its preparation or its presentation. From the start, Youmans had difficulties with both Ziegfeld (who added Walter Donaldson's "You're Driving Me Crazy" and "Keep Smiling and Carry On" to the score during its brief New York run), and Marilyn Miller (who, for some inexplicable reason, refused to sing "Time on My Hands," the hit song of the show). On the bright side there was a dance routine to "Say, Young Man of Manhattan," in which Fred Astaire, in top hat and tails, danced around chorus boys in similar costume and shot them down with his cane. The idea was later used in the film *Top Hat*, with which it has since become identified.

Through the Years, based on *Smilin' Through*, was another ambitious musical and another flop. Youmans produced it himself, gave it a painstaking production (including a forty-five piece orchestra), but the story was heavy and old-fashioned. The title song was always the composer's favorite.

In 1932, Youmans was called in to bolster the score of a musical called *Humpty Dumpty*, then floundering in its pre-Broadway tryout. Renamed *Take a Chance*, its original score by Richard A. Whiting, Herb Brown Nacio (better known as Nacio Herb Brown), and B. G. DeSylva was then augmented by seven songs by Youmans, two of which were dropped before New York. The show was one of Ethel Merman's early triumphs. The final curtain was delayed almost every night by Merman's exciting delivery of

TAKE A CHANCE (1932). *One of the musical numbers in a Broadway-bound revue called* Humpty Dumpty *was "Eadie Was a Lady," sung by Ethel Merman. "She sings it," wrote Percy Hammond, "in an ante-prohibition New Orleans supper club, where, surrounded by chorus girls disguised as amorous sailors from the U.S. battleship* Tampico, *she mourns the death of Eadie, a sister in sin. Ere she is through with the jocular threnody her audience is clapping its hands and waving its handkerchiefs in deserved approval." (Costumes by Kiviette and Charles LeMaire; setting by Cleon Throckmorton.)*

such show-stopping numbers as the Whiting-DeSylvia-Nacio "Eadie Was a Lady" (with additional lyrics by Roger Edens), and the Youmans-DeSylva optimistic, revivalistic "Rise 'n Shine." Other Youmans efforts included the schizophrenic dilemma of "pop" singers, "Should I Be Sweet?" (". . . or hot? It's up to yooooou!"), and two attractive duets, "So Do I" and "Oh, How I Long to Belong to You," both sung by June Knight and Jack Whiting.

In all, the Vincent Youmans catalogue consists of less than one hundred songs, published within a thirteen-year period. But in this group are some of the most continually performed "standards" of popular music. Because his more ambitious works such as *Rainbow, Great Day!,* and *Through the Years* failed to win popular support, Youmans has become far better remembered for the quality of his music than for his innovations in the musical theatre. His intriguing harmonies and syncopations combined with a disarming economy of notes have become something of a trademark, as have such spiritual-inspired, emotionally compelling pieces as "Hallelujah!," "Great Day," and "Rise 'n Shine." But Youmans could also create songs that overflowed with rich melody and sentiment, distinguished by warmth and genuine musicianship.

Although he died on April 5, 1946, at the age of forty-seven, "new" songs by Vincent Youmans may yet be heard. During his years as an invalid, he spent almost all of his time studying and writing. There are approximately 175 manuscripts of music in his "trunk," most of which were composed after his retirement. If suitable musical comedy librettos can be found, these songs, outfitted with new lyrics, will then be used. The years ahead will surely be musically enriched if once again the credit line, "Music by Vincent Youmans," is associated with a Broadway musical.

Lorenz Hart and Richard Rodgers.

CHAPTER TEN

Richard Rodgers
and Lorenz Hart

APART FROM THOSE men who not only create music but also write their own lyrics, the theatre composer, as a rule, has outshone the lyricist. In the early days of the twentieth century, words of popular songs were usually so uninspired that the reputations of Victor Herbert, Sigmund Romberg, and others were far greater than those of their lesser endowed collaborators. Even more modern song-writers, such as Kern or Youmans, were better known than most of the writers who joined words to their melodies. Although the Gershwin brothers were a closely welded team, the billings usually listed "Music by George Gershwin" ahead of all other credits, and, in some cases, in larger letters than those allotted to Ira. The first composer-lyricist team that made a change in this trend and created musicals for which both men were given equal billing was that of Rodgers and Hart.

In his entire career, Richard Rodgers has had only two partners, Lorenz Hart and Oscar Hammerstein II. In each case, the partnership has been entirely equal. No one has ever referred to a "Richard Rodgers musical"; it has always been "Rodgers and Hart" or "Rodgers and Hammerstein." This "collaborative fidelity of Rodgers," Hammerstein has written, "is significant, I think, because it illustrates a sense of pattern and constructive purpose which never leaves him. This is not just professional habit, but a view of life."*

It also illustrates why a song by Rodgers, whether its lyric was written by Hart or Hammerstein, seems to have been the product of just one man. There is always the effect of not only a singleness of expression but of a single-mindedness as well. For to fuse lyrics with music so that each seems to belong totally and indivisibly with the other, both composer and lyricist must yield a little so that neither element in the song is given sustained prominence. It is this ability to compromise that has marked the most successful song-writing teams. That Rodgers has been able to achieve a close unity with two such disparate lyricists as Hart and Hammerstein, and to produce brilliant music with both, is a mark of his dedication and his uniqueness.

Richard Charles Rodgers was born on June 28, 1902, near Arverne, Long Island, where his parents, William and Mamie Rodgers, were spending the summer. His mother was a fine pianist and his father, a doctor, was a good baritone. They frequently held family concerts in their New York apartment of all the latest musical comedy and operetta successes. By the time Dick was four, he could pick out melodies on the piano; at six, he was able to play with both hands. From an early age he was enchanted by the theatre, particularly the musical theatre. When he was in his teens, Saturday afternoon would find him at the matinée of a musical; if it were by Jerome Kern, he would see it over and over again. As he recently told Arnold Michaelis in a recorded interview, "If you were at all sensitive to music, Kern had to be your idol. You had to worship Kern."

It was at a summer camp in Maine, Camp Wigwam (later to be attended by Frank Loesser), that the fourteen-year-old Richard Rodgers wrote his first song, the words and music to "Campfire Days." The same year he multigraphed and distributed his first copyrighted song, "Auto Show Girl," with a lyric by David Dyrenforth.

Unlike most song-writers, Rodgers was fortunate in having a father who encouraged and helped him in his musical interests. Dick's older brother, Mortimer, however, was responsible for giving him his first chance to write for the theatre. Mortimer belonged to a social group known as the Akron Club. In 1917, when the club decided to put on an original musical comedy for the benefit of the New York *Sun* Tobacco Fund for servicemen, he managed to convince his fellow members that his fifteen-year-old brother should be allowed to write the songs. Called *One Minute Please*, the show was presented at the Grand Ballroom of the Plaza Hotel. Among the numbers were such intriguingly titled compositions as "When They Rub Noses in Alaska," "I'm a Vampire," and "At the Movies" ("If your sweetie should prove fickle, You can love her for a nickel").

* From *The Rodgers and Hart Song Book*, with Foreword by Oscar Hammerstein II. New York: Simon and Schuster, Inc., 1951.

Rodgers' score was so well received that the following year he was asked to contribute the music and lyrics for the second Akron show, *Up Stage and Down*. With his father assisting him on some of the melodies, and his brother helping out with the lyrics, Rodgers contributed sixteen numbers to the show. Five of them were considered good enough to be published, but the young composer did not have to find a receptive music company. His father gave him the money and he published the songs himself.

When Rodgers was only seventeen, the first Rodgers and Hart song was sung in a Broadway musical. The two young men had been brought together the previous year by a mutual friend, Philip Leavitt, who felt that they would make a good song-writing team.

Lorenz Milton Hart was born May 2, 1895, in New York City. His parents were Max and Frieda Hart, and, on his father's side, Larry descended from Heinrich Heine, the German poet. He was an inveterate reader with a great interest in both classical literature and the classical theatre. Hart was only seven when he saw his first play; from then on, he attended the theatre as regularly as he could. At Columbia University, he was active in the Varsity Shows, but he left Morningside Heights after three years to work for the Shubert brothers as a play translator. In recalling his first meeting with Hart, Rodgers once wrote in *Theatre Arts Monthly:* "He was violent on the subject of rhyming in songs, feeling that the public was capable of understanding better things than the current monosyllabic juxtaposition of 'slush' and 'mush.' It made great good sense, and I was enchanted by this little man and his ideas. Neither of us mentioned it, but we evidently knew we'd work together, and I left Hart's house having acquired in one afternoon a career, a partner, a best friend and a source of permanent irritation."

The new partners began to work together almost immediately. Leavitt, the man who had introduced them, was a neighbor and a good friend of Lew Fields, the famous comedian and producer. In the summer of 1919, he arranged an audition for the new team to be held at Fields's Far Rockaway home. "In those days," Rodgers recalls, "all a show tune needed to be acceptable was attractiveness and a potential hit quality." Thus, after listening to all the material, Fields promptly decided to add one song, "Any Old Place with You," to the score of *A Lonely Romeo*, a musical in which he was then appearing on Broadway. The number was fitted into the show rather handily, and it became the first published song by Rodgers and Hart. "Any Old Place with You" remains an enjoyable, bouncy piece with a clever lyric that makes use of the names of geographic locations ("I'll go to hell for ya—or Philadelphia!") to create a series of original and unexpected rhymes.

Rodgers entered Columbia University in the fall of 1919. When Deems Taylor once asked him why he chose Columbia, his answer was simple: the Varsity Show. He was there only a few months when he and Hart wrote the score for a musical, *Fly with Me*, which was accepted by the Varsity Show

POOR LITTLE RITZ GIRL (1920). *Lulu McConnell, of the* Poor Little Ritz Girl *company, does some heavy emoting for the benefit of stage manager Grant Simpson. Aileen Poe, another member of the cast, looks rather disdainfully at the performance.*

CULVER PICTURES, INC.

committee. Oscar Hammerstein II, a member of the committee, even collaborated with Rodgers on one song for the show, "Room for One More." *Fly with Me* was a satire on undergraduate life on an island ruled by the Soviets. It was greeted so enthusiastically that S. Jay Kaufman of the *Globe* wrote of the young composer: "Several of his tunes were capital. We have not heard of Mr. Rodgers before. We have a suspicion we will hear of him again."

Another member of the audience who was impressed was Lew Fields. Once again he made a quick decision: he would use some of the songs in his next musical comedy, *Poor Little Ritz Girl*. This, of course, was exciting news to Rodgers and Hart. In addition to three songs from *Fly with Me* ("Don't Love Me Like Othello," "Peek in Pekin," and "Dreaming True," which became, respectively, "You Can't Fool Your Dreams," "Love's Intense in Tents," and "Love Will Call"), the team turned out twelve new songs for the production. That was as far as their association with *Poor Little Ritz Girl* went. Fields bought the songs outright, and never felt it necessary to consult such inexperienced talent during the show's preparation. Consequently, Rodgers and Hart were not advised of the producer's decision to cut eight of their numbers right after the Boston tryout, replacing them with eight by the more experienced Sigmund Romberg and Alex Gerber. Perhaps Fields had become nervous about entrusting an entire score to an eighteen-year-old college freshman and his twenty-five-year-old partner. Whatever the reason, the first the partners knew about the change was when they arrived at the Central Theatre for the première on July 27, 1920.

Poor Little Ritz Girl was a lightweight comedy of mistaken identity, using the musical-show-within-a-musical-show technique to present many of the songs. In spite of their decimated contribution, Rodgers and Hart did succeed in gaining some recognition. Kenneth Macgowan and the *Globe* liked Rodgers' "hard, brisk tunes," and Heywood Broun of the *Tribune* commented that "the neglected lyric also gets more of its due than usual, for 'Mary, Queen of Scots' seems to us the most rollicking ballad we have heard in a twelvemonth. It is perhaps fitting to mention that Richard C. Rodgers composed the music for this ditty as well as that for another excellent song, 'What Happened Nobody Knows.' The more serious songs are from Sigmund Romberg, and they are pleasing, but hardly as striking as the lighter numbers."

Such favorable comments, however, made little impression on Broadway producers who were reluctant to take a chance on two brash young men and their unorthodox approach to songs. Rodgers reluctantly returned to Columbia and, with Hart, wrote the next Varsity Show, *You'll Never Know* (which included two songs, "Will You Forgive Me?" and "Let Me Drink in Your Eyes," that had been written for *Poor Little Ritz Girl* but were never used). Oscar Hammerstein II directed the show. After his second year at Columbia, Rodgers left to enroll in the nearby Institute of Musical Art (now the Juilliard School of Music). During his two years there, he found time to continue writing musicals with Hart for the Akron Club and almost any other social group that asked him. In many of these undertakings, the partners were joined by Lew Fields's son, Herbert, as either book director or dance director.

In 1924, under the perhaps protective *nom de drame* of "Herbert Richard Lorenz," Fields, Rodgers, and Hart collaborated on a comedy for Lew Fields called *The Melody Man.* Though it was about the music-publishing business and included two songs ("I'd Like to Poison Ivy" and "Moonlight Mama"), the play was not really a musical. Nor was it a hit. But it did accomplish two things: it helped to launch the career of a young actor named Fredric March, and it inaugurated the most successful musical comedy-writing trio since Bolton, Wodehouse, and Kern.

Just before the beginning of the long string of Fields, Rodgers, and Hart book musicals, the trio was associated in the production of a now-legendary revue of the mid-Twenties, *The Garrick Gaieties.* Fields's position as dance director, however, made the show a far less important assignment for him than it was for Rodgers and Hart.

The Garrick Gaieties provided the song-writers with the opportunity they badly needed. Rodgers and Hart had started auspiciously enough with *Poor Little Ritz Girl* in 1920. Yet for five years they had been unable to interest producers or music publishers; except for *The Melody Man,* they had had to devote their energies exclusively to creating amateur shows. Benjamin Kaye, a lawyer and close friend of the Rodgers family, was anxious to do what he could to help the young composer. A sometimes writer himself (he had once written the words to a Rodgers song, "Prisms, Plums and Prunes," which was in the Akron Club show *Up Stage and Down*), Kaye was helping to organize an intimate revue with a group of young actors who had appeared in the Theatre Guild plays. It was their hope that the Theatre Guild itself might sponsor the entertainment; the Guild had just built the Guild Theatre (now the ANTA), but had run short of money and could not buy new tapestries. The revue would serve a double purpose: it would give young talent a chance to be seen, and it would raise the necessary amount for the tapestries.

At Kaye's suggestion, Rodgers was chosen as composer; at Rodgers' insistence, Hart was chosen as lyricist. Lawrence Langner and Theresa Helburn, the managers of the Guild, agreed to sponsor the show and to allow it to be shown for two Sunday performances at the Garrick Theatre. With a top price of $2.20 a ticket, *The Garrick Gaieties* featured a cast of unknown performers including Sterling Holloway, Elisabeth (Libby) Holman (in her first Broadway appearance), Edith Meiser, Romney Brent, Philip Loeb (who also directed), Lee Strasberg, and Sanford Meisner. Harold Clurman was the stage manager, and Rodgers himself conducted the tiny pit orchestra. Although it had been planned to show *The Garrick Gaieties* only on Sunday, May 17, 1925, the demand for tickets was so great that six extra performances were given. When the demand continued unabated, the show settled down for a six-month run.

The Garrick Gaieties followed the pattern set by the *Greenwich Village Follies* and *The Grand Street Follies*. It was a fresh, youthful, impudent, seemingly spontaneous revue with some of its satirical barbs aimed at the Theatre Guild itself and its fondness for heavy dramatic productions. There was in both the first and the second *Gaieties* (the second was given in 1926) such a high level of wit and melody that they have since become landmarks in the history of the revue. (Wells Root of the *World*, who attended that first Sunday performance, predicted with some accuracy that its program "will be dug up from nowhere in ten years and conned with reminiscent chuckles.")

"Manhattan," an almost wistfully bucolic tune combined with a bright, intricately rhymed lyric, was the hit of the 1925 edition, though "Sentimental Me," in which the excessively ardent emotions of popular love ballads were parodied, was also outstanding. In the 1926 *Gaieties*, the most popular item was "Mountain Greenery," a brisk number that was something of a companion piece to "Manhattan" as it sang the praises of vacations in the country. Each edition also contained a lengthy musical production as the first-act finale. In the first *Gaieties*, *The Joy Spreader* was an attempt at a jazz opera, with the inspiration for its book credited to Gilbert Seldes, "who is therefore primarily responsible for this outrage." The second *Gaieties* included a devastating lampoon of operettas called *Rose of Arizona*. As the title indicates, one of

THE GARRICK GAIETIES *(1925)*
Philip Loeb, Sterling Hollo-
way, and Romney Brent as
"The Three Musketeers."
(Costumes by Carolyn Han-
cock.)

PHOTO BY VANDAMM

the main targets was *Rose-Marie*. with the setting changed from the Canadian Rockies to the Mexico–Arizona border. The Rodgers and Hart work had a chorus line of muscular soldiers, eight chorus girls depicting different flowers, and a group of songs all obviously plagiarized from well-known tunes ("It May Rain When the Sun Stops Shining" was an especially wicked takeoff on "Till the Clouds Roll By.") *

Although most of the critics hailed the two revues, there seems to have been a slight preference for the first one. Robert Benchley felt that "Rodgers and Hart's music and lyrics, together with the burlesque sketches and the playing of half-a-dozen hitherto unknown youngsters, should be a standing taunt and source of chagrin to those uptown revue managers who keep putting on the same old thing each year." On viewing the second *Gaieties*, Percy Hammond commented, "Last year it seemed to be saying 'Ain't I Cute, I'm only six'; which it was. But this time it is a wise and flippant ingenue, well versed in the ways of the world, though a bit awkward in pursuing them."†

Between the 1925 and 1926 *Garrick Gaieties*, two Fields, Rodgers, and Hart book musicals, *Dearest Enemy* and *The Girl Friend*, were shown in New York. *Dearest Enemy*, which was written even before the first *Gaieties*,

---

* *Rose of Arizona*, apparently, was the grandmother of *Little Mary Sunshine*, Rick Besoyan's clever spoof of the same type of musical theatre, produced over thirty years later.

† In 1930, a third *Garrick Gaieties,* with songs by many different writers, was presented by the Theatre Guild. Although some of the members of the original company were present, and many of the original Rodgers and Hart songs were used, it was far less successful than its predecessors. The cast included Albert Carroll, Edith Meiser, Philip Loeb, Sterling Holloway, Imogene Coca, and, making her musical comedy debut, Rosalind Russell.

143

DEAREST ENEMY (1925) Charles Purcell, as Capt. Sir John Copeland, is temporarily at the mercy of Helen Ford, as patriotic Betsy Burke, in this tale of the American Revolution. (Costumes by James Reynolds; setting by Clark Robinson.)

was variously described as an "operetta with more than a chance flavor of Gilbert and Sullivan" (*Times*); "something very akin to a genuine comic opera" (Arthur Hornblow, *Theatre* magazine), and "a baby grand opera" (Percy Hammond, *Herald Tribune*). The trio had originally taken the manuscript to Lew Fields, but he had feared that its story of how Mrs. Robert Murray (of Manhattan's Murray Hill) detained General Howe during the American Revolution would not be commercial. The musical was eventually sponsored by the husband of Helen Ford, the star of the show.

There was a well-sustained attempt to fit the music into both the story and the period. The ballads, "Here in My Arms," "Bye and Bye," and "Here's a Kiss," were dainty, charming pieces, while the comic numbers, among them "Old Enough to Love" (a gayer approach to mature love than Kurt Weill's "September Song") and "War Is War," were both funny and appropriate. "Sweet Peter" went back to an even earlier New York as it told how the boom-boom-boom of Peter Stuyvesant's wooden leg always alerted his wife when he came home drunk. In summing up his opinion of *Dearest Enemy*, Frank Vreeland of the *Telegram* wrote: "We have a glimmering notion that someday they [Fields, Rodgers, and Hart] will form the American counterpart of the once great triumvirate of Bolton, Wodehouse, and Kern."

The new triumvirate's next show, *The Girl Friend*, was indeed in the spirit of the bright, up-to-date productions once offered at the Princess Theatre. Presented by Lew Fields, with Sammy White and Eva Puck in the leads, the musical won critical and popular favor. Its book, according to Abel

Green of *Variety*, "is the best libretto Fields has contributed so far and is only parred by the songs with ultra-smart lyrics and oddly rhythmed and fetching tunes." Among them were the classic of city-life contentment, "The Blue Room," and the jagged ode to "The Girl Friend."

"From the beginning," wrote an unspecified *Times* critic in his review of *Peggy-Ann*, "Fields, Rodgers, and Hart have brought freshness and ideas to the musical comedy field, and in their new piece they travel a little further along their road." The show, which opened in December, 1926, was daring in almost every respect but its title. Roughly based on a 1910 Marie Dressler musical called *Tillie's Nightmare*, the entire story was a dream, with the exception of a prologue and an epilogue. Many of the conventions of musical comedy were both shattered and satirized as the slightly Freudian saga took the heroine (Helen Ford) from her home in Glens Falls, New York, to New York City's Fifth Avenue, out to sea in a yacht and then a raft, and finally to a Havana race track. There was no opening chorus, nor were there any songs at all for the first fifteen minutes. When the dancing girls did arrive, they were used functionally within the plot rather than as unrelated ornaments. The ending, when Peggy-Ann finally awoke from her three-hour dream, was actually performed in semidarkness.

That such an adult and original work could succeed commercially in the mid-Twenties so encouraged its trio of writers that they followed it with another dream fantasy. Early in 1921, Fields, Rodgers, and Hart had taken a six-month option on Mark Twain's *A Connecticut Yankee in King Arthur's Court*, but they were unable to interest a producer. Six years later, they had little difficulty in getting Lew Fields and Lyle D. Andrews, the co-producers of *Peggy-Ann*, to sponsor it as the next attraction at the Vanderbilt Theatre. In inventiveness and wit it may have been a less-inspired offering than its predecessor, but *A Connecticut Yankee* nevertheless attracted audiences in such throngs that it became the first Rodgers and Hart musical to run over

PHOTO BY VANDAMM

A CONNECTICUT YANKEE *(1927). "That irrepressible young trinity" (as Gilbert Gabriel called them), Herbert Fields, Richard Rodgers, and Lorenz Hart, photographed backstage at the Vanderbilt Theatre.*

145

400 performances. The music and lyrics were an important factor in its popularity. "My Heart Stood Still" (originally sung earlier in the year by Jessie Matthews and Richard Dolman in a London revue, *One Dam Thing After Another*) was a warm, rich melody wedded to an uncommonly expressive lyric, made all the more effective by Hart's use of simple monosyllabic words. Another hit of the score, "Thou Swell," revealed the lyricist in a more characteristic vein as he mixed old English and new American.

In 1943, after Rodgers and Hammerstein had begun their collaboration with *Oklahoma!*, Rodgers himself produced an up-dated version of *A Connecticut Yankee*. This time, the Yankee was a lieutenant in the Navy and the girl a corporal in the W.A.C. Another change enlarged the relatively minor character of Queen Morgan Le Fay to fit the major talents of Vivienne Segal. It was in this production that she introduced the hilariously macabre inventory, "To Keep My Love Alive," which, in Rodgers's words, showed "the inability on Larry's part to succumb to a cliché or to rhyme any way but brilliantly."

Rodgers and Hart had three shows on Broadway in 1928, *She's My Baby*, *Present Arms*, and *Chee-Chee*. Following the quick failure of *She's My Baby* (in spite of the efforts of Beatrice Lillie, Clifton Webb, and Irene Dunne), the composer and lyricist went back to the Fields family for their next musical. Herbert Fields, having recently written a libretto about the Navy in *Hit the*

A CONNECTICUT YANKEE *(1927). Queen Morgan Le Fay (Nana Bryant) seems to have hypnotized the Yankee (William Gaxton). (Costumes by John Hawkins, Jr.)*

Deck, now turned his attention to the Marines in *Present Arms.* This, too, became a well-attended attraction, with critics comparing it to both *Hit the Deck* and the DeSylva-Brown-Henderson musical *Good News.* The songs, happily, were pure Rodgers and Hart—among them the unregretful "You Took Advantage of Me."

Chee-Chee, also with a book by Herbert Fields, was an ambitious work that tried to make all the songs adhere firmly to the story line. Rodgers and Hart had been anxious to write this kind of show for a long time. As Hart described it before the opening, it would be "a new form of musical show," in which "the songs are going to be a definite part of the progress of the piece, not extraneous interludes without rhyme or reason." Even its program note—similar to that of *Rose-Marie*—contained the following information: "The musical numbers, some of them very short, are so interwoven with the story that it would be confusing for audiences to peruse a complete list." Only six, including "Moon of My Delight" and "I Must Love You," were then specified by title. Everything, in fact, seemed promising about *Chee-Chee* except a plot that related the fairly indelicate account of how the son of the Grand Eunuch of old China avoided inheriting his father's exalted position. The show lasted thirty-one performances.

The quick failure of *Chee-Chee* ended Rodgers and Hart's association with Lew Fields and temporarily halted their collaboration with Herbert Fields. It also made them a little cautious. *Spring Is Here* and *Heads Up!,* their next two shows, were formula entertainments, both produced by Alex A. Aarons and Vinton Freedley. *Spring Is Here* did have "With a Song in My Heart" (though it had to be sung by the "other man," John Hundley, because the star, Glenn Hunter, could not sing); *Heads Up!* offered the gently lapping "Ship without a Sail." This was also the first Broadway musical to provide a young dancer named Ray Bolger with sufficient opportunity to demonstrate his remarkable talent.

Nor was there anything outstanding about *Simple Simon,* a lavish Ziegfeld production of 1930 in which Ed Wynn starred. Of the Rodgers and Hart songs, the maudlin "Ten Cents a Dance" has become the most popular. It was introduced by Ruth Etting, who had succeeded Lee Morse only twenty-four hours before the New York opening. During the tryout, Ziegfeld insisted that one song, "Dancing on the Ceiling," would have to be cut. Luckily, Rodgers and Hart were able to salvage it for Jessie Matthews to sing in a London musical, *Ever Green.*

America's Sweetheart, in 1931, was the last original musical comedy written by Fields, Rodgers, and Hart. As the Mary Pickford allusion in the title suggests, it was a satire on Hollywood, where the trio had just spent some time working on a film called *The Hot Heiress.* For the leading female role of an aspiring movie actress, the authors chose an unknown singer, Harriette

SIMPLE SIMON *(1930). Ed Wynn comes to the rescue of Cinderella in this musical Mother Goose fantasy. "Wynn has never seemed so indisputably great," wrote Brooks Atkinson.*

AMERICA'S SWEETHEART *(1931). Rodgers and Hart's musical about the movies had Jack Whiting and Harriette Lake (better known as Ann Sothern) as two ambitious young actors. In this scene, Miss Lake is obviously not amused at Mr. Whiting's gift of a success horseshoe consisting of fruits and vegetables. (Costumes by Charles Le-Maire; setting by Donald Oenslager.)*

Lake, whom they had seen in a brief part in *Smiles* during its Boston tryout. Described by *Time* as "a lovely synthesis, one part Ginger Rogers, one part Ethel Merman," Miss Lake soon emerged with a definite personality of her own under the name of Ann Sothern.

In general, although Dorothy Parker commented in *The New Yorker* that Hart's rhymes were "less internal than colonic," greater praise was bestowed on the score than on the script. According to Brooks Atkinson, there was "a rush about the music and a mocking touch in the lyrics that make the score more deftly satirical than the production."

Despite the attitude they had shown toward the movie industry in *America's Sweetheart*, Rodgers and Hart spent the next three and one-half years in Hollywood. Upon their return to New York in 1935, their first assignment was to create the songs for Billy Rose's mammoth *Jumbo*, the final production to play at the Hippodrome Theatre. With John Murray Anderson as over-all director and George Abbott staging the book (his first musical), *Jumbo* was, according to Percy Hammond, "a sane and exciting compound of opera, animal show, folk drama, harlequinade, carnival, circus, extravaganza, and spectacle." Jimmy Durante headed the cast of ninety humans and almost as many animals.

The myriad problems of such a huge undertaking—financial as well as creative—compelled Billy Rose to delay the première for almost three months beyond its scheduled date. Surprisingly, after it did open, Broadway customers kept it running for only five months. After closing in New York, it

JUMBO (1935). The "Circus Wedding" finale with Donald Novis and Gloria Grafton as the groom and bride. (Costumes by Raoul Pène du Bois; production designed by Albert Johnson.)

PHOTO BY VANDAMM

reopened at the Dallas Exposition with Eddie Foy, Jr., in the Durante part. But eventually, as a headline in *Variety* sadly revealed:" 'JUMBO' DISINTE-GRATES INTO 50-CENT CIRCUS; TEXAS DATE ANOTHER FLOP, RAN SHOW $30,000 FURTHER INTO RED."

Although they were always anxious to explore novel ideas for the musical stage, Rodgers and Hart were never completely successful in contributing to the structure of the musical theatre until *On Your Toes* in 1936. This time the partners decided to write the book themselves, which they did in collaboration with George Abbott. Thus, they were able to create a strikingly unified production that not only offered a coherent story but also utilized dancing as an integral part of the action. For the important post of dance director, they secured George Balanchine, the ballet choreographer, whose only previous Broadway experience had been in staging some of the dances for the *Ziegfeld Follies of 1936*. The most memorable sequence in *On Your Toes* was the *Slaughter on Tenth Avenue* ballet, in which Balanchine's choreography, the dancing of Ray Bolger and Tamara Geva, the sleazy ex-citement of Rodgers' music, and the ballet's dramatic importance all com-bined to lift *On Your Toes* to a position as one of the supreme theatrical achievements of the mid-Thirties.

The producer of *On Your Toes* was Dwight Deere Wiman. For the next two years he followed it with annual spring musicals bearing the credits,

ON YOUR TOES (1936). *George Balanchine's* Slaughter on Tenth Avenue *ballet. Tamara Geva as the Strip Tease Girl, George Church the Big Boss, and Ray Bolger the Hoofer. (Costumes by Irene Sharaff; setting by Joe Mielziner.)*

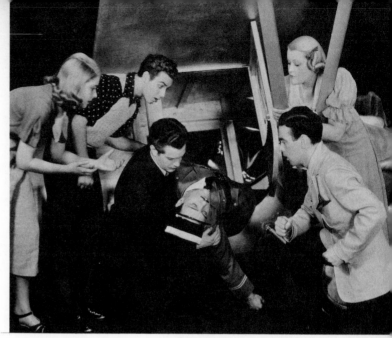

BABES IN ARMS (1937). *Aljan de Loville, as a French pilot, makes a forced landing in the midst of Mitzi Green, Rolly Pickert, Alfred Drake, Duke McHale, and Wynn Murray. (Costumes by Helene Pons; setting by Raymond Sovey.)*

"Book, music, and lyrics by Rodgers and Hart," and "Choreography by George Balanchine." In 1937, their combined efforts created *Babes in Arms;* in 1938, it was *I Married an Angel.*

Babes in Arms was full of *Garrick Gaieties* youthfulness, with a cast headed by such youngsters as Mitzi Green, Ray Heatherton, the Nicholas Brothers, Wynn Murray, and, in minor roles, Alfred Drake and Dan Dailey. More important, it was another serious attempt to make each song serve a purpose in the story, which, conveniently, was concerned with young people putting on an amateur musical. Seldom has one show produced so many enduring hits—the saga of the vocal phenomenon known as "Johnny One Note"; the almost psychological "Where or When"; "My Funny Valentine," in which the warmth of the music conveys so perfectly the true intent of the slightly exaggerated lyric; the duet, "I Wish I Were in Love Again," with its unusual combination of disillusionment and ebullience; and the brazen confession of the nonconformist, "The Lady Is a Tramp."

John Anderson in the *Journal-American* hailed *I Married an Angel* as "a winged wonderwork from the musical heavens of Rodgers and Hart," an appraisal that may have been only slightly excessive. The story, which Rodgers and Hart had originally adapted for the movies in collaboration with Moss Hart, was an imaginative tale of a Budapest banker (Dennis King) who vows that he will marry only an angel, and the awkward situations that arise when a real angel (Vera Zorina) actually becomes his bride. The cast was particularly notable. Both King and Walter Slezak had recently distinguished themselves in straight dramas. After an eight-year self-imposed exile from the musical stage, Vivienne Segal returned to Broadway in the kind of light comedy part she had been trying to get ever since *The Three Musketeers*, her last musical, in which she had also appeared opposite Dennis King. Vera

151

I MARRIED AN ANGEL (1938). *Audrey Christie, Walter Slezak, and Dennis King. (Costumes by John Hambleton; setting by Jo Mielziner.)*

"Beauty is truth, truth beauty / Gabriel blow your root-toot-tooty," sing Vera Zorina and fellow angels in "Angel without Wings."

Zorina, who had scored a hit in the Tamara Geva role in the London production of *On Your Toes*, gave her most fondly remembered performance as the lovely angel-bride.

I Married an Angel was the first musical to be directed by Joshua Logan. Jo Mielziner's decor, which incorporated treadmills and a curtain that functioned like a huge Venetian blind, was an especially important contribution to the effectiveness of the play.

The score offered such glittering Rodgers and Hart gems as "Did You Ever Get Stung?" ("Where the doctor can't help you"), "I Married an Angel," "I'll Tell the Man in the Street," "A Twinkle in Your Eye," and the poignant "Spring Is Here," in which the beauties of spring are found to have little appeal when one is unloved. Of all, perhaps, the real show-stopper was the audacious travesty of every Roxy and Radio City Music Hall stage spectacle, "The Roxy Music Hall" ("It's a Wonderland where everyone is Alice/Where the ladies room is bigger than a palace".*)

Between *Babes in Arms* and *I Married an Angel*, Rodgers and Hart and librettists George S. Kaufman and Moss Hart collaborated on a musical social satire, *I'd Rather Be Right*. Following the precedent set by Moss Hart's and Irving Berlin's *As Thousands Cheer*, actual living people were portrayed. Instead of offering impersonations in a number of blackout sketches, however, *I'd Rather Be Right* was a regular book musical with President Franklin D. Roosevelt as the leading character. Portraying the role was the semiretired, but still agile, George M. Cohan.

Because of the news value of such a production, newspapers and news magazines treated the preparation of *I'd Rather Be Right* as a major event. There were headlines when, during the Boston tryout, Cohan refused to sing an uncomplimentary line about his friend, Al Smith, in the song, "Off the Record." There were more headlines when Noël Coward was called in to help rewrite and restage some of the material. There were still more headlines concerning the friction between Cohan and Rodgers and Hart, whom the star disparagingly referred to as "Gilbert and Sullivan." Even the New York *Times* devoted an editorial to "Spoofing the Great" (they were for it). All these helped give the show a record advance sale of $300,000. ("Why the idea of calling George M. Cohan Franklin D. Roosevelt should have engendered so intense an interest I cannot figure out," wrote George Jean Nathan in *Newsweek*, "unless it was because Franklin D. Roosevelt, on the other hand, has been called everything under the sun but George M. Cohan.")

Almost inevitably, when *I'd Rather Be Right* at last arrived at the Alvin Theatre in New York on November 2, 1937, there were some who felt disappointed. Richard Lockridge, whose review was carried on page 1 of the *Sun* and contained almost every punch line in the show, commented that it was

* Copyright © 1938 Robbins Music Corporation. Used by special permission.

I'D RATHER BE RIGHT *(1937). Gathered around the piano in Sam Harris' office are producer Harris, lyricist Lorenz Hart, composer Richard Rodgers, colibrettists Moss Hart and George S. Kaufman, and star George M. Cohan.*

not always brilliant satire. In comparing it with *Of Thee I Sing*, which almost everyone did, the general feeling was that Gershwin, Gershwin, Kaufman, and Ryskind were more skillful than Rodgers, Kaufman, and the *Zwei Herzen* (as John Mason Brown referred to the unrelated Moss and Lorenz). George M. Cohan, however, scored a great personal triumph that might well have elected *him* President, and audiences were made acutely aware that nowhere else in the world could so outspoken a production be shown.

The score for *I'd Rather Be Right* was written in just three weeks. It contained only one moderately popular song, "Have You Met Miss Jones?"; the rest of the numbers being too satirical and too close to the theme for any of them to catch on.

After their three-in-a-row springtime musicals for Dwight Deere Wiman, Rodgers and Hart evened their seasonal average by writing three successive fall shows for producer-director George Abbott—*The Boys from Syracuse* (libretto by Abbott) in 1938, *Too Many Girls* in 1939, and *Pal Joey* in 1940. The first of these, an uninhibited but skillful adaption of Shakespeare's *The Comedy of Errors,* so impressed Richard Watts, Jr., of the *Herald Tribune,* that he wrote: "If you have been wondering all these years just what was wrong with *The Comedy of Errors*, it is now possible to tell you. It has been waiting for a score by Rodgers and Hart and direction by George Abbott."

The long-awaited score still remains one of the team's finest, high-lighted by "This Can't Be Love," "You Have Cast Your Shadow on the Sea," "Falling in Love with Love" (one of Rodgers and Hart's best waltzes), and the romantic tribute to the winter solstice, "The Shortest Day of the Year." The two Dromios were played by Jimmy Savo and Teddy Hart (Larry's brother), and their masters were Eddie Albert and Ronald Graham.

Too Many Girls had a collegiate setting (Pottawatomie College, Stop Gap, New Mexico) which gave it a football backfield of Hal LeRoy, Eddie Bracken, Desi Arnaz, and Richard Kollmar, cheered on by coeds Marcy West-cott, Mary Jane Walsh, and Diosa Costello. One of the energetic undergradu-ates was Van Johnson, who later succeeded Kollmar for the tour. The pro-duction had so much vitality and so many fine Rodgers and Hart songs that few were troubled by its old-fashioned book or the awkward way some of the numbers were incorporated into it.

The idea of fashioning a musical out of a series of short stories about a conniving hoofer named Joey Evans was first suggested by the author himself, John O'Hara, in a letter to Rodgers. It took Rodgers and Hart only five minutes to decide to do it, and they promptly notified O'Hara that they would be glad to write the songs if he supplied the book. For the leading part, Rodgers chose a young actor named Gene Kelly, whom he had seen in a dancing role in William Saroyan's *The Time of Your Life*. As his middle-aged, worldly patroness there could be no other actress than Vivienne Segal, who had recently demonstrated her gifts as a brittle comedienne in *I Married an Angel*.

In many ways, *Pal Joey* was the pinnacle of the Rodgers and Hart col-laboration. The score was purposely unsentimental and sardonic, allowing only one love song, "I Could Write a Book," and even that was an insincere

THE BOYS FROM SYRACUSE (1938). *Dromio of Syracuse (Jimmy Savo) is obviously in need of a little extra spending money from his master, Anti-pholus of Syracuse (Eddie Albert). The lady draped on Albert's shoulder is Betty Bruce. (Costumes by Irene Sharaff.)*

TOO MANY GIRLS *(1939). Desi Arnaz, as the football hero of Pottawatomie College, leads the students in the torrid "Spic and Spanish" number. On the right is an equally animated Diosa Costello, and behind them is Van Johnson. (Costumes by Raoul Pène du Bois.)*

PAL JOEY *(1940). Joey's dream of the Chez Joey night club at the end of the first act. Gene Kelly and Vivienne Segal are in the center. Van Johnson is at the extreme right. (Costumes by John Koenig; setting by Jo Mielziner.)*

expression. Throughout, there was a cohesion of mood between music and plot that was remarkable, though not all the songs were used to advance the action. Some of the best ("Happy Hunting Horn," "The Flower Garden Of My Heart," "That Terrific Rainbow") were part of a nightclub floor show; "Zip" was an out-of-nowhere, in-front-of-the-curtain routine; "Do It the Hard Way" was a specialty number for tumbler Jack Durant. Others, however, such as "In Our Little Den of Iniquity," "Bewitched, Bothered, and Bewildered," and "Take Him," were all intelligently introduced as part of the story. In whatever manner they were introduced, however, all the songs shed light on the smoky characters who sang them and about whom they were sung.

Peopled by characters who were either unattractive or just stupid, *Pal Joey* was too far from musical comedy orthodoxy for many of the patrons and some of the critics. "Although it is expertly done, can you draw sweet water from a foul well?" asked Brooks Atkinson. To Wolcott Gibbs, however, it was that rarity, "A song-and-dance production with living, three-dimensional figures, talking and behaving like human beings."

Pal Joey may well have been ahead of its time. When it was revived in 1952 by Jule Styne and Leonard Key, it met with much greater success. "While Joey himself may have been fairly adolescent in his thinking and his morality," Rodgers observed shortly before the second opening, "the show bearing his name certainly wore long pants, and in many respects forced the entire musical comedy theatre to wear long pants for the first time." With Vivienne Segal in her original role, with Joey played by Harold Lang (understudied by Bob Fosse), and with hardly a line changed, the musical had the longest run (542 performances) of any Rodgers and Hart production. The once divided critics were now almost unanimous in their praise. Words like "masterpiece" and "classic" were in their reviews, and some compared it to the Kurt Weill–Bert Brecht *Die Dreigroschenoper.* Even Brooks Atkinson could now feel that "it renews confidence in the professionalism of the theatre," while a slightly gloating Wolcott Gibbs noticed that "standards

PAL JOEY *(1952). Vivienne Segal recreates her original role of Vera Simpson, and Harold Lang is the new Joey Evans. Here they sing "In Our Little Den of Iniquity." (Costumes by Miles White; setting by Oliver Smith.)*

BY JUPITER *(1942). Ray Bolger as Sapiens and Benay Venuta as Hippolyta in a musical remake of Julian Thompson's* The Warrior's Husband. *(Costumes by Irene Sharaff.)*

apparently have changed, because up to now I have met nobody who found anything embarrassing in the goings on."

The April before the first *Pal Joey* opened, Dwight Deere Wiman tried to revive his streak of spring musical successes with Rodgers and Hart's *Higher and Higher,* but it was a failure. The producer was more fortunate in the summer of 1942 when he joined Rodgers (in association with Richard Kollmar) to present *By Jupiter.* Starring the nimble Ray Bolger, it was a formula Rodgers and Hart show full of what the customers could easily appreciate as pre-World War II glamour, and it became one of the team's most profitable undertakings.

The partnership of Rodgers and Hart, however, was all but finished. Hart, a brilliant, unstable man given to mysterious disappearances for weeks at a time, was becoming extremely difficult for Rodgers to work with. In 1941, the composer had secretly aligned himself with George Abbott as co-producer of *Best Foot Forward* (score by Hugh Martin and Ralph Blane), and early in September of that year had discussed with his old friend, Oscar Hammerstein II, the possibility of a partnership if the time ever came when Hart could no longer continue. When Theresa Helburn of the Theatre Guild approached Rodgers with the idea of adapting Lynn Riggs's play, *Green Grow the Lilacs*, into a musical, he immediately became enthusiastic about the project. Hart demurred. He didn't feel well, it wasn't their kind of show, and if Rodgers really wanted to do the show, why didn't he choose another lyricist. It was then that Rodgers and Hammerstein agreed to work together on the play that eventually became *Oklahoma!* Hammerstein, in fact, had long wanted to make a musical out of *Green Grows the Lilacs*, and had even tried unsuccessfully to interest Jerome Kern in collaborating on it.

The last show Lorenz Hart worked on was the 1943 production of *A Connecticut Yankee*. Throughout the opening-night performance, Hart remained in the rear of the theatre, walking back and forth and muttering to himself. When Rodgers looked for him after the final curtain, he was nowhere to be found. Two days were spent in frantic efforts to locate him. When he was finally found unconscious in a hotel room, Hart was immediately rushed to Doctors Hospital, suffering from acute pneumonia. Rodgers and his wife were with him almost constantly for three days, but he never regained consciousness. On November 22nd, in the midst of an air-raid-drill blackout, Lorenz Hart died. He was forty-eight years old.

The collaboration between Rodgers and Hart was a unique one in many ways. Aside from its productivity and longevity, it was a near-perfect combination of frequently sharp, sophisticated lyrics set to music that was just as frequently warm and lyrical. The remarkable thing, of course, is how well each man complemented the other's style, adding something both inseparable from, and indispensable to, the total effect. (The Rodgers and Hart technique, incidentally, was somewhat opposite from that of the Gershwin brothers. George's hard-driving, jagged rhythms were often smoothed down by what Vernon Duke has called the "lazy, good-natured, placidly *gemutlich* fun with words that was Ira's characteristic.")

Freshness, charm, and daring, coupled with an unquenchable spirit of youthfulness, were present in almost everything that Rodgers and Hart wrote. The methodical, outwardly calm composer and his excitable, cigar-chewing partner were continually seeking new ideas in songs and in stories, and the range of subject matter in their musicals attests to their inquisitive, experimental nature. *Time* magazine wrote, in 1938: "As Rodgers and Hart see it, what was killing musicomedy was its sameness, its tameness, its eternal rhyming of June with moon. They decided it was not enough to be just good at the job; they had to be constantly different also. The one possible formula was: *Don't have a formula;* the one rule for success: *Don't follow it up."*

Cole Porter.

CHAPTER ELEVEN

Cole Porter

T HE LIVES OF the most prominent theatre composers have been distinguished by extreme dedication to their occupations. Apart from Rodgers, who got his apprenticeship writing amateur shows, the leading figures during the Twenties usually followed a set routine as they went from song plugger (usually for Max Dreyfus), to vaudeville accompanist, to rehearsal pianist. Then, if they were lucky, they would have a song interpolated in a show, or, if they were even luckier, they would be asked to compose an entire score. But no matter what the exact path may have been, all the major talents first decided on their goal when they were in their early or middle teens, and then went after it with diligence and determination.

Cole Porter was the notable exception. He never had to struggle or to perform lowly tasks either in Tin Pan Alley or in Shubert Alley. He never had to bother with amateur shows to attract attention. He never had to make the rounds of producers and publishers. Competition never disturbed him, nor was he particularly concerned about money. He was twenty-three when his first Broadway show, *See America First,* opened in 1916, but for the next twelve years he spent most of his time living in Europe, traveling around the world, and, in general, making sure that there was not one pleasurable place anywhere that he had not visited. Chronologically, his initial offering places

Porter after Romberg, Friml, and Berlin, and before Gershwin, Youmans, and Rodgers, but his theatrical career only began in earnest at the very end of the 1920's. From then on, however, Porter's rise was rapid. He turned out a series of scores—both words and music—for musical comedies celebrated for their glossy opulence, outstanding performances, melodic inventiveness, and sophisticated wit.

During the Thirties, when other composers were writing social satires and experimenting with new and different theatrical forms, Porter was creating songs that did what they could do to perpetuate all that was glamorous in the Twenties. For Porter, that was the decade of luxurious apartments in Paris, special trains to the Lido, ballets staged by Diaghilev for his own private parties, years spent at the Palazzo Rezzonico in Venice (at a rental of $4,000 a month), cruises down the Rhine, and incessant traveling to distant, exotic places. During this period, whenever a friend would suggest that he try Broadway again, Porter's answer was that he much preferred writing his songs for the amusement of his friends. His attitude was summed up once when, to an entreaty that he turn professional song-writer, he answered simply, "Suppose I had to settle down on Broadway for three months just when I was planning to go to the Antibes."

Nonetheless, wherever Porter was, or whatever he was supposed to be doing, he was always busily composing songs. These songs, among them "Two Little Babes in the Wood," "Let's Do It," and "What Is This Thing Called Love?," were certainly not the product of an amateur or a dabbler. In melody and in lyrics, his work at the time showed a professionalism made all the more impressive by his absence from Broadway. For though he was aware of what the Gershwin brothers and Rodgers and Hart were accomplishing, he was not directly under the influence of the rising young generation of song-writers of the Twenties. Completely independently and far from the Broadway scene, Cole Porter was creating his own distinctive style, one that would later characterize all his contributions to the musical theatre.

Cole Albert Porter was born on a 750-acre farm in Peru, Indiana, on June 9, 1893. His parents were Samuel Fenwick and Kate (Cole) Porter. By the time he was ten, young Cole had already composed two songs, a feat that so delighted his proud mother that she had one of them, "The Bobolink Waltz," published in Chicago. This musical interest, however, did not please Porter's wealthy grandfather, J. O. Cole. Cole, who had made a fortune in the lumber business in West Virginia, was anxious to leave his grandson a large inheritance, but only on the condition that the boy become a lawyer.

Porter's grandfather sent him to Worcester Academy in Massachusetts, and to Yale, with the hope that he would become interested in his studies and get his mind off music. Porter still found time to write. When he was seventeen, Remick published an early effort called "Bridget", and within the next two years he created those immortal college tunes, "Bingo Eli Yale" and "Yale Bulldog Song." Although music interested him for more than his regular studies, Porter dutifully entered Harvard Law School. His obvious lack of interest in the law soon became apparent to the dean, who suggested that he might make a more impressive scholastic record at the Harvard School of Music. Once grandfather Cole finally gave his grudging consent, Porter enthusiastically began his study of music.

While still at Harvard, Porter and a fellow student, T. Lawrason Riggs, collaborated on a professional Broadway show, *See America First.* On one of his frequent trips to visit friends in East Hampton, Porter had met Elisabeth Marbury, the socially prominent literary agent who had recently co-sponsored the immensely successful *Very Good Eddie.* Hoping to do as much for Porter's career as she had for Kern's, Miss Marbury agreed to produce the show that Porter and Riggs had recently written. *See America First* ("A Patriotic Comic Opera") may have seemed like a clever idea on paper, but when it was performed on the stage it was a complete failure. The story dealt with the efforts of an anti-British U. S. senator to keep his daughter from meeting anyone from across the Atlantic. Of course, inevitably, after being taken out West, the girl does meet a titled Englishman (Clifton Webb), they fall in love, and, eventually, the senator loses his prejudices. Apparently, the fact that this was a spoof of the George M. Cohan flag-wavers—particularly *George Washington, Jr.*—was lost on the unnamed critic of the *New York Dramatic Mirror,* who wrote: "The lyrics are studiously copied after the Gilbertian pattern in the long and complicated rhyme effects achieved. The music, however, gives the impression that its composer, after the first hour, gave up the task of recreating a Sullivan atmosphere, preferring to seek his inspiration in our own George M. Cohan."

Following the brief run of *See America First,* Porter, partly out of disappointment and partly out of a desire for adventure, joined the French Foreign Legion.* While in service in North Africa, he entertained the troops by playing his songs on a specially constructed portable piano which could be carried on his back with the rest of his equipment. When the United States entered the First World War, Porter was transferred to the French Artillery School at Fontainebleau. The charms of Paris soon proved irresistible to him; after the war, he rented a large apartment and decided to remain there.

Although he was rather well provided for, Porter felt that he needed a still larger allowance from his grandfather, especially since he wanted to marry the wealthy Linda Lee Thomas. Such an important request required a personal confrontation, and Porter sailed back to the United States in 1919.

---

* T. Lawrason Riggs also gave up thoughts of a musical career after *See America First.* He soon entered the priesthood, and later became Roman Catholic chaplain at Yale.

Also on board ship was Raymond Hitchcock, the popular comedian and producer. After hearing Porter play some of his songs (and possibly not un-
mindful of the young man's financial status), Hitchcock commissioned the
young composer to write the music and lyrics for the third edition of his
Hitchy-Koo revues. Joe Cook made his New York debut in the show singing
"When I Had a Uniform On," but it was the uncharacteristically sentimental
"An Old-Fashioned Garden" that gave Cole Porter his first song hit.

Grandfather Cole's refusal to allow him more money was of little concern to Porter now. With his royalty checks from "An Old-Fashioned Garden"
giving his bank account a much-needed boost, he returned to Paris, married
Linda Lee, and began his life of party-giver and pleasure-seeker. He did not
abandon music, however, devoting much time to the study of harmony and
counterpoint under Vincent d'Indy at the Schola Cantorum in Paris. In 1923,
Porter's affluence was enhanced even more when J. O. Cole died and left his
grandson over $1 million. Then, as Porter once put it, "I could go to Venice."

During the early Twenties, Porter interrupted his life of ease only twice:
to write songs for another *Hitchy-Koo* revue that never came to New York,
and to contribute the score for John Murray Anderson's *Greenwich Village
Follies of 1924*. Of the numbers in the *Follies*, "I'm in Love Again," sung by
the Dolly Sisters and danced by future Broadway choreographer Robert
Alton, was the only one to win popularity.

Among the many people who never gave up their efforts to induce
Porter to return to the Broadway theatre, the only one to succeed was E. Ray
Goetz. Goetz, an enterprising producer and occasional song-writer himself,
journeyed to the Lido in the summer of 1928 with the express purpose of
talking the reluctant composer into creating another score. Finding Porter
sunning himself on the Lido beach, Goetz introduced himself and immediately offered what he was sure would be an attractive proposal. The score
would be for a musical that was so Parisian it was actually called *Paris*, the
star of the show would be Goetz's vivacious wife, Irene Bordoni, and Porter
would only have to compose eight songs. Somewhat to his own surprise,
Porter found himself agreeing to take the assignment.

Paris, though it was billed, *Time*-fashion, as "A Musicomedy," and
though it did well at the box office, was little more than an incidental comedy
with incidental music. In fact, of the eight Cole Porter songs, only five were
used, with two others supplied by the producer. All the numbers were sung
by Miss Bordoni accompanied by Irving Aaronson's Commanders, an eleven-
piece orchestra seated on stage in what was supposed to be a hotel suite.

In the song, "Let's Misbehave" (cut from *Paris* before it reached New
York), Porter's lyric mentioned briefly the love life of lovebirds, bears, and
camels. This interest in the animal kingdom was slight compared to the
zoölogical survey in "Let's Do It," the number that replaced "Let's Misbe-

PARIS *(1928). Irene Bordoni surrounded by Irving Aaronson's Commanders. (Setting by William Castle.)*

have." Bluebirds, bluebells, sponges, oysters, clams, jellyfish, electric eels, shad, sole, goldfish, dragonflies, centipedes, mosquitoes, katydids, lady bugs, moths, locusts, bees, fleas, chimpanzees, kangaroos, giraffes, hippopotamuses, sloths, guinea pigs, bears, and Pekinese dogs—in addition to various types of humans—all had their amatory habits covered in a manner that immediately established Cole Porter as one of the most ingenious creators of sly and imaginative lyrics.

The reception to his songs for *Paris* convinced Porter that there were pleasures to be had in the world of musical comedy as well as in the world of international society. The next year, he and Goetz again worked together on another musical with a Parisian locale, *Fifty Million Frenchmen.* Featuring William Gaxton, Genevieve Tobin, and Helen Broderick, it was the first of seven Cole Porter musicals to have librettos written or co-written by Herbert Fields. It was also the first musical directed by Edgar Montillion "Monty" Woolley, who had been an instructor at Yale while Porter was an undergraduate.

Fifty Million Frenchmen, which became a bigger box office success than *Paris,* had a score that abounded in unhackneyed sentiments. "I Worship You" revealed Porter's interest in the mythology of the Greeks, Phoenicians, and Egyptians, while "Find Me a Primitive Man" went back to an earlier age for inspiration. There was even a jaunty, insouciant air about the more traditional love duets, "You Do Something to Me" and "You've Got That Thing."

165

"When it comes to lyrics," wrote George Jean Nathan in *Judge*, "this Cole Porter is so far ahead of the other boys in New York that there just is no race at all."

Just one month after the première of *Fifty Million Frenchmen*, an English show, *Wake Up and Dream!*, opened with Jack Buchanan, Jessie Matthews, and Tilly Losch. Porter did not contribute all the songs to it, but he was responsible for the dark, brooding "What Is This Thing Called Love?," which was based on a native chant he had first heard in Marrakech, Morocco, and the somewhat more emotionally fulfilling "Looking at You." Although the eternal dilemma of the modern maiden called "Which?" had been intended originally for *Paris*, it was first sung on Broadway by Miss Matthews in *Wake Up and Dream!*

The New Yorkers, in 1930, was another Porter musical written by Herbert Fields for E. Ray Goetz. Monty Woolley again directed. There were some interpolations in it from the repertory of Clayton, Jackson, and Durante, and also that of Fred Waring's Pennsylvanians, but the score was chiefly Porter's. Hope Williams and Charles King sang "Where Have You Been?," a rather heavy ballad, and Kathryn Crawford intoned the dolorous saga of a street walker in "Love for Sale." The composer also described the rival pleasures of staying at home ("The Great Indoors") and of taking off for a tropical island ("Let's Fly Away").

Porter's skill at combining opposites within a single song was strikingly demonstrated in "Night and Day," which was first sung by Fred Astaire in the 1932 success, *Gay Divorce*. The song, a somewhat extended piece, was another example of a less ethereal, more carnal approach to love, with its verse suggesting a heartbeat and its release a tegumentary revelation of the yearning burning under one's hide. Luella Gear and Eric Blore contributed most of the comedy, with Miss Gear making something both funny and touching of the mad life of the social-climbing "Mister and Missus Fitch."

After the debacle of the Gershwin brothers' *Pardon My English* ended the Alex A. Aarons–Vinton Freedley partnership in 1934, Freedley and his

FIFTY MILLION FRENCHMEN (1929). *William Gaxton and a bevy of beauties. (Costumes by James Reynolds.)*

GAY DIVORCE *(1932). There were many complications in this tale of an unhappy wife who hires a professional co-respondent to help her secure a divorce. In this scene, Luella Gear discovers the wife (Clairé Luce) with both the presumed corespondent (Fred Astaire) and the real one (Erik Rhodes). (Setting by Jo Mielziner.)*

wife took a lengthy ocean voyage to enable him to reflect on the possibility of a career as a solo producer. As Freedley recalls: "The idea came to me when I was fishing peacefully in the Pacific Ocean near the Pearl Islands. While waiting for a bite, I began, with no special purpose, to consider the ideal people for a musical show." William Gaxton and Victor Moore were obvious choices, particularly as a result of their Wintergreen and Throttle-bottom characterizations in *Of Thee I Sing* and *Let 'Em Eat Cake.* So was Ethel Merman, whom Freedley had discovered for *Girl Crazy.* George and Ira Gershwin would have been the logical song-writers, but it was apparent from their toiling over *Porgy and Bess* that they would have little interest in doing another musical comedy. The bright and brittle rhythms of Cole Porter suggested themselves immediately; so did the idea of having a book created by the Princess Theatre masters, P. G. Wodehouse and Guy Bolton.

The more he thought of the idea, the more plausible it became. When he arrived back in New York, Freedley immediately signed the stars, the composer, and, finally, the librettists. In those days, as Ethel Merman wrote in her autobiography, *Who Could Ask for Anything More,* "the writers who used to think up the books that were wrapped around Gershwin or Cole Porter scores, started from scratch, with only their bare cupboards and an unmanageable sense of humor to guide them. First a producer signed a cast; then he hired writers to rustle up some material for that cast to use. 'I've got Bert Lahr,' he'd say; 'write me a part for Bert Lahr.' Or 'I've signed Victor Moore. Get goin' buddy. Make with the Moore-type yoks.' "*

* From *Who Could Ask for Anything More* by Ethel Merman. Garden City, N. Y.: Doubleday & Company.

ANYTHING GOES (1934). *Ethel Merman sings "Anything Goes" accompanied by Marshall Smith, Ray Johnson, Dwight Snyder, and Del Porter. (Costume by Jenkins.)*

The story Wodehouse and Bolton concocted for the new show was based on some general ideas Freedley had given them. The producer wanted it to take place on board a ship, but when the script arrived he found that the authors had written a libretto about a shipwreck. Such a theme would not have been disastrous in itself, but just two months before the scheduled opening of the musical, the S.S. *Morro Castle* went down in flames off Asbury Park, New Jersey, with a loss of 125 lives. With Wodehouse in London and Bolton in Paris, the harried producer had to find someone quickly to rewrite the book. His director, Howard Lindsay, had had some experience as a playwright, but with so little time Lindsay insisted on having a collaborator. Through a mutual friend he was introduced to Russel Crouse, a Theatre Guild press agent and occasional librettist. The two agreed to be partners. "We went into rehearsal with only two-thirds of a first act and there was no second act at all," Lindsay later admitted. Somehow, everything was miraculously pulled into shape before the opening night; once the curtain went up on November 21, 1934, there was little doubt that *Anything Goes* would become one of the decade's superior achievements in musical comedy.

"A thundering good song-and-dance show," thundered Brooks Atkinson; and so it was. With Moore in the incongruous role of Public Enemy Number 13 (a superstitious man, he was anxious to bump off Number 12 so that he might rise in the hierarchy), with Gaxton bursting with kinetic energy, and with Ethel Merman trumpeting her way through some of Cole Porter's most inspired numbers, *Anything Goes* was the quintessence of the lavish, bawdy, swift-paced, uninhibited Music Comedy of the mid-Thirties. Almost every musical number was a highly polished gem, including "All through the Night," with its throbbing description of an imaginary nocturnal romance; the propulsive "Blow, Gabriel, Blow"; the blasé, but sincere "I Get a Kick out of You"; and "You're the Top," the classic of catalogued superlatives set to music.

Most of the songs for *Anything Goes* were written while Porter was cruising down the Rhine. For *Jubilee,* the following year, he extended his quest for geographical inspiration by composing the score during a world-wide tour with librettist Moss Hart. Wherever he went, Porter was able to find ideas for his songs. The melody for "Begin the Beguine" came to him as he was listening to native music on the island of Kalabahi, in the Dutch East Indies; "The Kling-Kling Bird on the Top of the Divi-Divi Tree" was actually seen and heard in Jamaica, British West Indies; the music for the "Judgment of Paris" ballet emanated from ethnic themes heard on the island of Bali. Among the less exotic rhythms, "A Picture of Me without You" strung out a varied list of improbable separations to affirm love's constancy (Fritzi Kreisler without his fiddle, Philadelphia without a Biddle); "Why Shouldn't I?" expressed the youthful desire for even a temporary romance; and "Just One of Those Things" conveyed a disillusioned, though realistic, acceptance of a passing affair.

Mary Boland and Melville Cooper were the queen and king of an Anglified (though unspecified) country in *Jubilee*. Members of the royal family included Charles Walters, Margaret Adams, and fifteen-year-old Montgomery Clift. Unfortunately, when a film contract forced Miss Boland to return to Hollywood, a satisfactory replacement could not be found, and the musical was forced to close after only 169 performances.

In 1936, hoping to repeat the success of *Anything Goes*, Vinton Freed-

JUBILEE *(1935). The collaborators: Cole Porter (music and lyrics) and Moss Hart (libretto).*

JUBILEE (1935). *King Melville Cooper is momentarily distracted from his rope trick to glance at a picture of Queen Mary Boland's favorite Hollywood star. (Costumes by Irene Sharaff and Connie De Pinna; setting by Jo Mielziner.)*

PHOTO BY VANDAMM

RED, HOT AND BLUE! *(1936). Vivian Vance, Jimmy Durante, Ethel Merman, Bob Hope, and Grace Hartman have a large audience for their conversation. (Costumes by Constance Ripley; setting by Donald Oenslager.)*

PHOTO BY VANDAMM

ley signed Cole Porter, Howard Lindsay, and Russel Crouse to create *Red, Hot and Blue!* It was originally intended as a vehicle for Ethel Merman, Jimmy Durante, and William Gaxton, but, according to Miss Merman, Gaxton refused to appear in it after overhearing Lindsay and Crouse telling her what a big part she would have. To replace Gaxton, Freedley hired Bob Hope, who had previously revealed his comic talent in *Roberta* and the *Ziegfeld Follies of 1936.*

In spite of its authors and performers, *Red, Hot and Blue!* was not a success. The chief fault was the book, a fairly elementary piece concerned with the search for a missing heiress whose identity could only be determined by a waffle-iron mark on her behind. Porter's contributions were more inspired. "Down in the Depths (on the 90th Floor)," sung by Miss Merman in a gold lamé gown illuminated by a single gold spotlight, brilliantly heightened the heroine's loneliness by contrasting it with her surrounding luxury. The exultant "Ridin' High," however, brought Miss Merman back to her more accustomed sanguine emotions. There was also the cleverly intricate "It's De-Lovely," which told, via a self-kidding verse and four choruses, the blissful saga of a boy and girl from the night they fell in love, through their marriage and wedding trip, and right up to the arrival of their first born.

Apart from its songs, *Red, Hot and Blue!* is remembered today chiefly because of the ridiculous battle of the billing. Both Miss Merman's and Durante's agents wanted their clients to have top billing, i.e., the name on the left-hand side above the title of the show. Although it still seemed to give the preferential billing to Durante, the following compromise was finally worked out:

In the summer of 1937, while Porter was horseback riding on a friend's estate on Long Island, his horse suddenly slipped, threw him, and then fell on top of him. Both of his legs were broken, and extreme damage was done to his nervous system. After submitting to thirty-one operations over a period of about twenty years in order to save his legs, Porter eventually had to have his right leg amputated in 1958.

Shortly after the accident, the Shubert brothers tried to take Porter's mind off his misfortune by commissioning him to supply the score for *You Never Know*. It was not, however, one of his—or their—major efforts. The next year, the composer had far better luck with *Leave It to Me!*, which was also written while he was bed-ridden. Adapted by Sam and Bella Spewack from their play *Clear All Wires*, the musical had a stellar cast including William Gaxton, Victor Moore, Sophie Tucker, and Tamara. While Moore, as usual, was singled out for his hilarious performance as Alonzo P. Goodhue, the American ambassador to the Soviet Union, a twenty-four-year-old singer named Mary Martin made an auspicious Broadway debut as she sang, and coyly stripped to, "My Heart Belongs to Daddy," while waiting at a freezing Siberian railway station. (Some people even noticed a dancer in that scene named Gene Kelly, who was also appearing on the New York stage for the first time.)

Leave It to Me! was a generally funny spoof of communism and American diplomacy, with such irreverences as "The Internationale" performed as the first-act finale and Stalin dancing around in true musical comedy fashion. The sight of the timid Mr. Moore kicking the Nazi ambassador in the stomach was treasured by audiences as both a wish-fulfillment and a reminder of the unique freedom that the Broadway theatre has always enjoyed.

LEAVE IT TO ME! *(1938). "A new girl named Mary Martin is gay, fresh, and attractive," wrote Richard Watts, Jr., in the* Herald Tribune. *Here at a freezing Siberian railroad station she sings "My Heart Belongs to Daddy," accompanied by a quintet including (to her immediate right) Gene Kelly. (Costumes by Raoul Pène du Bois; setting by Albert Johnson.)*

PHOTO BY VANDAMM

DUBARRY WAS A LADY (1939). Bert Lahr, as the washroom attendant at the Club Petite, dreams that he is King Louis XV and that Ethel Merman is DuBarry. (Costumes by Raoul Pène du Bois.)

From December, 1939, to January, 1944, Cole Porter created the songs for five box-office smashes in a row—*DuBarry Was a Lady, Panama Hattie, Let's Face It!, Something for the Boys,* and *Mexican Hayride.* Each one of these shows ran over 400 performances, and all were co-authored by Herbert Fields (he wrote the first two with B. G. DeSylva, the other three with his sister, Dorothy Fields). Although only *Let's Face It!* was produced by Vinton Freedley, all five musicals seemed to capture the bright, star-studded, flavor of the Gershwin shows that Aarons and Freedley had offered in the Twenties. Like Gershwin at that time, Porter was particularly adept at writing for star personalities (Ethel Merman, Bert Lahr, Danny Kaye, Bobby Clark), without too much concern for the logic of plot development or the manner in which the songs were suited to the story. But just as the early Gershwin entertainments were attuned to the period in which they were presented, so the five Porter musicals of the early Forties could offer the amusement-seeking audiences of the Second World War a much-needed escape into a spangled, melodic, and glamorous world.

DuBarry Was a Lady was described by John Mason Brown as "a rowdy, boisterous, high-spirited extravaganza which stops at just this side of nothing and makes much of little." Ethel Merman played May Daley, a nightclub

DUBARRY WAS A LADY (1939). Charles Walters and Betty Grable in a burlesque routine at the Club Petite. (Costumes by Raoul Pène du Bois.)

PANAMA HATTIE (1940). Rags Ragland registers complete approval of Ethel Merman's rather garish outfit. (Costumes and setting by Raoul Pène du Bois.)

singer, and Bert Lahr was the washroom attendant at the Club Petite who dreams that he is Louis XIV and Ethel is DuBarry. Among the songs, "Do I Love You?" was another beguine-tempoed ballad; "Katie Went to Haiti" related the rhythmic saga of a girl who was, according to critic John Anderson, "obviously a business and musical relation of the immortal Eadie"; and "Well, Did You Evah?" was made up of a series of gossipy social notes, delivered by Betty Grable (in her only stage role) and Charles Walters. Surprisingly, the song with the greatest popular appeal was the mocking hillbilly duet in which Miss Merman and Mr. Lahr vowed their eternal "Friendship."

Ethel Merman received solo star billing for the first time in *Panama Hattie*. Again she played the part of a nightclub singer (this time called Hattie Maloney) whose heart of gold could only be revealed through a voice of brass. In "I've Still Got My Health," she gaily proclaimed that her physical soundness was ample compensation for her lack of social graces, but in "Make It Another Old Fashioned, Please," she sadly concluded that the only thing to do with her sorrow was to drown it. The most fondly remembered sequence in the show involved Miss Merman and eight-year-old Joan Carroll, an occasion so touching that Brooks Atkinson predicted: "Gruff old codgers are going to choke a little this winter when tot and temptress sing 'Let's Be Buddies' and bring down the house."

The performance that Danny Kaye had given in *Lady In the Dark* fully merited the stardom he won in *Let's Face It!* Its tale of three middle-aged married ladies who go on a spree with three young servicemen was found to be, in the words of John Mason Brown, "an exuberant and irresistible show which does not hesitate to call a shovel a spade." In addition to Kaye, the cast was comprised of a superior roster of musical comedy talent, including Mary Jane Walsh, Eve Arden (with Carol Channing as understudy), Edith

PHOTO BY VANDAMM

LET'S FACE IT! *(1941). Extra marital entanglements among three discontented wives and three eager servicemen. Eve Arden, Danny Kaye, Edith Meiser, Benny Baker, Jack Williams, and Vivian Vance. (Costumes by John Harkrider; setting by Harry Horner.)*

MEXICAN HAYRIDE *(1944).*
Bobby Clark (alias Joe Bas-
com, alias Humphrey Fish)
and June Havoc as the bull-
fighter known as Montana.
(Costumes by Mary Grant.)

Meiser, Vivian Vance, Nanette Fabray, and Benny Baker. Among the outstanding Porter songs were "Farming," which ridiculed celebrities who had
just discovered the soil; "Ev'rything I Love," a straight love duet for Kaye and
Miss Walsh, and "You Irritate Me So," a comic love duet sung by Miss Fabray
and Jack Williams.

Cole Porter's two musicals for Michael Todd, *Something for the Boys*
and *Mexican Hayride* were successful as moneymakers, though neither one
represented the composer's best work. Originally known as *Jenny Get Your
Gun, Something for the Boys* doubtlessly benefited from the presence of
Ethel Merman who was cast as a defense worker who could receive wartime
radio messages through the fillings in her teeth. The show-stopping routine
was one in which Miss Merman and Paula Laurence, decked out as squaws
for no apparent reason, romped through a number about their husbands who
wait for them "By the Mis-sis-sis-sis-sis-sis-sis-sis-sin-e-wah."

Just as *Something for the Boys* was indebted to Ethel Merman for its
success, so *Mexican Hayride* was equally indebted to Bobby Clark. As Joe
Bascom (alias Humphrey Fish), Clark was cast as a numbers racketeer who
flees to Mexico, assumes various disguises, and becomes involved with a
female bullfighter (played by June Havoc). "I Love You," which followed
the pattern of "Do I Love You?" has been the most durable song from the
score, but two others, "Sing to Me, Guitar" and "Carlotta," were especially
successful in capturing the atmosphere of a languid and romantic Mexico.

By the mid-Forties, the belief was that Cole Porter was no longer capable
of creating the outstanding scores that had distinguished most of his early

176

musicals. Neither *Something for the Boys* nor *Mexican Hayride* was a major effort, and there was little of merit in Porter's music and lyrics for Billy Rose's revue, *Seven Lively Arts*, or Orson Welles's adaptation of Jules Verne's *Around the World in Eighty Days*. Few, therefore, had high expectations when it was announced in 1948 that librettists Sam and Bella Spewack were collaborating with Porter on *Kiss Me, Kate*, a musical based on Shakespeare's *The Taming of the Shrew*. Nor did the stars indicate success. Since his first important role in *Oklahoma!*, Alfred Drake had appeared in four failures in a row, and Patricia Morison, who was to play opposite him, had not been in a Broadway musical in over ten years. (Her last appearance had been in *The Two Bouquets*, in which Drake also had had a part.)

Like Irving Berlin with regard to *Annie Get Your Gun*, Porter was apprehensive about the new project, which was completely unlike the usual gossamer star vehicles with which he was customarily associated. Moreover, in common with everyone else in the musical theatre, he was well aware of the strides taken since the formation of the Rodgers and Hammerstein partnership. "The librettos are much better," he once told reporter Gilbert Millstein, "and the scores are much closer to the librettos than they used to be. Those two made it much harder for everybody else." Nevertheless, partially spurred on by Berlin's example ("His having so much music in *Annie Get Your Gun* made me feel like trying a similar thing"), Porter created a score for *Kiss Me, Kate* that is universally conceded to be his masterpiece. Although, as was his customary professional habit, he still remained somewhat aloof from the actual production, he was extremely concerned with the way his music and lyrics fit the characters and the situations, and frequently called upon the Spewacks for opinions and suggestions.

Porter's unique accomplishment in *Kiss Me, Kate* lay in his facility for creating melodies and lyrics of uncommonly high standards while, at the same time, successfully bridging the completely different worlds of Broadway and the Bard. From the general area of Times Square, he produced "Another Op'nin', Another Show," a rousing show business anthem to rival Berlin's "There's No Business like Show Business"; the plaintive torch ballad, "Why Can't You Behave?"; "Too Darn Hot," with its galvanic melody in direct contrast to the inaction proposed in the lyric; and the tender confession, "So in Love," another melody in Porter's soft beguine tempo. "Always True to You in My Fashion" was pure Broadway also, even though its title stemmed from a line in a poem by Ernest Dowson. In its avowel of fidelity to one true love, the song expressed a reverse sentiment to the composer's previous "My Heart Belongs to Daddy," in which fidelity was pledged to the wealthy "daddy."

The Taming of the Shrew itself provided the direct inspiration for four of the songs. "I've Come to Wive It Wealthily in Padua" was based on

KISS ME KATE (1948). "We open in Venice," sing Patricia Morison, Alfred Drake, Lisa Kirk, and Harold Lang as a group of strolling players about to appear in Shakespeare's The Taming of the Shrew. (Costumes and setting by Lemuel Ayers.)

Petruchio's first revelation of his quest for a rich wife, in which the concluding lines were:

> . . . were she as rough
> As are the swelling Adriatic seas:
> I come to wive it wealthily in Padua;
> If wealthily then happily in Padua.

"Where Is the Life That Late I Led?" was a line in a song actually sung by Shakespeare's hero, while the rather mystical "Were Thine That Special Face" was prompted by Bianca's admission:

> Believe me, sister, of all the men alive,
> I never yet beheld that special face
> Which I could fancy more than any other.

For the last number in the show, "I Am Ashamed That Women Are So Simple," Porter set almost all of Shakespeare's original words to music for the reformed Kate to explain how women should behave toward their husbands.

Such numbers as "Tom, Dick or Harry," "We Open in Venice," and "I Hate Men," while they are all completely Porter, fit perfectly into the story and spirit of the ancient tale. Indeed, Brooks Atkinson has termed "I Hate Men" "the perfect musical sublimation of Shakespeare's evil-tempered Kate."

"Wunderbar" is, of course, far from either Shubert Alley or Shakespeare. Though Porter wrote the melody in strict three-quarter time, the song is actually a satire on all the sentimental waltzes ever performed in a Viennese operetta. This is immediately revealed in the first line of the verse, "Gazing down on the Jungfrau," which is a rather difficult feat, the Jungfrau being one of the highest peaks in the Alps.

Arnold Saint Subber and Lemuel Ayers, the producers of *Kiss Me, Kate*, also produced Cole Porter's next musical, *Out of This World*. As *Kiss Me, Kate* had contrasted show business with Shakespeare, so *Out of This World* combined the Amphitryon legend with the adventures of a modern American couple visiting Greece on their wedding trip. In the role of Juno, Charlotte Greenwood made a gangling, triumphal return to the musical stage after an absence of almost twenty-four years.

The now-standard "From This Moment On" was dropped from the score before the musical opened in New York, but there were still many superb songs among those left—"Where, Oh Where?," with its sweet, lilting melody mated to a coldly calculating lyric; the ever-present beguine, "I Am Loved" (with a release almost identical to that of the earlier "I Love You"); the forthright stand of the contented wife called "No Lover"; and the paean to the satisfactions of old age, "I Sleep Easier Now," which Miss Greenwood sang with particular relish. There were also some delightful Cole Porter incongruities: "I Jupiter, I Rex" ("Reck-eck-o-weck-o-wex!") brought the spirit of the Yale cheering section to Mount Olympus, while "Climb Up the Mountain" turned a quasi-Negro spiritual into the perfect musical expression for gods and goddesses. Two bright sagas of itemization were "Cherry Pies Ought to Be You" (in the "You're the Top" vein), and the Rabelaisian, rapid-fire account of Mercury's romantic conquests, "They Couldn't Compare to You."

Can-Can (1953) and *Silk Stockings* (1955) were presented by Cy Feuer and Ernest Martin, the team that had previously produced *Where's Charley?*

KISS ME, KATE (1948). *Fred Graham (Alfred Drake) gives vent to his feelings toward his leading lady, Lilli Vanessi (Patricia Morison), by administering a sound spanking during a performance of* The Taming of the Shrew. *Lisa Kirk is beneath the balcony at the right. (Costumes and setting by Lemuel Ayers.)*

CAN-CAN *(1953). Gwen Verdon, Hans Conried, and Lilo. (Costumes by Motley.)*

and *Guys and Dolls*. Both shows were written and directed by Abe Burrows, although in the case of *Silk Stockings* he revised a script already completed by George S. Kaufman and Leueen McGrath. *Can-Can* dealt with Parisian life in the days of Toulouse-Lautrec. Its story may have been inconsequential, but the dances created by Michael Kidd and the show's breezy pace helped make it a huge financial success. The songs, if not among Porter's best work, nonetheless enabled him to recapture the Parisian flavor of some of his earliest scores with such pieces as "Allez-Vous-En," "I Love Paris" (written, according to Porter, because Jo Mielziner had designed such a beautiful scenic sky line of the city), "Montmart'," and "C'est Magnifique." Of the rest, "I Am in Love" was constructed from the "Do I Love You?–I Love You–So in Love–I Am Loved" matrix, and "It's All Right with Me" was a wry serenade sung by a disillusioned young man whose heart still longs for another.

Lilo, the French star, was imported especially to play La Mome Pistache, which she did in a strikingly ebullient manner. However, a greater success was scored by a twenty-eight-year-old dancer named Gwen Verdon, despite the fact that her part had been cut drastically to please the star. Miss Verdon's two previous Broadway appearances had been as a dancer in *Alive and Kicking*, a revue, and in the Villa-Lobos operetta, *Magdalena*.

Silk Stockings, an adaptation of the movie, *Ninotchka*, was set in modern Paris, with the leading roles played by Hildegarde Neff, Don Ameche, and Gretchen Wyler. Porter's lyrics had fun at the expense of the movies ("Josephine," "Stereophonic Sound") and the Russians ("Too Bad," "Siberia," and the exercise in verbal frugality, "The Red Blues"). Amatory emotions were expressed cartographically in "All of You," selflessly in "Without Love," and dispassionately in "It's a Chemical Reaction."

Of all the major musical comedy composers and lyricists, Cole Porter has a style that has altered least through the years. If we listen to his early efforts and compare them with his most recent songs, we find little change in his basic attitudes; there is still something of the glittering Twenties about even his newest compositions. For, in spite of the changes in the world and

SILK STOCKINGS *(1955). Don Ameche as Steve Canfield and Hildegarde Neff as Ninotchka, in the musical version of one of Garbo's most popular films. (Costumes by Lucinda Ballard.)*

his own serious accident, the world of Cole Porter has never really changed. When he describes a certain locale or refers to a well-known personality in his lyrics, he is doubtlessly well acquainted with both. Indeed, he has even been able to combine his professional life with his social life. "I've done lots of work at dinner, sitting between two bores," he has said. "I can feign listening beautifully. I can work anywhere. I work very well while I'm shaving or when I'm in a taxi."

In his worldly outlook revealed through his ingenious verses and his compelling music, Porter is still writing the kind of songs he once did merely to amuse his friends. He is no dilettante, but a meticulous, painstaking craftsman, although he seldom has become involved with the day-to-day production of a musical as have most of his colleagues. His detached manner has, in fact, allowed him to take pleasure from his own works in much the same ingenuous manner of George Gershwin; the premières of Cole Porter musicals invariably have found the composer, surrounded by friends, enjoying himself thoroughly from an orchestra seat, rather than pacing feverishly in the men's room of the theatre.

As Jule Styne once said, "Cole Porter has a brand of sophistication that is commercial, the type that makes a shopgirl know 21 or El Morocco without having been there." This sophistication can be communicated only because it is not the acquired sophistication of the outsider; it is the genuine expression of what has always been, to Cole Porter, the only way of life.

Howard Dietz and Arthur Schwartz.

CHAPTER TWELVE

Arthur Schwartz
and Howard Dietz

THE OPPORTUNITIES AVAILABLE to aspiring young writers of the musical theatre have always been limited. By the mid-Twenties, they could no longer depend on the heavy European operettas of the kind that had served Jerome Kern so propitiously in the early decades of the century. However, there were still the revues. Whether extravagant or intimate, on-Broadway or off-Broadway, hackneyed or imaginative, these shows were the chief outlets for the budding talents of young composers and lyricists, their first chance to get their work on the professional stage.

The composer and lyricist who have been most closely identified with this form of musical theatre are Arthur Schwartz and Howard Dietz. Moreover, from their very first collaboration, *The Little Show*, they were among the leaders in creating a new form of revue. Eschewing the opulence of Ziegfeld or the make-shift modesty of the off-Broadway attractions, the new shows were closer to the spirit of the impeccably produced *Charlot's Revues,* which had introduced Beatrice Lillie, Gertrude Lawrence, and Jack Buchanan to American audiences in the mid-Twenties. Intimate, sophisticated, and callid, these revues were marked by the brilliant performances of their stars, some revolutionary innovations in stagecraft, and a general air of sleek but exuberant professionalism.

In addition to *The Little Show*, Schwartz and Dietz were associated with other memorable revues—*Three's a Crowd, The Band Wagon, Flying Colors, At Home Abroad,* and *Inside U.S.A.* All of these attractions were well suited to the skillful cohesion of words and music created by the team. For both men were of similar background and outlook, and their urbane, literate songs caught perfectly the flavor of the shows for which they were created. Though his music has always shown great variety, Schwartz's most distinguished ballads are frequently marked by a brooding soulfulness that is perhaps matched only by some of Cole Porter's work. Dietz's lyrics are characterized by their brittle wit and subtle poetic imagery; while they may lack a certain warmth, they nevertheless contain a keenness and originality that make them ideally suited to Schwartz's music.

Arthur Schwartz was born in Brooklyn, on November 25, 1900. His father, a lawyer, was so strongly opposed to his son's early interest in music that he punished the youth whenever he found him trying to play the family piano. Secretly encouraged by his mother, young Arthur learned to play well enough to make his professional debut at the age of fourteen when he was hired to furnish musical accompaniment to silent films at the Cortelyou Movie Emporium in Flatbush.

After graduating from New York University, Schwartz continued his studies at Columbia University. Although he briefly considered a writing career, he acceded to his father's wishes and entered Columbia Law School. During his four years there, he helped support himself by teaching English at various high schools in New York. He also began to devote whatever free time he had to composing popular songs. At twenty-three, he wrote his first published song, "Baltimore, Md., You're the Only Doctor for Me." It netted him about eight dollars, but the urge to write melodies continued to be strong. One thing was obvious even from the title: he needed a good lyricist.

At first, Schwartz hoped to form a partnership with Lorenz Hart. The summer after graduating from Columbia Law School, he took a job as a counselor at a summer camp for the sole reason that Hart was also a counselor there. They wrote several songs together for camp shows, plus one, "I Know My Girl by Her Perfume," that was later used in a vaudeville act.

The success Hart achieved with Rodgers when they wrote the songs for *The Garrick Gaieties* ended the possibility of a permanent Schwartz-Hart collaboration. In 1926, Schwartz had some songs in *The Grand Street Follies* and the following year he was one of three composers responsible for another off-Broadway revue, *The New Yorkers* (not to be confused with the Cole Porter musical of three years later). Finding himself being drawn more to music than to law, Schwartz felt that he had to make a definite choice between the two. Encouraged by Larry Hart, he quit his law practice in 1928 to devote himself exclusively to music and the theatre.

Although some of his earliest assignments—for vaudeville acts and "tab" shows (tabloid versions of Broadway plays that played the vaudeville circuits)—were not profitable, he continued to feel that things would change once he found the right lyricist. The man he eventually decided on was a part-time writer for the theatre and a full-time publicist for M-G-M named Howard Dietz.

Dietz was born in New York City, on September 8, 1896. He attended Columbia University at the same time as Oscar Hammerstein II and Lorenz Hart. While still an undergraduate, he had his first light verse published in Franklin P. Adams' *Conning Tower* and Don Marquis' *Sun Dial* newspaper columns. He also won a $500 prize for submitting the winning advertising copy in a contest sponsored by Fatima cigarettes. This led to his getting a job as copywriter for an advertising agency. One of the agency's accounts was the Goldwyn Pictures Corporation, and one of Dietz's first assignments was to give the new company a trademark (Leo the Lion, inspired by the mascot of Columbia University) and a slogan (*Ars Gratia Artis*). After serving in the Navy during World War I, Dietz did free-lance publicity for various film companies until Samuel Goldwyn appointed him director of advertising and publicity. When, in 1924, the Goldwyn company merged with Metro and Mayer, Dietz continued with the new company in a similar capacity. (Goldwyn, however, sold his interest soon after the merger to continue as an independent producer.) Dietz remained an executive at M-G-M for over thirty years; during that period he also wrote sketches, librettos, and lyrics for twelve Broadway musicals, plus English versions of *La Bohème* and *Fledermaus* for the Metropolitan Opera.

Dietz first began to write for the theatre in 1923, when he fashioned a lyric to Arthur Samuel's music for the song "Alibi Baby." It was sung by Luella Gear in *Poppy*, one of W. C. Fields's greatest stage successes. (Fame was not Dietz's, however, because Dorothy Donnelly, the librettist-lyricist of the show, would not allow his name on either the program or the sheet music.)

The following year, Jerome Kern agreed to collaborate with the young lyricist on the score for *Dear Sir*. One evening when Dietz reported to the composer at his home in Bronxville, Kern played twelve numbers of the score on the piano, and asked him to get to work and return in a few days. Somewhat overawed by writing his first complete score with such an illustrious composer, Dietz thought he was expected to have all twelve sets of lyrics completed by that time. He then worked for fifty hours straight to finish the assignment, only to discover upon his return to Kern's home that the composer had expected him to have just one lyric ready.

Dear Sir was a quick failure, but *Merry-Go-Round*, a revue which Dietz wrote with Jay Gorney and Morrie Ryskind in 1927, did have a long enough run to make many people recognize his talent. One of those most impressed was Arthur Schwartz.

Schwartz became convinced that in Dietz he would have a partner equally as inventive and as bright as Larry Hart. So determined was he to form a collaboration that he barraged the lyricist with telegrams and telephone calls. Dietz, however, was not receptive to the entreaties; he felt that since both men were relatively new to the theatre they would benefit more from associating with writers of greater experience.

The matter was allowed to rest until 1929 when Tom Weatherly joined with William A. Brady, Jr., and Dwight Deere Wiman to produce a revue called *The Little Show*. This was the outgrowth of a series of Sunday evening *Divertissements* that Weatherly and James Pond had presented at the Selwyn Theatre. "They were really nothing more than high-class vaudeville shows," recalls Weatherly, "but they were far more artistic than the Sunday night variety programs then being offered at the Winter Garden. They became so successful that I was convinced there would be an audience for a really smart and sophisticated revue." Upon reading the first newspaper announcement of the plans for *The Little Show*, Schwartz immediately went to see Weatherly. After some further persuasion on Schwartz's part, Dietz finally yielded and agreed to become associated with the project.

The Little Show, which played at the Music Box, was an elegantly intimate affair featuring Clifton Webb, Libby Holman, and Fred Allen. Most of the songs were composed by Schwartz and Dietz, but, as in most revues, there were many interpolated numbers. In fact, Schwartz had nothing to do with two of Miss Holman's biggest hits, "Can't We Be Friends?" and "Moanin' Low." "Can't We Be Friends?" was written by Kay Swift and her husband, James Warburg, a banker and occasional lyricist who wrote under the name of Paul James; "Moanin' Low" was the work of Howard Dietz and Ralph Rainger, one of the two featured pianists in the pit orchestra. During the out-of-town tryout of the revue, prospects did not seem very promising until Dietz suggested that "Moanin' Low" be given the next-to-closing spot on the program; somehow this strengthened the entire entertainment and helped assure its success. The scene in which Libby Holman expressed this excruciating sentiment was a squalid Harlem tenement flat. After rousing her lover (Clifton Webb) from a drunken stupor, she brings him to his feet and they perform a particularly torrid dance. As a climax to the scene, and to prove the line in the song about being mean as can be, Webb strangles his devoted paramour.

The Schwartz-Dietz creations, however, were not completely overlooked. Among them was the open-hearted tribute to New York's celebrated nuts-and-bolts emporium, "Hammacher Schlemmer, I Love You," and the

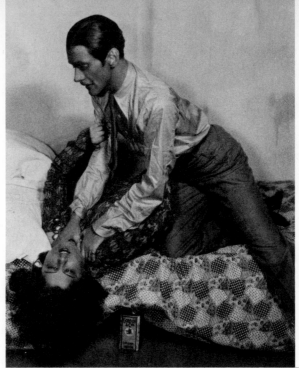

THE LITTLE SHOW *(1929)"One of the most striking things in the revue," wrote critic Richard Lockridge, "is a song that is neither amusing nor forgettable. It is 'Moanin' Low,' which Libby Holman sings in that powerfully throbbing voice of hers while Clifton Webb dances with her in mad grotesque." The climax of that dance is shown here. (Costumes by Ruth Brenner.)*

CULVER PICTURES, INC.

debonair admission of the spurned lover, "I Guess I'll Have to Change My Plan."*

With *The Little Show* such an impressive hit, Messrs. Brady, Wiman, and Weatherly soon made plans for a sequel to be produced in the fall of 1930. At first they considered starring Webb, Holman, and Allen again. Then, remembering that even with Lillie, Lawrence, and Buchanan, the second *Charlot's Revue* had run less than half the number of performances of the first, the producers decided upon an entirely new cast for *The Second Little Show*. The show lasted just two months.

Once it became known that Webb, Holman, and Allen would not be in the new production, Max Gordon, a former agent and associate of Sam Harris, promptly signed the three for his own production, *Three's a Crowd*. He also hired Schwartz and Dietz to supply most of the songs, and gave Dietz the additional task of selecting all the material and the other performers to be in the show.

Again, although Schwartz and Dietz wrote most of the songs together, Dietz also collaborated on numbers with Phil Charig, Burton Lane, and Vernon Duke. The piece that made the biggest hit, however, was the only one that Dietz was not associated with—"Body and Soul," by Johnny Green,

---

* "I Guess I'll Have to Change My Plan" was based on a melody Schwartz had written the summer he spent at the camp with Lorenz Hart. Hart's original lyric went, in part:
I love to lie awake in bed.
Right after taps
I pull the flaps
Above my head . . .

187

THREE'S A CROWD (1930). *Clifton Webb, Libby Holman, and Fred Allen.*

Robert Sour, and Edward Heyman. As intoned by Libby Holman, this masochistic lament became the "Moanin' Low" of the new revue. The best of the Schwartz and Dietz inspirations was "Something to Remember You By,* a ballad of unhappy leave-taking sung by Miss Holman to a sailor who stood with his back to the audience. He was played by Fred MacMurray. Fred Allen achieved new stature as a comedian with his uproarious sketch about Admiral Byrd at the South Pole.

By the time they signed with Max Gordon to supply the songs for *The Band Wagon,* Schwartz and Dietz were the acknowledged masters of the revue form. Dietz again agreed to supervise the production but only on two conditions: George S. Kaufman would have to write most of the sketches, and Fred and Adele Astaire would have to be signed for the leads. "In many ways, it was an experimental production," Dietz has observed, "combining as it did the best features of the so-called intimate type of revue that had come into vogue with *The Garrick Gaieties* and *The Little Show,* with the more spectacular backgrounds associated with the productions of Ziegfeld."

One of its most unusual innovations was the use of the revolving stage, which before that had been used mainly to change scenery. Now, as created by Albert Johnson, it was employed to enhance the musical and dramatic effectiveness of a scene. The sketches by Kaufman and Dietz were well above the average in wit and substance, particularly the satire on the Old South called "The Pride of the Claghornes."

Shortly after the June 3, 1931, opening of *The Band Wagon,* Olin Downes, the music critic of the New York *Times,* handed down the following verdict: "Each scene or episode serves to display a new angle of approach and craftsmanship. And—mirabile dictu—we have a composer whose melodic

* "Something to Remember You By," with a much faster tempo, was called "I Have No Words" when it was first sung in an English musical, *Little Tommy Tucker,* the previous year.

vein is not only graceful but characterized at its best by refinement and artistic quality. . . . He is able in many places to deliver a quality of musical workmanship which would command the respect of the most serious composer, and perhaps also the envy."

The still-enviable score—possibly the finest ever written for a revue—included the gaily optimistic "New Sun in the Sky" for Astaire to sing as he preened before a mirror; the saucy "Hoops" for Fred and Adele as two frolicking Parisian *enfants;* the almost ethereal "High and Low"; and the contagious oom-pah rhythm of "I Love Louisa" which ended the first act on a roistering Bavarian scene with the cast astride a swirling, festively decorated merry-go-round.

During rehearsals one day, it was discovered that there was need for what Schwartz describes as a "dark song, somewhat mystical, yet in slow, even rhythm." The following morning, he awoke with the entire melody so fixed in his mind that he was able to go immediately to the piano and play it through without faltering. The song, "Dancing in the Dark," was sung by John Barker, and danced by Tilly Losch on a slanted, mirrored floor illuminated by continually changing colored lights.

The third and final Max Gordon revue was *Flying Colors.* Judging by its cast (Clifton Webb, Tamara Geva, Patsy Kelly, Charles Butterworth, Larry Adler), it was the equal of *Three's a Crowd* and *The Band Wagon.* Yet,

THE BAND WAGON (1931). "I Love Louisa," sung by the cast on a merry-go-round at a Bavarian amusement park, was the first act finale. Adele and Fred Astaire are seated on the tortoise, Frank Morgan wears the lederhosen, and Helen Broderick is on the lamb. (Costumes by Kiviette; setting by Albert Johnson.)

PHOTO BY VANDAMM

though Dietz (chief sketch writer, director, and lyricist) and Schwartz made notable contributions, there were many who felt that the show was merely repeating some of the proven formulas of their previous offerings. "Meine Kleine Akrobat," for example, sought to recapture the flavor of "I Love Louisa," while the sultry "Alone Together" was performed in a manner so similar to "Dancing in the Dark" that John Mason Brown referred to it as "Dancing in the Schwartz." "A Shine On Your Shoes," a piece of didactic exuberance tapped out by Monette Moore and Vilma and Buddy Ebsen around a shoe-shine stand, and the joyous chorale, "Louisiana Hayride," were also originally heard in this revue.*

The sameness that was creeping into their revues and their natural desire to try something fresh prompted Schwartz and Dietz to write their first book musical, *Revenge with Music,* in 1934. Inspired by a trip to Spain, Dietz adapted his libretto from the same Spanish novel, *El Sombrero de Tres Picos* by Pedro de Alarcón, that had previously served as the basis for Manuel de Falla's ballet of the same name and Hugo Wolf's comic opera, *Der Corregidor.* The story, a fairly elementary tale, concerned the attempt of a governor of a Spanish province to make love to the wife of a poor miller, and the miller's counter (and more successful) attempt to make love to the governor's wife.

Schwartz's score was distinguished by its melodic richness and its faculty for capturing all the fire and romance of Spain. Because Libby Holman, as the miller's wife, was given the fervent "You and the Night and the Music," it was necessary to have an equally strong solo for Georges Metaxa, as her husband. Among the many songs Schwartz and Dietz had written the previous year for a radio serial, *The Gibson Family,* was one called "If There Is Someone Lovelier Than You," which they felt would be perfectly suited to the requirements of *Revenge with Music.* Although melodically it may have lacked the proper Spanish coloration, Mr. Metaxa's European accent and the orchestral arrangement combined to give it just the right atmosphere for the locale.

There were two other collaborations by the team in the Thirties. *At Home Abroad* (1935) used one of the oldest frameworks for a revue, the around-the-world tour. Thus, Beatrice Lillie was given the opportunity to extoll the charms of "Paree," become hopelessly confused in London while ordering "two double-damask dinner napkins," and, in "Get Yourself a Geisha," slyly reveal some of the quaint customs of Japan, the land where "it's better with your shoes off." Ethel Waters, Eleanor Powell, Herb Williams, and Reginald Gardiner (he mimicked trains and gave an impersonation of wallpaper) were also members of the tour.

* Agnes de Mille was to have done the choreography—her first for a Broadway musical—for *Flying Colors,* but because of differences with almost everyone but Howard Dietz, she quit during the tryout and was succeeded by Albertina Rasch.

REVENGE WITH MUSIC *(1934).*
Libby Holman and Georges
Metaxa as the young Spanish
couple in a musical based on
an old Spanish tale of cuckolds
and cuckolders. (Costumes by
Constance Ripley.)

Between the Devil (1937), the last Schwartz–Dietz musical for eleven years, was their second book show. Its tale of an English bigamist whose life was complicated by an English wife (Evelyn Laye) and a French wife (Adèle Dixon) was a time-worn farce situation (it turned up again twenty-one years later in *Oh Captain!*), and neither the authors nor the players could extract much life from it. As the bigamist, Jack Buchanan sang the jauntily self-pitying "By Myself" while being pursued by bobbies through London's foggy streets. The show ran three months.

Because of increased pressure on Dietz to concentrate on his salaried chores at M-G-M, Schwartz was compelled to seek other collaborators during the latter part of the Thirties. Shortly before *Between the Devil,* he became associated with an elaborate production called *Virginia* which the Rockefeller family produced at the Center Theatre in Radio City. As the Rockefellers had already invested a considerable sum toward the restoration of the Colonial village of Williamsburg, Virginia, they thought it would be a fine idea to offer a musical set in that locale during the American Revolution. To write the book they chose Laurence Stallings (later succeeded by Owen Davis), and as Schwartz's partner they assigned Albert Stillman, the Radio City's staff lyricist.

The musical, which turned out to be a costly but dull extravaganza, was the last stage musical shown at the theatre. After becoming a showplace for Sonja Henie's ice revue and a television studio, the Center Theatre was torn out in 1954 to be converted into office space.

Stars In Your Eyes, in 1939, was Schwartz's first score with Dorothy Fields. Miss Fields, the daughter of Lew Fields and the sister of Joseph and Herbert, had first won success in 1928 when she teamed with Jimmy McHugh

PHOTO BY JEROME ROBINSON

STARS IN YOUR EYES (1939). *Every night, in the midst of the song called "It's All Yours," Ethel Merman and Jimmy Durante would break each other up with supposedly spontaneous wisecracks and stories. (Costumes by John Hambleton.)*

to write the score for *Blackbirds of 1928*. For the past ten years, she had written lyrics (mostly to melodies by McHugh and Jerome Kern) for many Hollywood films, an experience that made her well suited to work on the new project with Schwartz. For this was to be a movie satire with a particularly novel idea. It was Schwartz's notion that a very funny show could be built around the making of a Hollywood musical by leaders of New York's left-wing theatre, with the humor derived from superimposing social significance on a glamorous Hollywood production. After J. P. McEvoy completed the script—then called *Swing to the Left*—Dwight Deere Wiman agreed to produce it with Ethel Merman as a movie queen and Jimmy Durante as a labor-union organizer. Upon reading the book and listening to the songs, however, director Joshua Logan objected to the social commentary. Liberal themes were fine for revues, he told the authors, but why clutter up a gay story with anything so weighty? Eventually, Schwartz, Fields, and McEvoy capitulated. The labor leader became a studio idea man, a song about the South's economy was thrown out, and, in general, what might have been a sharp, unconventional spoof of the movies became a standard product by the time *Swing to the Left* was transformed into *Stars in Your Eyes*. Nevertheless,

192

with all the concessions to what the public was supposed to want, the show lasted only 127 performances.

Soon after *Stars in Your Eyes* opened, Schwartz accepted an offer to work in Hollywood. He remained there until 1946. Among the films for which he wrote complete scores were *Thank Your Lucky Stars* (lyrics by Frank Loesser) and *The Time, the Place and the Girl* (lyrics by Leo Robin). For Columbia, he produced the Gene Kelly–Rita Hayworth *Cover Girl* (score by Jerome Kern and Ira Gershwin), and for Warners, the romanticized biography of Cole Porter, *Night and Day.*

By the mid-Forties, the Broadway musical theatre had become saturated with serious costume musical plays. As something of an antidote to *Bloomer Girl, The Song of Norway, Up in Central Park, Carousel,* and the like, George S. Kaufman and Nunnally Johnson decided to collaborate on a sophisticated modern musical comedy. *Park Avenue,* the show they wrote, was concerned with nothing more serious than the compulsion of socialites to shed their mates with as much frequency as possible. As the production was also to mark the return to Broadway of both Arthur Schwartz and Ira Gershwin in their first assignment as a team, there was, understandably, great expectation for the enterprise. Unfortunately, although the songs were attractive, the book was too much of a one-joke affair, and the show had a very brief run.

Schwartz's duties in both New York and in Hollywood have compelled him to cross the country many times. Yet it was not until the summer of 1947, when he drove from the East Coast to the West Coast, that he actually saw something of the country and the people. This gave him an idea: a musical revue that, instead of using the format of an around-the-world tour as in *At Home Abroad,* would be restricted to topics and locales indigenous to the United States. John Gunther presented him with a perfect title for it—*Inside U. S. A.*

Inside U. S. A., which co-starred Beatrice Lillie and Jack Haley, was the only musical Schwartz ever produced himself. It also reunited him with Howard Dietz, and their score gave undeniable proof that in the wit and originality of their songs the collaborators had lost none of the skill that had marked their earlier efforts. In "Haunted Heart," they returned to the kind of throbbing torch ballad to which they have always given a certain distinction; in "Rhode Island Is Famous for You," they created a punning inventory of the most famous products of almost every state in the Union; in "Come, O Come to Pittsburgh," they supplied Beatrice Lillie with a mocking madrigal celebrating the industrial wonders of that city. Two particularly original musical notions were "Blue Grass," the lament of a girl who has lost her boy friend to the horses at Churchill Downs, and "My Gal Is Mine Once More," a loping Western number sung by a cowboy celebrating his remarriage to his first wife.

For his two most recent scores, *A Tree Grows in Brooklyn* in 1951, and

193

By the Beautiful Sea in 1954, Schwartz again became affiliated with lyricist Dorothy Fields. Both shows starred Shirley Booth (whose previous musical comedy experience had been as Louhedda Hopsons in *Hollywood Pinafore* five years earlier), both were set in Brooklyn just after the turn of the century, and both lasted exactly 270 performances.

Judged on musical merits, *A Tree Grows in Brooklyn* was the more impressive work. The famous Betty Smith novel provided both Schwartz and Miss Fields with the opportunity to create songs of far greater depth and meaning than they had previously done. In place of sophisticated patter and soulful ballads of the type they had provided for *Stars in Your Eyes*, the writers produced a score overflowing with nostalgia and sentiment, one that caught all the poignance and emotion of the gallant Nolan family. For Schwartz, it was an opportunity to return to the people and the places he had once known during his boyhood in Brooklyn, and he took long walks through the tenement areas of the city in order to steep himself in the proper atmosphere. Miss Fields also strove for authenticity. "The lyrics reflect the simplicity of these people," she once said. "There are no high-flown poetic sentiments." Yet, though there may not be any deliberate attempts at poetry, there

INSIDE U.S.A. *(1948). The gay opening number of the second act with Beatrice Lillie as the queen of the Mardi Gras. The kneeling swain at the right is Jack Cassidy. (Costumes by Eleanor Goldsmith and Castillo; setting by Lemuel Ayers.)*

PHOTO BY EILEEN DARBY—GRAPHIC HOUSE

A TREE GROWS IN BROOKLYN
(1951). Aunt Cissy breaks out
into a spirited rendition of
"Look Who's Dancing." The
scene is a furniture store
where she and newlyweds
Kate and Johnny Dolan have
gone to purchase a bed. Shirley Booth, Marcia VanDyke,
and Johnny Johnston. (Costumes by Irene Sharaff.)

PHOTO BY EILEEN DARBY—GRAPHIC HOUSE

is a rich vein of the poetry of everyday speech in the lyrics, just as there is a feeling of genuine eloquence in the music. Indeed, the characters and locale came more vividly to life in the songs than in the somewhat awkward libretto devised by George Abbott and Betty Smith.

Because it had an even weaker book and score, *By the Beautiful Sea* was more dependent on the charm and personality of Shirley Booth. As Lottie Gibson, a vaudeville performer who owned a theatrical boarding house in Coney Island, her performance was so disarming that Brooks Atkinson had to confess, "Everyone has long since lost his heart to Miss Booth." It is interesting to note that while both *A Tree Grows in Brooklyn* and *By the Beautiful Sea* were financial failures, they ran ten performances longer than had the hugely successful *Band Wagon* in 1931.

The striking irony in the career of Arthur Schwartz is that in spite of the general excellence of his music for such book shows as *Revenge with Music, Virginia, Between the Devil, Stars in Your Eyes, Park Avenue,* and especially *A Tree Grows in Brooklyn,* the composer's only commercial successes have been the revues he wrote with Howard Dietz. The fault has never been his or his lyricist's; in every case it has been the librettist who has somehow failed to supply a script worthy of its score. Thus, at this writing, Schwartz still remains a man looking for a good librettist, just as in the mid-Twenties he was a man looking for a good lyricist. Now that he is again united with Howard Dietz, the search may prove a good deal easier.

But no matter what the team's future collaborations may produce, the contributions of Arthur Schwartz and Howard Dietz to the revue form will probably remain their most significant achievement in the musical theatre. Chiefly due to their efforts, the revue reached a peak of perfection that has never been surpassed. Indeed, if this type of musical entertainment ever does return to its former eminence, it will need the very qualities of smartness, originality, and wit that the partners once brought to it. Quite possibly, it will also need Schwartz and Dietz.

E. Y. Harburg.

CHAPTER THIRTEEN

E. Y. Harburg,
Vernon Duke, Harold Arlen,
Burton Lane

IN ADDITION TO Arthur Schwartz, there were many other composers who first won recognition for their work in the Broadway revues of the late Twenties and early Thirties. Chief among them were Vernon Duke, Harold Arlen, and Burton Lane, though none of these men was as closely identified with this form of entertainment as Schwartz.

In fact, each one of these composers won far more lasting fame with serious musical plays during the Forties—Duke with *Cabin in the Sky*, Arlen with *Bloomer Girl*, and Lane with *Finian's Rainbow*. Apart from the similarity of their progress in the theatre, what is interesting about these men is that they were part of the rising group of writers—which included Schwartz—who were inspired by George Gershwin. Just as Jerome Kern had been the idol of Rodgers, Gershwin, and other composers of the Twenties, so it was now Gershwin himself who was the inspiration for the new generation. The relationship of these men to the Gershwin family has even been professional, as all have collaborated with George's brother, Ira. The lyricist, however, who has been most closely associated with the careers of Duke, Arlen, and Lane— and who has also been a close friend of the Gershwins—is the prodigious E. Y. Harburg.

E. Y. Harburg

E. Y. (Edgar "Yip") Harburg was born on April 8, 1898, in New York City. His parents were poor, and as a boy he sold newspapers, lighted street lamps, and did other odd jobs to help pay for his education. At Townsend Harris High School, he was co-editor with Ira Gershwin of the literary column in the school newspaper. The friendship of the two men continued when they both attended the City College of New York. While at college, Harburg, like Ira Gershwin and Howard Dietz, began to contribute light verse to Franklin P. Adams' *Conning Tower* column. After graduation, he traveled through South America for about three years, spending a year writing for a newspaper in Montevideo, Uruguay.

While in South America, he made up his mind to become a lyricist. On his return to New York in the early Twenties, he was advised by Ira Gershwin that he would do well to find a more remunerative way of earning a living. Harburg then started an electrical appliance business and did well until the 1929 stock market crash wiped him out. "I had my fill of this dreamy abstract thing called business," he once said," and I decided to face reality by writing lyrics."

Fortunately, at that time, composer Jay Gorney was looking for a lyricist. A few years before, having read some poems in F.P.A.'s column signed "Freckles," Gorney had discovered the man behind the nickname to be Howard Dietz, and an informal partnership had developed. But because Gorney had recently been appointed head of the music department of Paramount Picture's Astoria Studio and Dietz was the chief publicist for M-G-M, the composer had to find another lyricist. Again he scanned F.P.A.'s column, where some verses signed "Yip" attracted his attention. Abetted by a high recommendation from Ira Gershwin, Harburg soon had both a partner and a contract with a motion picture company. About the same time, five songs by Gorney and Harburg were accepted for *Earl Carroll's Sketchbook*, an extremely successful revue which ran for a year and one-half. So outstanding were Harburg's initial efforts that he was given assignments to contribute the major share of lyrics to *The Garrick Gaieties, Earl Carroll Vanities of 1930, Shoot the Works, Ballyhoo,* and *Americana*. In *Americana,* produced in 1932, Harburg was represented by contributions written with Vernon Duke ("Let Me Match My Private Life with Yours"), Harold Arlen and Johnny Mercer ("Satan's Li'l Lamb"), and Burton Lane ("You're Not Pretty but You're Mine"). The biggest hit of the show was the memorable Depression anthem, "Brother, Can You Spare a Dime?," which Harburg wrote with Jay Gorney. The song was one of the first examples of the kind of socially conscious viewpoint that would mark many of Harburg's later lyrics.

Vernon Duke.

Vernon Duke

Along with Kurt Weill, Vernon Duke had the most thorough musical education of any of the leading theatre composers who won recognition during the Thirties. Yet, unlike most well-trained composers, Duke has led a somewhat schizophrenic musical life, writing symphonies, ballets, and concertos in a style completely unlike that employed in his musical comedies and revues. Indeed, for many years, he even used two different names: his real name, Vladimir Dukelsky, for the concert hall, and Vernon Duke, a pseudonym suggested by George Gershwin, for Broadway.

Duke was born in Parafianovo, Russia, on October 10, 1903. His early studies were under Reinhold Glière and Marian Dombrovsky, and at the age of thirteen was admitted to the Kiev Conservatory of Music. After the Russian Revolution, his family fled the country. For a time, Duke tried to pursue his musical career in the United States, but found few opportunities. He returned to Europe, where he soon became acquainted with Sergei Diaghilev, the director of the Ballet Russe. Diaghilev was so impressed with

WALK A LITTLE FASTER (1932).
Bobby Clark, Beatrice Lillie,
and Paul McCullough.

the twenty-year-old composer that he commissioned him to write the music for the ballet, *Zéphyr et Flore*, which was subsequently performed throughout Europe. In the mid-Twenties, Duke moved to London. There his first assignment for the musical theatre was to supply additional music for *Katja, the Dancer*. The following year he performed a similar task for *Yvonne*, which won immortality when Noël Coward dubbed it "*Yvonne* the Terrible." Duke's first complete score was written in 1928 for *The Yellow Mask*, an English musical with a book by Edgar Wallace.

Soon after settling permanently in the United States in 1929, Duke wrote his first "American" song, "I Am Only Human after All," with a lyric by Ira Gershwin and E. Y. Harburg. Although the song was accepted for Ruth Selwyn's *9:15 Revue*, it was dropped from the score even before rehearsals began. Later, it was introduced in the 1930 edition of *The Garrick Gaieties* and became Duke's first commercial success.

Duke's romantic background as a Russian emigré soon made him a popular figure in the social life of New York. Courtney Burr, a wealthy young man with a great interest in the theatre, was anxious to produce a revue in the sophisticated style inaugurated by *The Little Show*. Burr was impressed by Duke's musical talent and hoped to induce Dorothy Parker to contribute the lyrics. On Duke's insistence, however, the assignment went to Harburg. The revue, *Walk a Little Faster*, opened in December, 1932, with the leading parts played by Beatrice Lillie and Clark and McCullough. The show may have been hindered by its continual striving for unusual artistic effects, but there was no sign of strain in the smoothly constructed melodies or in their deft lyrics.

"April in Paris," which quickly established the reputation of Duke and Harburg (even though Evelyn Hoey, who introduced it, had laryngitis on opening night), was written one April afternoon while Duke and some friends were reminiscing about Paris in a small restaurant in New York. Suddenly, someone paraphrased Browning by crying out "Oh, to be in Paris now that April's here." "April in Paris" struck the composer as a perfect title for a song; he dashed over to an upright piano and, within a relatively short time, created the refrain that still remains the most popular melody he has ever composed.

In the mid-Thirties, the Shuberts were the successors to Ziegfeld in the creation of elaborate revues. In fact, after Ziegfeld's death in 1932, his former rivals secured the rights to produce the *Ziegfeld Follies*. The first Shubert-sponsored *Follies* was presented in 1934, with Mrs. Billie Burke Ziegfeld as titular producer. Duke and Harburg created most of the score for this revue. Two years later, an equally resplendent edition reunited Duke with Ira Gershwin. Fanny Brice was the stellar attraction in both productions, though the second served to introduce American audiences to the charms of the St. Louis-born and Paris-acclaimed Josephine Baker. The 1936 *Follies* was also the first Broadway attraction to have choreography by George Balanchine.

On Christmas night, 1936, the Shuberts offered another opulent revue, *The Show Is On*, which was designed and directed by Vincente Minnelli. The bulk of the score was the product of Vernon Duke and Ted Fetter (Cole Porter's cousin). By the time the show reached New York, however, many of their numbers had been cut and replaced by contributions by some of the most illustrious song-writers of the theatre: George and Ira Gershwin, "By Strauss"; Rodgers and Hart, "Rhythm" (for an aggressively rhythmic Beatrice Lillie); Hoagy Carmichael and Stanley Adams, "Little Old Lady"; and Harold Arlen and E. Y. Harburg, "Song of the Woodman" (bellowed out by Bert Lahr). Among the remaining Duke-Fetter songs was one of their loveliest inspirations, the graceful, economically titled "Now."

PHOTO BY MURRAY KORMAN

ZIEGFELD FOLLIES OF 1936. *The irrepressible Baby Snooks (Fanny Brice) is beginning to get on the nerves of a Hollywood director (Bob Hope) in one of the sketches from the revue. This was Miss Brice's last appearance on the Broadway stage.*

THE SHOW IS ON (1936). *Beatrice Lillie invites the audience to "Buy yourself a balloon, fly up to the moon," as she is swung way out over the orchestra. As a climax to the number, Miss Lillie unfastened a garter and flung it to a favored gentleman. (Costume by Vincente Minnelli.)*

Although his previous works would not have indicated his suitability for the task, Vernon Duke became associated in 1940 with a musical fantasy of Negro life called *Cabin in the Sky.* The Lynn Root libretto was initially brought to George Balanchine, who was anxious to do it as his first assignment as director of an entire Broadway production. Balanchine took the script to Duke, who became fascinated by the story. Nevertheless, he hesitated to write the music as he feared that his lack of familiarity with the Negro people would be too much of a handicap. (The word around Broadway at the time was that the wrong Duke had been chosen.)

The more he thought about it, however, the more Duke became intrigued by the challenge. Because both he and Balanchine were Russian and Root was a Hollywood script-writer, the composer wanted a lyricist with some direct contact with Southern Negroes. Duke first thought of Ira Gershwin because of *Porgy and Bess,* but Gershwin was already committed to *Lady in*

CABIN IN THE SKY *(1940). Dooley Wilson listens as Ethel Waters sings "Cabin In the Sky." "Without once stepping out of character or assuming the airs of a star performer," wrote Brooks Atkinson, "Miss Waters captures all the innocence and humor of a storybook character, investing it also with that rangy warmth of spirit that distinguishes her acting."*

PHOTO BY BOB GOLBY

the Dark. E. Y. Harburg, Duke's second choice, diplomatically told the composer that he thought the story lacked significance, though his true feeling was that the composer was incapable of writing the kind of score the play required. (Later, Harburg readily admitted he was wrong.) Finally, Duke turned to the willing John Treville Latouche, a twenty-three-year-old poet from Richmond, Virginia, whose lyric to *Ballad for Americans* (music by Earl Robinson) had recently won wide acclaim.

When it was finally presented in October, 1940, *Cabin in the Sky* offered audiences an imaginative tale that combined elements of both *The Green Pastures* and *Liliom.* As a parable of the struggle between good and evil, the play may have been, as Richard Watts, Jr., wrote, "merely a white man's self-conscious attempt to write a pseudo-folk fable of another race." Yet in its pioneering effort to create something bold and unconventional, it did provide Ethel Waters with her only dramatic role in the musical theatre, while also demonstrating the remarkable versatility of the composer. Despite the fact there were no blues or rhythm songs to convey the authentic emotions of American Negroes, the score was still authentic enough as purely theatre music to delineate characters skillfully and to set the proper mood. Such varied, yet appropriate creations as the deeply felt "Cabin in the Sky," or the slinky "Honey in the Honeycomb" (for temptress Katherine Dunham), or the hedonistic "Do What You Wanna Do," all demonstrated their creators' talents for using music and lyrics to achieve maximum dramatic effectiveness.

Shortly before the New York opening, the authors felt that a comic number was badly needed for Miss Waters to offset some of her more impassioned solos. With the New York première only three days off, Duke came up with a song called "Foolin' around with Love," which he had once written with Ted Fetter. Latouche rewrote the lyric and retitled it "Takin' a Chance on Love." With Miss Waters delivering it through chorus after chorus, it became one of the most memorable show-stoppers in the history of Broadway musicals.

One of the great enigmas of the American musical theatre is that, to this writing, Vernon Duke has been unable to follow up his work for *Cabin in the Sky* with anything else that has revealed so much creative talent for the stage. As in the case of Arthur Schwartz, Harold Arlen, and other gifted composers, the fault has not been in the quality of Duke's contributions but rather in the quality of the productions for which they were written. Just one year after *Cabin in the Sky*, Duke became involved in a minor vehicle for Eddie Cantor called *Banjo Eyes*, which was also Cantor's final Broadway appearance. In 1944, great expectations were held for *Sadie Thompson*, a musical version of Somerset Maugham's *Rain* that had a libretto by Howard Dietz (he also did the lyrics) and Rouben Mamoulian. However, the production was foredoomed when Ethel Merman, the intended star, refused to appear in it because she objected to Dietz's lyrics. June Havoc was an excellent replacement, but the damage had been done: *Sadie Thompson* lasted only two months on Broadway.

In the Fifties, Duke became involved in the ill-advised Bette Davis revue, *Two's Company*, which also included an abbreviated musical treatment of *Rain* as the first-act finale. Two of the composer's most exquisite numbers, "Roundabout" and "Out of the Clear Blue Sky" (both with lyrics by Ogden Nash), were also sung in this revue. Ben Bagley's off-Broadway *Littlest Revue* in 1956 was a modest effort with an equally modest run.

Probably no other composer, with the possible exception of Arthur Schwartz, contributed so many good songs to the revues of the Thirties than Vernon Duke. With *Cabin in the Sky*, however, he showed definite indications of the broadening of his scope as a creator of well-integrated scores for adult, meaningful book musicals. The bad luck that has since plagued him in the commercial theatre cannot obliterate the sound musicianship and superior quality that have distinguished his work for the musical stage. Graceful, elegant, imaginatively constructed, the songs of Vernon Duke have a durability and individuality that has made them part of the permanent literature of American popular songs.

Harold Arlen.

Harold Arlen

Harold Arlen became a composer almost by accident. He was born in Buffalo, New York, on February 15, 1905. At seven, he sang in the choir of the synagogue where his father was a cantor. Because his parents wanted him to become a music teacher, they encouraged young Harold's interest in music. In his early teens, Arlen began to play piano at local clubs and on lake steamers. When he was fifteen, he helped organize an instrumental group known as The Snappy Trio. He later joined another group, The Yankee Six, which eventually expanded into a full-sized dance orchestra known as the Buffalodians. While performing as a pianist, vocalist, and arranger for the group during an engagement at a New York nightclub, Arlen attracted the attention of Arnold Johnson, a well-known orchestra leader. Johnson liked Arlen's singing and playing so much that he hired him for his own orchestra, which was then about to appear in *George White's Scandals of 1928*.

Because Arlen's chief ambition at the time was to become a singer, Johnson allowed him to sing one of the songs from the DeSylva-Brown-Henderson score during the intermission. Thus for the six-and-one-half-month run of the *Scandals,* Arlen serenaded nonsmoking spectators with his crooning of Harry

Richman's hit song, "On the Crest of a Wave." One of those who were impressed with the twenty-three-year-old between-the-acts entertainer was Vincent Youmans, who was just beginning to organize the cast for his forthcoming production, *Great Day!* Youmans promptly hired Arlen to play the role of Cokey Joe, the piano player, in the musical. Arlen never quite made it on the Broadway stage, however; after the first tryout performance on Long Island, both the character and the song he sang, "Doo-Dah-Dey," were eliminated.

Great Day! may have ended Arlen's career as a performer, but it was responsible for beginning his career as a full-time composer. One day at rehearsal, the regular pianist had become ill. As Arlen recalls: "I was asked to sit at the piano and play ta-tum, ta-tum-tum, TUM—the phrase that's always used to start a dance chorus off at rehearsals. I gave them the standard pick-up the first day, but the next day I played it a little differently. On the third day, I worked it around a bit more, and suddenly the whole company was asking, 'Say, what *is* that you're playing?' "

Urged to turn his variation into a commercial song, the neophyte composer took the piece to his friend, Harry Warren, then on the staff at Remick's. Warren introduced Arlen to Ted Koehler, who gave the melody a lyric and the title, "Get Happy." When they learned of Ruth Selwyn's plans for the *9:15 Revue,* the two men auditioned the song. Unlike the less-fortunate team of Duke, Harburg, and Gershwin, whose "I Am Only Human after All" had not been used, Arlen and Koehler had their new song accepted and given to Ruth Etting to sing in the first-act finale. George Gershwin, who saw the show during its tryout, was so impressed with "Get Happy" that he told the composer it was the most exciting finale he had ever heard. After receiving such encouragement—especially since the *9:15 Revue* was a dismal failure—Arlen promptly decided to end his career as a singer and pianist to devote all his time to composing.

Though he contributed songs to a few minor Broadway attractions in the early 1930's, Harold Arlen first won fame for the songs he and Koehler wrote for a series of Cotton Club revues. These were probably the only night-club floor shows ever to produce so many numbers of enduring appeal, among them "Between the Devil and the Deep Blue Sea," "Kickin' the Gong Around," "I Love a Parade," "I've Got the World on a String," "Stormy Weather," and "Ill Wind."

In 1938, "Yip" Harburg had an idea for a musical that was eventually turned into a successful vehicle for Ed Wynn and called *Hooray for What!* Concerned with the chaotic world situation at that time, the lyricist was anxious to become associated with a musical comedy that would not only be entertaining but would also have something to say about the need for preserving peace and the dangers of the armament race. Unsure of his own ability as a librettist, he took the idea to Howard Lindsay and Russel Crouse, who agreed to write the book. Arlen then joined Harburg to write the score. In spite of its overtones of a message (it even made reference to the atom bomb), *Hooray for What!* was still very much within the framework of conventional musical comedy. Ed Wynn again played his customary zany clown, although this time the character was called upon to save the world from destruction by using laughing gas. In the score were many superior numbers, including "God's Country," a merry flag-waver in which Popeye and Gypsy Rose Lee were extolled as ample compensation for being deprived of Mussolini and Oswald Mosley.*

From the Thirties to the mid-Forties, the uncertain condition of the Broadway theatre forced most of the creative musical talent, including Arlen and Harburg, to accept Hollywood contracts. By the early Forties, however, writers on the West Coast were becoming eager to return to a Broadway that was being transformed as a result of the impact of *Cabin in the Sky, Pal Joey, Lady in the Dark,* and, most significantly, *Oklahoma!* A book show now had to have a really sturdy libretto, with songs and dances an inseparable part of the entire production. During World War II, there was also a greater emphasis on American themes from which audiences might derive some measure of hope for the future.

While still in California, "Yip" Harburg became intrigued with the idea of doing a musical with a Civil War setting. Lilith and Dan James had written a play about the introduction of bloomers during that period. Harburg liked the story, but he felt the theme needed further development and suggested to writers Sig Herzig and Fred Saidy that they strengthen it by putting greater emphasis on the issues of women's rights and Negro rights. In that way, he felt, audiences of 1944 could accept the theme as pertaining to the struggle for freedom everywhere. To provide the score, Harburg was joined by Arlen, with whom he had last collaborated on the film *The Wizard of Oz.*

Bloomer Girl emerged as a charming and colorful musical play with an almost inescapable kinship to *Oklahoma!* This, however, was due more to its cast and production staff than to its subject matter or music. Both Celeste Holm (in her first starring role) and Joan McCracken had previously been in the Rodgers and Hammerstein musical and both plays shared the same set designer (Lemuel Ayers), costume designer (Miles White), choreographer (Agnes de Mille), and orchestral arranger (Robert Russell Bennett). Miss de Mille's chief contribution, a Civil War Ballet, was particularly impressive in its moving depiction of the longing of women who must wait at home while their men are at war.

* *Hooray for What!* was the second musical intended to begin the Broadway career of choreographer Agnes de Mille. As in *Flying Colors,* however, she withdrew prior to the show's New York opening.

BLOOMER GIRL (1944). Agnes de Mille's eloquent Civil War Ballet. Joan McCracken is the girl with her arms upraised, third from the left. (Costumes by Miles White; setting by Lemuel Ayers.)

The songs by Arlen and Harburg caught the mood and the spirit of the story. "The Eagle and Me" and "I Got a Song" sang eloquently of the Negro's yearning for freedom, while "It Was Good Enough for Grandma" burst out in animated defiance of old-fashioned convention. The eternal subject of love was melodiously treated in "Evelina," with its quasi-folk flavor, and in the more conventional "Right as the Rain." "Sunday in Cicero Falls" was a mocking, stately march that conveyed so perfectly the starched atmosphere of the Sabbath in a small, mid-nineteenth-century American town.

After *Bloomer Girl*, Harold Arlen continued to divide his time between film assignments and Broadway. In 1946, he joined Johnny Mercer in creating the songs for *St. Louis Woman*,* an all-Negro musical in which Pearl Bailey made an auspicious Broadway debut singing "Legalize My Name" and "A Woman's Prerogative." In spite of a superior score, however, the show was not a success. Neither was Arlen's next musical, *House of Flowers*, produced almost nine years later. Truman Capote made the adaptation from his own short story, and collaborated with Arlen on the lyrics. Although the idea was

* *St. Louis Woman* was subsequently expanded into a "blues opera," *Free and Easy*, which incorporated some early songs by the composer. After opening in Amsterdam, Holland, in the fall of 1959, it was forced to close soon afterward in Paris.

promising, the story of an innocent girl living in a brothel on a Caribbean island proved to be too weak and undramatic to be successful as a musical comedy libretto. This was particularly unfortunate; Arlen's score was one of his most distinguished, the Oliver Messel décor was stunning, and the cast, headed by Pearl Bailey and Diahann Carroll, was widely acclaimed.

When Harburg first approached Arlen to write the music for *Jamaica*, the composer was reluctant. The Caribbean locale of the story was almost identical with that of *House of Flowers*, and, though his music has always shown a certain Negroid influence, he was understandably anxious to try something different. But the prospect of again working with Harburg was hard to resist, and he was intrigued by the simple charm of the story. Originally, Harburg's script was about a poor fisherman on a tropical island (to be played by Harry Belafonte) who was unique among his fellow islanders in that he had no desire to live in the United States. Why, he reasoned, should he trade his values for those of the people on the mainland when tourists obviously like his way of life so much that they continuously visit his island?

Because the producer, David Merrick, had different ideas about the show, this theme was completely lost by the time *Jamaica* opened on Broadway in the fall of 1957. The character of the fisherman (now played by Ricardo Montalban) was made subordinate to that of the leading female character (Lena Horne), and the plot was almost nonexistent. Although the

PHOTO BY EILEEN DARBY—GRAPHIC HOUSE

ST. LOUIS WOMAN *(1946). Pearl Bailey made her first appearance on Broadway in this musical. Here she is seen urging Fayard Nicholas to "Legalize My Name." (Costumes by Lemuel Ayers.)*

HOUSE OF FLOWERS (1954). Ottilie (Diahann Carroll) and the townspeople of a Caribbean island give a joyous welcome to Royal (Rawn Spearman), who has just barely escaped being drowned at sea. (Costumes and setting by Oliver Messel.)

show was a financial success because of the lure of Miss Horne in her first starring role, in almost every department it was a curiously heavy-handed production.

Faults of production were also apparent in *Saratoga*, for which Arlen was joined by his *St. Louis Woman* lyricist, Johnny Mercer. In his first attempt as librettist, director Morton Da Costa evolved a rather plodding book out of Edna Ferber's novel, *Saratoga Trunk*, which left Cecil Beaton's almost overpoweringly elegant settings as the chief feature of the attraction.

In Harold Arlen, the musical theatre has, quite possibly, the most distinguished native composer to emerge since the Twenties. George Gershwin called him "the most original of us all." Irving Berlin, with typical succinctness, has said, "Harold's best *is* the best." To E. Y. Harburg, Harold Arlen is

JAMAICA (1957). Ricardo Montalban and Lena Horne. Of Miss Horne, Life Magazine wrote, "She shines like a tigress in the night, purring and preening and pouncing into the spotlight." (Costumes by Miles White.)

SARATOGA (1959). "Cecil Beaton's sets and costumes depicting New Orleans and the title resort in the lavish glories of the '80s provide a really breathtaking pictorial loveliness," was the opinion of Richard Watts, Jr. The above scene shows Howard Keel, Carol Lawrence, Odette Myrtil, Tun Tun, and Carol Brice at the Waterfront Market in New Orleans.

a genius. "He writes with his own genes. An Arlen song is completely individual, completely uninfluenced by anyone else. His songs are the kind that last. His contributions are colorfast."

Though he can write in a variety of moods, Arlen is best known for his blues and rhythm songs that have a strong affinity with the emotions of Negroes. Many of his numbers have been written specifically for shows with all-Negro or predominantly Negro casts—the Cotton Club revues, *St. Louis Woman* (and *Free and Easy*), *House of Flowers,* and *Jamaica.* Other musicals, such as *Bloomer Girl* and *Saratoga,* were concerned with Negro themes. Yet Arlen's ability to invest his songs with so much inventiveness and musicianship has kept them from seeming repetitive, and his great theatrical sense has endowed them with an indisputable fitness for the stage.

"Does it work theatrically?" is the question he continually asks himself about his songs. "Does it motivate the action? Is the song, in a sense, a part of the dialogue? Does the music capture character without getting out of the framework of the show?" The hard, relentless questioning of the requirements of his music has, happily, resulted in songs that can be appreciated even apart from the circumstances for which they were written. For though he understands fully the theatrical requirements of music, Arlen has frequently been associated with enterprises that have not always utilized his gifts to their fullest. A dedicated, sensitive artist, he has put the stamp of his own creativity far more on the songs he has written than on the productions for which they were created. The obstacles of a weak libretto cannot be surmounted even by a composer such as Harold Arlen. That so many of his songs have outlasted their original surroundings is a testament to the inherent quality with which they have been endowed.

Burton Lane.

Burton Lane

Although *Bloomer Girl* was a success, commitments in Hollywood forced Harburg to remain on the West Coast for the next few years. While there, he continued to think of ideas for the stage. He had tentative ideas for two nonmusical plays, but neither one seemed to work out. One was about a bigoted Southern senator who miraculously turns black and thus becomes a victim of his own discriminatory laws. The other was a fantasy about a leprechaun with three wishes. "Then it occured to me," Harburg recalls, "Why not combine the two stories by having one of the leprechaun's wishes be to turn the senator black? Then I knew I had something!"

Harburg decided to write the story himself in collaboration with Fred Saidy. After finishing the libretto, he approached composer Burton Lane to supply the music. "All it needs is something like *Porgy and Bess*," Harburg told him. Lane, a highly regarded song-writer, but one who had never before attempted anything of this scope, at first felt that Harburg had gone to the wrong man. But Harburg was so positive that Lane eventually joined the project that resulted in *Finian's Rainbow*.

Burton Lane was another composer who had begun his career in the early Thirties by having songs interpolated in revues. He was born in New York City, on February 2, 1912, of well-to-do parents. While still in high school, he showed so much musical talent that J. J. Shubert hired him to compose the score for a proposed edition of the *Greenwich Village Follies*. The sixteen-year-old composer had more than twenty songs ready for the show, but when the intended star, James Barton, fell ill, Shubert abruptly cancelled the production. After getting a job as a pianist at Remick's, Lane became acquainted with many rising young song-writers. One of them, Howard Dietz, liked two of his melodies so much that he put words to them and added the songs to *Three's a Crowd*. The composer was still in his teens when "Forget All Your Books" and "Out in the Open Air" were sung in the revue.

Many of the numbers for the 1931 edition of the *Earl Carroll Vanities* were written by Lane in collaboration with lyricist Harold Adamson. Two years later, Lane went to Hollywood. He remained there until 1954, creating many film songs with such lyricists as Adamson, Harburg, Ted Koehler, Frank Loesser, Alan Jay Lerner, and Ira Gershwin.

During the twenty-one years he lived in California, Lane returned to New York for three Broadway assignments. In 1940, he and Harburg wrote a bright score for *Hold On to Your Hats*, a satire on radio Westerns, in which Al Jolson made a highly acclaimed return to the stage after an absence of almost ten years. Jolson scored a personal hit, but the show lasted only about four months because of the star's ill health at the time. It was his last appearance in a musical comedy. Lane returned to Broadway again in 1944 when he contributed both words and music to Olsen and Johnson's madhouse variety show, *Laffing Room Only*. Created from the same mold as the immensely successful *Hellzapoppin* and *Sons o' Fun*, the attraction is probably best remembered for the song "Feudin' and Fightin'," later made famous by Dorothy Shay.

In 1947, *Finian's Rainbow* brought Lane back to New York for the third time. That its intermingling of fantasy and social comment could cohere so smoothly into a unified musical attests to the uncommon skill brought to it by all those responsible for its creation. The feeling of a message may have been apparent throughout, but *Finian's Rainbow* was never allowed to become a sermon. It was light, it was imaginative, and it had its own brand of simpleminded logic. For example, Finian, an Irishman newly arrived in the state of Missitucky, is anxious to bury a crock of gold at Fort Knox. His reason is that if gold is buried there it will have to grow, for what other purpose would the United States government have to put all of its gold in the ground? Harburg was anxious to make two important points in the story: one was that people would find riches not in burying gold but in trusting one another more, and the other, as exemplified by the situation of the senator, was the inanity of racial intolerance.

The score aided immeasurably in keeping the various elements complementing rather than competing with each other. The Irish motif was found in the wistful "How Are Things in Glocca Morra?" and "Look to the Rainbow," both sung by Ella Logan in her customary Scottish burr. The whimsical spirit of the leprechaun, played by David Wayne, came through in "Something Sort of Grandish" and "When I'm Not Near the Girl I Love." Two rousingly optimistic numbers describing the vision of a bright future were the satirical "When the Idle Poor Become the Idle Rich," and the more impassioned "That Great Come-and-Get-It-Day."

Burton Lane has been represented on Broadway less frequently than any other major composer who first won recognition in the Thirties. Nevertheless, his contributions to *Finian's Rainbow* undoubtedly place him among the most talented of the post-Twenties composers, with a score that still remains a classic of the musical theatre. Harburg has observed that of all the modern composers, Burton Lane has come the closest to capturing that certain effervescence so characteristic of the works of George Gershwin.

Of the composers discussed in this chapter, Arlen has been the most prolific, though the contributions of Duke and Lane, particularly with respect to their work for *Cabin in the Sky* and *Finian's Rainbow*, have ensured their lasting fame. Yet the inability of these men to continue the pursuit of their careers in the theatre with the constancy of the composers of the first three decades of the century is unfortunate. The drastic reduction in the number

FINIAN'S RAINBOW *(1947). Og, a leprechaun (played by David Wayne), sings a reprise of* "Something Sort of Grandish" *to the children of Rainbow Valley, Missitucky. (Costumes by Eleanor Goldsmith.)*

of musicals being produced, the length of time that it takes to prepare a musical, and the almost prohibitive cost of such a venture have all been factors resulting in the relative infrequency of their efforts on Broadway.

Another important change has been the growing importance of the librettist. No other writer has appreciated this more than E. Y. Harburg. His entire career has reflected the transformations through which the musical theatre has gone. Starting as a writer of sophisticated lyrics for revues in the early Thirties, he soon moved away from revues to concentrate his attention on book musicals. In the Forties, he originated the plot of *Bloomer Girl* and also directed it. With *Finian's Rainbow* he became his own librettist. Since then, he has been both co-author and lyricist of all his subsequent musicals.

By his growing concern with every phase of a production, Harburg has been able to make his musicals more totally a part of himself than have the composers with whom he has worked. Rather than merely setting words to another man's melody or blocking out the rudiments of a story to hold the songs together, he has become the motivating force behind each production of which he is a part. Usually it is Harburg who first gets the idea and then finds collaborators he believes will be best suited to a particular project. Moreover, particularly in the cases of Harold Arlen and Burton Lane, he has been able to inspire composers to turn out their most successful efforts.

Though he is occasionally accused of injecting too much social consciousness in his plays, "Yip" Harburg is one of the most consistently adventurous men of the theatre today, both in his lyrics and in his librettos. To him, his purpose in writing for the musical stage is neither to provide escapist entertainment nor to depict life realistically. "I don't believe the theatre is a place for photographic reproduction," he says. "That's why I'm attracted to fantasy, to things with a poetic quality. Through fantasy, I feel that a musical can say things with greater effectiveness about life. It's great for pricking balloons, for exploding shibboleths. Of course, I want to send people out of the theatre with the glow of having had a good time, but I also believe the purpose of a musical is to make people think."

Harold Rome.

CHAPTER FOURTEEN

Harold Rome

THE ECONOMIC CLIMATE of the early Thirties inevitably nurtured the socially conscious revues and musical comedies that came along during the second half of the decade. Of course, there had been such pioneering work as *Strike Up the Band, Of Thee I Sing,* and *Face the Music,* but these did not hit specific individuals or situations; the country had to wait until after the worst years of the Depression for serious topics to again be treated with a certain amount of detachment and humor.

Parade, in 1935, was intended as the first revue of social significance, though its edge was considerably blunted by its sponsor, the Theatre Guild. The season of 1937–1938 provided theatregoers with four political musicals containing viewpoints ranging from mildly liberal to radical: *I'd Rather Be Right* (President Roosevelt and his administration); Marc Blitzstein's *The Cradle Will Rock* (the evils of capitalism and the virtues of the working class); *Hooray for What!* (the need for international disarmament); and *Pins and Needles.*

Of them all, it was *Pins and Needles* that won the largest following. Produced by the International Ladies Garment Workers Union and with a cast composed entirely of union members, the revue ran for more than three years, went through at least three editions, toured the major cities of the

United States, and was responsible for giving composer-lyricist Harold Jacob Rome the most auspicious debut of any song-writer of the decade.

Rome was born in Hartford, Connecticut, on May 27, 1908. He began to play the piano at an early age and, in his teens, joined many local dance bands. At Yale, he was a member of the University Orchestra, with which he made four trips to Europe. After graduation, he spent a year at the Yale Law School. Like Cole Porter, he had little interest in poring over law books, and soon switched to the School of Architecture. In 1934, he became a draftsman with an architectural firm in New York. As the Depression was then at its most severe, he augmented his small salary by playing the piano at social functions.

After quitting his job as a draftsman, Rome joined the entertainment staff at Green Mansions, an adult summer camp in upstate New York. There he wrote many topical songs for camp revues. Encouraged by the reception the guests gave his efforts, he returned to New York determined to succeed as a song-writer. Producers and publishers, however, were almost unanimous in their reactions: Nobody, they chorused, wanted to hear songs about the nation's current problems while the economic situation was still so serious. Though he did manage to get a few numbers published—one was sold to Gypsy Rose Lee—it was not until Louis Schaffer, the head of the I.L.G.W.U. drama activities, heard his songs that Rome at last was given his opportunity.

Schaffer was then preparing a revue to be shown at the Labor Stage (the new name of the Princess Theatre), with the cast recruited entirely from the ranks of the union. After assembling all the sketches and songs necessary for the show, Schaffer discovered that his union actors were against doing anything so frivolous as a musical revue. They wanted a grim drama depicting the hardships of the economically exploited masses. In order to convince them that a song-and-dance show would be even more effective in presenting the union's point of view, Schaffer hired a group of W.P.A. actors to perform the show exclusively for the benefit of the cast. With Harold Rome and Earl Robinson providing two-piano accompaniment, the first showing of *Pins and Needles* took place on June 14, 1936, in a small studio above the regular Labor Stage auditorium.

As soon as they saw the sketches and heard Rome's bright, pungent music and lyrics, those who had objected to the entertainment were won over. For a year and a half, the I.L.G.W.U. Players rehearsed almost every night after they had finished their day's work in New York's garment center. They were eager to learn, but their lack of experience and the brevity of rehearsal periods were responsible for many delays. When the show finally had its première, neither critics nor a large audience turned out to greet it. Within weeks, however, word-of-mouth reports turned *Pins and Needles* into such a popular attraction that the small playhouse soon had a hit equal to those it had once enjoyed during the days of Bolton, Wodehouse, and Kern.

The revue was intelligent and funny, with the enthusiasm of the cast making up for what it may have lacked in professional skill. Perhaps the show's most winning trait was the ability to laugh at the labor movement itself while also, of course, taking jabs at the foibles of those on the other side of the bargaining table. After running about a year and one-half, a somewhat altered version, *Pins and Needles 1939*, was introduced. Later that year, it moved uptown to the larger, on-Broadway Windsor Theatre ($1.65 top) where a third edition, *New Pins and Needles*, was presently displayed. Including all its versions, the show had a run of 1,108 performances, though this impressive record must be "weighted" as the Labor Stage seated only about 300.

"Sing me a song of social significance" demanded the opening chorus in feigned earnestness. Rome obliged with a group of songs that were remarkable in their ability to express a fresh, original viewpoint within a colloquial speech pattern that was completely natural for the untrained performers. "It's Better with a Union Man" was a turn-of-the-century tearjerker given a sly, up-to-date twist; "Nobody Makes a Pass at Me" revealed the plight of the girl whose love life is completely unaided by any of the advertised products she tries; "Sunday in the Park" (as if in answer to Irving Berlin's elegant "Easter Parade") proclaimed the verdant pleasures of Central Park as a haven for the working man; and "One Big Union for Two" expressed eternal love through the language of collective bargaining.

The sketches and songs tried to keep up with the daily headlines as much as possible. "Four Little Angels of Peace" were Hitler, Mussolini, Eden, and an unnamed Japanese. After Munich, the composer substituted Chamberlain

PINS AND NEEDLES *(1937). Two of the "Four Little Angels of Peace": Berni Gould as Hitler and Harry Clark as Stalin. (Setting by S. Syrjala.)*

for Eden. With the signing of the Hitler–Stalin nonaggression pact, another angel was added. "Britannia Waives the Rules" had to be cut when World War II started. In "The Red Mikado," Rome and sketch-writer Joseph Schrank had fun at the expense of both communism and the two jazz versions of the same Gilbert and Sullivan operetta, *The Hot Mikado* and *The Swing Mikado,* then running concurrently in New York.

Even before *Pins and Needles* ended its run, *Sing Out the News,* another topical revue with words and music by Harold Rome, was offered on Broadway. This time, although the view was still from the left of the political stage, the show was a completely professional affair produced by Max Gordon in association with George S. Kaufman and Moss Hart. Rome's observations continued to be remarkably trenchant, but the novelty of his kind of revue had apparently already worn off. Although *Sing Out the News* lasted only three months, it did contain one truly electric number—the exultant "F.D.R. Jones," sung by Rex Ingram and chorus at a joyous Harlem christening.

Rome was inducted into the Army in 1943. During most of his time in the service, he wrote and organized soldier shows. While still in uniform, Rome and Arnold Auerbach, a former radio script-writer, began planning a Broadway revue. The show's theme would be soldiers returning to civilian life, with songs and sketches depicting in a generally lighthearted manner various aspects of life in and out of the Army. Only ex-servicemen, ex-WACs, and ex-USO entertainers would be in the cast, which was headed by Betty Garrett. (Her credentials were numerous appearances in the *G.I. Jane* shows that toured Army bases and hospitals.)

Titled *Call Me Mister,* the revue was presented in the spring of 1946 under the combined sponsorship of Herman Levin (who was to produce *My Fair Lady* ten years later) and Melvyn Douglas. The mood of the show was almost completely optimistic. Although Rome's songs were less concerned with the class struggle, they were equally as original as those of his previous revues. "The important element of a song is neither the words nor the tune, but the basic idea," Rome explained at the time *Call Me Mister* opened. "Take 'Little Surplus Me.' Once I had the picture of the girl pleading with the President to bring back her uniformed boy friends, the rest was merely a matter of variations on the original thesis. Similarly with 'Military Life.' Having conceived the notion that the soldier who went away a jerk might return still a jerk, all that remained was improvisations on the established theme."

The two serious numbers (both sung by Lawrence Winters) in *Call Me Mister* illustrated the composer's sociopolitical outlook. Contrasted with the jubilation of "F.D.R. Jones" in *Sing Out the News,* was the quietly touching tribute to Roosevelt called "The Face on the Dime." There was also a bitter sequence in which Winters, a Negro, after singing of the wartime exploits

CALL ME MISTER (1946). Betty Garrett, as a U.S.O. hostess, expresses her opinion of Latin American music in "South America, Take It Away." The attentive soldiers are Alan Manson, Chandler Cowles, George Hall, and Harry Clark.

of the Transportaton Corps in the stirring "Red Ball Express," was the only one of a group of applicants to be refused a job.

Harold Rome was the last of the major revue writers of the Thirties to compose a score for a book musical. In 1950, he and Arthur Kober decided to adapt Kober's play *Having Wonderful Time* into a musical appropriately called *Wish You Were Here*. The story dealt with middle-class New Yorkers on a two-week vacation at a summer camp in the mountains, and it gave Rome the chance to draw from his youthful experiences at Green Mansions.

Wish You Were Here was also an early example of the importance that directors were to assume in the musical theatre during the Fifties. When Joshua Logan agreed to produce the show, he also became its director, co-librettist, and choreographer. His insistence on putting in a $15,000 swimming pool made it impossible to take the musical on the customary tryout tour. Consequently, without the necessary "break-in" period, the play was greeted with generally unfavorable reviews following its June 25, 1952, première.

Logan still thought he had a potential hit. With the cooperation of Kober and Rome, he completely rewrote the script, changed many songs, and had the dances restaged by Jerome Robbins. *Wish You Were Here* became a sell-out within three weeks, and ran for two years. (So many alterations had taken place after its faltering start that Harold Clurman once called it the only experimental theatre left in New York.)

Logan was also associated with Rome on his next musical, *Fanny*. In 1951, Producer David Merrick had brought the property, which was based on Marcel Pagnol's trilogy *Marius, César,* and *Fanny*. The musical took three

PHOTO BY SLIM AARONS

WISH YOU WERE HERE (1952). *Joshua Logan directing. So many changes were continually being made even after the show opened that Harold Clurman once called it "the only truly experimental theatre in New York."*

Happy vacationers at Camp Karefree, a summer camp for adults, "where friendships are formed to last a whole lifetime through." In the center are Jack Cassidy, Patricia Marand, and Sheila Bond. (Costumes by Robert Mackintosh; setting by Jo Mielziner.)

PHOTO BY SLIM AARONS

years of preparation before it reached Broadway, with Ezio Pinza and Walter Slezak in the leads. After working more than a year with other writers and composers, Merrick called in Logan, who promptly became co-producer, co-author (with S. N. Behrman), and director. Because of their association on *Wish You Were Here*, Logan brought in Rome.

The score of *Fanny* presented the composer with a greater challenge than any other work for which he had written. Previously, he had been more celebrated for the ingenuity and wit of his lyrics than for his gifts as a composer. For *Fanny* he was called upon to create an expansive, melodious score, matched by lyrics that expressed deep emotions. As Marseilles was the locale and the people were uneducated waterfront characters, it was necessary to give the music a certain French feeling, while keeping the lyrics both simple and direct. Another major problem, according to Logan, was ". . . how to get jubilation into an essentially tragic story. Here was the tale of two lovers who are so completely separated that it is difficult to dream of them ever getting together. The songs in *Fanny* did not solve the problem completely, but Harold Rome's resourceful score was able to satisfy the audience's need for happy music without sacrificing the integrity of the story."

PHOTO BY ZINN ARTHUR

FANNY (1954). *Ezio Pinza as César and Walter Slezak as Panisse. This was Pinza's last role in the theatre.*

During the run of *Fanny*, David Merrick was struck with the thought that there had never been a real Western musical comedy. Kern's *The Red Petticoat*, Youmans' and Hammerstein's *Rainbow*, the Gershwin brothers' *Girl Crazy*, Rodgers and Hammerstein's *Oklahoma!*, Lerner and Loewe's *Paint Your Wagon* all had Western settings, but what Merrick wanted was something in the classic good-guys-versus-bad-guys movie tradition. The producer immediately thought of the durable sagebrush saga, *Destry Rides Again*, and, after some delay, secured the rights from Universal Pictures. He also insisted that Rome supply the songs for the new show.

The musical opened in the spring of 1959, with Andy Griffith as the violence-hating deputy sheriff, and Dolores Gray as the singer in the frontier

DESTRY RIDES AGAIN (1959). *Tom Destry (Andy Griffith) causes Frenchy (Dolores Gray) some momentary embarrassment by accidentally tearing off part of her skirt. The villainous Kent (Scott Brady) thinks it's all rather amusing. (Costumes by Alvin Colt.)*

PHOTO BY FRIEDMAN-ABELES

saloon. Although the show brought neither satire nor any new dimension to the familiar story, it was skillfully staged by Michael Kidd, whose explosive dances were infused with crackling vitality. Rome's music and lyrics captured the spirit of the old and rugged West but, unfortunately, the book provided him with little inspiration for a distinguished score.

The revues that Harold Rome was identified with during the Thirties and Forties were reactions to current events. *Pins and Needles* and *Sing Out the News* were outgrowths of the Depression. *Call Me Mister* reflected the spirit of the country immediately after the war. When timely revues were no longer in style, and Rome at last began to write scores for book shows, he was able to bring to them the same understanding and natural warmth that had shown through in his earlier works. Moreover, to his already well established skill with words, Rome soon added a greater richness of musical style, one that served him with equally winning effect in his scores for *Wish You Were Here* and *Fanny*. The ability to express in songs the honest emotions of those who are least articulate has been one of his most distinguishing characteristics. For Rome is, essentially, a people's composer and lyricist, one who, without being sentimental or patronizing, provides the common man with uncommon musical expressions.

Kurt Weill

CHAPTER FIFTEEN

Kurt Weill

U NLIKE OTHER EUROPEAN-BORN composers who have settled in the United States, Kurt Weill had achieved a worldwide reputation even before he began to write for the American musical theatre. His *Die Dreigroschenoper* (*The Threepenny Opera*), written in 1928, was performed over 10,000 times throughout Central Europe within a period of five years. It was translated into eighteen languages and, in 1933, even had a brief run on Broadway. The musical was universally accepted as the most revealing depiction of the moral decadence that was then eating away the fabric of society at almost every level all over Europe. Bertolt Brecht's libretto may have been a social preachment but, particularly when combined with Weill's jingly, beer-hall tunes, it emerged as popular entertainment that reflected the cynicism and desperate gaiety of the times.

To the Nazis, however, the work was that of a *Kultur-Bolshevist*, and one of the first things the new regime did when it came to power in Germany in 1933 was to ban the production. Weill and his wife, Lotte Lenya, were soon forced to flee the country. For a time they settled in Paris where the composer quickly learned the techniques of the French theatre. Within two years, he had collaborated with French playwright Jacques Deval on *Marie Galante* and, with fellow-refugee Bertolt Brecht, he composed the ballet *The Seven Deadly Sins*.

Though his career in France seemed assured, Weill was anxious to leave Europe as quickly as possible. He had little confidence that France or England could stand up to Hitler; only in the United States, he felt, was there hope for the future. His opportunity to leave the Continent came in 1935. Max Reinhardt, the Viennese director and producer, was then preparing a Biblical pageant, *The Eternal Road,* for a Broadway production. Knowing of Weill's urgent desire to go to America, he offered the composer the commission of creating the background music.

Almost as soon as he arrived in New York, Weill became so much a part of his adopted country that he made up his mind never to return to Europe. Indeed, it was characteristic of the man, in both his work and in his personal life, that he never looked backward. The challenge of the present was what concerned him, whether it was a new country or a new musical project. His impatience with self-pity, combined with his complete disinterest in anything that was not of immediate concern, enabled him to adjust to every new situation within the shortest possible time and with the most efficient results.

Kurt Weill was born in Dessau, Germany, on March 2, 1900. Like Irving Berlin and Harold Arlen, he was the son of a cantor. As a youth, he showed such musical aptitude that at sixteen he was sent to Berlin to study under Engelbert Humperdinck. When Humperdinck retired from teaching, Weill accepted the post of director of a small opera company at Ludenscheid. During his one year there, he gained valuable experience in every phase of theatrical production.

Weill returned to Berlin in the early Twenties to continue his studies under Ferruccio Busoni. His first important attempts at composition resulted in many concert pieces greatly influenced by the modern atonal technique. At the time, Weill cared little for audience acclaim. His ideas began to change, however, when he was commissioned to compose a children's ballet, *Die Zaubernacht.* Upon seeing the reactions of the children to the work, Weill, with characteristic decisiveness, made up his mind to devote his career to creating music that would make a direct appeal to the largest number of people. "I am not struggling for new forms or new theories," he said in the mid-Twenties. "I am struggling for a new public."

Three years later, Weill's first opera, *Die Protagonist,* with a libretto by playwright Georg Kaiser, won such favorable notice that he received a commission from the Berlin State Opera. This resulted in *Royal Palace,* in which may be detected some of the earliest influences of jazz in an opera.

With *Die Dreigroschenoper* and the even more sardonic *Aufsteig und Fall der Stadt Mahagonny* (*Rise and Fall of the City of Mahagonny*), the composer broke completely with the classical past. Even the opera house had become too confining for these examples of *Zeitoper,* a form of popular opera created to reflect the spirit of the times in which it was written.

228

After he had come to America in 1935, Weill found that the Broadway theatre offered him a greater latitude than he had ever had before. There was no censorship, no storm troopers, nothing to stand in his way of reaching the wide public he so fervently desired. He reacted to this freedom by shedding some of the astringent pessimism inherent in his German works and by revealing a far greater lyricism than had previously been apparent.

One of the exciting developments of the Broadway theatre during the mid-Thirties was the formation of the Group Theatre, a repertory company dedicated to introducing new works by promising playwrights. Because he admired the aims of the organization, Weill confided in Lee Strasberg, one of the Group's directors, that he would like to work on an original musical play with a dramatist Strasberg would recommend. Strasberg suggested Paul Green. The result of the Weill-Green collaboration was *Johnny Johnson,* a bitter yet funny anti-war "folk legend," with a cast including many who later won fame as both actors and directors: Russell Collins (in the title role), Lee J. Cobb, John (then Jules) Garfield, Robert Lewis, Elia Kazan, Luther Adler, and Morris Carnovsky. The production also marked the first Broadway assignment of musical director Lehman Engel.

PHOTO BY ALFREDO VALENTE

JOHNNY JOHNSON *(1936). The scene in the French churchyard in which Johnny Johnson, an American soldier, captures a German sniper who has been hiding behind a statue of Christ. When Johnny learns that the German (whose name is also Johnny) longs for peace, he releases him. John Garfield played the German and Russell Collins had the title role. (Setting by Donald Oenslager.)*

KNICKERBOCKER HOLIDAY (1938). *Led by Councilman Roosevelt (George Watts), the City Council of New Amsterdam turns against Governor Pieter Stuyvesant (Walter Huston) and refuses to pull the rope that would hang the outspoken Brom Broeck (Richard Kollmar). (Costumes by Frank Bevan; setting by Jo Mielziner.)*

Although *Johnny Johnson* was not a commercial success, its daring fusion of music and satiric fantasy won many champions. At the opening-night performance, Lorenz Hart, who was seated behind Weill, tapped the composer on the shoulder and inquired in mock rage: "What are you trying to do, put people like me out of business?" And Robert Benchley, indignant at the indifference of both critics and the public, particularly in a mediocre theatrical season, exclaimed: "My God, if we don't grab onto something really big when it comes along, even if it does have flaws, the theatre may go right on as it started this year. This is the first anti-war play to use laughing gas in its attack on the stupidity of mankind, and to my mind it is the most effective of all satires in its class."

Knickerbocker Holiday, in 1938, united Kurt Weill with playwright Maxwell Anderson. As both men were deeply concerned with the world situation, they longed to say something pertinent, yet entertaining, about the evils of dictatorship and the value of freedom. To express their convictions they drew modern parallels with the attempts of the tyrannical Pieter Stuyvesant to suppress the liberties of the people of New Amsterdam. The theme of the play was posed in the song, "How Can You Tell an American?" To Anderson and Weill, the answer was simple: an American is someone who loves freedom and hates any restrictions on his thoughts or on his actions.

At the suggestion of director Joshua Logan, the role of Stuyvesant was given to the fifty-four-year-old Walter Huston, a former vaudeville song-and-dance man who had never before appeared in a Broadway musical. Because Huston was living in California when he signed the contract, Weill sent him the following telegram: "WHAT IS RANGE OF YOUR VOICE." The actor's reply came promptly: "I HAVE NO RANGE STOP APPEARING TONIGHT ON BING CROSBY PROGRAM WILL SING SONG FOR YOU." Upon hearing Huston's transcontinental radio audition that night, Weill turned to Anderson and said, "Let's write a sentimental, romantic song for him." Both men went to work at once and within a few hours produced the most enduring number of the show, "September Song."

In spite of its brief run of about four months, *Knickerbocker Holiday* is generally accepted as a significant milestone in the development of the American musical theatre. Apart from its close integration of music and story, it was one of the first musicals to use a historical subject as a means through which pertinent observations could be made about contemporary political problems.

Moss Hart was the one who first thought of the idea of *Lady in the Dark*. Having recently undergone psychoanalysis, he was anxious to write a serious play about the subject and to cast Katharine Cornell in the central role of an emotionally disturbed fashion-magazine editor. As the work progressed, however, he found it taking shape more as a musical. With Miss Cornell eliminated by the play's metamorphosis, the author could think of no other actress for the part than Gertrude Lawrence. Kurt Weill, who was to have written some incidental music for the original concept, readily agreed to supply the entire score, and Ira Gershwin was signed as lyricist for his first Broadway musical since the death of his brother.

Lady in the Dark was an advanced work in both theme and music. Even allowing for the convenient device of keeping the musical portions within the dream sequences until the final scene, the music and lyrics, as Moss Hart has written, were "part and parcel of the basic structure of the play. One cannot separate the play from the music, and vice versa. More than that, the music and lyrics carry the story forward dramatically and psychologically."

The most memorable scene of *Lady in the Dark* takes place in the Circus Dream during the second act. Here the inability of the magazine editor, Liza Elliott, to make up her mind becomes the motivation for a trial presided over by the Ringmaster (Danny Kaye), with the handsome movie star (Victor Mature) as Liza's lawyer. For no apparent reason (except that tongue-

LADY IN THE DARK *(1941). Musical director Maurice Abravanel, composer Kurt Weill, and lyricist Ira Gershwin.*

"As for Gertrude Lawrence," wrote Brooks Atkinson in his review, "she is a goddess, that's all." Miss Lawrence is shown here in the Circus Dream sequence as she related all the misadventures of the unfortunate lady known as Jenny. (Costumes by Irene Sharaff.)

twisting numbers were a Danny Kaye specialty), the Ringmaster rattles off the names of forty-nine Russian composers in thirty-nine seconds in a piece called "Tschaikowsky."* Soon after this feat of vocal dexterity, Liza follows it with her own lubriciously uninhibited "Saga of Jenny," in which she relates all the misfortunes that once befell a lady because she "would make up her mind." Doing "Jenny" so soon after Kaye's ovation-winning rendition was a challenge to Miss Lawrence; she met it by giving an interpretation of such unbounded magnetism that audiences were once again brought to their feet.

Lady in the Dark, which opened January 23, 1941, was the third major musical to move onto Broadway within a period of three months. Following so soon after *Cabin in the Sky* and *Pal Joey*, it inspired Brooks Atkinson to predict: "The American musical stage is a sound basis for a new centrifugal dramatic form, and *Lady in the Dark* takes a long step forward in that direction."

If *One Touch of Venus* was not the daring work usually associated with Kurt Weill, the musical nevertheless provided many unusual touches on the familiar Pygmalion-Galatea theme. The S. J. Perelman libretto may have floundered occasionally between low comedy and highly polished wit, but the songs by Weill and poet-turned-lyricist Ogden Nash maintained a high level of musicianship and verbal ingenuity. Although *One Touch of Venus* was originally written with Marlene Dietrich in mind, the part was eventually given to Mary Martin as her first starring role on Broadway. Apart from the brooding, haunting "Speak Low," the most impressive musical interlude came when Miss Martin, in elegant simplicity, leaned over the back of an ordinary straight chair to describe her ideal man in the tender, amusing (and intentionally ungrammatical) "That's Him."

From the very beginning of his theatrical career, Kurt Weill zealously recruited outstanding writers from other fields to become active in the musical theatre. By the time he began work on the musical version of *Street Scene*, some of his American collaborators had been playwrights Paul Green, Maxwell Anderson, and Edwin Justus Mayer (with whom Weill had adapted the short-lived *Firebrand of Florence* from Mayer's own play, *The Firebrand*), humorist S. J. Perelman, and poet Ogden Nash. For *Street Scene*, produced in 1947, the composer persuaded Elmer Rice to supply the libretto based on his own Pulitzer Prize-winning play, and secured Langston Hughes to write the lyrics. "Not until *Street Scene*," Weill once wrote, "did I achieve a real blending of drama and music in which the singing continues naturally

* "Tschaikowsky" was based on a humorous poem called "The Music Hour," which Ira Gershwin had written under the pen name of Arthur Francis. It was published in the June 12, 1924, issue of the old *Life* magazine. Before listing the Russian composer's names, Gershwin introduced them with the following couplet:

I'll mention some composers who are known to us as Russian.
Please note them down. Tomorrow we shall have them for discussion.

ONE TOUCH OF VENUS *(1943)*. *Mary Martin singing "That's Him." (Costume by Mainbocher; setting by Howard Bay.)*

STREET SCENE *(1947). Norman Cordon, as the suspicious husband, threatens his wife, Polyna Stoska, as Anne Jeffreys, their daughter, tries to intervene. (Costumes by Lucinda Ballard; setting by Jo Mielziner.)*

where the speaking stops, and the spoken word, as well as the dramatic action, is embedded in the over-all musical structure."

Even though it was billed as "A Dramatic Musical," *Street Scene* was very close to genuine opera. Taking a compassionate look at the varied inhabitants of a single New York tenement (much as DuBose Heyward and George and Ira Gershwin had done with the citizens of Catfish Row in *Porgy and Bess*), the authors created a work that was, in the opinion of critic Olin Downes, "the most important step toward significant American opera yet encountered in the musical theatre." Of its arias, "Somehow I Never Could Believe" (sung by Polyna Stoska) was an overpowering exposition of the causes of a woman's bitterness and frustration, and there were deeply affecting passages in Anne Jeffreys' and Brian Sullivan's duets, "Remember That I Care" and "We'll Go Away Together." The musical even had a "pop" hit, "Moon-faced, Starry-Eyed," energetically danced by Sheila Bond and Danny Daniels over fire hydrants, garbage pails, and a front stoop.

A temporary cessation in the partnership of Alan Jay Lerner and Frederick Loewe enabled Lerner to become associated with Weill for an imaginative musical called *Love Life*. Designated simply as "A Vaudeville," it depicted the disintegration of marriage in the United States—from the colonial era up to that time (1948)—in a series of sketches and vaudeville acts. The couple through whom the story was told never grew any older during the entertainment; they were still the same age in the last scene, when the tensions of modern life had made it increasingly difficult for them to remain in the same blissful matrimonial state, they were at the play's beginning. If its stagecraft technique occasionally seemed like too much of a theatrical device, *Love Life* was nevertheless a welcome departure from conventional musical fare, containing many sharp observations on marital mores in America.

Weill was reunited with Maxwell Anderson for his last work, *Lost in the Stars*, produced in 1949. For years, Weill and Anderson had been looking for the right story on which to base a musical dealing with racial problems. At the recommendation of Mrs. Oscar Hammerstein II, they read Alan Paton's novel, *Cry, the Beloved Country*, and immediately felt that it was the story they needed. Through this drama of negro-white relations in South Africa, Weill sought to convey a "message of hope that people, through a personal approach, will solve whatever racial problems exist." Avoiding obvious "native" devices in his score, the composer made effective use of music to set the proper emotional atmosphere, though the integration of music as part of the action of the story was never completely realized.

Kurt Weill was only fifty years old when he died of a heart attack on April 3, 1950. During the fifteen years that he devoted himself to the American musical theatre, he brought to it an affection and pride that was, perhaps,

LOST IN THE STARS (1949). *Rev. Stephen Kumalo (Todd Duncan) visits his brother (Warren Coleman) in Shantytown, outside of Johannesburg, in a vain attempt to enlist his help in finding his missing son. (Setting by George Jenkins.)*

partly motivated by the circumstances responsible for his becoming part of it. His undeviating faith in the commercial theatre was effectively summed up when, in an interview, he said, "You hear a lot of talk about the 'American opera' that's going to come along some day. It's my opinion that we can and will develop a musical-dramatic form in this country, but I don't think it will be called 'opera,' or that it will grow out of the opera which has become a thing separate from the commercial theatre. It will develop from, and remain a part of, the American theatre—'Broadway' theatre, if you like. I'm convinced that many modern composers have a feeling of superiority toward their audiences. But the great 'classic' composers wrote for their contemporary audiences. As for myself, I write for today. I don't give a damn about writing for posterity."

Posterity, however, does give a damn about the writing of Kurt Weill. *Street Scene* and *Lost in the Stars* have become part of the repertory of the New York City Opera Company, and *The Seven Deadly Sins* is one of the most popular attractions of the New York City Ballet Company. *Down in the Valley*, a half-hour opera based on American themes that Weill wrote with Arnold Sundgaard, is continually being performed in schools throughout the country. Kurt Weill concerts are sell-out programs in New York, both at Lewisohn Stadium and at Carnegie Hall.

Just four years after the composer's death, Stanley Chase and Carmen Capalbo raised $10,000 to present an off-Broadway production of Marc Blitzstein's English adaptation of *The Threepenny Opera*. With Lotte Lenya appearing in the same role she had created in Berlin in 1928, the show ran for twelve weeks before it was forced to vacate the theatre due to a prior booking of another play. But interest in *The Threepenny Opera* would not die. In response to genuine public demand, it reopened, a year and a half later, on September 20, 1955. At this writing, it is still being performed at the 299-seat Theatre de Lys.

What is the reason for its continued durability? In the twilight years of the Weimar Republic in Germany, audiences could see in its raffish, sardonic story all the venality and bitterness then so much a part of daily life in Central Europe. An empathy was created between the play and audience that no other work of that period could approach. The social illnesses within the United States thirty years later may not be so pronounced, but they have caused many sociologists to express concern at the decline of moral values within an apparently healthy society. Thus, *The Threepenny Opera* still has something pertinent to say, while, at the same time, delivering its message with broad humor, a certain romantic charm, and an unflagging musical appeal.

Kurt Weill was a complete man of the theatre. The only major composer since Victor Herbert to do his own orchestrations, he was also vitally interested in every phase of theatre production. Moreover, from his very first American score, he was a motivating force in organizing and giving direction to every musical with which he was associated. Never lured to Hollywood for a lengthy stay, this soft-spoken, timid-looking man was able to devote all his considerable energies to the creation of a popular musical theatre that, he felt, had as its essence "a simple, strong story told in musical terms, inter-

THE THREEPENNY OPERA (1954). *Lotte Lenya, Kurt Weill's widow, as Jenny. As Jay Harrison wrote: "During the second act, Lotte Lenya stepped to the front of the stage to sing her air about Pirate Jenny. At that moment the miniature confines of the theatre stretched and were replaced by a broad and sweeping arena of genuine sentiment. For that's what art can do, and that's what an artist does."*

weaving the spoken word and the sung word so that the singing takes over naturally whenever the emotion of the spoken word reaches a point where the music can 'speak' with greater effectiveness."

Weill's devotion to the commercial theatre never made him deaf to uncommercial ideas. In fact, the theory of the *Zeitoper* theatre that he had brought to such acceptance in Germany continued to dominate his thinking in his American works. Though he believed in the mass appeal of music, he would never condescend to his audiences. Nothing was too daring for him. He built his musicals around such "unpopular" subjects as war, dictatorship, psychoanalysis, tenement living, race relations, and political and moral decay. That so many of his works are still performed today attests not only to the durability of the popular theatre in which Weill had so much faith, but also to his own indestructible place in this theatre.

Richard Rodgers and Oscar Hammerstein II.

CHAPTER SIXTEEN

Richard Rodgers
and Oscar Hammerstein II

AT A FEW SECONDS past eight-thirty on the evening of March 31, 1943, the house lights at the St. James theatre dimmed, the excited chatter of the audience died down, musical director Jacob Schwartzdorf* raised his baton, and the orchestra struck up the overture to the first New York performance of *Oklahoma!*

Everyone connected with the production had reason to feel especially apprehensive at that moment. To Theresa Helburn and Lawrence Langner, the co-directors of the Theatre Guild which produced it, the new work represented their last hope. The once affluent Guild had only $30,000 in the bank when it occurred to Miss Helburn that a twelve-year-old play by Lynn Riggs, *Green Grow the Lilacs*, might make a good musical. A series of theatrical failures had depleted the number of financial backers who would even consider investing in a Guild project; countless time-consuming auditions had to be given before, little by little, the required amount was raised.

To actors Alfred Drake, Joan Roberts, and Celeste Holm, *Oklahoma!* was their first opportunity to be seen in major roles in a Broadway musical. To director Rouben Mamoulian, it was a challenge to repeat the great success he had achieved with *Porgy and Bess*, his last Broadway assignment more

* During the run of *Oklahoma!*, Mr. Schwartzdorf anglicized his name to Jay S. Blackton.

than seven years before. To choreographer Agnes de Mille, it was the first real chance to create something meaningful in the musical theatre.

To composer Richard Rodgers and librettist-lyricist Oscar Hammerstein II, *Oklahoma!* had probably the greatest significance of all. For twenty-five years, Rodgers had never written a note with any lyricist other than Lorenz Hart. They had been an inseparable team that had created some of the greatest musical comedy scores ever heard on Broadway. It was almost impossible to think of one without the other. As for Hammerstein, though he had had many successes in the Twenties, his record since *Music In the Air*, in 1932, had consisted of an almost unbroken chain of failures.

The new partners also knew they were giving the public a work that broke with conventional musical comedy on many levels. While it was no longer an innovation to begin a show without a high-kicking chorus line, it was unusual for the curtain to rise on a simple farm scene of a woman sitting alone on the stage churning butter, with the opening song, "Oh, What a Beautiful Mornin'," begun offstage by the leading baritone. About forty minutes later, when the dancing girls finally did arrive, they were all garbed in correct, though less-than-appealing, period costumes. No great conflicts were posed in Act I; the action was concerned primarily with finding out which man, Curly McLain or Jud Fry, would take Laurey Williams to a

OKLAHOMA! *(1943). The Post Cards in Agnes de Mille's dream ballet, "Laurey Makes Up Her Mind": Joan McCracken, Kate Friedlich, Margit DeKova, Bobby Barrentine, and Vivian Smith. (Costumes by Miles White; setting by Lemuel Ayers.)*

PHOTO BY VANDAMM

OKLAHOMA! (1943). *The final scene just before Curly and Laurey (Alfred Drake and Joan Roberts) drive off in the surrey with the fringe on top. Kneeling in front of the happy couple is Joseph Buloff as Ali Hakim, the peddler. Other well-wishers are Marc Platt (Chalmers), George Church (Jess), Katharine Sergava (Ellen), Lee Dixon (Will Parker), Celeste Holm (Ado Annie), Betty Garde (Aunt Eller), Owen Martin (Cord Elam), and four of the bridesmaids. (Costumes by Miles White; setting by Lemuel Ayers.)*

The lively "Farmer and the Cowman" dance at the party at the Skidmore ranch. Photo below is of the National Company which toured for ten and a half years, beginning in New Haven, October 15, 1943, and ending in Philadelphia, May 1, 1954. It was seen in 153 cities in the United States and 10 in Canada, with frequent return performances in most of the larger cities. In 1951, it was presented in Berlin, Germany, as part of the International Theatre Festival. The longest run of the National Company was 60 weeks in Chicago.

PHOTO BY VANDAMM

dance. The second act introduced only three new songs, all the others being reprised from the first.

Many of the facts concerning the production were known to the audience at the first-night performance. Indeed, as the reports from Boston—where the show had opened under the title of *Away We Go!*—were not overwhelmingly enthusiastic, there were empty seats at the première. But almost as soon as they heard the rich, true baritone of Alfred Drake singing "Oh, What a Beautiful Mornin'," the audience succumbed to the open-air charm of the production. After the intermission, as the people were returning to their seats for the second act, Hammerstein recalls that "the glow was like the light from a thousand lanterns. You could *feel* the glow, it was that bright."

The critical reception the next morning was equally incandescent. "Wonderful," exclaimed Lewis Nichols of the *Times*. "Jubilant and enchanting," cheered Howard Barnes of the *Herald Tribune*. "The most thoroughly and attractive American musical comedy since *Show Boat*," was the verdict of the *News's* Burns Mantle. To Burton Rascoe of the *World-Telegram*, it was "fresh, lively, colorful and enormously pleasing." Wolcott Gibbs of *The New Yorker* happily admitted, "I feel nothing but the greatest affection for everybody in it. To the Theatre Guild my gratitude is practically boundless."

Oklahoma! ran for five years and nine weeks, to achieve a total run of 2,212 performances. At this writing, this is still the greatest number of continuous performances ever recorded for a musical play on Broadway.*

The first lyric Hammerstein wrote for *Oklahoma!* was for "Oh, What a Beautiful Mornin'." "When Oscar handed it to me," Rodgers recalls, "and I read it for the first time, I was a little sick with joy because it was so lovely and so right. When you're given words like 'the corn is as high as a elephant's eye,' you've got something to say musically." In its happy description of a sun-drenched morning on a farm in the American Southwest, the song set the proper mood for both play and audience.

The mood continued throughout. Early in the first act there was need for a love duet between the hero and the heroine. As they had just had a quarrel, however, it was necessary for them to express their emotions in an indirect way. Rodgers and Hammerstein adroitly solved the problem in "People Will Say We're in Love" by having the boy and girl warn each other against appearing too friendly lest they give people the impression that they are really in love. "The Surrey with the Fringe on Top" was a brilliant piece of scene painting in the way it fused music and lyric to convey the simple pleasures of a young couple riding in a horse and buggy. In "Pore Jud," the authors succeeded in creating something both ludicrous and touching in the

* This record, however, was finally surpassed by *My Fair Lady* on July 12, 1961.

imagined death of the story's villain. As a finale, they produced a roaring title song that was so charged the audience could almost feel the wind come sweeping down the plain.

Apart from the charm and inventiveness of the individual songs, what was unique about *Oklahoma!* was the synthesis of its component parts into a complete theatrical entity of great beauty and imagination. Everything fit into place. For the first time, not only were songs and story inseparable, but the dances devised by Agnes de Mille heightened the drama by revealing the subconscious fears and desires of the leading characters.

One factor in the success of *Oklahoma!* that cannot be overlooked was the attitude of the American people at the time it was presented. World War II was more than a year old when the musical opened, and those who remained at home were becoming increasingly aware of the heritage they enjoyed as a free people. Seeing the happier, sunnier days that were so much a part of this heritage gave spectators both an escape from daily headlines and a feeling of optimism for the future.

Rodgers was forty years old and Hammerstein forty-seven when *Oklahoma!* began its historic run on Broadway. Though they had never written together professionally before, they had known each other almost all of their lives. In fact, Rodgers had met Hammerstein about a year before he met Larry Hart. Mortimer Rodgers, Dick's older brother and Oscar's fraternity brother, had taken Dick to see a Columbia Varsity Show in which Hammerstein was appearing. Later, backstage, the awestruck twelve-year-old Rodgers was introduced to his future partner, then a worldly nineteen-year-old Junior.

Oscar Greeley Clendenning Hammerstein was born July 12, 1895, in New York City. Named for his paternal grandfather, the opera impressario and producer of *Naughty Marietta*, young Oscar soon adopted the "II" in order to rid himself of the cumbersome middle names. His father, William Hammerstein, was the manager of the Victoria Theatre, a vaudeville house owned by Oscar I. It was there that the youth first experienced the fascination of the theatre. But his parents were well aware of the hazards of show business and thought that their son might be happier if he became a lawyer. At Columbia, Oscar's first writing for the stage was an additional scene in the Varsity Show of 1916, *The Peace Pirates*, in which both he and Lorenz Hart appeared.

Even though the theatre was becoming increasingly important to him, Hammerstein acceded to his parents wishes and entered Columbia Law School. After a few months, however, he left to enter the professional theatre. His uncle, producer Arthur Hammerstein, gave him his first job as stage manager for three Rudolf Friml musicals—*You're in Love, Sometime,* and *Tumble In.*

Hammerstein also continued to be active in Columbia Varsity Shows.

245

He shared credit for writing the book and lyrics of the 1917 edition, *Home, James,* and the following year assumed full responsibility for the book, lyrics, and direction of the "War Show," *Ten for Five.* He was also on the committee that-chose Rodgers and Hart's *Fly with Me* as the Varsity Show of 1920. In addition to having the first complete Rodgers and Hart score, the musical also had the first song by Rodgers and Hammerstein, "Room for One More," a rather debonair piece with just a touch of John Donne in the lyric:

> My heart is an airy castle
>   Filled with girls I adore.
> My brain is a cloud of memories
>   of peaches galore.
> There were Jane and Molly,
>   And Ruth and Sue;
> Camilla, Kit,
>   and Patricia, too.
> My heart is filled to the brim with you—
> But there's always room for one more!

In 1919, Hammerstein created his first professional work for the theatre, a nonmusical play called *The Light.* It lasted four performances in New Haven, where it was described by one critic as *"The Light* that failed." The following year, Hammerstein wrote the book and lyrics for his first musical, *Always You,* with music by Herbert Stothart. The show had a very brief Broadway run. Because Hammerstein exhibited far greater talent as a lyricist than as a librettist, Arthur Hammerstein, who had produced both of his nephew's plays, suggested that he collaborate with the more experienced Otto Harbach, who had written both book and lyrics for most of the early Friml operettas. Their maiden effort, *Tickle Me,* had a good run due chiefly to its star, Frank Tinney. Later they worked on four of the leading musicals of the Twenties—*Wildflower, Rose-Marie, Sunny,* and *The Desert Song.* Still later, as the sole author of both libretto and lyrics, Hammerstein joined Jerome Kern in creating *Show Boat, Sweet Adeline, Music In the Air,* and *Very Warm for May.*

When Rodgers first proposed to Hammerstein that they collaborate on the musical version of *Green Grow the Lilacs,* the librettist was immediately enthusiastic—he had already tried in vain to interest Jerome Kern in the same project. Rodgers believed that their basically similar outlook on the theatre and on life itself would help to make theirs a harmonious partnership. With Larry Hart, it had been a matter of combining warm, tender melodies with frequently biting lyrics. With Hammerstein, it would now be a matter of combining these same musical qualities with lyrics that also possessed great warmth and tenderness. This fact, coupled with Rodgers' sound musicianship, his explorative nature, and his maturity as a composer, indicated how well he would be able to suit his style to that of his new collaborator. To a writer of such innate gifts, turning from the sardonic quality of a *Pal Joey*, or the slickness of a *By Jupiter*, to the rustic pleasures of an *Oklahoma!* was both natural and, perhaps, even inevitable.

The lyrics of Oscar Hammerstein II differ from those of Lorenz Hart in many ways, just as in appearance, working habits, and temperament, the men themselves were entirely different. For example, unless it is something like "Thou Swell," it is hard to recall a dialect lyric by Hart. Hammerstein, however, has always made use of dialects and idioms; his rare gift for enhancing the varied, colloquial speech patterns of an Oklahoma cowboy or a Siamese monarch is equally as brilliant as Hart's more facile ability with polysyllabic and internal rhymes. A Hammerstein lyric seldom calls attention to itself; at its best it seems to be the spontaneous and honest expression of the character who sings it. Yet there is always an inherent quality that once prompted Irving Berlin to remark, "The difference between Oscar and the rest of us lyric writers is that he is a poet." Moreover, Hammerstein has been able to convey his basic philosophy more firmly in his work than did Hart. "I believe not that the whole world and all of life is good," he has said, "but I do believe that so much of it is good, and my inclination is to emphasize that side of life. It's a natural inclination, not one that I've developed."

Shortly after *Oklahoma!* opened, the team split up temporarily—Rodgers to produce the new version of *A Connecticut Yankee* and Hammerstein to complete work on *Carmen Jones*, adapted from Georges Bizet's opera *Carmen*. While adhering faithfully to the original tempos (except in the wildly exciting "Beat out Dat Rhythm on a Drum"), Hammerstein updated the story more than one hundred years and changed the characters and locale from Basques in southern Spain to Negroes in the southern United States. What resulted was a vividly idiomatic theatrical piece, beautifully sung and acted, and stunningly produced.

Rodgers and Hammerstein resumed their partnership to create *Carousel*, a musical version of Ferenc Molnar's play, *Liliom*. As in *Oklahoma!*, it was Theresa Helburn of the Theatre Guild who first suggested the idea. At first, the partners thought it was too tragic for the musical stage, but they finally decided that the story could be made acceptable by adding a strong note of hopefulness at the end. They also felt that the play's locale of Budapest should be changed to somewhere in the United States; Rodgers' suggestion of the New England coast met with a favorable response because they could then have choruses of mill workers, sailors, and fishermen. Another task was in keeping the leading character, a carnival barker, basically sympathetic even though he is shiftless and frequently unattractive. But the authors were able

CAROUSEL (1945). *Mrs. Mullin, the owner of the carousel, warns Julie Jordan and Carrie Pipperidge to stay away from her barker, Billy Bigelow. John Raitt, Jean Casto, Jan Clayton, and Jean Darling. (Costumes by Miles White; setting by Jo Mielziner.)*

to treat the theme with so much insight and compassion that the work emerged as a remarkably affecting musical drama, one that could be accepted on its individual merits without comparison to the play from which it had been adapted.

The use of music as in integral part of the story was maintained to an even greater degree than in the authors' first collaboration. Early in the play, when two young girls, Julie Jordan and Carrie Pipperidge, are seated on a park bench, their dialogue is first synchronized over the music. As their conversation continues, it develops naturally into song: first the duet, "You're a Queer One, Julie Jordan," and then Carrie's starry-eyed revelation that she is in love with Mr. Snow. Shortly thereafter, Julie meets Billy Bigelow, the barker. Because it is too soon for them to admit their love, Rodgers and Hammerstein created "If I Loved You," a song in which the characters imagined how they would act if they really were in love.

As with "Oh, What a Beautiful Mornin'," "June Is Bustin' Out All Over" was inspired by the effect of weather. However, while the song in *Oklahoma!* was a lazy, arm-stretching ode to the beauties of a farm in summertime, the song in *Carousel* is a sprightly account of the odd effects summer has on the behavior of normally well-adjusted individuals. The final feeling of hope, so essential to the story, is conveyed through the simple, moving hymn, "You'll Never Walk Alone."

The most ambitious musical undertaking of the score was Billy Bigelow's "Soliloquy," which had taken Hammerstein several weeks to write and Rodgers just two hours to compose. The song contains many contrasting melodic and emotional themes as the barker imagines what it would be like to be the father of a boy and what it would be like to be the father of a girl. Expressing the frequently conflicting feelings of the joys and fears of fatherhood, the authors created one of the most probing expositions of a man's inner thoughts ever written for the Broadway stage.

In addition to its Theatre Guild sponsorship, *Carousel* kept intact most of the production staff that had worked on *Oklahoma!* Rouben Mamoulian directed, Agnes de Mille did the choreography, and Miles White designed the costumes. Again the cast consisted of comparatively unknown performers, among them John Raitt, Jan Clayton, Murvyn Vye, Jean Darling, and, from *Oklahoma!*, Bambi Linn. The new musical opened on April 19, 1945, at the Majestic Theatre, directly across the street from the St. James where *Oklahoma!* was playing. Thus, for about two years, Rodgers and Hammerstein had two musicals facing each other on West 44th Street.

CAROUSEL *(1945). The final scene of the musical in which the graduating class of a local school sings "You'll Never Walk Alone." Bambi Linn, as Louise, is seated at the far right of the front row. At the far right of the stage are Jan Clayton, John Raitt, and Jay Velie. (Costumes by Miles White; setting by Jo Mielziner.)*

PHOTO BY VANDAMM

Allegro, produced by the Theatre Guild in 1947, was Rodgers and Hammerstein's first original musical play. Directed entirely by Agnes de Mille, it was a boldly experimental work detailing the life of a young doctor from his birth to his thirty-fifth year. The authors used the story to probe the reasons why dedicated men sometimes begin to lose their integrity after they have won success. "I wanted to write a large, universal story, and I think I overestimated the phsychological ability of the audience to identify itself with the leading character," Hammerstein admits.

The story was told with many original theatrical effects, particularly in the elimination of formal sets and in the use of a modern Greek chorus to comment on the happenings in the play. The authors also made a deliberate attempt to make the score serve the function of the plot, although some pieces, "A Fellow Needs a Girl," "So Far" (the only number that was not germane to the story), and "The Gentleman Is a Dope," have won favor as individual popular songs.

Allegro had the critics divided. Brooks Atkinson thought it "just missed the final splendor of a perfect work of art," while Howard Barnes felt it was a "show to be remembered with *Show Boat* and *Oklahoma!*" However, Wolcott Gibbs referred to it as "spectacular banality," and George Jean Nathan called it "as pretentious as artificial jewelry, and just as valuable."

ALLEGRO (1947). *"Yatata, yatata, yatata, yatata" sing the guests at a party at the home of Dr. and Mrs. Joseph Taylor. John Battles and Roberta Jonay, as the host and hostess, are in the center foreground. John Conte, as Joe's best friend, is third from the left holding the brandy snifter. (Costumes by Lucinda Ballard.)*

PHOTO BY VANDAMM

South Pacific, which opened in 1949, is probably the most universally admired achievement of Rodgers and Hammerstein. In a realistic wartime setting, they created a warm, credible romance between a worldly French planter and a naïve Army nurse from Little Rock, while managing to keep this somewhat idyllic relationship in perfect balance with the far-from-idyllic circumstances that brought them together.

The idea of turning James A. Michener's collection of stories, *Tales of the South Pacific,* into a dramatic work first occurred to Kenneth MacKenna, then the head of M-G-M's story department. When the studio decided against filming it, MacKenna suggested to his friend, Joshua Logan, that it would make an excellent property for the stage. Logan read the book and took the idea to producer Leland Hayward; when it seemed to be developing into a musical, they approached Rodgers and Hammerstein. All four men agreed to become associated as co-producers, with Logan also serving as director. Originally, the libretto was to have been written entirely by Hammerstein, but because of Logan's experience in the Navy, he joined Hammerstein as co-author. One thing everyone was agreed on from the start: there would be no formal choreography to jar the mood.

Almost four months were devoted to conferences before a word or a note was put on paper. The tale they decided to use for the story was the one

251

called "Fo' Dollah," which related the unhappy love affair between Lieutenant Joe Cable and a Tonganese girl, Liat. The writers soon felt, however, that there was too much *Madama Butterfly* in the romance to make it acceptable as the main plot. Another tale, "Our Heroine," about the planter Emile DeBecque and the nurse Nellie Forbush, seemed to work out better. The story of Cable and Liat was retained as a secondary theme and the two stories were fused by adding the dramatic situation of Cable and DeBecque going off together on a secret mission behind enemy lines.

For the part of DeBecque, Rodgers and Hammerstein needed a mature man with an excellent singing voice. When they heard that Metropolitan Opera basso Ezio Pinza was anxious to appear in a Broadway musical, they promptly signed him to a contract. For Nellie, they chose Mary Martin, who had just finished touring in the National Company of *Annie Get Your Gun*, another Rodgers and Hammerstein production.

The skill with which the action flowed from the music just as smoothly as the music flowed from the action prompted some music critics to liken Rodgers' technique to that of an operatic composer. Moreover, the authors created each song to fit perfectly with the occasion and the character singing it. Nellie's straightforward, buoyant, warmhearted quality is expressed through "A Cockeyed Optimist," "I'm Gonna Wash That Man Right outa My Hair," and "I'm in Love with a Wonderful Guy." In fact, this last song

SOUTH PACIFIC *(1949). Myron McCormick leads the Seabees in singing "There Is Nothing like a Dame." (Setting by Jo Mielziner.)*

had such a contagious effect on audiences that Harold Clurman once wrote: "When Mary Martin tells us, with radiant good nature, 'I'm in love, I'm in love, I'm in love with a wonderful guy,' one doesn't murmer 'Who cares?' but 'Congratulations, congratulations, congratulations to you both! ' "

DeBecque's impulsive, romantic emotions come through in his ardent affirmation of love at first sight, "Some Enchanted Evening," and in the touching song of a fleeting romance, "This Nearly Was Mine." The raucous, restless Seabees beautifully contrast this idealized attitude with their single-minded desires in the rollicking "There Is Nothing like a Dame." The haunting dissonance of "Bali Ha'i" (which the composer wrote in less than ten minutes during lunch one day) captures the flavor of the entire South Pacific, while "Younger Than Springtime" and the plea for understanding, "Carefully Taught," give meaning to the character of the earnest young Joe Cable.

South Pacific had a New York run of 1,925 performances and, until *My Fair Lady,* held the record for the highest gross receipts ($9,000,000) of any Broadway musical. In 1950, it became the second musical ever to win the Pulitzer Prize for drama. As the *Herald Tribune* editorialized, it was one award that "will receive confirming cheers from coast to coast."

After traveling to Oklahoma, New England, the Middle West, and the South Pacific, Rodgers and Hammerstein journeyed to the Far East in 1951 for *The King and I.* The play was adapted from the book, *Anna and the King of Siam* by Margaret Landon, which had been based on the real adventures of a Victorian Englishwoman who went to Siam to become tutor and governess to the royal children. The novel made such an impression on Gertrude Lawrence that she approached Rodgers and Hammerstein about adapting it as a musical for her. Miss Lawrence was persuasive, and the partners were especially intrigued by the prospect of doing a play with an Oriental locale.* Finding an actor to play the part of the king proved to be more difficult. They finally decided on a little-known, bald-headed actor named Yul Brynner who, for his audition, sat cross-legged on the stage, played a guitar, and sang gypsy songs.

The possibility of creating a story around the characters of the straight-laced Anna Leonowens and the semibarbaric monarch fascinated Rodgers and Hammerstein. "The intangibility of their strange union," they once wrote, "was a challenge to us as librettist and composer. In dealing with them musically, we could not write songs which said 'I love you' or even 'I love him' or 'I love her.' We were dealing with two characters who could indulge themselves only in oblique expressions of their feeling for each other, since they themselves do not realize exactly what these feelings mean."

* Gertrude Lawrence died on September 6, 1952, during the run of *The King and I.* She was succeeded by Constance Carpenter.

THE KING AND I (1951). The
royal Siamese children bow
down as the king enters their
classroom. Standing are Gertrude Lawrence, Yul Brynner,
and Dorothy Sarnoff. (Costumes by Irene Sharaff; setting by Jo Mielziner.)

To the
music of "Shall We Dance?,"
Gertrude Lawrence teaches
Yul Brynner how couples
dance in Western countries.
Wrote John Mason Brown:
"Her incredible grace remains
with her as she moves about
in her great hoopskirts. So do
her glamour, her beauty, and
her charm."

RICHARD RODGERS AND OSCAR HAMMERSTEIN II

Again Rodgers and Hammerstein created a score to implement the action and to reveal characters and motivations, but at times with even greater effectiveness than in previous works. The king's soliloquy, "A Puzzlement," so different from the emotional outpouring of Billy Bigelow in *Carousel*, illuminates much of the personality of the untutored yet crafty ruler; "My Lord and Master" is a moving expression of pent-up secret defiance; the light, dainty "Getting to Know You" is an affirmative answer to Cable's troubled "Carefully Taught" in *South Pacific;* Anna's "Hello, Young Lovers" is a gentle, eloquent song of consolation and encouragement.

No better example of the way Rodgers and Hammerstein use a song to illuminate a dramatic situation can be found than the scene from *The King and I* in which Lady Thiang, the king's number-one wife, pleads with Anna to remain at court after she has decided to leave. Nothing can sway the determined governess. Then, as a final effort, Lady Thiang sings "Something Wonderful." In the song, while admitting all the ruler's faults, she emphasizes his hopes and aspirations and expresses her own belief that with Anna's help he could accomplish "something wonderful." This alone changes Anna's mind, and she agrees to remain at court.

The exotic locales of *South Pacific* and *The King and I* made Rodgers and Hammerstein anxious to try something completely different. As both men had been stagestruck from early youth, they decided to express their feelings about the theatre in a modern musical comedy. *Me and Juliet*, produced in 1953, was their valentine to show business. For their cast, they chose such bright young performers as Isabel Bigley, Bill Hayes, and Joan McCracken, and for their director, George Abbott.

PHOTO BY EILEEN DARBY—GRAPHIC HOUSE

ME AND JULIET *(1953). A tense moment backstage, as Bob, the electrician (Mark Dawson), warns Larry, the assistant stage manager (Bill Hayes), to keep away from his girl. In the center of the group of onlookers are Joan McCracken and Arthur Maxwell. (Costumes by Irene Sharaff.)*

Hammerstein's libretto was his first original script since *Allegro*. Unfortunately, it was an occasionally awkward combination of backstage story and onstage story that never quite succeeded in fitting together as a completely realized plot. The real distinction of the production was the spectacular scenic effects devised by Jo Mielziner, which enabled audiences to see both backstage and onstage simultaneously. "No Other Love," originally written as a theme for Rodgers' thirteen-hour television score for *Victory at Sea*, was the song with the greatest popularity.

Pipe Dream, in 1955, had the shortest run of any Rodgers and Hammerstein musical—246 performances. Originally, the rights to do a musical version of John Steinbeck's *Sweet Thursday* were held by producers Cy Feuer and Ernest Martin; when they were unable to secure Frank Loesser to write the score, they suggested to Rodgers and Hammerstein that it might be suitable for them. R & H agreed, but the public did not. A leisurely story with little conflict, *Pipe Dream* took such a warmhearted look at the denizens of a West Coast skid row that there was little opportunity for theatrical excitement or genuine gaiety. In the leading female role of the owner of a brothel, the Metropolitan's Helen Traubel found herself in rather strange surroundings.

In 1957, playwright Joseph Fields read the novel, *The Flower Drum Song*, by Chin Y. Lee, and felt that it was an almost-perfect property for the stage. After securing the rights, he and his friend Oscar Hammerstein discussed the possibility of turning it into a musical. Hammerstein believed that while it did not have a strong plot, it was "strong on character and background, like a Chinese *Life with Father*. I just fell in love with it." With Rodgers in agreement, Hammerstein and Fields then became collaborators on the libretto.

PIPE DREAM *(1955). Helen Traubel leads the group in "The Bums' Opera." Seated at the left are Mike Kellin and George Wallace. (Costumes by Alvin Colt; setting by Jo Mielziner.)*

FLOWER DRUM SONG (1958). *Oscar Hammerstein II leans across the footlights to polish a lyric.*

Flower Drum Song opened on December 1, 1958. It told a placid, some-what predictable tale of the conflicts between Old World and New World Chinese living in San Francisco's Chinatown. Miyoshi Umeki, who was born in Japan, played the part of a tradition-bound Chinese girl, while Pat Suzuki, an American of Japanese descent, played a Chinese-American strip-tease dancer. Of the songs, the masterfully constructed "I Enjoy Being a Girl" has probably become the most popular, but the gliding, pseudo-Oriental "You Are Beautiful" and the searching lament, "Love, Look Away," are equally fine examples of the art of Rodgers and Hammerstein. *Flower Drum Song* was a box-office success in spite of wide differences among the critics— from Robert Coleman's "everything about it is just right," to Brooks Atkinson's "a pleasant interlude," to Kenneth Tynan's "a world of woozy song."

Even before the opening of *Flower Drum Song*, Rodgers and Hammer-stein had become associated with one of those rare productions that seems, from the outset, to be incapable of failure. Theatre director Vincent J. Done-hue, after being approached by Paramount Pictures to direct a movie based on a German film, *The Trapp Family Singers*, became convinced that the story should be done only as a Broadway musical. Once the film company allowed

257

FLOWER DRUM SONG (1958). *Pat Suzuki and the chorus of the Celestial Bar singing of the wonders of Grant Avenue, the main street of San Francisco's Chinatown. (Costumes by Irene Sharaff; setting by Oliver Smith.)*

its option to lapse, Donehue contacted Mary Martin; as soon as she saw the German film, she too became excited about the project.

Securing the rights, however, turned out to be rather difficult. Miss Martin's husband, Richard Halliday, spent eight fruitless months trying to locate Baroness Von Trapp, who was somewhere in the South Pacific doing missionary work. Eventually, he found her in an Austrian hospital, where she was being treated for malaria. Co-producer Leland Hayward made six trips to Munich before he came to terms with the German film company that had made the original movie. Then the producer had to search for the widely scattered Trapp children to secure their permission to be portrayed on the stage.

After all of this preliminary work was over, there was still the important task of finding the writers best suited to tell the story of the courageous Trapp family. The first to be signed were librettists Howard Lindsay and Russel Crouse. For the score, the producers wanted to use the authentic folk and religious songs that the family actually sang in its concerts, plus some additional songs. When Hayward suggested to Rodgers and Hammerstein that they supply the new material, the partners were against the idea. If you are going to use authentic Trapp family music, that's fine, Rodgers told the producer; the important thing is that old songs should never be mixed with new. It did not take Hayward long to come to a decision: if Rodgers and Hammerstein would supply an entirely new score, he would be glad to postpone production until they had completed *Flower Drum Song*.

The effect of the new alliance was not hard to foresee. The combination of Mary Martin and Rodgers and Hammerstein (who also became co-producers) was enough to guarantee an advance ticket sale for *The Sound of Music* of $3,325,000, the highest ever achieved for a Broadway production.

Opening on November 16, 1959, the play that audiences waited for so eagerly was cheerful, wholesome entertainment, possibly more in the style of a Sigmund Romberg operetta than in the integrated style that Rodgers and Hammerstein themselves had done so much to develop. Wisely, the team decided against a formal overture. Instead, nuns at an abbey sang a moving *a capella* "Preludium," which helped set the tone and spirit of the play. The title song told appealingly of the beauties of music and nature, while a bubbly quartet, "Maria," was described by Walter Kerr as having "the lilt and sprightliness proper to lucky princesses living in an enchanted castle." Of the

THE SOUND OF MUSIC *(1959). To allay the Van Trapp children's fears during a storm. Maria (Mary Martin) teaches them a song about "The Lonely Goatherd." (Costumes by Lucinda Ballard; setting by Oliver Smith.)*

PHOTO BY FRIEDMAN-ABELES

numbers Miss Martin sang with the seven Trapp children, the most popular has become "Do-Re-Mi," a brisk march which served to teach the children the rudiments of music by having the lyric develop from the notes on the scale. "My Favorite Things," possibly the loveliest song in the play, deftly employed an abruptly contrasting release to emphasize the wistfulness of the chief melodic line. The moving theme of the story, "Climb Ev'ry Mountain," had something of the simple faith expressed in "You'll Never Walk Alone" from *Carousel*.

Again, as in most recent Rodgers and Hammerstein works, the critics were divided. Although he lamented the book, Brooks Atkinson found that "the sound of music is always moving. Occasionally, it is also glorious." Richard Watts, Jr., thought the entire production "wonderfully endearing," and John McClain of the *Journal-American* called it "the most mature product of the Rodgers-Hammerstein team." However, Walter Kerr felt that it "will be most admired by people who have always found Sir James M. Barrie pretty rough stuff," and Henry Hewes of the *Saturday Review* questioned whether everything about the play "was decided by a committee of craftsmen all too willing to please each other and to avoid risk." Nevertheless, audiences have been far less divided, and *The Sound of Music* may well become one of Broadway's longest running attractions.

THE SOUND OF MUSIC *(1959).*
Maria and Capt. Von Trapp
first begin to realize that they
are in love as they dance to
the "Laendler" during a party
at the captain's home. (Cos-
tumes by Lucinda Ballard.)

From the beginning of their association, Rodgers and Hammerstein have made their influence felt both in the audience and behind the footlights. Once, when Cole Porter was asked to name the most profound changes in musical comedy in forty years, he replied simply, "Rodgers and Hammerstein." Chiefly because of them, writers for the musical stage who might have spent the rest of their lives in Hollywood suddenly began to think again of the challenge and the opportunities inherent in the Broadway musical theatre. By their pioneering, Rodgers and Hammerstein have conditioned the public to accept the kind of adventurous musicals that have been presented since *Oklahoma!* For in spite of the gradual changes that were taking place before that memorable production, it was *Oklahoma!* that demonstrated to composers, librettists, and lyricists the indisputable truth that if they do create something of merit, no matter how unconventional, there will be a large and responsive audience waiting for it.

As did the team of Rodgers and Hart, Rodgers and Hammerstein have always avoided formula musicals. "We believe that writers who repeat themselves will eventually bore themselves," they once said. "And this condition is a short and automatic step toward boring the public." In spite of the variety of their plays, however, there is always something of the basic philosophy of the two men present in their works. Ironically, although they have helped bring about a more realistic musical theatre through their contributions both before and after their partnership, Rodgers and Hammerstein are frequently accused of radiating too much sweetness and light. Rodgers is quick to answer. "What's wrong with sweetness and light? It's been around quite a while. Even a cliché has a right to be true. I'm not interested in cracking out at anything and I'm certainly not interested in kicking sentiment around. I love satire but I just couldn't write it." Hammerstein readily admits that he is a sentimentalist. "There's nothing wrong with sentiment because the things we're sentimental about are the fundamental things in life, the birth of a child, the death of a child, or anybody falling in love. I couldn't be anything but sentimental about these basic things. To be anything but sentimental about them is being a poseur."

Apart from their influence and philosophy, the special distinction of Rodgers and Hammerstein has always been their creative integrity. Once they have decided on their subject and the manner in which it will be developed, they have proceeded in a direction that conforms solely to their own ideas. "I think it is disaster to try to do what the public wants, if you don't feel that way yourself," Rodgers says. "It's only when you and the public have the same mind that you are successful." To which Hammerstein adds "You can't deliberately say, "I will please the public, although I don't like what I'm doing.' There must be a faith behind every work to make it succeed."

NOTE: *On August 23, 1960, as this book was about to go to press, Oscar Hammerstein died of cancer. His age was 65.*

Leonard Bernstein.

CHAPTER SEVENTEEN

Leonard Bernstein

WITH THE GROWING emphasis on well-constructed librettos, young writers of the Forties and Fifties could no longer rely on the gradually disappearing revue as a means of getting their first songs on Broadway. Diverse media of entertainment, however, were still available to provide training for many aspiring composers and lyricists. The profusion of movie musicals in the Thirties and Forties gave Jule Styne and Frank Loesser the opportunity to write their first hits. Betty Comden and Adolph Green began their careers performing their own material in night clubs. Radio script-writing was Alan Jay Lerner's first professional job. For many years, Meredith Willson was known coast to coast as a radio conductor and composer. The most ancient training locale of all, Tin Pan Alley, was responsible for the emergence of Richard Adler and Jerry Ross, and Bob Merrill.

Although it is no longer a rarity for the concert hall to produce composers for the musical stage, not since Victor Herbert has there been anyone quite as successful in both areas as Leonard Bernstein. As a conductor, pianist, lecturer, and composer for the concert hall, he is an acknowledged leader in the world of classical music; as the composer of *On The Town, Wonderful Town, Candide,* and *West Side Story,* he is also an acknowledged leader in the world of musical comedy.

Born in Lawrence, Massachusetts, on August 25, 1918, Leonard Bernstein first became interested in music at a relatively advanced age. He was ten when an aunt presented his parents with a discarded upright piano; the gift so fascinated the youth that his father eventually yielded to his entreaties and permitted him to take lessons. At Harvard, where he majored in music, Bernstein became acquainted with Dimitri Mitropoulos, who was so impressed by the young man's talents that he urged him to become a conductor. After graduating from Harvard, Bernstein studied under Fritz Reiner at the Curtis Institute of Music in Philadelphia. In the summer of 1940, Serge Koussevitzky hired him as an assistant at the Tanglewood Summer Music Festival. The famed conductor soon developed a fatherly affection for Bernstein, who returned to Tanglewood for the next two summers.

Artur Rodzinski, then the musical director of the New York Philharmonic, thought the twenty-five-year-old conductor showed so much promise that he made him his assistant. One evening in the fall of 1943, Bruno Walter, the scheduled guest conductor of the Philharmonic, was suddenly taken ill. With Rodzinski out of town, and with no time for a rehearsal, Bernstein was suddenly called on to take over as conductor of the concert. His success prompted a front page story in the New York *Times* and an editorial in the *Daily News*. Hailed as a *Wunderkind,* Bernstein quickly found himself sought after for a wide variety of musical commissions.

The first one he accepted was to compose the music for a ballet, *Fancy Free,* choreographed by a young man named Jerome Robbins. The work, which depicted the escapades of three brash sailors on a twenty-four-hour spree in New York, became such a popular attraction of the Ballet Theatre that its creators decided to enlarge it into a Broadway musical. At Bernstein's suggestion, producers Oliver Smith and Paul Feigay signed Betty Comden and Adolph Green to write the libretto and lyrics.

Bernstein and Green had known each other since 1937 when Bernstein had been the music counsellor at a summer camp where Green had been hired to play the pirate king in a production of *The Pirates of Penzance.* Two years later, they shared an apartment in Greenwich Village. At the time, Green wrote for a nightclub act, The Revuers, which consisted of himself, Betty Comden, and Judy Holliday. Bernstein spent almost every evening with the group, which was then performing at the Village Vanguard.

Because of the inexperience of all those connected with *On the Town,* they chose as over-all director one of the most experienced men in the theatre, George Abbott. The show, which opened in December, 1944, was bright, swift-paced, and engagingly youthful. Its skillful blending of music, lyrics, book, and dances was the result of the unusually close rapport among the creators. The score was not only melodically and rhythmically appealing, but it had a technical mastery and unity of design that was uncommon. For

ON THE TOWN (1944). *The collaborators at work. Leonard Bernstein (composer), Jerome Robbins (choreographer), Betty Comden, and Adolph Green (co-librettists and co-lyricists).*

Three sailors enjoying the night life of New York. Adolph Green, Cris Alexander, and John Battles are the sailors; Allyn Ann McLerie, Betty Comden, and Nancy Walker are the girls. (Costumes by Alvin Colt; setting by Oliver Smith.)

PHOTO BY VANDAMM

example, the melody of "New York, New York," which opens the show and sets its invigorating pace, was later used by Bernstein in a much slower tempo to establish the proper mood for the contrasting expression, "Lonely Town." Comden and Green also had parts in the show (to bellow out their song of suppressed desires, "I Get Carried Away"), and Nancy Walker, as a female taxi driver, was especially funny as she boasted of her culinary and amatory prowess in "I Can Cook, Too."

Bernstein's major occupation as a symphony conductor (with the short-lived New York City Symphony and, since 1956, with the New York Philharmonic) has severely limited his theatrical output since *On the Town*. His second musical, *Wonderful Town*, was written eight years later and came about when he was called in to replace another composer. Because of differences with Joseph Fields and Jerome Chodorov (who had adapted the story from their own play, *My Sister Eileen*), the original lyricist and composer had quit five weeks before rehearsals were to start. This posed a problem; if rehearsals did not begin by December 15, 1953, producer Robert Fryer would lose his star, Rosalind Russell. In desperation, director George Abbott called in Betty Comden and Adolph Green. They agreed to undertake the assignment on the condition that Leonard Bernstein would compose the music.

According to Green, neither he nor Miss Comden was optimistic about the show. *My Sister Eileen* had seemed to him "so awfully Thirties-bound, sort of a post-Depression play, full of overexploited plot lines and passé references." Bernstein, however, was bursting with enthusiasm. "The Thirties! My God, those were the years! The excitement that was around! The political awareness! F.D.R.! Fiorello! Real personalities! And the wonderful fashions! Glorious! And the songs! What beat!" The composer's attitude proved so contagious that the trio seldom left his studio during the five weeks it took to finish the score.

All the numbers in *Wonderful Town* caught the pace and spirit of New York of the mid-Thirties, with such tunes as "Swing!" and "Conga!" written in the specific style of the then-current rhythmic phenomena. "Conversation Piece," in which five people at a party make self-conscious, embarrassed attempts at conversation, has always been one of the composer's favorites. "That's the kind of thing I like to do in the theatre. The background is pure theatre music, operating exclusively in theatre terms, not with an eye on Tin Pan Alley, and not to create a memorable tune, but something which is an integral part of the story."

As in *On the Town*, Bernstein used many devices to give the score unity. For example, themes from "What a Waste" were adroitly repeated at the beginning of "Pass that Football" and "A Quiet Girl," while the melody of "A Little Bit in Love" was used in the introductions to "Conversation Piece" and "It's Love."

WONDERFUL TOWN (1953). *Rosalind Russell, in the arms of a Brazilian naval officer, gives some pointers on the American dance called the conga. Wrote Walter Kerr: "Instead of attacking a song, she inhabits it, moving around in it with such confidence, grace, and honest exuberance as to make it entirely her own."*

PHOTO BY BOB GOLBY

The most important single element that assured the box-office success of *Wonderful Town* was the performance of Rosalind Russell. After eighteen years in Hollywood, the forty-five-year-old actress romped through her part with such magnetic verve that audiences happily overlooked her limitations as a singer and dancer.

Being a thorough musician, Bernstein has not been limited by either subject matter or locale. For the unsuccessful *Candide* in 1956 he was able to capture the flavor of the Voltaire classic in a score that abounded in melodic grace and satiric invention. Such rhythms as the tango, mazurka, waltz, gavotte, and schottische were employed with striking effect, as were parodies of the styles of various classical composers. In particular, "Glitter and Be Gay" provided a delightful operatic coloratura aria in which the heroine, who has temporarily become a *demimondaine,* trills gaily of the materialistic compensations of her sad life.

For many years, Bernstein and Jerome Robbins had discussed the idea of doing a special kind of musical. Was it possible, they wondered, to tell a tragic story with a theme of some depth in terms of musical comedy without becoming operatic? A specific idea occurred to Robbins early in 1949: an up-to-date version of *Romeo and Juliet,* with the lovers played by a Jewish girl and an Italian Catholic boy living on the lower East Side of Manhattan. Playwright Arthur Laurents, a friend of Robbins, was called in to write the libretto of *East Side Story,* as it was then called, but the project soon had to be abandoned because of conflicting schedules.

About six years later, the writers decided to try again. By this time, it was apparent that the original concept was dated; the clashes between native-born teenagers and newly arrived Puerto Ricans offered them a far more timely and dramatic conflict. Now, in partnership with a young television writer named Stephen Sondheim as lyricist, they moved the play's locale across town and retitled it *West Side Story*. Although the work had to be interrupted because of Bernstein's commitment to compose the score for *Candide*, the four men were reunited early in 1957.

To Bernstein, creating *West Side Story* was like walking on a tightrope. The important thing was to keep it from ever getting too poetic or too realistic. In the "Rumble," for instance, the composer felt that if it "had been too balletic, we would have fallen off on one side—all you'd have is just another ballet. And if it had been too realistic, we would have fallen off on the other side— there would have been no poetry to it, no art."

The great triumph of *West Side Story*, which eventually was presented on Broadway in September, 1957, is that it is impressionistic but at the same time it gives the illusion of reality. The costumes, the settings, the dialogue, the music, and the dances were all combined with a theatrical expressiveness that transcended mere naturalism to establish a truly lyrical mood. Here were young city toughs moving with agility through the dance patterns, spewing out their pent-up hatreds and revealing secret longings through music that could be, by turns, both nervously agitated and almost ethereal. Moreover, the story was told without resorting to wisecracks or a happy ending. It made few compromises, yet *West Side Story* contained sufficient entertainment value to last more than two years on Broadway, and to return in 1960 after a successful cross-country tour.

PHOTO BY FRED FEHL

WEST SIDE STORY *(1957). Larry Kert and Carol Lawrence, as the Romeo and Juliet lovers, use a fire escape as a balcony. (Costumes by Irene Sharaff; setting by Oliver Smith.)*

WEST SIDE STORY (1957). *The Jets and their girls dance in the local drugstore just before their rumble with the rival gang known as the Sharks. Larry Kert, seated alone at a table, is worried about the outcome. (Costumes by Irene Sharaff; setting by Oliver Smith.)*

With time for only four musicals within thirteen years, Bernstein has nevertheless left a strong mark on the theatrical scene, particularly as something of a *minnesinger* of Manhattan. The brash spirit of *On the Town*, the nostalgia of *Wonderful Town*, and the jagged impact of *West Side Story* reveal a city of many faces and a composer of many facets. Perhaps only one not native to the city could capture it so well in music. "This town still gets me," Bernstein exclaims. "No wonder I keep composing about it. It's so dramatic and alive. New York! The amazing, confusing beauty of the place!"

Paradoxically, this concern with one geographical locale has not endowed Bernstein's creations with any discernible personal style. Partly due to his knowledge of, and his involvement in, all kinds of music, Bernstein has shown a certain eclecticism in his work for the theatre that has made it less of an individual expression than highly technical, remarkably effective music with each score sounding almost as if it were the work of different men.

Leonard Bernstein has become the most public personality of today's composers. On television, his witty, incisive commentaries have shown him to be a zealous crusader for a wider appreciation of almost every type of music, including the music of the theatre. "Out of our natural musical theatre," he once said, "which is wholly an outgrowth of our culture, is emerging our opera, intelligible to all." The firmness of this belief would suggest that Bernstein is the successor to Kurt Weill, and, indeed, *West Side Story* is a direct extension of the *Zeitoper* that Weill had been instrumental in creating in Germany. Unfortunately, Bernstein has been unable to devote all his prodigious energies to the musical theatre. In spite of his multiple activities, however, he has always brought to his work for the Broadway stage the same kind of affection, originality, and painstaking care that has distinguished his career in every one of the numerous musical pursuits to which he is devoted.

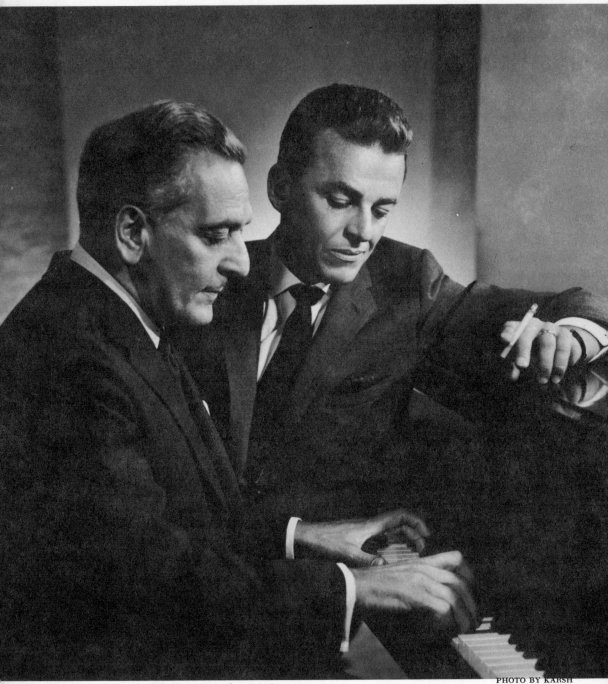

Frederick Loewe and Alan Jay Lerner.

CHAPTER EIGHTEEN

Alan Jay Lerner
and Frederick Loewe

THE SPECIAL CHEMISTRY that takes place between two individuals to enable them to produce a successful blending of words and music has never been distilled in any laboratory's test tube. Some famous song-writing teams—Rodgers and Hammerstein, for example, or Schwartz and Dietz—have had markedly similar backgrounds and outlook; others—Rodgers and Hart, the Gershwin brothers—may have had similar, and even identical, backgrounds, but they have been made up of men with almost completely different personalities and tastes.

In background, in personality, and in temperament, Alan Jay Lerner and Frederick Loewe would seem to be two of the most dissimilar men in the theatre. Loewe, Lerner's senior by fourteen years, was born in Vienna, on June 10, 1904. He was the son of Edmund Loewe, a well-known tenor who sang in many of the popular Viennese operettas. By the time he was seven, young Fritz could pick out tunes on the piano. He studied in Berlin under Ferruccio Busoni (Kurt Weill's teacher), Eugène d'Albert, and Emil Nikolaus von Reznicek. At thirteen, he was the youngest piano soloist ever to appear with the Berlin Symphony. Two years later, he wrote a popular song, "Katrina," which became one of the biggest song hits throughout Europe.

In 1924, Frederick Loewe confidently journeyed to New York to continue his career. His difficulties with the English language and his seeming inability to write in an "American" style made it extremely hard for him to adjust to the new country. Instead of continuing his career as a composer, he was soon forced to take a job as a pianist at a Greenwich Village nightclub, and, for a time, he was even a bus boy in a cafeteria.

With his career in music apparently over, Loewe, a solidly built, athletic man, next became a riding instructor at a New Hampshire resort and, later, a prize fighter at a Brooklyn athletic club. His pugilistic career, however, was painfully terminated when his teeth were knocked out in his ninth bout. After a few years in the West (where he was a cow puncher, gold prospector, and horseback mail deliverer), Loewe took a job as a pianist on board ships transporting thirsty citizens from Miami to Havana during Prohibition. When repeal ended this ferrying service in the early Thirties, he became a pianist at a *Brauhaus* in Yorkville, New York City's German section.

During this period, he again began to compose. As one acquaintance remembers, "Even though Fritz wasn't doing well in those days, I knew he had a tremendous inner fire just burning to create great songs." To help his career, Loewe joined the Lambs, the famous theatrical club. There he became friendly with Dennis King, who was so fond of one of Loewe's songs, "Love Tiptoed through My Heart," that he sang it in the play *Petticoat Fever*.

The following year, 1935, Loewe formed a partnership with Earle Crooker, a radio and Hollywood script-writer, who had contributed lyrics to *The Little Show*. Their first song, "A Waltz Was Born in Vienna," was danced by Gomez and Winona in the unsuccessful *Illustrators' Show*. It was subsequently added to the score for *Salute to Spring*, an original musical Loewe and Crooker wrote for the St. Louis Opera Association.

Salute to Spring was one of the most popular attractions offered in St. Louis in the summer of 1937. Producer Dwight Deere Wiman was so delighted with their work that he signed Loewe and Crooker to create the songs for *Great Lady*, a costly operetta which he produced on Broadway the following year. Neither music nor lyrics was distinguished, nor was there much merit in the story of how Eliza Bowan, a notorious adventuress of the early nineteenth century, broke into New York society by marrying the wealthy Stephen Jumel. Musical comedy sentimentalists may have been delighted to see Norma Terris, Irene Bordoni, and Helen Ford in the same play, but the future stars of the ballet, opera, and musical theatre were in the singing and dancing groups. The dancers, led by André Eglevsky, included Alicia Alonso, Nora Kaye, Paul Godkin, and Jerome Robbins; Dorothy Kirsten and Walter Cassel were among the singers.

It had taken Loewe almost fourteen years to get the opportunity to compose his first Broadway score. Unfortunately, *Great Lady* closed after twenty performances, and he was once again forced to return to his job as a piano player in a restaurant. Then, one day in 1942, he introduced himself to a young writer named Alan Jay Lerner.

Unlike Loewe, Lerner had never had to spend years toiling at strange occupations in an alien country. He was born in New York City, on August 31, 1918, the son of the founder of a chain of women's specialty shops, the Lerner Shops. Instead of smothering his ability, the advantages of wealth and education only instilled in him a strong determination to succeed unaided by any parental assistance. Lerner was only eight when he first made up his mind to become a writer for the theatre. His father neither opposed nor encouraged this ambition; his only advice to his son was that he would have to work hard at his profession if he really wanted to succeed. Young Lerner learned to play the piano at an early age, and later took courses at the Juilliard School of Music. At Harvard, he wrote music and lyrics for two Hasty Pudding shows. Two songs were even considered worthy enough to be commercially published: "Chance to Dream" from the 1938 production, *So Proudly We Hail,* and "From Me to You" from the 1939 show, *Fair Enough.* After graduating Lerner became a radio script-writer, turning out about five hundred scripts in two years.

Desperation brought Loewe to Lerner in 1942. Henry Duffy, a producer, wanted to present a series of original musical comedies at a theatre he owned in Detroit. The previous year he had offered a musical adaptation of Barry Connors' play, *The Patsy,* in San Francisco, but he wanted an entirely different treatment of the same story for the Detroit production. Two weeks before rehearsals were to begin, Duffy met with Loewe at the Lambs Club to discuss the possibility of using the bulk of the Loewe-Crooker score for *Salute to Spring.* What Loewe needed to ensure the commission, however, was a librettist who could also update some of the earlier lyrics. Because he admired the sketches and lyrics Lerner had contributed to *The Lambs Gambol,* a revue put on by Lambs Club members, Loewe immediately thought of him for the new project. Seeing Lerner at the club that day playing cards, the composer introduced himself with the businesslike: "You are Alan Jay Lerner? You write good lyrics. I am Frederick Loewe. I have something to say to you."

Two days later, they were on a train bound for Detroit, the show was written within the prescribed two weeks, and in October, 1942, Detroit audiences saw the initial collaboration of Alan Jay Lerner and Frederick Loewe—*Life of the Party,* starring Dorothy Stone and Charles Collins. There was nothing memorable about the musical, but Lerner's work convinced Loewe that they might succeed as a team. For their next musical, *What's Up*—and for every one of their collaborations since then—Alan Jay Lerner has written the book and lyrics and Frederick Loewe has composed the music.

273

What's Up opened in November, 1943. Even with Jimmy Savo in the cast and George Balanchine as director, it was not an auspicious debut. Their next work, however, *The Day before Spring,* turned out to be a highly literate and imaginative fantasy which just missed being a hit. Wolcott Gibbs called it "my kind of show," adding that "the songs that go with it are fresh and bright and seem to spring spontaneously from the action rather than from spasmodic impulses on the part of the singers."

The Day before Spring was more of an artistic than a commercial success. *Brigadoon* was both. Lerner, long fond of the works of Sir James M. Barrie, had been eager to write a musical with a Scottish setting. "One day, while working on *The Day before Spring,* Fritz mentioned something about faith moving mountains. This started me thinking. For a while, I had a play about faith moving a mountain. From there we went to all sorts of miracles occurring through faith, and, eventually, faith moved a town."

In less skilled hands, the legend of the sleeping Scottish town that awakens once in every one hundred years could easily have been too precious or maudlin, but so ably were the theatrical ingredients blended—story, music, lyrics, dancing, settings, costumes—that the result became what Brooks Atkinson unequivocably labeled a "vibrant work of art." Never before had Agnes de Mille's talents been better realized than in the way she made each dance sequence an integral part of the story, most notably in the Sword Dance, the Chase, and the Funeral Dance. Robert Lewis directed *Brigadoon* with rare sensitivity, and Oliver Smith's evocative settings enhanced the total effect.

The score that Frederick Loewe and Alan Jay Lerner created was especially distinguished for its appropriateness to locale, story, and characters. Lerner's lyrics captured much of the highland flavor, and his ability to use simple, genuine imagery was marked in the songs "Brigadoon," "Come to Me,

WHAT'S UP *(1943). Johnny Morgan as an American sergeant and Jimmy Savo as an East Indian potentate.*

BRIGADOON (1947). *James Mitchell about to begin the Sword Dance. (Costumes by David Ffolkes; setting by Oliver Smith.)*

Bend to Me," and "The Heather on the Hill." Loewe's music was equally suffused with the atmosphere of the play, and, when required, attained a certain eloquence. The wisdom of the authors' approach was notably demonstrated in the way the one sophisticated song, "Almost Like Being in Love," was first introduced by the rich American tourist (played by David Brooks) before being reprised by the simple highland maid (Marion Bell).

Soon after writing *Love Life* with Kurt Weill in 1948, Lerner began thinking of an idea for a musical he could write with Loewe. He was determined that it would have a story with a positive point of view, "a musical that would embrace all the robustness and vitality and cockeyed courage that is so much a part of our American heritage." To both Lerner and Loewe, the saga of the California gold rush filled that specification.

Paint Your Wagon opened in New York in November, 1951. With the exception of director Daniel Mann, almost all of the principal members of the production staff had been associated with *Brigadoon*—producer Cheryl Crawford, choreographer Agnes de Mille, designer Oliver Smith, musical director Franz Allers, and musical arranger Ted Royal. James Barton, who had not appeared in a Broadway musical in over twenty years, played the part of a grizzled old prospector, and Olga San Juan appeared as his daughter. Throughout the score, the songs projected a genuine flavor of Americana; many of them, in fact, seemed to be not Broadway show tunes but authentic folk ballads handed down from the miners themselves. The booming theme song, "Wand'rin' Star," sung at the beginning and end of the play, served as an appropriate frame for such numbers as the stirring "I'm on My Way"; the rushing legend "They Call the Wind Maria"; the misty-eyed "I Still See

PAINT YOUR WAGON *(1951). Agnes de Mille's lively dance to "Hand Me Down That Can o' Beans." (Costumes by Motley; setting by Oliver Smith.)*

Elisa," touchingly sung by Barton; the rousing dances "Whoop-Ti-Ay" and "Hand Me Down That Can o' Beans"; and the almost chilling expression of loneliness, "Another Autumn."

In their research for *Paint Your Wagon,* Lerner and Loewe became so steeped in the subject that they incorporated actual incidents and miners' dialogue as part of the play. Possibly, as Lerner later admitted, they may have done too much research. According to Walter Kerr, "Writing an *integrated* musical comedy—where people are believable and the songs are logically introduced—is no excuse for not being funny from time to time. But the librettist of *Paint Your Wagon* seems to be more interested in the authenticity of his background than in the joy of his audience."

Including *Paint Your Wagon,* Lerner's books for his first five musicals had all been based on original stories. He became convinced that the main reason why some of his musicals were not more successful was that they had faulty librettos. Quite logically, he decided that henceforth he would adapt his stories from plays or novels that had already won favor with both critics and the public. His opportunity came in 1952, when Gabriel Pascal, the celebrated Hungarian movie producer, suggested to him that he transform Bernard Shaw's *Pygmalion* into a musical play.

Pascal, the only man ever to win Shaw's permission to film his plays, had made a motion picture of *Pygmalion* in the mid-Thirties. Sometime after that he became interested in producing a musical version of the work. Shaw, who had voiced public indignation over Oscar Straus's *The Chocolate Soldier* (based on his *Arms and the Man*), had always been unalterably opposed to the idea of a musical *Pygmalion*. In 1948, when a friend once interceded in behalf of two other writers, the playwright shot back a typically Shavian response: "I absolutely forbid such outrage. If *Pygmalion* is not good enough for your friends with its own verbal music, their talent must be altogether extraordinary. Let them try Mozart's *Cosi fan tutti*, or at least Offenbach's *Grand Duchess*."

After Shaw's death in 1950, Pascal felt free to proceed with his plan. In rapid succession, he importuned such distinguished writers of the musical stage as Noël Coward, Cole Porter, E. Y. Harburg and Fred Saidy, Schwartz and Dietz, and Rodgers and Hammerstein. Each one, however, turned him down.* When Lerner and Loewe finally agreed to undertake the project, the producer did not even have the rights to present the play as a musical. So persuasive were his arguments, however, that the Shaw estate granted him a two-year option.

Lerner and Loewe at first could not agree on the proper approach to the Shaw work. After struggling with it for about three months, they had to admit to Pascal that they saw no way in which the adaption could be accomplished. For the next two years, Lerner and Loewe went their separate ways, each becoming involved in projects that were never realized. Lerner tried to transform *Li'l Abner*† into a musical, first with Burton Lane and later with Arthur Schwartz. Loewe joined with Joseph Fields, Jerome Chodorov, and Leo Robin in attempting a musical version of Paul Vincent Carroll's *Saints and Sinners*.

While Lerner and Loewe were occupied with other pursuits, Pascal continued his vain hunt for other writers who might be induced to make a musical of *Pygmalion*. It had become such an obsession with him that he obtained a two-year extension after his option had expired. The tenacious producer, however, never lived to see his dream fulfilled. He died in New York in the summer of 1954, soon after beginning another search.

Ironically, it was about the time of Pascal's death that Lerner and Loewe resumed their partnership to make one last attempt at setting *Pygmalion* to music. The problem, according to Lerner, "was how to enlarge it into a big musical without hurting its content. It was a big surprise—we hardly had to enlarge the plot at all. We just added what Shaw had happening offstage." Once they found the way to do it, the authors went ahead with their adapta-

* Harburg refused to do the adaptation because he felt *Pygmalion* was a perfect work of art and should not be touched. Hammerstein's reason was based on Shaw's insistence that it was not a love story, and he did not want to oppose the author's wishes.
† The rights to *Li'l Abner* were presently acquired by Norman Panama, Melvin Frank, and Michael Kidd. With a score by Johnny Mercer and Gene de Paul, the musical opened in New York in the fall of 1956. It had a run of almost 700 performances.

MY FAIR LADY (1956). *The first day of rehearsals on the roof of the New Amsterdam Theatre. Julie Andrews, Rex Harrison, Alan Jay Lerner, and Frederick Loewe. Moss Hart can be seen just behind Lerner and Loewe.*

tion, even though they no longer had Pascal or the rights. They took the finished script to producer Herman Levin. After some delays, he was able to secure the rights from the Pascal estate.

From the very beginning, Rex Harrison was the choice of Lerner and Loewe to play Professor Higgins. Following Shaw's specifications that Eliza Doolittle should be played by an actress between eighteen and twenty, the authors diligently auditioned every girl in her late teens they could find. While so occupied, they received word that Mary Martin was interested in the part. "Forgetting Shaw's directions," Levin recalls, "we paged Mary. She wasn't twenty, but she was box-office dynamite. Mary quickly dissipated any qualms we may have had about flouting Shaw's blueprint. Lerner and Loewe played five songs for her and she didn't like any of them." They next tested a young English actress, Julie Andrews, then making an impressive Broadway debut in Sandy Wilson's *The Boy Friend*. Although she fitted Shaw's concept perfectly, they still were not completely sure that she was right for the part. After auditioning about fifty English girls in London, however, the producer and the writers returned to New York and signed Miss Andrews to a two-year contract.

In October, 1955, a press release announced the forthcoming adaptation, then known as *My Lady Liza*. Rehearsals began early the following January. Moss Hart was the director, Hanya Holm the choreographer, Oliver Smith the set designer, Cecil Beaton the costume designer, and Franz Allers the musical director. The supporting cast was headed by Stanley Holloway

MY FAIR LADY (1956). *The first scene between Eliza Doolittle (Julie Andrews) and Professor Higgins (Rex Harrison), as they meet outside Covent Garden. (Costumes by Cecil Beaton.)*

Stanley Holloway (as Alfred P. Doolittle) explains his philosophy in "With a Little Bit of Luck" to cronies Gordon Dilworth and Rod McLennan.

Eliza (Julie Andrews) Professor Higgins (Rex Harrison), and Col. Pickering (Robert Coote) join in a spontaneous dance to the tune of "The Rain in Spain." This was, in Wolcott Gibbs's opinion, "just about the most brilliantly successful scene I remember seeing in a musical comedy."

279

MY FAIR LADY *(1956). The scene at the Ascot Races. Freddy Eynsford-Hill and Henry Higgins's mother are amused at Liza's difficulties with the English language. John Michael King, Julie Andrews, and Cathleen Nesbitt. (Costumes by Cecil Beaton.)*

PHOTO BY FRIEDMAN-ABELES

(Alfred P. Doolittle), Cathleen Nesbitt (Professor Higgins' mother), and Robert Coote (Col. Pickering). After opening in New Haven, two songs, "Say a Prayer" (later used in the film *Gigi*) and "Come to the Ball," and a ballet, "Decorating Eliza," were cut from the score.

Since its première on March 15, 1956, the legends about the difficulties of getting tickets to *My Fair Lady* and the reports of weekly box-office grosses have become part of the folklore of the theatre. In December, 1958, the show established the all-time record for gross receipts with $10 million, thus exceeding the record of $9 million established by *South Pacific* at a lower price scale.

"For years, Fritz and I floundered around, trying to find our natural way of writing," Lerner once confessed in an interview in the New York *Times*. "*My Fair Lady* revealed it to us. The property dictates it. The characters in the story. We are the means by which they express themselves, not vice versa. When we felt we really knew them, then we began to work on the score. We try to find some thought of a character that motivates him and, in turn, the story."

This approach is evident throughout. In the songs for Professor Higgins, there is the biting disdain for his inferiors in "Why Can't the English?"; his witty defense of his own way life in "I'm an Ordinary Man"; his petulent admiration for masculine traits in "A Hymn to Him"; and, in the simply stated "I've Grown Accustomed to Her Face," his admission that he has finally fallen in love with Eliza. Eliza's character is also revealed through song. First, as a poor flower-seller, she dreams only of a life of physical comforts in "Wouldn't It Be Loverly?" Later, after having gone through the rigors of the professor's speech classes, she expresses her secret defiance in "Just You Wait," and her thrill at having succeeding in speaking correctly in "I Could Have Danced All Night." The girl's impatience with all men bursts through in "Show Me," and, at the end, in a bolt of sarcastic fury, she tells Higgins her real opinion of him in "Without You."

The secondary characters are equally well served by the songs. For Alfred Doolittle, Eliza's philosophical, high-spirited father, Lerner and Loewe created two appropriate music-hall turns, "With a Little Bit of Luck" and "Get Me to the Church on Time." For the faithful Freddy Eynsford-Hill (played by Dennis King's son, John Michael King) they wrote the worshipful ballad "On the Street Where You Live."

The most musically and dramatically effective episode comes midway through the first act when Eliza is at last able to say "The rain in Spain stays mainly in the plain" without a Cockney accent. As Walter Kerr described the scene, "You listen astonished—because you believe in her so completely that you didn't really suppose she could make it. Suddenly, her delight becomes yours. And when Mr. Harrison, together with an equally astonished Robert Coote, bounces irresistibly to the center of the stage and begins to kick out a tango rhythm to the sound she has just made, there is no controlling the joy in the theatre."

The unprecedented success of *My Fair Lady*, which has given Lerner and Loewe a stature almost equal to that of Rodgers and Hammerstein, has produced a rather philosophical attitude in both men. "Neither Fritz nor I believe we're *that* good," says Lerner. "It's just that the time was ripe for something gay and theatrical, something that was not two lonely people finding each other in a dark alley. *My Fair Lady* filled the bill."

They had, in fact, purposely set out to make their musical as glamorous, as stylish, as visually stunning as they possibly could, something that would be in the grand manner of the romantic musicals of the past. (Even their story was a variation on the oldest plot of all, the Cinderella legend, including the ball.)

The musicals of Lerner and Loewe are, to a great extent, the successors to the Viennese school of Lehár and Strauss and Herbert—only welded more firmly together with all the theatrical arts developed through the years. Instead of pasteboard characters, theirs have depth and believability. Instead of illogical, frequently infantile stories, theirs deal coherently with a wide variety of subjects. Instead of bland, artificial lyrics mated to usually unmotivated melodies, their songs are created to serve a purpose in the story and spring naturally from the characters who sing them.

Modern though their plays are in inspiration and execution, the distinguishing trait of Lerner and Loewe has been in their preservation of the values and traditions of the past. It has been this fidelity to places and periods —a 200-year-old Scottish town that has vanished in the highland mist, the colorful gold fields of California in the 1850's, London society just before the First World War—that has endowed their works with the rare feeling of authenticity. The musical world of Alan Jay Lerner and Frederick Loewe is not concerned with the problems of today; but it is created for today's audiences. It is a world in which the past comes excitingly alive, while still remaining romantic, and gay, and eternally appealing.

Jule Styne.

CHAPTER NINETEEN

Jule Styne

THERE ARE MANY reasons for the reduction in the number of Broadway musicals since the 1920's and the corollary lessening in the output of major theatrical composers. Among the most apparent have been the increasingly longer runs of hit shows, the greater care given all the component parts of a production, the competition from other entertainment media, and, possibly the strongest deterrent of all, the mounting production costs.

As a consequence, some striking paradoxes emerge between the musical theatre of the Twenties and the Fifties, particularly as reflected in the career of Jule Styne. By working on twelve Broadway musicals over a period of about eleven and one-half years, Vincent Youmans was the least prolific among the leading composers of his day; by working on eight Broadway musicals over a period of eleven and one-half years, Styne has become the most prolific composer currently writing for the theatre. In fact, judging by the popularity of his shows, he is one of the most successful musical comedy composers of all time. When *Gypsy* closes, the total number of original Broadway performances of the eight musicals with scores by Styne will exceed that of the entire twenty-three musicals with scores by George Gershwin.

This, of course, does not necessarily mean that Styne has yet achieved the eminence of a Youmans or a Gershwin. But it is strange that with a record of such productivity and popularity, he should be one of the least acclaimed composers of the current theatre. The reason may be found in the changing styles of the musical stage. In general, only those composers who have been associated with truly noteworthy productions have won fame. Most of Styne's shows, successful though they may be, have frequently remained well within the boundaries of formula Broadway musical comedy. Moreover, almost every one of his successes has been dominated by the personality of one or two performers. *High Button Shoes* had the swaggering clowning of Phil Silvers and the charm of Nanette Fabray. *Gentlemen Prefer Blondes* became a vehicle for the talents of a wide-eyed comedienne named Carol Channing. *Two on the Aisle* starred Bert Lahr and Dolores Gray. *Peter Pan* relied on the appeal of Mary Martin. *Bells Are Ringing* owed its marathon run to the delightful performance of Judy Holliday.

Although *Gypsy* stars the redoubtable Ethel Merman, it may at last win Styne the recognition that has long been his due. Exhibiting far greater gifts for dramatic writing than he had shown before, the composer has created a musical score that is equally as important to the artistic merits of a production as the star. Complemented by a strong libretto by Arthur Laurents and pungent lyrics by Stephen Sondheim, the music of *Gypsy* has made it apparent that in artistic quality as well as in proficiency Jule Styne is one of the foremost composers for the modern musical theatre.

Styne was born in London, England, on December 31, 1905. He had his first taste of the theatre at the age of three when he ran up on the stage to sing a duet with Sir Harry Lauder. When he was eight, his parents moved to Chicago. There the youth quickly showed such musical talent that within a year he was guest piano soloist with the Chicago and Detroit Symphonies. At thirteen, he won a scholarship to the Chicago College of Music where he studied piano, harmony, composition, and theory.

In the Twenties, Styne became fascinated by the songs being written by the rising young composers of Tin Pan Alley and Broadway. Because he responded to popular music to a far greater extent than he did to the works of classical composers, he abandoned his concert career to become a pianist with a dance band. In 1931, he organized his own orchestra, for which he created the arrangements and also composed some songs. Writing music eventually became more important to Styne than leading an orchestra; in the mid-Thirties he disbanded his group to accept a contract with Twentieth Century-Fox as both composer and vocal coach.

During the Thirties and Forties, Styne wrote many successful movie songs. His first hit, "I Don't Want to Walk without You, Baby," had lyrics by Frank Loesser. Later, he formed a close working relationship with Sammy Cahn. Living in California was pleasant and profitable, but the lack of recognition or of artistic fulfillment made him long to compose the complete score of a Broadway musical. (As Styne has said: "In Hollywood, you're a song-writer; in New York, you're a composer.") Styne and Cahn received their first opportunity in 1944, when they were signed to supply the songs for the Broadway-bound *Glad to See You*. Unfortunately, the show folded in Boston.

High Button Shoes, three years later, not only opened on Broadway but had a run of about two and one-half years. With a book by Stephen Longstreet, it was a pleasant formula musical with a good deal of nostalgic charm. Its main appeal, however, was in the brash performance of Phil Silvers and in the hilarious Keystone Kops Ballet devised by Jerome Robbins. Of the songs, "Papa, Won't You Dance with Me?" and "I Still Get Jealous," engagingly performed by Nanette Fabray and Jack McCauley, are still recalled for their winning period flavor.

In spite of the success of *High Button Shoes*, Cahn preferred to return to Hollywood, and Styne found a new lyricist in Leo Robin. For *Gentlemen Prefer Blondes*, produced in 1949, they contributed a bright, atmospheric score that was perfectly suited to Anita Loos's hedonistic tale of the torrid Twenties. Yet it was Carol Channing, as the gold-digging Lorelei Lee, who captivated both the critics and the public, particularly by her rendition of "Diamonds Are a Girl's Best Friend" and "I'm Just a Little Girl from Little Rock." Miss Channing, whose only previous experience in Broadway musicals had been as Eve Arden's understudy in *Let's Face It!* and in Charles Gaynor's revue, *Lend an Ear*, was elevated to stardom during the run of the musical. It was chiefly due to her that *Gentlemen Prefer Blondes* had an even longer run than did *High Button Shoes*.

HIGH BUTTON SHOES *(1947). Phil Silvers, as Harrison Floy, and Nanette Fabray, as Sara Longstreet. Of Mr. Silvers, Brooks Atkinson wrote: "He is an uproarious comic. He has the speed, the drollery, and the shell-game style of a honky tonk buffoon." (Costumes by Miles White.)*

GENTLEMEN PREFER BLONDES *(1949). Lorelei Lee (Carol Channing) demonstrates her prowess on a diminutive Frenchman (Mort Marshall). Looking on is another Frenchman (Howard Morris). According to John Chapman, Miss Channing "got the most enthusiastic notices of any musicomedienne of this generation."*

In 1951, Jule Styne began his association with his most frequent collaborators, Betty Comden and Adolph Green. Their first production was *Two on the Aisle,* a revue for which Comdon and Green also supplied most of the sketches. The show gave Bert Lahr some wonderful opportunities for his special brand of humor, particularly in the scene written by Nat Hiken and William Friedberg in which he played a member of New York's Department of Sanitation who lived in constant fear that he would be demoted to the dump. Among the songs sung by Dolores Gray was "If You Hadn't but You Did," a rapid-fire apologia detailing the reasons why a distraught woman had just killed her husband.

Styne was both producer and composer of *Hazel Flagg,* a rather disappointing musical version of the celebrated movie, *Nothing Sacred.* Ben Hecht adapted the story from his own screenplay, and Bob Hilliard supplied the lyrics. The score was not on a level with most of Styne's work, but it did contain an affectionate tribute to New York City, "Every Street's a Boulevard in Old New York." Is was sung and soft-shoed by Jack Whiting as a dapper, Jimmy Walker-type mayor of the city.

When Jerome Robbins decided to stage a new production of Sir James M. Barrie's *Peter Pan* with Mary Martin as Peter and Cyril Ritchard as Captain Hook, he first planned to use only a few incidental songs by composer Mark ("Moose") Charlap and lyricist Carolyn Leigh. When the production began to develop into a full musical, however, he asked Jule Styne, Betty Comden, and Adolph Green to supply the additional songs. After its world première in San Francisco, *Peter Pan* opened in New York, in October, 1954. The reviews were generally favorable, and Miss Martin won special acclaim for her ability to sing and fly through the air at the same time. The play's short run (152 performances) was chiefly because it opened only about four

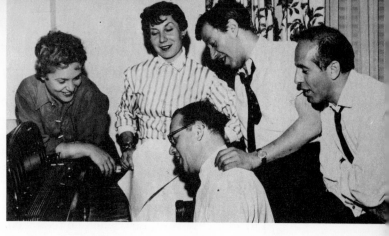

BELLS ARE RINGING *(1956)*. *Going through the songs are star Judy Holliday, co-author Betty Comden, composer Jule Styne, co-author Adolph Green, and director Jerome Robbins.*

PHOTO BY B. C. MITTLEMAN

and one-half years after the highly successful Jean Arthur–Boris Karloff version, which had had incidental songs by Leonard Bernstein.

Styne, Comden, Green, and Robbins were reunited in 1956 for *Bells Are Ringing*. Ever since Betty Comden and Adolph Green first became associated with Judy Holliday in the nightclub act, The Revuers, they had hoped someday to write a musical for her. When they thought of the idea of doing a story about a switchboard operator at a telephone-answering service, they immediately knew that this would be the proper vehicle. The libretto they devised owed much to the already proven *Wonderful Town* formula of depicting New York as just a gay, warmhearted small town, where people dance and sing in subways, and where a nosey telephone operator can find both adventure and the man of her dreams.* Miss Holliday, in her first musical, had an appealing winsomeness that helped audiences overlook some of the defects in the plot. Even her untrained singing voice proved remarkably suitable at interpreting the sentiments of such diverse Styne–Comden–Green contributions as the amusing "Is It a Crime?," which satirized bathetic pleas for happiness, the poignant "The Party's Over," and the rousing, "Mammy"-styled "I'm Going Back" ("To the Bonjour Tristesse Brassière Company").

Say, Darling, the fourth Jule Styne–Betty Comden–Adolph Green collaboration, was something of a theatrical oddity. After having co-authored *The Pajama Game*, a musical version of his novel *7½ Cents*, Richard Bissell wrote a novel based on his adventures in the world of musical comedy. It was called *Say, Darling*. This story also suggested itself as a production for the theatre, and Bissell, his wife, Marian, and Abe Burrows promptly set about writing the adaptation. Though it was a "comedy about a musical," not a musical comedy, it did have nine songs by Styne, Comden, and Green, none of which was distinguished.

After *Say, Darling* opened on Broadway in the spring of 1958, audiences took special pleasure in trying to identify some of the people actually connected with *The Pajama Game*. David Wayne, as the unsophisticated

* The leading character in *Bells Are Ringing* was not too dissimilar from the one in *The Five O'Clock Girl*, a Bert Kalmar–Harry Ruby hit of 1927. In that show, the heroine worked in a cleaner's shop and carried on a telephone flirtation with an unknown man every day at five.

author, was obviously Bissell himself. Robert Morse, as a young producer, was doubtlessly Harold Prince, and Jerome Cowan, as an experienced musical comedy director, could only be George Abbott. However, there was considerable speculation regarding the true identity of the glamorous star of the show (played by Vivian Blaine), and the egotistical song-writer (played by Johnny Desmond).

Producer David Merrick first became aware of *Gypsy*, the autobiography of Gypsy Rose Lee, when he read a chapter from it in *Harper's Magazine*. Merrick liked what he read so much that without even waiting to read the entire book, he quickly secured the theatrical rights. Ethel Merman, who did read the complete biography, became so determined to play the part of Gypsy's mother, Rose, that she threatened to shoot anyone else who got the part. She got it without firing a shot. At first, *Gypsy* was to have been another Styne–Comden–Green–Robbins enterprise, but other commitments forced the book-and-lyrics writing team to give up the project. Because Robbins had previously worked with librettist Arthur Laurents and lyricist

BELLS ARE RINGING *(1956). Sydney Chaplin and Judy Holliday perform an impromptu entertainment for passersby in New York's Central Park.*

PHOTO BY FRIEDMAN-ABELES

SAY, DARLING *(1958). Jerome Cowan, as the director, gives instructions to the cast of* The Girl from Indiana, *a new musical about to go into rehearsal. To the right are Johnny Desmond as the composer, David Wayne as the author, and Vivian Blaine and Mitchell Gregg as the stars. (Costumes by Alvin Colt; setting by Oliver Smith.)*

Stephen Sondheim on *West Side Story*, he was able to persuade them to undertake the new assignment.

The book of *Gypsy* may have been another variation of the familiar rags-to-riches Cinderella tale, but all those responsible resisted the temptation to make it just another backstage story of an ambitious mother. "This woman is a classic," says Laurents. "What we've got here is a mother who has to learn that if you try to live your children's lives, you'll end by destroying yourself." Creating music to match the uncompromising libretto was the most severe challenge Styne ever had as a composer. To achieve the proper musical setting Styne and Sondheim evolved a superbly congruous score that illuminated all the courage, misplaced ambition, and singleness of purpose of the central character. They did this chiefly through three numbers—"Some People," "Ev'rything's Coming Up Roses," and "Rose's Turn"—each individually compelling, yet each firmly linked to the other, with the haunting "I had a dream" passage as a leitmotif.

On a lighter though equally meaningful level, the composer and lyricist were able to capture all the tinselled gaudiness of small-time vaudeville and big-time burlesque. One original and effective touch was their use of a single melody, "May We Entertain You" (later called "Let Me Entertain You") to serve as the "onstage" music for all the scenes involving Gypsy Rose Lee and her sister, June Havoc. First, it is sung by two frightened little girls as they audition for a vaudeville show; later it becomes more aggressive as the girls acquire greater experience; finally, it turns into the slinky, blaring accompaniment to Gypsy's first strip tease. Other remarkably effective pieces dealing with different aspects of show business are "All I Need Is the Girl," the slightly pathetic attempt of a young dancer to do a suave Fred Astaire routine, and the vulgar, riotous show-stopper, "You Gotta Have a Gimmick," in which three strippers give a highly animated expatiation of their art.

Gypsy has given Styne his long-awaited recognition. It may still have Ethel Merman to attract the customers, but *Gypsy* could not be called a

GYPSY (1959). *Rose, the ambitious stage mother, coaches her children, Louise and June, in the first scene of the play. Karen Moore, Ethel Merman, and Jacqueline Mayro. (Costumes by Raoul Pène du Bois.)*

PHOTO BY FRIEDMAN-ABELES

GYPSY (1959). Louise, who has grown up to be Gypsy Rose Lee, makes up with her mother after a fight. Sandra Church and Ethel Merman in the final scene of the play. "Miss Merman," wrote Walter Kerr, "seems to have piled all her past successes together and to be standing on top of them."

PHOTO BY FRIEDMAN-ABELES

Merman vehicle. For just as the musical required more of Styne, it also required more of Miss Merman; both have met the demands of the story with gifts never before revealed because they were never before required.

"Without the rendition there is no song," states Jule Styne emphatically, and his career proves it. With Nanette Fabray, Carol Channing, Dolores Gray, Mary Martin, Judy Holliday, and Ethel Merman to sing them, his songs have benefited from some of the most individual and exciting renditions ever heard in the theatre. But what would the rendition be without the songs? To compose songs to fit particular talents — especially when those talents are as distinguished as the ones for whom Styne has written—requires a creativity no less outstanding than composing songs to fit particular characters or situations. When a composer can create a melody that fits all three — the performer, the character portrayed, and the dramatic situation — he demonstrates the rarest kind of musical ability in the theatre. The measure of Jule Styne's contributions to the world of musical comedy can best be appreciated not alone by what performers have done to his songs, but also by what his songs have meant to the careers of the performers who have sung them.

Frank Loesser.

CHAPTER TWENTY

Frank Loesser
Richard Adler and Jerry Ross
Meredith Willson

THE FREQUENTLY BACK-BITING rivalry usually associated with the theater is, of course, very real, and there is no point in denying that it exists. Yet with regard to composers, the rule seems to be more one of mutual admiration, even mutual assistance. Victor Herbert took a keen interest in the career of Jerome Kern, and, for a while, Kern had an almost paternal feeling toward George Gershwin. Gershwin himself did what he could to help many budding talents; in the early Thirties, he even introduced new works by various young composers on his radio program. More recently, Rodgers and Hammerstein offered *Annie Get Your Gun* with a score by Irving Berlin, and Jule Styne was responsible for reviving Rodgers and Hart's *Pal Joey*. He also presented *Mr. Wonderful* and *First Impressions*, both with scores by other song-writers. Of all the composers discussed in this book, however, it is Frank Loesser who has probably been in the most advantageous position of being of help to others, a fact that is strikingly revealed in the careers of Richard Adler, Jerry Ross, and Meredith Willson.

Frank Loesser

The multiple activities of Frank Loesser in the musical theatre—composer, lyricist, librettist, producer — have given him a special distinction among his colleagues. Of equal importance to his own accomplishments, however, has been his unflagging interest in, and assistance to, new writers for the stage. Loesser is, in fact, able to offer very tangible aid. As president of the Frank Music Company, one of the leading music-publishing companies in the country, he has published the works of many promising composers and lyricists—in addition, of course, to his own songs.

It has been a particular mark of his foresight that Frank Loesser has been instrumental in furthering the careers of the three most successful songwriters of the theatre to emerge during the Fifties—Richard Adler, Jerry Ross, and Meredith Willson. In 1951, anxious to find the most promising talent among the young writers of Tin Pan Alley, he signed the team of Richard Adler and Jerry Ross to a contract. A few years later, after Loesser was approached to write the score for *The Pajama Game*, he suggested to George Abbott that Adler and Ross would make excellent replacements. In the case of Meredith Willson, it was Loesser who first urged him to turn the story of his Iowa boyhood into a musical. Loesser even introduced Willson to Cy Feuer and Ernest Martin, who were originally to have been the producers of *The Music Man*. Eventually, when it opened in New York in 1957, Frank Productions was the associate producer with Kermit Bloomgarden and Frank Music was the music publisher.

Such a variety of activities is completely natural to the restless, energetic Loesser. A hard-working, hard-driving man, he gets no more than four hours sleep a night and is usually awake by six-thirty in the morning. "I get bored otherwise," he says. "I like to have a song, a list of figures, and a business problem all around me."

Frank Henry Loesser was born in New York City, on June 29, 1910. His father was a piano teacher whose only interest was in the classics. His older brother, Arthur, has been a concert pianist, critic, and music teacher. In this environment, Loesser became interested in music at an early age. At six, he wrote a song called "The May Party" in celebration of the children's processions he saw in Central Park. A year later, he amused himself by fitting words to the clicking of the elevated railroad as it roared through his neighborhood.

Because his father disapproved of popular music, Loesser had to teach himself how to play the piano when he was in his early teens. After failing in his studies at the City College of New York, he took a variety of jobs. One that he particularly liked was as a reporter for a short-lived New Rochelle newspaper. When he was assigned to cover a local dinner of the

Lions Club, he obliged one of the officers by supplying rhymed couplets celebrating the exploits of all the members at the dinner. According to his brother Arthur, the local fame he achieved as the author of such lines as "Secretary Albert Vincent, Read these minutes right this instant," gave him his first inspiration to become a lyricist.

Soon Loesser began to write sketches and lyrics for vaudeville acts. During the Depression, he wrote occasional material for radio. In those days, Loesser recalls, "Somehow you had to find a way of getting a job. You had to keep alert all of the time. I suppose that's where this tremendous energy of mine originated."

In 1931, Loesser wrote his first published song, "In Love with a Memory Of You." It had a melody by William Schuman, who was to become a celebrated composer of concert music. A few years later, Loesser got a job singing and playing at the Back Drop, a 52nd Street nightclub. Many of the songs he sang where original numbers with music by Irving Actman. Five of these were used in *The Illustrators' Show*, the same revue in which Frederick Loewe's "A Waltz Was Born in Vienna' was first heard.

As a result of their work for *The Illustrators' Show*, Loesser and Actman were signed to a contract by Universal Pictures. Soon afterward, Loesser joined Paramount. His first song hit, "The Moon of Manakoora," (music by Alfred Newman) was written for *The Hurricane* in 1937. Among his most frequent collaborators during his eleven years in Hollywood were Burton Lane, Hoagy Carmichael, Frederick Hollander, Jimmy McHugh, Victor Schertzinger, Jule Styne, and Arthur Schwartz.

Loesser often wrote the words to songs before composers had written the music. Because the very construction of his lyrics almost dictated the melodies that would carry them, many of his collaborators urged him to write music as well as words. The first song with music and lyrics created exclusively by Frank Loesser was "Praise the Lord and Pass the Ammunition," written while he was in the Army during World War II. Its success gave Loesser the confidence to compose all of his own melodies from then on.

After his army stint was over, Loesser returned to Hollywood in 1946. His friends, Cy Feuer, the former head of the music department at Republic Pictures, and Ernest Martin, a former television executive, had formed a partnership to produce musical plays. Through attorney Howard Reinheimer (who is also Rodgers and Hammerstein's lawyer), they had secured the rights to Brandon Thomas' ancient farce, *Charley's Aunt*, as a vehicle for Ray Bolger, and they wanted Loesser to contribute the music and lyrics. In common with many other theatrical beginners, the producers then called upon the experienced George Abbott to serve as both director and librettist.

Where's Charley?, as the play was retitled, opened on October 11, 1948, and became an unqualified hit. It was the first of Feuer and Martin's five

WHERE'S CHARLEY? *(1948).*
George Abbott directing Ray
Bolger.

successful musicals in a row (the other four were *Guys and Dolls, The Boy Friend, Can-Can,* and *Silk Stockings*), and it also established Loesser as a Broadway composer and lyricist of great promise. His ballads ("My Darling, My Darling" and "Once in Love with Amy") had a simple, direct appeal, though even more impressive musical gifts were revealed in "The Red Rose Cotillion" and "The New Ashmoleon Marching Society and Student Conservatory Band." Moreover, in "Make a Miracle," he created a number in which words and music were brilliantly combined to produce a complete musical vignette as the ardent suitor tries vainly to gain the attention of his daydreaming sweetheart.

For their next musical, Feuer and Martin decided on a more ambitious work. Long fond of Damon Runyon stories and characters, they decided to do a Runyon fable based on a short story, *The Idyll of Miss Sarah Brown.* They also had a good title for it: *Guys and Dolls.* Their first choice for librettist was a Hollywood scenarist named Jo Swerling, but the producers were dissatisfied with the result. By the time they approached Abe Burrows, then a radio script-writer, they had already read librettos by eleven different authors. Although the Burrows script at last provided them with the right approach, contractural arrangements compelled them to retain Swerling's name on the program as co-author.

Feuer and Martin had signed Loesser even before they hired Burrows. Later, they secured George S. Kaufman as director and Michael Kidd to stage the dances. What emerged, when the show opened in 1950, was one of the most tightly coordinated musicals ever created. As Howard Barnes of the *Herald Tribune* wrote: "The work uses music and dancing as embellishments to the libretto, rather than making the latter a loose clothesline for assorted capers and vocal numbers."

GUYS AND DOLLS (1950). *The oldest established permanent floating crap game in New York takes up temporary residence in a sewer. Throwing the dice is Sky Masterson (Robert Alda), and standing behind him is Big Julie (B. S. Pully). Nicely Nicely Johnson (Stubby Kaye) and Nathan Detroit (Sam Levene) are kneeling on either side of them. (Costumes by Alvin Colt; setting by Jo Mielziner.)*

PHOTO BY EILEEN DARBY—GRAPHIC HOUSE

In writing the score, Loesser found inspiration in many of the actual guys and dolls he had known when he was a pianist at the Back Drop. It was his ability to capture the racy, hard-shelled, but basically soft-hearted characters of the gamblers and racketeers of the Runyon fable that gave his songs their special distinction. These people speak in awkwardly cultivated tones, their emotions are explosive but unassailably pure, and when Sister Sarah Brown of the Save a Soul Mission comes along to urge them into living more respectable lives, there is never any doubt that she will eventually succeed.

Loesser's score had great variety, yet it also had a singleness of design and purpose that caught the appealing ambivalence of the highminded lowlifes. Dignified and classical forms, such as a college alma mater for "The Oldest Established," or the Bachlike fugue for a description of a horse race, were completely right because, in spite of the incongruity, the characters themselves were essentially dignified and classical. So too, a grandly operatic duet, "Sue Me," was used with unerring effect as Adelaide, a nightclub singer, (played by Vivian Blaine) flails away at Nathan Detroit, her fiancé of fourteen years (played by Sam Levene), only to be met by his unnerving acquiescence. For the two sequences at the Hot Box nightclub, Loesser had his fun on two levels. "A Bushel and a Peck" is a purposely inane number which becomes all the more ridiculous as it is squealed by the chorus girls, while "Take Back Your Mink" achieves its humor from the shocked attitude of the girls whose virtues are about to be imperiled.

One song, "Adelaide's Lament," was written well before the final libretto was completed. Originally, Adelaide was to have been a stripper who catches cold from overexposure; later, when it was decided that she would be more sympathetic as a singer, Loesser changed the lyric to make her suffer from psychosomatic ailments because her marriage to Nathan has been postponed so often. "Adelaide's Lament," one of the most brilliant of all comic love songs, is a perfect example of Loesser's dictum: "I try to examine characters, not events."

THE MOST HAPPY FELLA
(1956). *Robert Weede as
Tony, the aging winegrower
of Napa Valley, California,
and Jo Sullivan as Rosabella,
his mail-order bride.*

PHOTO BY ARTHUR CANTOR

In 1952, a friend suggested to Loesser that he create a musical out of
Sidney Howard's *They Knew What They Wanted*. Loesser read it and was
immediately intrigued with the idea. "I figured take out all this political talk,
the labor talk, and the religious talk. Get rid of all that stuff and you have a
good love story." The tender tale of the elderly Italian winegrower in California who falls in love at first sight with a waitress seemed to Loesser to have
an emotional intensity especially well suited to a musical adaptation. "Go
spell what you sound like when you're laughing or crying. You have to say it
in music."

Writing *The Most Happy Fella*—music, lyrics, libretto—took Loesser
more than four years. He felt like giving it up many times, but inevitably a
period of depression would be followed by one of extreme enthusiasm, and
he would again plod forward. Once the work was finished, there still remained the problem of finding a suitable actor for the leading role of the
winegrower. Loesser even made a trip to Italy in a vain search for someone
with the right quality of voice and acting ability. Eventually, he engaged
Robert Weede, formerly of the Metropolitan Opera, who made his Broadway
debut in the musical.

The Most Happy Fella, which opened in New York on May 5, 1956, was
probably the most ambitiously operatic work ever created for the Broadway
musical theatre. Included among its more than thirty separate musical numbers were recitatives, arias, duets, trios, quartets, and choral passages, yet all
of them were created to fit within the framework of the commercial musical
theatre. Big, booming arias, such as "Rosabella" and "My Heart Is So Full of
You," are interspersed with such traditional Broadway specialty numbers as
"Big 'D'" and "Standing on the Corner." Other selections, particularly
"Abbondanza" and "Benvenuta," reveal their composer's knack of parodying
the effulgences of Neapolitan singers. Perhaps most charming of all are the
duet between Weede and Jo Sullivan (as his mail-order bride), "Happy to
Make Your Acquaintance," and the evocative quartet, "How Beautiful the
Days."

Although in the manner of an opera, the program for *The Most Happy Fella* did not list the individual songs, the work was designated simply as "A Musical." To those who prod him on the matter, Loesser says, "I may give the impression this show has operatic tendencies. If people feel that way—fine. Actually all it has is a great frequency of songs. It's a musical with music." Or, as arranger Don Walker has put it, "This is a musical comedy expanded. Not an opera cut down."

Apparently, once Frank Loesser becomes identified with a particular type of music or musical, he feels he must move on to something more challenging. In his next production, *Greenwillow*, starring Anthony Perkins in his first appearance in a musical, Loesser abruptly abandoned the colorful big-city world of Damon Runyon and the melodramatic world of Sidney Howard in favor of the pastoral world of novelist B. J. Chute. This time, Loesser (and co-librettist Lesser Samuels) sought to capture the elusive flavor of an imaginary community located somewhere along the banks of the Meander River. With little plot, the musical relied on a certain synthetic charm derived from imaginary quaint rural customs (the baptism of a cow, for example), that were perhaps somewhat difficult to accept on the musical stage. "Folklore," wrote Walter Kerr following its March 8, 1960, première, "may just be one dish that can't be cooked to order."

Loesser's score provided a rich variety of bucolic themes, demonstrating again that the composer is a master at recreating familiar musical styles, while still endowing his songs with his own individual style. Included are wistful old English ballads ("Walking Away Whistling," "Faraway Boy"), a religious hymn (an amusing bit in which two ministers offer contrasting sermons

THE MOST HAPPY FELLA *(1956). The "Big D" number led by Texans Susan Johnson and, at the far right, Shorty Long. (Costumes by Motley.)*

PHOTO BY FRIEDMAN-ABELES

on the same theme), and a Christmas carol ("Greenwillow Christmas"). Loesser also created two moving songs for Mr. Perkins, "Summertime Love," which fairly bursts out its message of love's constancy, and the touching renunciation, "Never Will I Marry." Though alien to the composer's personal experience, these numbers have an authenticity and feeling for mood that somehow escaped the production as a whole.

Frank Loesser's many careers have limited him to four musicals since 1948. Yet so profound are his talents that he is accepted among the most creative men of the musical theatre today. Moreover, his career has been marked by the most steady advance of any composer since George Gershwin. From formula musical comedy, (*Where's Charley?*), he went immediately to a Broadway comic opera (*Guys and Dolls*). Then, as Gershwin had done, he created a Broadway opera (*The Most Happy Fella*). If *Greenwillow* proved to be a little too coy for popular taste, it nevertheless demonstrated its author's impatience with the convenional, his desire to try something new that is no less an expression of his individual gifts. Also noteworthy is that, just as he has extended himself in themes, Loesser has also expanded his activities—from lyricist to composer-lyricist to composer-lyricist-librettist-producer.

Frank Loesser has established his own high standards in the Broadway theatre. Combining the sensitivity of the artist with the acumen of the businessman, he has helped preserve these standards not alone through his own creations but through the creations of others whom he has encouraged and assisted.

GREENWILLOW *(1960). Anthony Perkins vows his devotion to his "Summertime Love." (Costumes by Alvin Colt.)*

PHOTO BY FRED FEHL

Richard Adler and Jerry Ross.

Richard Adler and Jerry Ross

When, in 1951, Frank Loesser asked another music publisher to send him the most promising young song-writers he knew, the publisher immediately thought of Richard Adler and Jerry Ross. Loesser was so impressed with their songs that he promptly signed the two young composers to an exclusive contract with his publishing company. Many things about the versatile team—each man could write both music and lyrics—made Loesser confident that they would eventually fulfill his expectations. Their music showed both originality and a rhythmic accessibility that indicated commercial appeal. Their lyrics were full of the argot of modern, idiomatic speech that Loesser himself has captured so well. Above all, both men, like Loesser, were anxious to break down the walls that had, for so many years, created barriers between Tin Pan Alley and the Broadway theatre.

During their relatively brief partnership (Ross died of a lung ailment in 1955), these "two young Loessers," as Leonard Bernstein has called them, showed a special aptitude for communicating with contemporary audiences. "Subconsciously, and from our training, we're writing for the man in the street," Ross once remarked. To which Adler added: "We try to write universal truths in colloquial terms. We're just trying to bring out the expression of the times in which we live in terms of the people with whom we're dealing. We're writing the way our generation demands we write."

Both men were born in New York—Adler on August 23, 1923, and Ross on March 9, 1926. Adler's family life was quite similar to Frank Loesser's, as his father, Clarence Adler, was a concert pianist and music teacher. Classical music, however, never interested the young Adler; in fact, his original ambition was to become a writer. After graduating from the University of North Carolina (where he studied playwrighting under Paul Green), he spent three years in the Navy. Upon his discharge, he got a job writing advertising copy for a large corporation. About this time he began to compose songs; at first, during his spare time and later even during office hours. Inevitably, this resulted in his dismissal, but, as Adler had already decided to become a song-writer, he welcomed the opportunity to devote all of his time to music. He met with little success, however, until he met Jerry Ross in 1950.

Ross was born in the East Bronx of poor parents. At ten, while singing in a synagogue choir, he was approached to join the Bronx Art Theatre, a Yid-dish acting company. After acting in one of its productions, he joined other companies then presenting plays on the Jewish stage. Because Ross attended high school in the Bronx and most of these groups were on the lower East Side of Manhattan, he was forced to stay up until all hours commuting. As a result, during this period he developed chronic bronchietasis, which was eventually responsible for his death. Ross was still in his teens when he wrote his first song. He continued composing at New York University, where he took courses in music, and at summer resorts in the Catskills. Like Adler, Ross had little luck as a song-writer until he met his partner.

Adler and Ross's first success for Frank Loesser was "Rags to Riches," which they wrote in 1954. The same year, they were signed to write most of the songs for *John Murray Anderson's Almanac*, a revue starring Hermione Gingold, Billy DeWolfe, and Harry Belafonte. Even before this show opened, the team was hired by George Abbott to create the entire score for *The Pajama Game*. Adler and Ross had previously auditioned for Abbott on two occasions; each time, though he was encouraging, the old master told them that they were not yet ready. When Loesser recommended them for *The Pajama Game*, the partners again auditioned. This time, the director was

THE PAJAMA GAME (1954).
Eddie Foy, Jr., Janis Paige, and John Raitt.

DAMN YANKEES (1955). *Chore-ographer Bob Fosse rehears-ing the chorus.*

PHOTO BY TALBOT

so excited about their work that he rushed over to Frederick Brisson, Robert Griffith, and Harold Prince, the show's producers, and insisted that the team be hired.

The Pajama Game opened in May, 1954. Following the frequent pattern of George Abbott musicals, most of the people responsible for the production were newcomers to the theatre—including the producers (Griffith and Prince had been stage managers for many of Abbott's productions) and choreographer Bob Fosse. Apart from Abbott, the only other experienced member of the staff was Jerome Robbins, the co-director, though this marked his first assignment directing an entire show. By thus dividing the directing chores, Abbott was given more time to work on the libretto with Richard Bissell, the author of *7½ Cents,* the novel from which the book was adapted.*

The Pajama Game was a fast-paced, human story based on the unlikely subject of a threatened strike in a pajama factory. There was, however, nothing socially conscious about it in the manner of *Pins and Needles;* the rights of the workers were not nearly as important as their fun and romantic complications. Although the unmistakable George Abbott touch was evident throughout, the contributions of Adler and Ross were of sufficient merit to establish them as the brightest new song-writing team to emerge during the decade. *The Pajama Game* also provided new opportunities for its stars, John Raitt, Janis Paige, and Eddie Foy, Jr., as well as for Carol Haney, a young dancer making her Broadway debut. (For a few performances soon after the opening, Miss Haney was replaced by her understudy, Shirley MacLaine.)

The flavor—if not the ingredients—of *Damn Yankees,* produced exactly one year later, was similar to *The Pajama Game.* It had the same production

* Bissell subsequently based his novel, *Say, Darling,* on his experiences working on *The Pajama Game.* This, in turn, became "A Comedy about a Musical," with songs by Jule Styne, Betty Comden, and Adolph Green.

303

DAMN YANKEES *(1955). Wrote Louis Kronenberger: "In Ray Walston it had a fine stylish Devil, and in Gwen Verdon what was by all odds the musical comedy delight of the year—a vivacious redhead who can dance superbly, and be as hilarious about sex as she can be seductive."*

staff—producers, choreographer, musical director (Hal Hastings), arranger (Don Walker)—plus director George Abbott and Adler and Ross. Abbott also collaborated on the libretto with Douglass Wallop, whose novel, *The Year the Yankees Lost the Pennant,* furnished the basis for the musical. Again, the swift-moving show had the style and the spirit that has long distinguished its director's work; even the Faustian overtones of the story were treated in a breezy manner, particularly with Ray Walston playing the devil and Gwen Verdon (in her first starring role) as his most efficient temptress. The Adler and Ross contributions, while not as striking as those in their first score, nevertheless provided such commercially successful pieces as "Whatever Lola Wants" and "Heart."

There is little doubt that the firm hand of director and co-librettist George Abbott was chiefly responsible for the lengthy runs of both *The Pajama Game* and *Damn Yankees.* Yet the work of Adler and Ross cannot be overlooked in appraising their success. Just as Frank Loesser had before them, they brought a new commercial flair to the Broadway theatre; they were remarkably adept at combining a wide range of catchy, familiar rhythms —plus original sound effects—within the framework of a single score. Thus, in *The Pajama Game* there was a lively march ("7½ Cents"), a roaring Western ballad ("There Once Was a Man"), a novelty item with a hissing noise as part of its lyric ("Steam Heat"), a lilting waltz ("I'm Not at All in Love"), a solo love song that became a duet when played back over a dictaphone ("Hey, There"), and a spooky tango ("Hernando's Hideaway"). For *Damn Yankees,* the team created a satirical barbershop quartet ("Heart"), a spirited hoedown ("Shoeless Joe from Hannibal, Mo."), a sultry tango ("Whatever Lola Wants"), a soft-shoe vaudeville number ("Those Were the Good Old Days"), and a comic mambo ("Who's Got the Pain?").

This faculty for combining unrelated musical styles and rhythms may not have endowed the scores of Adler and Ross with any lasting distinction. Nevertheless, the writers did possess an unerring instinct for what was good theatre music and what was good commercial music. Although Adler has devoted most of his time to television since the death of his partner, the team, if only temporarily, succeeded in closing the apparently ever-widening gulf between Broadway and Tin Pan Alley.

304

Rini and Meredith Willson.

Meredith Willson

One day in 1949, Meredith Willson was indulging in one of his favorite indoor pastimes: reminiscing to a group of friends about his boyhood in Mason City, Iowa. Among his listeners was Frank Loesser. Suddenly, Loesser jumped to his feet. "What an idea!" he shouted, "Why don't you write a musical about it?" Then he started to pace up and down. "Maybe you can start with the fire chief. Let's make him the leader of the town band. Maybe *you* can play the fire chief. And maybe instead of a pit orchestra, you can have a real brass band in the pit. And you're the leader of the band. You could also be sort of a narrator and talk directly to the people in the audience. That way you could tell everybody about your town. It would be real Americana!"

When *The Music Man* finally opened on Broadway eight years later, it bore little resemblance to Loesser's original concept. But Loesser had planted an idea in Willson's mind about doing a musical with an Iowa background, something that would capture all the nostalgia and warmth inherent in a story of a small Midwestern town in the early days of the century. "Innocent, that was the adjective for Iowa," Willson has said. "I didn't have to make anything up for *The Music Man*. All I had to do was remember."

Meredith Willson was born in Mason City, on May 18, 1902. His mother gave piano lessons, and young Meredith dutifully studied that instrument as well as the piccolo and the flute. In his youth, he played piccolo in the high-school band, enjoyed the county fairs, had a job pumping water for Saturday night baths, and, in general, absorbed everything he could of the folk-lore of his small Iowa community. After high school, he went to New York to pursue a career in music. There he studied at the Institute of Musical Art (later Juilliard School of Music), and, at the age of nineteen, was hired by

305

John Philip Sousa as first flutist in his band. Three years later, he joined the New York Philharmonic, where he played under Toscanini. In 1929, Willson became musical director of the Northwest Territory for the American Broadcasting Company; soon afterward, he joined the staff of the National Broadcasting Company.

Willson's first symphony ("San Francisco") was written when he was thirty-three. From 1937 on, with the exception of the years spent in the Army during World War II, he was associated with many radio programs as both conductor and performer. His first song hit, "You and I," was written in 1941; nine years later, he wrote the popular "May the Good Lord Bless and Keep You" as the theme song for Tallulah Bankhead's radio program, *The Big Show*.

Because of his other work, Willson did not begin to write the musical about Iowa until nearly three years after Loesser had first suggested it. After abandoning the idea of the fire chief and also of appearing in the show himself, Willson then thought of telling a story about a kindly music teacher. Later, the main character was changed to a traveling salesman of nonexistent musical instruments. The leading female part, a librarian who also gives piano lessons, was modeled after Willson's mother.

Through Loesser, Willson met producers Cy Feuer and Ernest Martin. They became so enthusiastic about the script that they promised to put it into production immediately after the opening of *Silk Stockings* in February, 1955. They even suggested *The Music Man* as the title. Soon, however, the producers lost interest because of what they felt were basic weaknesses in the story. This was a serious blow to Willson, but he had already put so much effort and time on the musical by then that he was determined to continue to work on it and try to interest other producers. In the summer of 1956, he rewrote much of the libretto with playwright Franklin Lacey. By the following November, Willson had already gone through thirty-two drafts of *The Music Man* and he was still unable to find a producer. Then, remembering that Kermit Bloomgarden had co-sponsored Frank Loesser's *The Most Happy Fella*, he telephoned the producer from California. When Bloomgarden agreed to let him audition, Willson and his wife, Rini, flew to New York, and played and sang the entire production the following evening. The next morning, Bloomgarden called Willson to his office. "Meredith," he asked, "may I have the privilege of producing your beautiful play?"

Many actors were considered for the leading role of Professor Harold Hill, the persuasive but unscrupulous music man. According to Willson's book, *But He Doesn't Know the Territory*, Danny Kaye was the original choice, but Kaye did not feel he was right for the part. Dan Dailey never kept his appointment to discuss the matter with Willson. Phil Harris did not even return his telephone call. Gene Kelly just was not interested. Finally, at the insistence of director Morton DaCosta and musical director Herbert Greene, Robert Preston, best known for his performances in movie Westerns, was signed for the part.

In his score for *The Music Man*, Willson made great use of the technique of rhythmic, but not rhyming, lyrics. This is apparent in the very first number of the show, "Rock Island," in which the rhythm of a moving train is simulated in dialogue as a group of traveling salesmen discuss the problems of their trade. The same device later occurs in both "Piano Lesson," which uses the musical scale as accompaniment to a conversation between Barbara Cook, as the librarian–music teacher, and Pert Kelton, as her mother, and in "Trouble," a rousing sermon exploded into the midst of the townspeople by the fast-talking Professor Hill. Willson also adds a dramatic touch by employing the same melody for both Miss Cook's wistful "Goodnight, My Someone" and Preston's spirited "Seventy-Six Trombones," in order, as he has explained, "to suggest that these two people have something more in common than meets the eye."

Despite the fears of those who felt that *The Music Man* would be too old-fashioned for Broadway, it received unanimously favorable reviews following its December 19, 1957, opening. It then settled down for the first marathon run since *My Fair Lady*. What distinguished the show were the

THE MUSIC MAN *(1957). In "Seventy Six Trombones," Robert Preston, as a bogus instrument salesman, wins over the children of River City, Iowa, with his description of the most mammoth parade of all times. "Though he never danced or sang before on stage," wrote* Life Magazine, *"he displays both zing and polish and follows triumphantly in the tradition of George M. Cohan." (Costumes by Raoul Pène du Bois.)*

THE MUSIC MAN (1957). Professor Harold Hill (Robert Preston) has a serious talk with Marian Paroo, the town librarian(Barbara Cook).(Costumes by Raoul Pène du Bois.)

qualities of conviction and affection that so obviously went into its creation. Every type of musical expression used—soft-shoe, ragtime, barbershop quartet, march—had a feeling of genuineness that helped to bring alive the flavor of a naïve American town circa 1912. In his capacity as composer, lyricist, and librettist, Willson brought to his work a musical proficiency and a unity of purpose that made *The Music Man* a completely irresistible show.

Willson's special combination of breeziness and sentimentality are reminiscent of the works of another man of the theatre who wrote music, words, and books—George M. Cohan. There is the same fondness for American characters and locales, the same electric excitement in the swift-paced production, the same theatrical contrast between the city slicker and various rural types. *The Music Man* even takes place on Cohan's favorite holiday, the Fourth of July. Thus, in spite of the skills of production and the advances in theatrical techniques, the musical theatre still finds room for a production with the same basic appeal that was found in the earliest examples of strictly American musicals based on American themes.

Of course, what Willson goes on to achieve in the theatre cannot be judged by one play. It can be assumed, however, that the qualities of sincerity and charm that went into *The Music Man* will also be present in his future works. It may be corn, but it is honest corn. Although his roots are firmly in the rich soil of Iowa, Meredith Willson has proved that with skill and patience he can be at home on the steel and concrete of Broadway.

CHAPTER TWENTY-ONE

Epilogue

WRITING THE STORY of such a viable form of entertainment as musical comedy presents a particularly difficult problem in keeping up to date with the younger talent which is always vaulting into prominence. This epilogue is devoted to those composers, lyricists and librettists who have not only most recently come to the fore, but who show the greatest indication of remaining there.

Like Adler and Ross, Bob Merrill is a product of Tin Pan Alley. He has created the words and music for such novelty items as "Candy and Cake," "If I Knew You Were Comin' I'd 'ave Baked a Cake," and his biggest hit of all, "How Much Is That Doggie in the Window?" ("Yip! Yip!"). Paradoxically, Merrill had originally begun his career as a writer of sophisticated songs; it was only when publishers told him that they would never sell that he began to write nonsense. After meeting hostility on Broadway because of his Tin Pan Alley background, Merrill succeeded in signing a contract with M-G-M to produce and write film musicals. His first assignment, *A Saint She Ain't,* was a song-and-dance treatment of Eugene O'Neill's *Anna Christie.* Although the film was never made—nor were any others—the composer was able to interest George Abbott in the idea for a stage musical.

Retitled *New Girl in Town,* the work was not entirely successful in adjusting the O'Neill drama to the requirements of the musical stage. Nevertheless, it gave Gwen Verdon and Thelma Ritter ample opportunity to give memorable performances, and revealed Merrill's faculty as a creator of

Bob Merrill.

atmospheric and theatrical songs. His next musical, *Take Me Along*, was also based on an O'Neill play, *Ah Wilderness!* It opened in the fall of 1959, with the leading roles played by Jackie Gleason (in his first Broadway appearance since *Along Fifth Avenue* in 1949), Walter Pidgeon, Eileen Herlie, and Robert Morse. Merrill's score showed marked improvement over his work for *New Girl in Town;* particularly notable were "I Get Embarrassed," a duet for Miss Herlie and Mr. Gleason, and Miss Herlie's affecting solo, "We're Home."

NEW GIRL IN TOWN (1957). *Gwen Verdon as Anna Christie and Thelma Ritter as Marty. (Costumes by Rouben Ter-Arturian.)*

TAKE ME ALONG (1959). *"There are many quite wonderful moments in Take Me Along,"* Richard Watts, Jr., *wrote in his review, "but the one I think I treasure most is that in which the Messrs. Gleason and Pidgeon go into a soft shoe dance to the accompaniment of the title song."*

Composer Mary Rodgers and lyricist Marshall Barer first became partners at Camp Tamiment, an adult summer camp, in 1958. It was there that they wrote the score for a miniature musical which librettists Barer, Dean Fuller, and Jay Thompson adapted from an ancient fairy tale, *The Princess and the Pea*. Miss Rodgers, the daughter of Richard Rodgers, had previously written the lyrics to *Three to Make Music*, with music created by her sister, Linda Rodgers Melnick. The number was included in Mary Mar-

ONCE UPON A MATTRESS (1959). *Gathered around composer Mary Rodgers are lyricist and co-librettist Marshall Barer, director George Abbott, and co-librettists Dean Fuller and Jay Thompson.*

tin's cross-country concert tour in 1958. Marshall Barer, before teaming with Miss Rodgers, had written songs with Dean Fuller, a librettist-composer. Five Fuller-Barer songs were in Leonard Sillman's *New Faces of 1956*, including the highly acclaimed "La Ronde" (also known as "This Is Quite a Perfect Night").

When it was offered at the off-Broadway Phoenix Theatre in May, 1959, the show was expanded into a full evening's entertainment and titled *Once Upon a Mattress*. George Abbott directed it, and Carol Burnett, in her musical comedy debut, established herself as an adept stage comedienne. Upon leaving the Phoenix Theatre the musical was housed in a succession of on-Broadway theatres. Miss Rodgers' distinctive musical gifts are particularly revealed in "Sensitivity," "In a Little While," and "Normandy"; Mr. Barer's faculty as a lyricist is most notably apparent in "Many Moons Ago" and "Very Soft Shoes."

Both *Little Mary Sunshine* and *Fiorello!* had their New York premières in November, 1959, within five days of each other. The shows were instant successes, and Rick Besoyan, Sheldon Harnick, and Jerry Bock soon became the most acclaimed young writers of the season. Neither success was antici-

ONCE UPON A MATTRESS (1959). *Carol Burnett as Princess Winifred ("Fred" to her friends) bellows to the assembled courtiers that she's "Shy." (Costumes by William and Jean Eckart.)*

Rick Besoyan.

pated. *Little Mary Sunshine,* with its music, lyrics, and libretto written by
Besoyan, had an advance ticket sale of $8.70 when it opened at the 199-seat
Orpheum Theatre on Second Avenue. But its bright, affectionate spoofing of
the conventions of the operettas of Victor Herbert, Sigmund Romberg,
Rudolf Friml, and others quickly attracted enthusiastic audiences, and
tuurned it into one of off-Broadway's biggest box-office attractions.

The team of Rick Besoyan was born in California. After winning a scholarship to the
Trinity Music College, in London, he went to New York hoping for a career
as a singer and actor. His inspiration for writing "A New Musical about an
Old Operetta" came when he was a member of the touring Savoy Light Opera
Company. It took Besoyan three years to write *Little Mary Sunshine,* which
was first presented in an abbreviated version as part of a nightclub revue. In
order to raise the necessary $15,000 needed to produce the musical, Besoyan
and Eileen Brennan, who played the title role, had to give at least fifty audi-
tions before acquiring the 127 backers who put up the money.

The team of Jerry Bock (music) and Sheldon Harnick (lyrics) was
formed in 1957 to write the score for *The Body Beautiful,* which opened the
following year and lasted two months. Bock, like the quartet responsible for

313

LITTLE MARY SUNSHINE
(1959). *Little Mary Sunshine
(Eileen Brennan) demurely
turns her head as the brave
Capt. Big Jim Warington
(William Graham) serenades
her with "You're the Fairest
Flower." (Costumes by Howard Barker.)*

FIORELLO! (1959). *Backstage
shot of George Abbott (director and co-librettist), Jerome
Weidman (co-librettist), Sheldon Harnick (lyricist), and
Jerry Bock (composer).*

Once Upon a Mattress, received most of his theatrical training preparing revues at Camp Tamiment. In 1956, he joined George Weiss and Larry Holofcener to provide both music and lyrics for *Mr. Wonderful,* starring Sammy Davis, Jr. Jule Styne was the producer. Sheldon Harnick, after studying music at Northwestern University, began his theatrical career as both composer and lyricist. His "Boston Beguine" (sung by Alice Ghostley) was one of the hits of Leonard Sillman's *New Faces of 1952,* and the following year Orson Bean sang his "Merry Minuet" ("They're rioting in Africa . . .") in *John Murray Anderson's Almanac.* Heeding the advice of E. Y. Harburg, Harnick decided to devote himself exclusively to writing lyrics. It was music publisher Thomas Valando, with whom both Bock and Harnick were under contract, who brought the writers together for *The Body Beautiful.*

Fiorello! was the first musical since *I'd Rather Be Right* to have an actual political figure as its leading character. It was also the third musical to be awarded the Pulitzer Prize for drama, a distinction it shares with another show with a political subject, *Of Thee I Sing.* Rather than being the satirical work the others were, however, *Fiorello!* was generally a warm, honest story of the rise to eminence of New York's scrappy Mayor LaGuardia. With the

FIORELLO! *(1959). A young New York lawyer named Fiorello LaGuardia shows picketing workers how to put some spirit in what they are doing. In the opinion of critic Henry Hewes, "Actor Tom Bosley, as a fine artist should, captures more of LaGuardia's essence than the man did himself when he was alive." (Costumes by William and Jean Eckart.)*

COURTESY CAPITOL RECORDS

BYE BYE BIRDIE (1960). *Lyricist Lee Adams, director Gower Champion, librettist Michael Stewart, producer Edward Padula, and composer Charles Strouse.*

His teenage fans swoon whenever they hear rock and roll idol, Conrad Birdie (Dick Gautier), sing "Honestly Sincere." Michael J. Pollard and Susan Watson are at the left. (Costumes by Miles White.)

omnipresent George Abbott directing (and writing the book with Jerome Weidman), it featured a little-known actor, Tom Bosley, in the title role. The score made many sharp observations on big-city politics, the most hilarious being "Little Tin Box," a number full of the air of injured innocence most politicians feel whenever they are caught with their hands in the till.

The creators of *Bye Bye Birdie*—composer Charles Strouse, lyricist Lee Adams, librettist Michael Stewart—began writing together during their apprenticeship at Green Mansions, the same summer camp where Harold Rome first sang his songs. All three were first represented in New York by material in Ben Bagley's *Shoestring Revue* in 1955, for which Strouse served as musical director. At that time Stewart was primarily a lyricist and collaborated with Strouse on three of the songs. The following year, Adams and Strouse formed a partnership to create some of the numbers for *The Littlest Revue* and *Shoestring '57*, both produced by Bagley. Until they began to work on *Bye Bye Birdie*, Strouse earned a living as a pianist (including rehearsal pianist), Adams was an editor of *This Week* magazine, and Stewart wrote comedy material for television.

Bye Bye Birdie, the first book musical directed by Gower Champion, was a modern tale inspired by teenagers' fondness for rock 'n' roll music and their adoration of singing idols. In this case, the Elvis Presley-type singer is called Conrad Birdie, and the story deals with a publicity stunt that his manager uses when the singer is drafted into the Army. Its songs caught the accents and attitudes of young America, and its approach was more of a genial satire than a sociological exposition. Chita Rivera and Dick Van Dyke had the leading roles.

With the almost total absence of film musicals, the competition in the musical theatre is probably as great today as it once was during the Twenties. What is immediately striking, however, is the versatility of the new writers. Almost every successful composer, lyricist, and librettist has had some experience in another phase of creative writing. This does not mean that any individual is equally proficient in all fields, but it does indicate an important development in the constant striving for more unity and integration in the musical theatre. For a writer who understands fully the problems of his collaborators is a person with a greater understanding of the requirements of a production as a whole. The closer the coöperation among all the component parts of a musical, the greater is its chance for success today.

The large number of talented composers, lyricists, and librettists now in the theatre is a recent development that is both exciting and heartening. The skills they have acquired writing for summer-camp musicals, nightclub performers and revues, off-Broadway revues, and the like, give indication that the American musical theatre of the future will be led by the same kind of dedicated and talented men and women who were once responsible for its birth and its growth.

Musical Productions & Discography

The following lists include opening dates, number of performances, collaborators, leading cast members, and principal songs of every Broadway (and off-Broadway) musical with scores written by the composers and lyricists discussed in this book. In addition to productions with complete scores by these writers, others with four or more interpolated songs have been included.

All original cast (O.C.), film version cast (F.V.), television cast (TV), and studio cast (S.C.) 12-inch long playing records are noted and discussed briefly. When two record numbers are used, the second one represents the stereo release. An "X" indicates that the record has been cut from the catalogue.

The exact number of performances, especially, of some of the earlier musicals, is difficult to determine. In general, references have been *The Best Plays* series, *The Billboard, Variety,* and Daniel Blum's *Theater World* series. Wherever a noticeable discrepancy exists in these sources, the number has been used that most closely corresponds to the total months a show has played on Broadway.

Names of cast members have been listed according to the spelling found in programs of each musical. In cases where actors or writers have since changed their names so that they are no longer identifiable by this listing, the more familiar names appear in parentheses.

Victor Herbert

PRINCE ANANIAS
Opened: Nov. 20, 1894.
No record of performances.
BOOK & LYRICS BY FRANCIS NEILSEN.

Cast included: Mena Cleary, W. H. Mac-Donald, Eugene Cowles, Henry Clay Barnabee, George Frothingham.
Principal songs: It Needs No Poet; I Am No Queen; Amaryllis; Ah! Cupid, Meddlesome Boy!; Love Is Spring.

THE WIZARD OF THE NILE
Opened: Nov. 4, 1895.
105 *performances.*
BOOK & LYRICS BY HARRY B. SMITH.

Cast included: Frank Daniels, Walter Allen, Edwin Isham, Dorothy Morton.
Principal songs: Pure and White Is the Lotus; Star Light, Star Bright; My Angeline; Stonecutters' Song.

THE GOLD BUG
Opened: Sept. 21, 1896.
1 *week.*
BOOK & LYRICS BY GLEN MACDONOUGH.

Cast included: Marie Cahill, Max Figman, Molly Fuller.
Principal songs: One For Another; The Owl and the Thrush.

THE SERENADE
Opened: Mar. 16, 1897.
79 *performances.*
BOOK & LYRICS BY HARRY B. SMITH.

Cast included: Alice Nielsen, Eugene Cowles, Henry Clay Barnabee, W. H. MacDonald, George Frothingham.
Principal songs: With Cracking of Whip and Rattle of Spur; I Love Thee, I Adore Thee; The Monk and the Maid; Cupid and I.

THE IDOL'S EYE
Opened: Oct. 25, 1897.
7 *weeks.*
BOOK & LYRICS BY HARRY B. SMITH.

Cast included: Frank Daniels, Helen Redmond, Maurice Darcy, Alf. C. Whelan.
Principal songs: I'm Captain Cholly Chumley of the Guards; The Lady and the Kick; Song of the Priestess.

THE FORTUNE TELLER
Opened: Sept. 26, 1898.
40 *performances.*
BOOK & LYRICS BY HARRY B. SMITH.

Cast included: Alice Nielsen, Eugene Cowles, Joseph Herbert, Joseph Cawthorn, Frank Rushworth.
Principal songs: Always Do As People Say You Should; Romany Life; Gypsy Love-Song; Czardas.

CYRANO DE BERGERAC
Opened: Sept. 18, 1899.
28 *performances.*
BOOK & LYRICS BY HARRY B. SMITH.

Cast included: Francis Wilson, Lulu Glaser, Josephine Intropidi, Charles H. Bowers.
Principal songs: Since I Am Not for Thee; Cadets of Gascony; I Wonder; Let the Sun of My Eyes.

THE SINGING GIRL
Opened: Oct. 23, 1899.
80 *performances.*
BOOK BY STANISLAUS STANGE; LYRICS BY HARRY B. SMITH.

Cast included: Alice Nielsen, Eugene Cowles, Joseph W. Herbert, Joseph Cawthorn, Richie Ling.
Principal songs: If Only You Were Mine; Love Is Tyrant; Well Beloved.

THE AMEER
Opened: Dec. 4, 1899.
51 *performances.*
BOOK & LYRICS BY FREDERIC RANKEN & KIRKE LASHELLE.

Cast included: Frank Daniels, Helen Redmond, George Devoll.
Principal songs: Sweet Clarissa; Fond Love, True Love.

THE VICEROY
Opened: Apr. 9, 1900.
28 *performances.*
BOOK & LYRICS BY HARRY B. SMITH.

Cast included: Henry Clay Barnabee, Helen Bertram, Grace Cameron, William H. MacDonald, Frank Rushworth.
Principal songs: The Robin and the Rose; Tell Me; 'Neath the Blue Neapolitan Skies; Just for Today.

BABES IN TOYLAND
Opened: Oct. 13, 1903.
192 *performances.*
BOOK & LYRICS BY GLEN MACDONOUGH.

Cast included: George W. Denham, Mabel Barrison, William Norris, Bessie Wynn, Amy Ricard.
Principal songs: Never Mind, Bo Peep; I Can't Do the Sum; Go to Sleep, Slumber Deep; March of the Toys; Toyland.

Recorded Version
Decca DL 8458 (S.C.)
Six numbers from this still-charming score are delightfully sung by Kenny Baker & Karen Kemple. The reverse side features selections from Herbert's *The Red Mill*.

BABETTE
Opened: Nov. 16, 1903.
59 *performances.*
BOOK & LYRICS BY HARRY B. SMITH.

Cast included: Fritzi Scheff, Eugene Cowles, Richie Ling, Louis Harrison.
Principal songs: Letters I Write All the Day; I'll Bribe the Stars; There Once Was an Owl.

IT HAPPENED IN NORDLAND
Opened: Dec. 5, 1904.
154 *performances.*
BOOK & LYRICS BY GLEN MACDONOUGH.

Cast included: Marie Cahill, Lew Fields, Joseph Herbert, Harry Davenport, May Robson, Bessie Clayton, Pauline Frederick.
Principal songs: Absinthe Frappé; Commanderess-in-Chief; Al Fresco; The Knot of Blue; Bandanna Land.

MISS DOLLY DOLLARS
Opened: Sept. 4, 1905.
56 *performances.*
BOOK & LYRICS BY HARRY B. SMITH.

Cast included: Lulu Glaser, Melville Stewart, Carter DeHaven, Elsie Ferguson, Ralph Herz.
Principal songs: A Woman Is Only a Woman but a Good Cigar Is a Smoke; An American Heiress.

WONDERLAND
Opened: Oct. 24, 1905.
73 *performances.*
BOOK & LYRICS BY GLEN MACDONOUGH.

Cast included: Sam Chip, Lotta Faust, Eva Davenport, Bessie Wynn.
Principal songs: The Nature Class; Love's Golden Day; The Only One.

MLLE. MODISTE
Opened: Dec. 25, 1905.
202 *performances.*
BOOK & LYRICS BY HENRY BLOSSOM.

Cast included: Fritzi Scheff, William Pruette, Walter Percival, Claude Gillingwater.
Principal songs: Kiss Me Again; The Time, the Place and the Girl; When the Cat's Away; I Want What I Want When I Want It; The Mascot of the Troop.

THE RED MILL
Opened: Sept. 24, 1906.
274 *performances.*
BOOK & LYRICS BY HENRY BLOSSOM.

Cast included: Fred Stone, David Montgomery, Augusta Greenleaf, Joseph Ratliff.
Principal songs: The Isle of Our Dreams; When You're Pretty and the World Is Fair; Everyday Is Ladies' Day with Me; The Streets of New York; Because You're You; Moonbeams.

Recorded Versions
Decca DL 8458 (S.C.)
Capitol T 551 (S.C.)
Eileen Farrell, Wilbur Evans, and Felix Knight are featured in six selections on the Decca album. In addition to its being coupled on the LP with *Babes In Toyland*, this version is also available on the same record with Romberg's *Up in Central Park* (Decca DL 8016). Capitol's release with Gordon MacRae offers much more of the music, and has Herbert's *Naughty Marietta* on the reverse.

DREAM CITY AND THE MAGIC KNIGHT
Opened: Dec. 25, 1906.
102 *performances.*
BOOK & LYRICS BY EDGAR SMITH.

Cast included: Joe Weber, Otis Harlan, Cecilia Loftus.
Principal songs: I Don't Believe I'll Ever Be a Lady; In Vaudeville; Nancy, I Fancy You.

THE TATTOOED MAN
Opened: Feb. 18, 1907.

59 *performances.*
BOOK BY HARRY B. SMITH & A.N.C. FOWLER;
LYRICS BY HARRY B. SMITH.

Cast included: Frank Daniels, Sallie Fisher,
Herbert Waterous, Harry Clarke, May Vokes.
Principal songs: Boys Will Be Boys and Girls
Will Be Girls; The Land of Dreams; Nobody
Loves Me.

ALGERIA
Opened: Aug. 31, 1908.
48 *performances.*
BOOK & LYRICS BY GLEN MacDONOUGH.

Cast included: Ida Brooks Hunt, William
Pruette, George Marion, George Leon Moore,
Harriet Burt.
Principal songs: Rose of the World; Twilight
in Barakeesh; Love Is like a Cigarette; Ask
Her While the Band Is Playing.

LITTLE NEMO
Opened: Oct. 20, 1908.
111 *performances.*
BOOK & LYRICS BY HARRY B. SMITH.

Cast included: Joseph Cawthorn, Billy B.
Van, Harry Kelly, Master Gabriel, Florence
Tempest.
Principal songs: Won't You Be My Valen-
tine?; The Happy Land of Once-upon-a-
Time; In Happy Slumberland.

THE PRIMA DONNA
Opened: Nov. 30, 1908.
72 *performances.*
BOOK & LYRICS BY HENRY BLOSSOM.

Cast included: Fritzi Scheff, William Raymond, William K. Harcourt, St. Clair Bay-
field.
Principal songs: I'll Be Married to the Music
of a Military Band; A Soldier's Love; Espag-
nola; If You Were I and I Were You.

THE ROSE OF ALGERIA
(revised version of *Algeria*)
Opened: Sept. 20, 1909.
40 *performances.*
BOOK & LYRICS BY GLEN MacDONOUGH.

Cast included: Lillian Herlein, Eugene
Cowles, Anna Wheaton, Frank Pollock.
Principal songs: Same as *Algeria.*

OLD DUTCH
Opened: Nov. 22, 1909.
88 *performances.*

BOOK BY EDGAR SMITH; LYRICS BY GEORGE
V. HOBART.

Cast included: Lew Fields, Alice Dovey, Ada
Lewis, Charles Judels, John Bunny, Eva
Davenport, Vernon Castle, John E. Henshaw,
William Raymond, Helen Hayes.
Principal songs: I Want a Man to Love Me;
Climb, Climb.

NAUGHTY MARIETTA
Opened Nov. 7, 1910.
136 *performances.*
BOOK & LYRICS BY RIDA JOHNSON YOUNG.

Cast included: Emma Trentini, Orville Har-
rold, Edward Martindel, Marie Duchene,
Peggy Wood.
Principal songs: Tramp! Tramp! Tramp!;
Naughty Marietta; 'Neath the Southern
Moon; Italian Street Song; I'm Falling in
Love with Someone; Ah! Sweet Mystery of
Life.

Recorded Version
Capitol T 551 (S.C.)
Gordon MacRae & Marguerite Piazza are
starred in arias from Herbert's celebrated
score. Selections from *The Red Mill* are on
the reverse.

WHEN SWEET SIXTEEN
Opened: Sept. 14, 1911.
12 *performances.*
BOOK & LYRICS BY GEORGE V. HOBART.

Cast included: Harriet Standon, Josie Intro-
pidi, Roy Purviance, Frank Belcher, William
Norris.
Principal songs: The Wild Rose; In the
Golden Long Ago.

THE DUCHESS
Opened: Oct. 16, 1911.
24 *performances.*
BOOK BY JOSEPH HERBERT; LYRICS BY JOSEPH
HERBERT & HARRY B. SMITH.
Cast included: Fritzi Scheff, George Ander-
son, John E. Hazzard, May Boley.
Principal songs: Cupid, Tell Me Why; The
Land of Sultans' Dreams; It's the Bump.

THE ENCHANTRESS
Opened: Oct. 19, 1911.
72 *performances.*
BOOK BY FRED DeGRESAC; LYRICS BY HARRY
B. SMITH.

Cast included: Kitty Gordon, Ralph Riggs, Harold Forde.
Principal songs: To the Land of My Own Romance; Rose, Lucky Rose; All Your Own Am I; They All Look Good When They're Far Away.

THE LADY OF THE SLIPPER
Opened: Oct. 28, 1912.
232 performances.
BOOK BY ANNE CALDWELL & LAWRENCE MCCARTY; LYRICS BY JAMES O'DEA.

Cast included: Fred Stone, David Montgomery, Elsie Janis, Vernon Castle, Queenie Vassar, Peggy Wood, Allene Crater, Douglas Stevenson, Vivian Rushmore.
Principal songs: Bagdad; Meow! Meow! Meow!; Punch Bowl Glide; Drums of All Nations.

SWEETHEARTS
Opened: Sept. 8, 1913.
136 performances.
BOOK BY HARRY B. SMITH & FRED DEGRESAC; LYRICS BY ROBERT B. SMITH.

Cast included: Christie MacDonald, Thomas Conkey, Tom McNaughton, Edwin Wilson.
Principal songs: Sweethearts; Angelus; Every Lover Must Meet His Fate; Jeannette and Her Little Wooden Shoes; Pretty As a Picture; The Cricket on the Hearth.

Recorded Version
RCA Camden CAL 369 (S.C.)
With Al Goodman conducting, soloists sing six numbers from the original production, plus "To the Land of My Own Romance" and "I Might Be Your Once-in-a-While."

THE MADCAP DUCHESS
Opened: Nov. 11, 1913.
71 performances.
BOOK & LYRICS BY DAVID STEVENS & JUSTIN MCCARTHY.

Cast included: Ann Swinburne, Glenn Hall, Josephine Whittell, Peggy Wood, Harry Macdonough.
Principal songs: Aurora Blushing Rosily; Love and I Are Playing; The Deuce, Young Man; Goddess of Mine.

THE ONLY GIRL
Opened: Nov. 2, 1914.
240 performances.

BOOK & LYRICS BY HENRY BLOSSOM.
Cast included: Thurston Hall, Wilda Bennett, Jed Prouty, Ernest Torrence, Adele Rowland.
Principal songs: When You're Away; Tell It All over Again; You're the Only Girl for Me; Personality; When You're Wearing the Ball and Chain.

THE DEBUTANTE
Opened: Dec. 7, 1914.
48 performances.
BOOK BY HARRY B. SMITH; LYRICS BY ROBERT B. SMITH.

Cast included: Hazel Dawn, Wilmuth Merkyl, Zoe Barnett, Robert G. Pitkin, William Danforth.
Principal songs: All for the Sake of a Girl; The Golden Age; The Love of the Lorelei; The Springtime of Life.

THE PRINCESS PAT
Opened: Sept. 29, 1915.
158 performances.
BOOK & LYRICS BY HENRY BLOSSOM.

Cast included: Eleanor Painter, Joseph R. Lertora, Al Shean, Eva Fallon, Robert Ober, Doris Kenyon.
Principal songs: Love Is the Best of All; Neapolitan Love Song; All for You; Two Laughing Irish Eyes.

THE CENTURY GIRL
Opened: Nov. 6, 1916.
200 performances.
MUSIC ALSO BY IRVING BERLIN; HERBERT LYRICS BY HENRY BLOSSOM.

Cast included: Hazel Dawn, Sam Bernard, Leon Errol, Elsie Janis, Harry Kelly, Gus Van & Joe Schenck, Frank Tinney, John Slavin, Lillian Tashman, Irving Fisher, James Doyle & Harland Dixon, Maurice & Walton.
Principal Herbert songs: You Belong to Me; When Uncle Sam Is Ruler of the Sea.

EILEEN
Opened: Mar. 19, 1917.
64 performances.
BOOK & LYRICS BY HENRY BLOSSOM.

Cast included: Walter Scanlan, Greek Evans, Edward Martindel, Olga Roller, Grace Breen.
Principal songs: Free Trade and a Misty Moon; When Shall I Again See Ireland; When Love Awakes; Thine Alone; The Irish

Have a Great Day Tonight; Eileen Alanna Asthore.

Recorded Version
RCA Camden CAL 210 (S.C.) X.

Six pieces from Herbert's own favorite score are heard on one side of the LP; the other side is devoted to music from *Polonaise*.

MISS 1917
Opened: Nov. 5, 1917.
48 *performances.*
MUSIC ALSO BY JEROME KERN; SKETCHES BY GUY BOLTON & P. G. WODEHOUSE; LYRICS BY WODEHOUSE.

Cast included: Lew Fields, Cecil Lean, Cleo Mayfield, Vivienne Segal, Andrew Tombes, Harry Kelly, Elizabeth Brice, Marion Davies, Charles King, Peggy Hopkins, Bessie McCoy Davis, Gus Van & Joe Schenck, Irene Castle, Lilyan Tashman, George White, Ann Pennington, Bert Savoy, Emma Haig, Herbert Fields.
Principal Herbert song: The Society Farmerettes.

HER REGIMENT
Opened: Nov. 12, 1917.
40 *performances.*
BOOK & LYRICS BY WILLIAM LeBARON.

Cast included: Donald Brian, Audrey Maple, Hugh Chilvers, Frank Moulan, Josie Intropidi.
Principal songs: Soldier Men; 'Twixt Love and Duty.

THE VELVET LADY
Opened: Feb. 3, 1919.
136 *performances.*
BOOK & LYRICS BY HENRY BLOSSOM.

Cast included: Fay Marbe, Alfred Gerrard, Ray Redmond, Ernest Torrence, Georgia O'Ramey, Jed Prouty, Eddie Dowling, Minerva Coverdale, Marie Flynn.
Principal songs: Life and Love; Fair Honeymoon; Spooky Ookum.

ANGEL FACE
Opened: Dec. 29, 1919.
57 *performances.*
BOOK BY HARRY B. SMITH; LYRICS BY ROBERT B. SMITH.

Cast included: Marguerite Zender, John E. Young, Tyler Brooks, Emilie Lea, George Schiller, Jack Donahue.

Principal songs: I Might Be Your Once-in-a-While; Someone like You; Lullaby.

MY GOLDEN GIRL
Opened: Feb. 2, 1920.
105 *performances.*
BOOK & LYRICS BY FREDERIC ARNOLD KUMMER.

Cast included: Victor Morley, Marie Carroll, Helen Bolton, George Trabert, Ned Sparks, Edna May Oliver.
Principal songs: Darby and Joan; I Want You; A Song without (Many) Words; Ragtime Terpsichore.

THE GIRL IN THE SPOTLIGHT
Opened: July 12, 1920.
56 *performances.*
BOOK & LYRICS BY RICHARD BRUCE (ROBERT B. SMITH).

Cast included: Mary Milburn, Johnny Dooley, Hal Skelly, John Reinhard.
Principal songs: I Cannot Sleep without Dreaming of You; I Love the Ground You Walk On.

ZIEGFELD FOLLIES
Opened: June 21, 1921.
119 *performances.*
MUSIC ALSO BY OTHERS; SKETCHES BY WILLARD MACK, RAYMOND HITCHCOCK & OTHERS; HERBERT LYRICS BY GENE BUCK.

Cast included: Gus Van & Joe Schenck, Fannie Brice, Raymond Hitchcock, Mary Milburn, W. C. Fields, Mary Eaton, Vera Michelena, Ray Dooley, Florence O'Denishawn, Channing Pollock, Consuelo Flowerton.
Principal Herbert songs: Princess of My Dreams; The Legend of the Golden Tree.

ORANGE BLOSSOMS
Opened: Sept. 19, 1922.
95 *performances.*
BOOK BY FRED DeGRESAC; LYRICS BY B. G. DeSYLVA.

Cast included: Edith Day, Queenie Smith, Hal Skelly, Robert Michaelis, Pat Somerset, Jack Whiting.
Principal songs: A Kiss in the Dark; This Time It's Love; The Lonely Nest; A Dream of Orange Blossoms.

ZIEGFELD FOLLIES
Opened: Oct. 20, 1923.
233 *performances.*
MUSIC ALSO BY OTHERS; SKETCHES BY EDDIE CANTOR & GENE BUCK; HERBERT LYRICS BY BUCK.

Cast included: Bert & Betty Wheeler, Fannie Brice, Brooke Johns, Harland Dixon, Lew Hearn, Olga Steck, Edna Leedom, Paul Whiteman Orchestra.
Principal Herbert songs: That Old-Fashioned Garden of Mine; I'd Love to Waltz through Life with You.

THE DREAM GIRL
Opened: Aug. 20, 1924.
117 *performances.*
BOOK & LYRICS BY RIDA JOHNSON YOUNG & HAROLD ATTERIDGE.

Cast included: Fay Bainter, Walter Woolf, George Lemaire, Billy B. Van, William O'Neal.
Principal songs: My Dream Girl; If Somebody Only Would Find Me; Bubble Song.

George M. Cohan

All music, books, and lyrics by Mr. Cohan unless otherwise noted.

THE GOVERNOR'S SON
Opened: Feb. 25, 1901.
32 *performances.*

Cast included: The Four Cohans, Ethel Levey.
Principal songs: Too Many Miles from Broadway; The Story of the Wedding March.

RUNNING FOR OFFICE
Opened: Apr. 27, 1903.
48 *performances.*

Cast included: The Four Cohans, Ethel Levey.
Principal songs: If I Were Only Mr. Morgan; I Want to Go to Paree, Papa.

LITTLE JOHNNY JONES
Opened: Nov. 7, 1904.
52 *performances.*

Cast included: George M. Cohan, Jerry Cohan, Helen Cohan, Ethel Levey, Donald Brian, Tom Lewis.
Principal songs: The Yankee Doodle Boy; Good-Bye Flo; Give My Regards to Broadway; Life's a Funny Proposition after All.

FORTY-FIVE MINUTES FROM BROADWAY
Opened: Jan. 1, 1906.
90 *performances.*

Cast included: Fay Templeton, Victor Moore, Donald Brian, Julia Ralph.
Principal songs: I Want to Be a Popular Millionaire; Mary's a Grand Old Name; So Long, Mary; Forty-Five Minutes from Broadway; Stand Up and Fight Like H---.

GEORGE WASHINGTON, JR.
Opened: Feb. 12, 1906.
81 *performances.*

Cast included: George M. Cohan, Jerry Cohan, Helen Cohan, Ethel Levey, Truly Shattuck.
Principal songs: You're a Grand Old Flag; I Was Born in Virginia; All Aboard for Broadway; If Washington Should Come to Life.

THE HONEYMOONERS
(revised version of *Running for Office*)
Opened: June 3, 1907.
167 *performances.*

Cast included: George M. Cohan, Jerry Cohan, Helen Cohan, Gertrude Hoffman.
Principal songs: I'm a Popular Man; If I'm Going to Die I'm Going to Have Some Fun; Nothing New Beneath the Sun.

THE TALK OF NEW YORK
Opened: Dec. 3, 1907.
157 *performances.*

Cast included: Victor Moore, Emma Littlefield, Gertrude Vanderbilt, Jack Gardner, Rosie Green.
Principal songs: When We Are M-A-Double R-I-E-D; When a Fellow's on the Level with a Girl That's on the Square; I Want the World to Know I Love You; I Want You; Under Any Old Flag at All.

FIFTY MILES FROM BOSTON
Opened: Feb. 3, 1908.
32 *performances.*

Cast included: Edna Wallace Hopper, Lawrence Wheat, Emma Janvier, George Parsons.

Principal songs: Harrigan; A Small Town Girl.

THE YANKEE PRINCE
Opened: Apr. 20, 1908.
28 performances.

Cast included: The Four Cohans, Tom Lewis, Stella Hammerstein, Jack Gardner, Donald Crisp.
Principal songs: Come on Down Town; I'm to Marry a Nobleman; The ABC's of the U.S.A.

THE AMERICAN IDEA
Opened: Oct. 5, 1908.
64 performances.

Cast included: George Beban, Gertrude Vanderbilt, Stella Hammerstein, Trixie Friganza, Rosie Green.
Principal songs: Too Long from Longacre Square; That's Some Love; F-A-M-E.

THE MAN WHO OWNS BROADWAY
Opened: Oct. 11, 1909.
128 performances.

Cast included: Raymond Hitchcock, Flora Zabelle, Stanley Forde.
Principal songs: There's Something about a Uniform; The Man Who Owns Broadway.

THE LITTLE MILLIONAIRE
Opened: Sept. 25, 1911.
192 performances.

Cast included: George M. Cohan, Jerry Cohan, Helen Cohan, Tom Lewis, George Parsons, Donald Crisp.
Principal songs: Barnum Had the Right Idea; Any Place the Old Flag Flies; Oh, You Wonderful Girl.

HELLO BROADWAY!
Opened: Dec. 25, 1914.
123 performances.

Cast included: George M. Cohan, William Collier, Louise Dresser, Peggy Wood, Lawrence Wheat, Rozsika Dolly, Florence Moore.
Principal songs: Hello, Broadway; My Flag.

THE COHAN REVUE 1916
Opened: Feb. 9, 1916.
165 performances.

Cast included: Elizabeth Murray, Fred Santley, Charles Winninger, Valli Valli, Richard Carle, Harry Bulger.

Principal songs: It's a Long Way from Broadway to Edinboro Town; You Can Tell That I'm Irish; Julia, Donald & Joe.

THE COHAN REVUE 1918
Opened: Dec. 31, 1917.
96 performances.
MUSIC & LYRICS ALSO BY IRVING BERLIN.

Cast included: Nora Bayes, Charles Winninger, Irving Fisher, Fred Santley.
Principal Cohan songs: The Eyes of Youth See the Truth; Their Hearts Are over Here.

THE VOICE OF McCONNELL
Opened: Dec. 25, 1918.
30 performances.

Cast included: Chauncey Olcott, Arthur Shields.
Principal songs: Ireland, the Land of My Dreams; When I Look in Your Eyes, Mavourneen.

THE ROYAL VAGABOND
Opened: Feb. 17, 1919.
208 performances
MUSIC ALSO BY ANSELM GOETZL; BOOK BY STEPHEN IVOR SZINNYEY; GOETZL LYRICS BY WILLIAM CARY DUNCAN.

Cast included: Tessa Kosta, Fred Santley, Mary Eaton, Dorothy Dickson, Carl Hyson.
Principal Cohan songs: Opera, Comic Opera; In a Kingdom of Our Own.

LITTLE NELLIE KELLY
Opened: Nov. 13, 1922.
276 performances.

Cast included: Elizabeth Hines, Robert Pitkin, Georgia Caine, Charles King, Arthur Deagon, Frank Parker.
Principal songs: You Remind Me of My Mother; Till My Luck Comes Rolling Along; Nellie Kelly, I Love You.

THE RISE OF ROSIE O'REILLY
Opened: Dec. 25, 1923.
87 performances.

Cast included: Virginia O'Brien, Jack McGowan, George Bancroft, Mary Lawlor, Emma Haig, Georgie Hale, Margaret Dumont, Bobby Watson.
Principal songs: Born and Bred in Brooklyn; When June Comes Along with a Song; Let's You and I Say Goodbye.

THE MERRY MALONES
Opened: Sept. 26, 1927.
208 *performances.*

Cast included: George M. Cohan, Polly Walker, Alan Edwards, Robinson Newbold.
Principal songs: Molly Malone; God's Good to the Irish; Like a Wandering Minstrel.

BILLIE
Opened: Oct. 1, 1928.
112 *performances.*

Cast included: Polly Walker, Robinson Newbold, Joseph Wagstaff, June O'Dea.
Principal songs: Every Boy in Town's My Sweetheart; Where Were You, Where Was I?; Billie.

Rudolf Friml

THE FIREFLY
Opened: Dec. 2, 1912.
120 *performances.*
BOOK & LYRICS BY OTTO HAUERBACH.

Cast included: Emma Trentini, Roy Atwell, Melville Stewart, Sammy Lee.
Principal songs: Giannina Mia; When a Maid Comes Knocking at Your Heart; Love Is like a Firefly; Sympathy.

HIGH JINKS
Opened: Dec. 10, 1913.
213 *performances.*
BOOK & LYRICS BY OTTO HAUERBACH.

Cast included: Elaine Hammerstein, Robert Pitkin, Mana Zucca, Tom Lewis, Elizabeth Murray.
Principal songs: Love's Own Kiss; Not Now but Later; The Bubble; Something Seems Tingle-ing-eling.

THE PEASANT GIRL
Opened: Mar. 2, 1915.
111 *performances.*
MUSIC ALSO BY OSKAR NEDBAL; BOOK BY EDGAR SMITH; LYRICS BY HERBERT REYNOLDS (M. E. ROURKE) & HAROLD ATTERIDGE.

Cast included: Emma Trentini, Clifton Crawford, Ernest Hare, John Charles Thomas.
Principal Friml songs: Listen, Dear; Love Is like a Butterfly; The Flame of Love.

KATINKA
Opened: Dec. 23, 1915.
220 *performances.*
BOOK & LYRICS BY OTTO HAUERBACH.

Cast included: Adele Rowland, Franklyn Ardell, A. Robbins, Count Lorrie Grimaldi, T. Roy Barnes.
Principal songs: 'Tis the End So Farewell; Allah's Holiday; Rackety Coo; My Paradise.

YOU'RE IN LOVE
Opened: Feb. 6, 1917.
167 *performances.*
BOOK & LYRICS BY OTTO HAUERBACH & EDWARD CLARK.

Cast included: Lawrence Wheat, Clarence Nordstrom, May Thompson, Harry Clarke.
Principal songs: I'm Only Dreaming; You're in Love.

KITTY DARLIN'
Opened: Nov. 7, 1917.
14 *performances*
BOOK BY OTTO HAUERBACH; LYRICS BY HAUERBACH & P. G. WODEHOUSE.

Cast included: Alice Nielsen, Glen Hall, Jackson Hines.
Principal songs: When She Gives Him a Shamrock Bloom; The Land Where Dreams Come True; Dear Old Dublin.

SOMETIME
Opened: Oct. 4, 1918.
283 *performances.*
BOOK & LYRICS BY RIDA JOHNSON YOUNG.

Cast included: Ed Wynn, Francine Larrimore, Mae West.
Principal songs: Sometime; Spanish Maid; The Tune You Can't Forget; Keep on Smiling.

GLORIANNA
Opened: Oct. 28, 1918.
96 *performances.*
BOOK & LYRICS BY CATHERINE CHISHOLM CUSHING.

Cast included: Eleanor Painter, Alexander Clark.
Principal songs: When a Girl; Toodle-oo; My Climbing Rose.

TUMBLE IN
Opened: Mar. 24, 1919.
128 *performances.*
BOOK & LYRICS BY OTTO HAUERBACH.

Cast included: Peggy O'Neil, Charles Ruggles, Zelda Sears.
Principal songs: The Thoughts I Wrote on the Leaves of My Heart; I've Told My Love; Snuggle and Dream.

THE LITTLE WHOPPER
Opened: Oct. 13, 1919.
224 *performances.*
BOOK BY OTTO HARBACH; LYRICS BY BIDE DUDLEY & HARBACH.

Cast included: Vivienne Segal, David Torrence, Harry C. Browne, Sydney Grant.
Principal songs: You'll Dream and I'll Dream; 'Round the Corner; Oh! What a Little Whopper.

JUNE LOVE
Opened: Apr. 25, 1921.
50 *performances.*
BOOK BY OTTO HARBACH & W. H. POST; LYRICS BY BRIAN HOOKER.

Cast included: Else Alder, Clarence Nordstrom, Johnny Dooley, W. B. Davidson.
Principal songs: Dear Love, My Love; June Love; The Flapper and the Vamp.

ZIEGFELD FOLLIES
Opened: June 21, 1921.
119 *performances.*
MUSIC ALSO BY OTHERS; SKETCHES BY WILLARD MACK, RAYMOND HITCHCOCK & OTHERS; FRIML LYRICS BY BUD DESYLVA, GENE BUCK, BRIAN HOOKER.

Cast included: Gus Van & Joe Schenck, Fannie Brice, Raymond Hitchcock, Mary Milburn, W. C. Fields, Mary Eaton, Vera Michelena, Ray Dooley, Florence O'Denishawn, Channing Pollock, Consuelo Flowerton.
Principal Friml song: Bring Back My Blushing Rose.

THE BLUE KITTEN
Opened: Jan. 13, 1922.
140 *performances.*
BOOK & LYRICS BY OTTO HARBACH & WILLIAM CARY DUNCAN.

Cast included: Joseph Cawthorn, Lorraine Manville, Victor Morley, Robert Woolsey, Lillian Lorraine, Marion Sunshine, Douglas Stevenson.
Principal songs: Cutie; I Found a Bud among the Roses; Blue Kitten Blues.

CINDERS
Opened: Apr. 3, 1923.
31 *performances.*
BOOK & LYRICS BY EDWARD CLARK.

Cast included: Queenie Smith, Nancy Welford, Jack Whiting, Douglas Stevenson, George Bancroft, Margaret Dale.
Principal songs: Cinders; One Good Time.

ROSE-MARIE
Opened: Sept. 2, 1924.
557 *performances.*
MUSIC ALSO BY HERBERT STOTHART; BOOK & LYRICS BY OTTO HARBACH & OSCAR HAMMERSTEIN II.

Cast included: Mary Ellis, Dennis King, William Kent, Edward Ciannelli, Dorothy Mackaye, Pearl Regay, Arthur Deagon.
Principal Friml songs: Rose-Marie; The Mounties; Indian Love Call; Totem Tom-Tom; The Door of My Dreams.

Recorded Versions
RCA Victor LOP 1001 / LSO 1001 (S.C.).
MGM E 3769 (F.V.) (1954).
Pathé 30146 (French S.C.).
On the RCA release, Julie Andrews and Giorgio Tozzi star in the only complete version of the enduring score. The sound-track LP, with Howard Keel, Ann Blyth and Fernando Lamas, has only three songs from the original production. It is backed by a sound-track of dePaul's & Mercer's *Seven Brides for Seven Brothers.* The French recording, backed by Youmans' *No, No, Nanette,* contains ten selections, all well sung.

THE VAGABOND KING
Opened: Sept. 21, 1925.
511 *performances.*
BOOK & LYRICS BY BRIAN HOOKER & W. H. POST.

Cast included: Dennis King, Carolyn Thomson, Max Figman.
Principal songs: Song of the Vagabonds; Some Day; Only a Rose; Huguette Waltz; Love Me Tonight; Nocturne.

Recorded Versions
RCA Victor LM 2004 (F.V.) (1956).
Capitol T 219 (S.C.).
Decca DL 8362 (S.C.).
Oreste & Jean Fenn (who was not in the film) cover most of the swashbuckling & romantic airs on the RCA release. Capitol's, featuring Gordon MacRae, is backed by *The*

New Moon (Romberg), while Decca's, with Alfred Drake and Mimi Benzell, is paired with *The Student Prince* (Romberg).

NO FOOLIN'
Opened: June 24, 1926.
(Title changed during run to *Ziegfeld's American Revue of 1926*)
108 *performances.*
MUSIC ALSO BY JAMES HANLEY; SKETCHES BY J. P. McEVOY & JAMES BARTON; LYRICS BY GENE BUCK & IRVING CAESAR.

Cast included: James Barton, Charles King, Andrew Tombes, Ray Dooley, Irving Fisher, Arthur "Bugs" Baer, Moran & Mack, Barbara Newberry, Louise Brown, Edna Leedom, Polly Walker, Peggy Fears, Claire Luce, Paulette Goddard.
Principal Friml songs: Florida, the Moon and You; Wasn't It Nice?

THE WILD ROSE
Opened: Oct. 20, 1926.
61 *performances.*
BOOK & LYRICS BY OTTO HARBACH & OSCAR HAMMERSTEIN II.

Cast included: William Collier, Desirée Ellinger, Joseph Santley, Joseph Macaulay, Gus Shy, Inez Courtney, Nana Bryant, Fuller Mellish.
Principal songs: Brown Eyes; Wild Rose; One Golden Hour; We'll Have a Kingdom.

THE WHITE EAGLE
Opened: Dec. 26, 1927.
48 *performances.*
BOOK & LYRICS BY BRIAN HOOKER & W. H. POST.

Cast included: Allan Prior, Marion Keeler, Jay Fassett.
Principal songs: Give Me One Hour; Gather the Rose; Regimental Song.

THE THREE MUSKETEERS
Opened: Mar. 13, 1928.
319 *performances.*
BOOK BY WILLIAM ANTHONY McGUIRE; LYRICS BY P. G. WODEHOUSE & CLIFFORD GREY.

Cast included: Dennis King, Vivienne Segal, Lester Allen, Yvonne D'Arle, Douglass Dumbrille, Detmar Poppen, Louis Hector, Reginald Owen, Clarence Derwent, Harriet Hoctor.

Principal songs: March of the Musketeers; Ma Belle; Your Eyes.

LUANA
Opened: Sept. 17, 1930.
21 *performances.*
BOOK BY HOWARD EMMETT ROGERS; LYRICS BY J. KEIRN BRENNAN.
Cast included: Ruth Altman, Joseph Macaulay, Donald Novis, Lillian Bond, Robert Chisholm, Doris Carson, Sally Rand.
Principal songs: Luana; My Bird of Paradise.

MUSIC HATH CHARMS
Opened: Dec. 29, 1934.
29 *performances.*
BOOK BY ROWLAND LEIGH & GEORGE ROSENER; LYRICS BY LEIGH & JOHN SHUBERT.
Cast included: Natalie Hall, Robert Halliday, Andrew Tombes, Paul Haakon, Constance Carpenter, William Kent.
Principal songs: My Palace of Dreams; It's You I Want to Love Tonight; My Heart Is Yours.

Sigmund Romberg

THE WHIRL OF THE WORLD
Opened: Jan. 10, 1914.
161 *performances.*
SKETCHES & LYRICS BY HAROLD ATTERIDGE.
Cast included: Lillian Lorraine, Bernard Granville, Ralph Herz, Eugene & Willie Howard, Walter C. Kelly, Rozsika Dolly.
Principal songs: Ragtime Arabian Nights; My Cleopatra Girl; Life Is Just a Dress Parade.

THE PASSING SHOW OF 1914
Opened: June 10, 1914.
133 *performances.*
MUSIC ALSO BY HARRY CARROLL; SKETCHES & LYRICS BY HAROLD ATTERIDGE.
Cast included: Bernard Granville, Jose Collins, Marilynn Miller, Bessie Crawford, Robert Emmett Keane, Lew Brice.
Principal Romberg songs: Omar Khayyam; Dreams of the Past.

DANCING AROUND
Opened: Oct. 10, 1914.
145 *performances.*
MUSIC ALSO BY HARRY CARROLL; SKETCHES & LYRICS BY HAROLD ATTERIDGE.

Cast included: Bernard Granville, James Doyle & Harland Dixon, Al Jolson, Clifton Webb, Cecil Cunningham, Melville Ellis.
Principal Romberg songs: My Lady of the Telephone; He Is Sweet, He Is Good.

MAID IN AMERICA
Opened: Feb. 18, 1915.
108 *performances.*
MUSIC ALSO BY HARRY CARROLL; SKETCHES & LYRICS BY HAROLD ATTERIDGE.

Cast included: Mlle. Dazie, Blossom Seeley, Harry Carroll, Harry Fox, Hal Forde, Lew Brice, Nora Bayes, Joe Jackson, Yansci Dolly, Yvette.
Principal Romberg songs: Sister Susie Started Syncopation; It's All for You; Oh, Those Days.

HANDS UP
Opened: July 22, 1915.
52 *performances.*
BOOK BY EDGAR SMITH; LYRICS BY E. RAY GOETZ.

Cast included: George Hassell, Alice Dovey, Irene Franklin, Ralph Herz, Will Rogers, A. Robbins, Maurice & Walton.
Principal songs: Orange Blossom Time in San José; Cling a Little Closer.

THE BLUE PARADISE
Opened: Aug. 5, 1915.
356 *performances.*
MUSIC ALSO BY EDMUND EYSLER; BOOK BY EDGAR SMITH; LYRICS BY HERBERT REYNOLDS (M. E. ROURKE).

Cast included: Cecil Lean, Cleo Mayfield, Vivienne Segal, Robert Pitkin, Ted Lorraine, Frances Demarest.
Principal Romberg songs: Auf Wiedersehn; One Step into Love; My Model Girl.

A WORLD OF PLEASURE
Opened: Oct. 14, 1915.
116 *performances.*
SKETCHES & LYRICS BY HAROLD ATTERIDGE.

Cast included: Kitty Gordon, Stella Mayhew, Clifton Crawford, Lew Holtz, Dan Healy, Sydney Greenstreet, Venita Fitzhugh, Sahari Djeli.
Principal songs: I Could Go Home to a Girlie like You; The Ragtime Pipe of Pan; Fascination.

ROBINSON CRUSOE, JR.
Opened: Feb. 17, 1916.
130 *performances.*
MUSIC ALSO BY JAMES HANLEY; BOOK & LYRICS BY HAROLD ATTERIDGE & EDGAR SMITH.

Cast included: Al Jolson, Barry Lupino, Kitty Doner.
Principal Romberg songs: Robinson Crusoe; When You're Starring in the Movies; Minstrel Days.

THE PASSING SHOW OF 1916
Opened: June 22, 1916.
140 *performances.*
MUSIC ALSO BY OTTO MOTZAN; SKETCHES & LYRICS BY HAROLD ATTERIDGE.

Cast included: Ed Wynn, Herman Timberg, James Hussey, Frances Demarest, Florence Moore.
Principal Romberg songs: Ragging the Apache; Sweet and Pretty.

THE GIRL FROM BRAZIL
Opened: Aug. 30, 1916.
61 *performances.*
MUSIC ALSO BY ROBERT WINTERBERG; BOOK BY EDGAR SMITH; LYRICS BY MATTHEW WOODWARD.

Cast included: Maude Odell, George Hassell, Hal Forde, Frances Demarest.
Principal Romberg songs: Stolen Kisses; Come Back Sweet Dream; My Senorita.

THE SHOW OF WONDERS
Opened: Oct. 26, 1916.
209 *performances.*
MUSIC ALSO BY OTTO MOTZAN & HERMAN TIMBERG; SKETCHES & LYRICS BY HAROLD ATTERIDGE.

Cast included: Willie & Eugene Howard, Ernest Hare, Marilynn Miller, McIntyre & Heath, Lew Clayton, Walter C. Kelly, Sam White, John T. Murray.
Principal Romberg songs: When Pavlova Starts Buck and Winging; Bring Your Kisses to Me.

FOLLOW ME
Opened: Nov. 29, 1916.
78 *performances.*
BOOK UNCREDITED; LYRICS BY ROBERT B. SMITH.

Cast included: Anna Held, Edith Day, Paul Porcasi, Harry Tighe.
Principal songs: Follow Me; I Am True to Them All; I Want to Be Good but My Eyes Won't Let Me.

HER SOLDIER BOY
Opened: Dec. 6, 1916.
198 *performances.*
MUSIC ALSO BY EMMERICH KALMAN; BOOK & LYRICS BY RIDA JOHNSON YOUNG.

Cast included: Clifton Crawford, John Charles Thomas, Adele Rowland, Ralph J. Herbert.
Principal Romberg songs: Mother; All Alone in a City Full of Girls; I'd Be Happy Anywhere with You; Kiss Waltz.

THE PASSING SHOW OF 1917
Opened: Apr. 26, 1917.
196 *performances.*
MUSIC ALSO BY OTTO MOTZAN; SKETCHES & LYRICS BY HAROLD ATTERIDGE.

Cast included: DeWolf Hopper, Irene Franklin, Zeke Colvan, Yvette Rugel, Johnny Dooley, Tom Lewis, Jefferson de Angeles.
Principal Romberg songs: Won't You Send a Letter to Me?; The Willow Tree.

MAYTIME
Opened: Aug. 16, 1917.
492 *performances.*
BOOK & LYRICS BY RIDA JOHNSON YOUNG.

Cast included: Peggy Wood, Charles Purcell, Ralph J. Herbert, William Norris.
Principal songs: The Road to Paradise; Jump Jim Crow; Will You Remember?

DOING OUR BIT
Opened: Oct. 18, 1917.
130 *performances.*
MUSIC ALSO BY HERMAN TIMBERG; SKETCHES & LYRICS BY HAROLD ATTERIDGE.

Cast included: Ed Wynn, Frank Tinney, Duncan Sisters, James J. Corbett, Charles Judels, Ada Lewis, Herman Timberg, Sam Ash.
Principal Romberg songs: Doing My Bit; Hello, Miss Tango; For the Sake of Humanity.

OVER THE TOP
Opened: Nov. 28, 1917.
78 *performances.*

MUSIC ALSO BY HERMAN TIMBERG; BOOK BY PHILIP BARTHOLOMAE & HAROLD ATTERIDGE; LYRICS BY CHARLES MANNING & MATTHEW WOODWARD.

Cast included: Justine Johnstone, Mary Eaton, Ted Lorraine, Fred & Adele Astaire, Joe Laurie, T. Roy Barnes.
Principal Romberg songs: The Justine Johnstone Rag; Where Is the Language to Tell?; Galatéa.

SINBAD
Opened: Feb. 14, 1918.
164 *performances.*
MUSIC ALSO BY OTHERS; BOOK & ROMBERG LYRICS BY HAROLD ATTERIDGE.

Cast included: Al Jolson, Kitty Doner, Forrest Huff.
Principal Romberg songs: A Thousand and One Arabian Nights; The Rag Lad of Bagdad.

THE PASSING SHOW OF 1918
Opened: July 25, 1918.
124 *performances.*
MUSIC ALSO BY JEAN SCHWARTZ; SKETCHES & LYRICS BY HAROLD ATTERIDGE.

Cast included: Willie & Eugene Howard, George Hassell, Fred & Adele Astaire, Charles Ruggles, Frank Fay, Lou Clayton, Sam White, Nita Naldi.
Principal Romberg songs: Dress, Dress, Dress; My Baby-Talk Lady; Galli Curci Rag.

THE MELTING OF MOLLY
Opened: Dec. 30, 1918.
88 *performances.*
BOOK BY MARIA THOMPSON DAVIES & EDGAR SMITH; LYRICS BY CYRUS WOOD.

Cast included: Charles Purcell, Gladys Walton, Ted Lorraine.
Principal songs: Jazz All Your Troubles Away; Floating Down a Moonlight Stream; You Remember Me.

MONTE CRISTO, JR.
Opened: Feb. 12, 1919.
254 *performances.*
MUSIC ALSO BY JEAN SCHWARTZ; BOOK & LYRICS BY HAROLD ATTERIDGE.

Cast included: Charles Purcell, Ralph Herz, Chic Sale, Sam Ash, Rose Rolando, Clem Bevins, Tom Lewis.
Principal Romberg songs: Are You Stepping out Tonight?; Broadway Butterfly.

THE PASSING SHOW OF 1919
Opened: Oct. 23, 1919.
144 *performances.*
MUSIC ALSO BY JEAN SCHWARTZ; SKETCHES
& LYRICS BY HAROLD ATTERIDGE.

Cast included: James Barton, Charles Winninger, Blanche Ring, Reginald Denny, Walter Woolf.
Principal Romberg songs: So Long, Sing
Song; Dreamy Florence.

THE MAGIC MELODY
Opened: Nov. 11, 1919.
143 *performances.*
BOOK & LYRICS BY FREDERIC ARNOLD KUM-
MER.

Cast included: Charles Purcell, Fay Marbe,
Julia Deane, Carmel Myers, Flavia Arcaro,
Tom McNaughton.
Principal songs: The Little Church around
the Corner; Down by the Nile; Once upon a
Time.

POOR LITTLE RITZ GIRL
Opened: July 28, 1920.
119 *performances.*
MUSIC ALSO BY RICHARD RODGERS; BOOK BY
GEORGE CAMPBELL & LEW FIELDS; ROM-
BERG LYRICS BY ALEX GERBER; RODGERS
LYRICS BY LORENZ HART.

Cast included: Charles Purcell, Eleanor Griffith, Lulu McConnell, Andrew Tombes.
Principal Romberg songs: I Love to Say
Hello to the Girls; When I Found You; In
the Land of Yesterday.

LOVE BIRDS
Opened: Mar. 15, 1921.
105 *performances.*
BOOK BY EDGAR ALLAN WOOLF; LYRICS BY
BALLARD MACDONALD.

Cast included: Pat Rooney, Marion Bent,
Elizabeth Hines, Elizabeth Murray, Vincent
Lopez.
Principal songs: I Love to Go Swimmin' with
Wimmen; Is It Hard to Guess?; Two Little
Love Birds; Trousseau Incomplete.

BLOSSOM TIME
Opened: Sept. 29, 1921.
516 *performances.*
MUSIC BASED ON FRANZ SCHUBERT THEMES;
BOOK & LYRICS BY DOROTHY DONNELLY.

Cast included: Bertram Peacock, Olga Cook,
Howard Marsh, William Danforth, Roy
Cropper.
Principal songs: Song of Love; Tell Me
Daisy; Only One Love Ever Fills the Heart;
My Springtime Thou Art; Three Little
Maids.

BOMBO
Opened: Oct. 6, 1921.
219 *performances.*
MUSIC ALSO BY OTHERS; BOOK & ROMBERG
LYRICS BY HAROLD ATTERIDGE.

Cast included: Al Jolson, Forrest Huff, Janet
Adair.
Principal Romberg songs: Oh, Oh, Colum-
bus; In Old Granada; Jazza-Da-Dadoo.

THE BLUSHING BRIDE
Opened: Feb. 6, 1922.
144 *performances.*
BOOK & LYRICS BY CYRUS WOOD.

Cast included: Cecil Lean, Cleo Mayfield,
Tom Lewis, Clarence Nordstrom, Edythe
Baker.
Principal songs: Mister and Missus; Rosy
Posy.

THE ROSE OF STAMBOUL
Opened: Mar. 7, 1922.
111 *performances.*
MUSIC ALSO BY LEO FALL; BOOK & LYRICS
BY HAROLD ATTERIDGE.

Cast included: Tessa Kosta, Marion Green,
James Barton.
Principal Romberg songs: My Heart Is Call-
ing; Lovey Dove.

SPRINGTIME OF YOUTH
Opened: Oct. 26, 1922.
68 *performances.*
BOOK UNCREDITED; LYRICS BY HARRY B.
SMITH, CYRUS WOOD, MATTHEW WOOD-
WARD.

Cast included: Olga Steck, J. Harold Murray,
Harry K. Morton, George MacFarlane.
Principal songs: Starlight of Hope; Just like
a Doll.

THE DANCING GIRL
Opened: Jan. 24, 1923.
126 *performances.*
MUSIC ALSO BY ALFRED GOODMAN; BOOK &
LYRICS BY HAROLD ATTERIDGE.

Cast included: Trini, Marie Dressler, Jack
Pearl, Arthur Margetson, Edythe Baker, Lou
Holtz, Ted & Kitty Doner, Benny Leonard.
Principal Romberg songs: Cuddle Me as We
Dance; That Romance of Mine; Why Am I
Sad?

THE PASSING SHOW OF 1923
Opened: June 14, 1923.
118 *performances.*
MUSIC ALSO BY JEAN SCHWARTZ; SKETCHES
& MOST LYRICS BY HAROLD ATTERIDGE.

Cast included: George Hassell, Walter
Woolf, George Jessel, Barnett Parker, Helen
Shipman, Alex Morrison.
Principal Romberg songs: Lotus Flower;
Rose of the Morning.

INNOCENT EYES
Opened: May 20, 1924.
126 *performances.*
MUSIC ALSO BY JEAN SCHWARTZ; BOOK BY
HAROLD ATTERIDGE; LYRICS BY ATTERIDGE
& TOT SEYMOUR.

Cast included: Mistinguett, Cecil Lean, Cleo
Mayfield, Frances Williams, Lew Hearn,
Edythe Baker, Ted Doner, Vera Lavrova
(Baroness Michael Royce Garrett), Vanessi,
Jack Oakie, Lucille Le Sueur (Joan Craw-
ford).
Principal Romberg songs: Love Is like a Pin-
wheel; Day Dreams.

THE PASSING SHOW OF 1924
Opened: Sept. 3, 1924.
106 *performances.*
MUSIC ALSO BY JEAN SCHWARTZ; SKETCHES
BY HAROLD ATTERIDGE; LYRICS BY ATTER-
IDGE & ALEX GERBER.

Cast included: James Barton, George Hassell,
Allan Prior, Lulu McConnell, Olga Cook,
Harry McNaughton, Lucille Le Sueur (Joan
Crawford).
Principal songs: When Knighthood Was in
Flower; Dublinola.

ARTISTS AND MODELS OF 1924
Opened: Oct. 15, 1924.
261 *performances.*
MUSIC ALSO BY J. FRED COOTS; SKETCHES
MOSTLY BY HARRY WAGSTAFF GRIBBLE;
LYRICS BY SAM COSLOW & CLIFFORD GREY.

Cast included: Trini, Frank Gaby, Barnett
Parker, Mabel Withee.

Principal songs: Tomorrow's Another Day;
Take Me Back to Samoa Some More.

ANNIE DEAR
Opened: Nov. 4, 1924.
103 *performances.*
MUSIC ALSO BY CLARE KUMMER; BOOK BY
MRS. KUMMER; ROMBERG LYRICS BY CLIF-
FORD GREY.

Cast included: Billie Burke, Ernest Truex,
Jack Whiting, Alexander Gray, Marion
Green, Spencer Charters, Bobby Watson,
May Vokes, Gavin Gordon, Catherine Little-
field.
Principal Romberg songs: Whisper to Me;
One Man Is like Another.

THE STUDENT PRINCE IN HEIDELBERG
Opened: Dec. 2, 1924.
608 *performances.*
BOOK & LYRICS BY DOROTHY DONNELLY.

Cast included: Howard Marsh, Ilse Mar-
venga, Greek Evans, George Hassell, Fuller
Mellish, Violet Carlson.
Principal songs: Golden Days; Drinking
Song; Deep in My Heart, Dear; Serenade;
Just We Two.

Recorded Versions
Columbia CL 826 (S.C.).
RCA Victor LM 2339 / LSC 2339 (F.V.)
(1954).
Capitol T 437 (S.C.).
Decca DL 8362 (S.C.).
Columbia ML 4060 (S.C.).
Romberg's melodic score is given an excel-
lent aural production in the first Columbia
release, starring Dorothy Kirsten and Robert
Rounseville. The RCA LP features Mario
Lanza and includes additional songs from the
1954 film. Capitol's (Gordon MacRae) has
Lehár's *The Merry Widow* on the reverse;
Decca's (Lauritz Melchior) is coupled with
Friml's *The Vagabond King;* the second
Columbia (Risë Stevens, Nelson Eddy)
shares the record with Straus's *The Chocolate
Soldier.*

LOUIE THE 14TH
Opened: Mar. 3, 1925.
319 *performances.*
BOOK & LYRICS BY ARTHUR WIMPERIS.

Cast included: Leon Errol, Doris Patston,
Ethel Shutta, Kathleen Doucet, Evelyn Law,

Catherine Littlefield, Lucy Monroe, Peggy Fears.
Principal songs: Little Peach; Homeland.

PRINCESS FLAVIA
Opened: Nov. 2, 1925.
152 *performances.*
BOOK & LYRICS BY HARRY B. SMITH.

Cast included: Harry Welchman, Evelyn Herbert, John Clarke, Joseph C. Spurin (Joseph Calleia), William Danforth, Alois Havrilla, Douglass Dumbrille, Margaret Breen, Maude Odell.
Principal songs: What Do I Care?; Only One; I Love Them All; I Dare Not Love You; Twilight Voices.

THE DESERT SONG
Opened: Nov. 30, 1926.
465 *performances.*
BOOK BY OTTO HARBACH, OSCAR HAMMERSTEIN II, FRANK MANDEL; LYRICS BY HARBACH & HAMMERSTEIN.

Cast included: Robert Halliday, Vivienne Segal, Eddie Buzzell, William O'Neal, Pearl Regay, Nellie Breen, Margaret Irving.
Principal songs: Riff Song; French Military Marching Song; Romance; I Want a Kiss; The Desert Song; One Flower Grows Alone in Your Garden; One Alone.

Recorded Versions
Columbia CL 831 (S.C.).
RCA Victor LOP 1000/LSO 1000 (S. C.).
RCA Victor LM 2440/LSC (S.C.).
Capitol T 384 (S.C.).
The Columbia and the first RCA versions are almost identical in content, and both are conducted by Lehman Engel. However, the singing on the former (Nelson Eddy, Doretta Morrow) is preferable to that on the latter (Giorgio Tozzi, Kathy Barr). The second RCA recording features Mario Lanza. Capitol's release (Gordon MacRae) has Jerome Kern's *Roberta* on the reverse.

CHERRY BLOSSOMS
Opened: Mar. 28, 1927.
56 *performances.*
BOOK & LYRICS BY HARRY B. SMITH.

Cast included: Desirée Ellinger, Howard Marsh, Bernard Gorcey, Gladys Baxter.
Principal songs: 'Neath the Cherry Blossom Moon; Tell Me Cigarette; Wait and See.

MY MARYLAND
Opened: Sept. 12, 1927.
312 *performances.*
BOOK & LYRICS BY DOROTHY DONNELLY.

Cast included: Evelyn Herbert, George Rosener, Nathaniel Wagner, Fuller Mellish, Warren Hull.
Principal songs: Boys in Gray; Won't You Marry Me?; Silver Moon; Mother; Your Land and My Land.

MY PRINCESS
Opened: Oct. 6, 1927.
20 *performances.*
BOOK & LYRICS BY DOROTHY DONNELLY.

Cast included: Hope Hampton, Leonard Ceeley, Donald Meek, Robert Woolsey, Luis Alberni.
Principal songs: When I Was a Girl like You; I Wonder Why; My Passion Flower.

THE LOVE CALL
Opened: Oct. 24, 1927.
88 *performances.*
BOOK BY HARRY B. SMITH & EDWARD LOCKE; LYRICS BY HARRY B. SMITH.

Cast included: Berna Dean, John Barker, W. L. Thorne, Barry Lupino, Joseph Macaulay, Veloz & Yolanda.
Principal songs: Eyes That Love; The Ranger's Song; I Live, I Die for You.

ROSALIE
Opened: Jan. 10, 1928.
327 *performances.*
MUSIC ALSO BY GEORGE GERSHWIN; BOOK BY WILLIAM ANTHONY MCGUIRE & GUY BOLTON; ROMBERG LYRICS BY P. G. WODEHOUSE; GERSHWIN LYRICS BY WODEHOUSE & IRA GERSHWIN.

Cast included: Marilyn Miller, Jack Donahue, Frank Morgan, Bobbe Arnst, Margaret Dale, Oliver McLennan, Clay Clement.
Principal Romberg songs: West Point March; Kingdom of Dreams; The King Can Do No Wrong.

THE NEW MOON
Opened: Sept. 19, 1928.
518 *performances.*
BOOK BY OSCAR HAMMERSTEIN II, FRANK MANDEL, LAURENCE SCHWAB; LYRICS BY HAMMERSTEIN.

Cast included: Robert Halliday, Evelyn Herbert, Gus Shy, William O'Neal, Max Figman, Esther Howard, Olga Albani.

Principal songs: Marianne; Softly, as in a Morning Sunrise; Stouthearted Men; One Kiss; Wanting You; Lover, Come Back to Me; Love Is Quite a Simple Thing.

Recorded Version

Capitol T 219 (S.C.).

Coupled with Friml's *The Vagabond King,* this is a well-sung collection featuring Gordon MacRae.

NINA ROSA
Opened: Sept. 20, 1930.
137 *performances.*

BOOK BY OTTO HARBACH; LYRICS BY IRVING CAESAR.

Cast included: Ethelind Terry, Leonard Ceeley, Guy Robertson, Clay Clement.

Principal songs: Nina Rosa; Your Smiles, Your Tears; My First Love, My Last Love; Serenade of Love.

EAST WIND
Opened: Oct. 27, 1931.
23 *performances.*

BOOK BY OSCAR HAMMERSTEIN II & FRANK MANDEL; LYRICS BY HAMMERSTEIN.

Cast included: Charlotte Lansing, J. Harold Murray, William Williams, Joe Penner, Greek Evans.

Principal songs: East Wind; You Are My Woman; I'd Be a Fool.

MELODY
Opened: Feb. 14, 1933.
79 *performances.*

BOOK BY EDWARD CHILDS CARPENTER; LYRICS BY IRVING CAESAR.

Cast included: Evelyn Herbert, Everett Marshall, Walter Woolf, George Houston, Hal Skelly, Victor Morley, Jeanne Aubert, Mildred Parisette, Consuelo Flowerton.

Principal songs: Give Me a Roll on the Drum; I'd Write a Song; I Am the Singer, You Are the Song.

MAY WINE
Opened: Dec. 5, 1935.
213 *performances.*

BOOK BY FRANK MANDEL; LYRICS BY OSCAR HAMMERSTEIN II.

Cast included: Walter Slezak, Nancy McCord, Walter Woolf King, Leo G. Carroll, Robert Fischer, Jack Cole.

Principal songs: Something in the Air of May; Just Once around the Clock; I Built a Dream; Somebody Ought to Be Told; Something New Is in My Heart.

FORBIDDEN MELODY
Opened: Nov. 2, 1936.
32 *performances.*

BOOK & LYRICS BY OTTO HARBACH.

Cast included: Carl Brisson, Ruby Mercer, Jack Sheehan, Leo Chalzel, June Havoc, Ruth Weston.

Principal songs: Lady in the Window; You Are All I've Wanted; No Use Pretending; Moonlight and Violins.

SUNNY RIVER
Opened: Dec. 4, 1941.
36 *performances.*

BOOK & LYRICS BY OSCAR HAMMERSTEIN II.

Cast included: Muriel Angelus, Bob Lawrence, Helen Claire, Ethel Levey, Tom Ewell, Ivy Scott, Vicki Charles (Vicki Cummings), Richard Huey, Oscar Polk, Dudley Clements, Joan Roberts, William O'Neal, Howard Freeman.

Principal songs: My Girl and I; Call It a Dream; Along the Winding Road; Let Me Live Today.

UP IN CENTRAL PARK
Opened: Jan. 27, 1945.
504 *performances.*

BOOK BY HERBERT & DOROTHY FIELDS; LYRICS BY MISS FIELDS.

Cast included: Wilbur Evans, Maureen Cannon, Noah Beery, Betty Bruce, Daniel Nagrin.

Principal songs: The Big Back Yard; When You Walk in the Room; April Snow; Close as Pages in a Book; It Doesn't Cost You Anything to Dream.

Recorded Version

Decca DL 8016 (S.C.).

Seven songs from the score are sung by Wilbur Evans, Celeste Holm, and Eileen Farrell. Excerpts from Herbert's *The Red Mill* are on the reverse.

MY ROMANCE
Opened: Oct. 19, 1948.
95 performances.
BOOK & LYRICS BY ROWLAND LEIGH.

Cast included: Anne Jeffreys, Lawrence Brooks, Luella Gear, Hazel Dawn, Jr., Rex Evans, Doris Patston, Hildegarde Halliday, Melton Moore, Melville Ruick.
Principal songs: Written in Your Hand; From Now Onward; In Love with Romance.

THE GIRL IN PINK TIGHTS
Opened: Mar. 5, 1954.
115 performances.
BOOK BY JEROME CHODOROV & JOSEPH FIELDS; LYRICS BY LEO ROBIN.

Cast included: Jeanmaire, Charles Goldner, Brenda Lewis, David Atkinson, Alexander Kalioujny, Joshua Shelley, Dania Krupska.
Principal songs: Lost in Loveliness; Up in the Elevated Railway; In Paris and in Love; My Heart Won't Say Goodbye.

Recorded Version
Columbia OL 4890 (O.C.).
The only original cast recording of a Romberg score, this has some agreeable melodies and the dynamic Jeanmaire.

Jerome Kern

MR. WIX OF WICKHAM
Opened: Sept. 19, 1904.
41 performances.
MUSIC ALSO BY HERBERT DARNLEY & GEORGE EVERARD; BOOK & LYRICS BY JOHN WAGNER.

Cast included: Julian Eltinge, Frank Lalor, Harry Clarke, Thelma Fair.
Principal Kern songs: From Saturday till Monday; Waiting for You.

FASCINATING FLORA
Opened: May 20, 1907.
113 performances.
MUSIC MOSTLY BY GUSTAVE KERKER; BOOK BY R. H. BURNSIDE & JOSEPH HERBERT; KERN LYRICS BY PAUL WEST, M. E. ROURKE & JAMES O'DEA; KERKER LYRICS BY BURNSIDE.

Cast included: Adele Ritchie, Ada Lewis, Louis Harrison.
Principal Kern songs: Ballooning; The Subway Express.

THE DAIRY MAIDS
Opened: Aug. 26, 1907.
86 performances.
MUSIC MOSTLY BY PAUL RUBENS & FRANK TOURS; BOOK BY A. M. THOMPSON & ROBERT COURTNEIDGE; KERN LYRICS BY M. E. ROURKE; RUBENS & TOURS LYRICS BY RUBENS & ARTHUR WIMPERIS.

Cast included: Julia Sanderson, George Gregory, Donald Hall.
Principal Kern songs: The Hay Ride; I've a Million Reasons Why I Love You.

FLUFFY RUFFLES
Opened: Sept. 7, 1908.
48 performances.
MUSIC MOSTLY BY WILLIAM FRANCIS; BOOK BY JOHN McNALLY; KERN LYRICS MOSTLY BY C. H. BOVILL; FRANCIS LYRICS BY WALLACE IRWIN.

Cast included: Hattie Williams, Violet Heming, John Bunny, Adele Rowland, Jack Gardner.
Principal Kern songs: Meet Her with a Taximeter; Won't You Let Me Carry Your Parcel?

THE KING OF CADONIA
Opened: Jan. 10, 1910.
16 performances.
MUSIC ALSO BY SIDNEY JONES; BOOK BY FREDERICK LONSDALE; KERN LYRICS MOSTLY BY M. E. ROURKE; JONES LYRICS BY ADRIAN ROSS.

Cast included: Marguerite Clark, William Norris, Melville Stewart, William Danforth, Robert Dempster.
Principal Kern songs: Catamarang; Every Girl I Meet.

LA BELLE PAREE
Opened: Mar. 20, 1911.
104 performances.
MUSIC ALSO BY FRANK TOURS; SKETCHES BY EDGAR SMITH; LYRICS BY EDWARD MADDEN.

Cast included: Mitzi Hajos, Mlle. Dazie, Kitty Gordon, Stella Mayhew, Al Jolson, Barney Bernard.
Principal Kern songs: I'm the Human Brush; Look Me Over Dearie.

THE KISS WALTZ
Opened: Sept. 18, 1911.
88 performances.

MUSIC MOSTLY BY CARL M. ZIEHRER; BOOK BY EDGAR SMITH; LYRICS BY MATTHEW WOODWARD.

Cast included: Adele Rowland, William Pruette.

Principal Kern songs: Fan Me With a Movement Slow; Love Is like a Little Rubber Band.

THE GIRL FROM MONTMARTRE
Opened: Aug. 5, 1912.
64 *performances.*

MUSIC ALSO BY HENRI BERENY; BOOK BY HARRY B. SMITH & ROBERT B. SMITH; LYRICS MOSTLY BY HARRY B. SMITH.

Cast included: Hattie Williams, Richard Carle, William Danforth, Lennox Pawle.

Principal Kern songs: Don't Turn My Picture to the Wall; Ooo, Ooo, Lena!

THE RED PETTICOAT
Opened: Nov. 13, 1912.
61 *performances.*

BOOK BY RIDA JOHNSON YOUNG; LYRICS BY PAUL WEST.

Cast included: Helen Lowell, William Pruette.

Principal songs: Little Golden Maid; Since the Days of Grandmama.

THE DOLL GIRL
Opened: Aug. 25, 1913.
88 *performances.*

MUSIC MOSTLY BY LEO FALL; BOOK & LYRICS BY HARRY B. SMITH.

Cast included: Hattie Williams, Richard Carle.

Principal Kern songs: If We Were on Our Honeymoon; A Little Thing like a Kiss; Will It All End in Smoke?

OH, I SAY!
Opened: Oct. 30, 1913.
68 *performances.*

BOOK BY SYDNEY BLOW & DOUGLAS HOARE; LYRICS BY HARRY B. SMITH.

Cast included: Joseph Herbert Cecil Cunningham, Nellie King, Wellington Cross, Walter Jones.

Principal songs: Each Pearl a Thought; Alone at Last; I Can't Forget Your Eyes.

THE LAUGHING HUSBAND
Opened: Feb. 2, 1914.
48 *performances.*

MUSIC MOSTLY BY EDMUND EYSLER; BOOK & EYSLER LYRICS BY ARTHUR WIMPERIS; KERN LYRICS BY HARRY B. SMITH.

Cast included: Fred Walton, William Norris, Roy Atwell, Josie Intropidi, Venita Fitzhugh.

Principal Kern songs: Take a Step with Me; You're Here and I'm Here.

THE GIRL FROM UTAH
Opened: Aug. 24, 1914.
120 *performances.*

MUSIC ALSO BY PAUL RUBENS & SIDNEY JONES; BOOK BY JAMES TANNER; KERN LYRICS MOSTLY BY HARRY B. SMITH; RUBENS & JONES LYRICS BY RUBENS, ADRIAN ROSS & PERCY GREENBANK.

Cast included: Julia Sanderson, Donald Brian, Joseph Cawthorn, Queenie Vassar, Venita Fitzhugh.

Principal Kern songs: Same Sort of Girl; Why Don't They Dance the Polka Anymore? They Didn't Believe Me.

90 IN THE SHADE
Opened: Jan. 25, 1915.
40 *performances.*

BOOK & LYRICS BY GUY BOLTON & CLARE KUMMER.

Cast included: Richard Carle, Marie Cahill, Edward Martindel, Victor Morley, Otis Harlan, Pedro de Cordoba.

Principal songs: Where's the Girl for Me?; A Package of Seeds.

NOBODY HOME
Opened: Apr. 20, 1915.
135 *performances.*

BOOK BY GUY BOLTON; LYRICS MOSTLY BY KERN & SCHUYLER GREENE.

Cast included: Adele Rowland, Lawrence Grossmith, Alice Dovey, Charles Judels, Maude Odell.

Principal songs: Any Old Night; In Arcady; The Magic Melody; You Know and I Know.

MISS INFORMATION
Opened: Oct. 5, 1915.
47 *performances.*

BOOK BY PAUL DICKEY & CHARLES GODDARD; LYRICS MOSTLY BY ELSIE JANIS & JOHN GOLDEN.

Cast included: Elsie Janis, Irene Bordoni, Melville Ellis.

Principal songs: Some Sort of Somebody; A Little Love.

VERY GOOD EDDIE
Opened: Dec. 23, 1915.
341 *performances.*
BOOK BY PHILIP BARTHOLOMAE & GUY BOLTON; LYRICS MOSTLY BY SCHUYLER GREENE.

Cast included: Alice Dovey, John E. Hazzard, Oscar Shaw, Ernest Truex, Ada Lewis, Helen Raymond.
Principal songs: Babes in the Wood; Some Sort of Somebody; On the Shore at Le Lei Wi; Thirteen Collar; Nodding Roses.

ZIEGFELD FOLLIES
Opened: June 12, 1916.
112 *performances.*
MUSIC ALSO BY OTHERS; SKETCHES BY GEORGE V. HOBART & GENE BUCK; KERN LYRICS BY BUCK.

Cast included: Frances White, Sam Hardy, Ina Claire, Carl Randall, Bernard Granville, Fanny Brice, W. C. Fields, Emma Haig, Bert Williams, Sam Hardy, Ann Pennington, Marion Davies, Lillian Tashman, Justine Johnstone.
Principal Kern songs: Have a Heart; Ain't It Funny What a Difference Just a Few Drinks Make?

HAVE A HEART
Opened: Jan. 11, 1917.
76 *performances.*
BOOK BY GUY BOLTON & P. G. WODEHOUSE; LYRICS BY WODEHOUSE.

Cast included: Louise Dresser, Margaret Romaine, Thurston Hall, Billy B. Van, Flavia Arcaro.
Principal songs: Honeymoon Inn; And I Am All Alone; The Road That Lies Before; You Said Something.

LOVE O' MIKE
Opened: Jan. 15, 1917.
192 *performances.*
BOOK BY THOMAS SYDNEY; LYRICS BY HARRY B. SMITH.

Cast included: Peggy Wood, Clifton Webb, Luella Gear, Alan Edwards, George Hassell, Lawrence Grossmith.
Principal songs: It Wasn't My Fault; Drift with Me; I Wonder Why; We'll See; Simple Little Tune; Who Cares?

OH, BOY!
Opened: Feb. 20, 1917.
463 *performances.*
BOOK BY GUY BOLTON & P. G. WODEHOUSE; LYRICS BY WODEHOUSE.

Cast included: Hal Forde, Marie Carroll, Tom Powers, Anna Wheaton, Edna May Oliver, Marion Davies, Justine Johnstone, Dorothy Dickson, Carl Hyson.
Principal songs: Till the Clouds Roll By; An Old-Fashioned Wife; You Never Knew about Me; Nesting Time in Flatbush; A Pal like You.

LEAVE IT TO JANE
Opened: Aug. 28, 1917.
167 *performances.*
BOOK BY GUY BOLTON & P. G. WODEHOUSE; LYRICS BY WODEHOUSE.

Cast included: Edith Hallor, Robert Pitkin, Oscar Shaw, Georgia O'Ramey, Olin Howland, Ann Orr.
Principal songs: Just You Watch My Step; Leave It to Jane; The Siren's Song; Cleopatterer; The Crickets Are Calling; The Sun Shines Brighter.

Recorded Version
Strand SL 1002 / SLS 1002 (O.C.) (1959).
Members of the 1959 off-Broadway revival give a scintillating performance of the score. Heading the cast are Kathleen Murray, Angelo Mango, Jeanne Allen, and Dorothy Greener.

MISS 1917
Opened: Nov. 5, 1917.
48 *performances.*
MUSIC ALSO BY VICTOR HERBERT; SKETCHES BY GUY BOLTON & P. G. WODEHOUSE; LYRICS BY WODEHOUSE.

Cast included: Lew Fields, Cecil Lean, Cleo Mayfield, Vivienne Segal, Andrew Tombes, Harry Kelly, Elizabeth Brice, Marion Davies, Charles King, Peggy Hopkins, Bessie McCoy Davis, Gus Van & Joe Schenck, Irene Castle, Lilyan Tashman, George White, Ann Pennington, Bert Savoy, Emma Haig.
Principal Kern songs: Go Little Boat; The Land Where the Good Songs Go.

OH, LADY! LADY!!
Opened: Feb. 1, 1918.
219 *performances.*

BOOK BY GUY BOLTON & P. G. WODEHOUSE; LYRICS BY WODEHOUSE.

Cast included: Vivienne Segal, Carl Randall, Margaret Dale, Harry C. Browne, Carroll McComas, Janet Velie, Constance Binney.
Principal songs: Before I Met You; Not Yet; When the Ships Come Home; Greenwich Village; You Found Me and I Found You.

TOOT TOOT
Opened: Mar. 11, 1918.
40 *performances.*
BOOK BY EDGAR ALLAN WOOLF; LYRICS BY BERTON BRALEY.

Cast included: William Kent, Flora Zabelle, Louise Groody, Greek Evans, Alonzo Price.
Principal songs: If You Only Care Enough; Honeymoon Land; When You Wake Up Dancing.

ROCK-A-BYE BABY
Opened: May 22, 1918.
85 *performances.*
BOOK BY EDGAR ALLAN WOOLF; LYRICS BY HERBERT REYNOLDS (M. E. ROURKE).

Cast included: Louise Dresser, Frank Morgan, Carl Hyson, Dorothy Dickson, Alan Hale, Edna Hibbard, Florence Eldridge.
Principal songs: Little Tune Go Away; No Better Use for Time Than Kissing; The Kettle Song.

HEAD OVER HEELS
Opened: Sept. 29, 1918.
100 *performances.*
BOOK & LYRICS BY EDGAR ALLAN WOOLF.

Cast included: Mitzi, Charles Judels, Dorothy Mackaye, Joe Keno, Robert Emmett Keane.
Principal songs: The Big Show; Head over Heels; Let's Build a Little Nest; Funny Little Something.

SHE'S A GOOD FELLOW
Opened: May 5, 1919.
120 *performances.*
BOOK & LYRICS BY ANNE CALDWELL.

Cast included: Ivy Sawyer, Joseph Santley, Olin Howland, Rosetta & Vivian Duncan.
Principal songs: First Rose of Summer; I've Been Waiting For You All the Time; The Bullfrog Patrol; Teacher, Teacher.

THE NIGHT BOAT
Opened: Feb. 2, 1920.
313 *performances.*
BOOK & LYRICS BY ANNE CALDWELL.

Cast included: Louise Groody, John E. Hazzard, Hal Skelly, Ernest Torrence, Wellington Cross, Ada Lewis, Lillian Kemble Cooper, Jeanette MacDonald.
Principal songs: Left All Alone Again Blues; Whose Baby Are You?; I Love the Lassies.

HITCHY-KOO 1920
Opened: Oct. 19, 1920.
71 *performances.*
SKETCHES BY GLEN MACDONOUGH; LYRICS BY MACDONOUGH & ANNE CALDWELL.

Cast included: Raymond Hitchcock, Julia Sanderson, Grace Moore, G. P. Huntley, Florence O'Denishawn, Bobby Connolly.
Principal songs: Buggy Riding; Ding-Dong It's Kissing Time; Moon of Love.

SALLY
Opened: Dec. 21, 1920.
570 *performances.*
BOOK BY GUY BOLTON; LYRICS MOSTLY BY CLIFFORD GREY.

Cast included: Marilynn Miller, Leon Errol, Walter Catlett, Irving Fisher, Mary Hay, Stanley Ridges, Dolores, Catherine Littlefield.
Principal songs: Wild Rose; Look for the Silver Lining; Whip-Poor-Will; The Lorelei; Sally; The Church 'round the Corner.

GOOD MORNING DEARIE
Opened: Nov. 1, 1921.
347 *performances.*
BOOK & LYRICS BY ANNE CALDWELL.

Cast included: Louise Groody, Oscar Shaw, John Price Jones, Ada Lewis, William Kent, Marie Callahan, Harland Dixon, Mary Read, Consuelo Flowerton, Leo Reisman Quartet.
Principal songs: Ka-lu-a; Blue Danube Blues; Didn't You Believe?; Easy Pickin's.

THE BUNCH AND JUDY
Opened: Nov. 28, 1922.
63 *performances.*
BOOK BY ANNE CALDWELL & HUGH FORD; LYRICS BY MISS CALDWELL.

Cast included: Fred & Adele Astaire, Ray

Dooley, Johnny Dooley, Grace Hayes, Philip Tonge, Six Brown Brothers.
Principal songs: Pale Venetian Moon; Every Day in Every Way; Morning Glory; How Do You Do, Katinka.

STEPPING STONES
Opened: Nov. 6, 1923.
241 *performances.*
BOOK BY R. H. BURNSIDE & ANNE CALDWELL; LYRICS BY MISS CALDWELL.
Cast included: Fred Stone, Dorothy Stone, Allene Stone, Jack Whiting, Evelyn Herbert, Oscar Ragland.
Principal songs: In Love with Love; Once in a Blue Moon; Raggedy Ann.

SITTING PRETTY
Opened: Apr. 8, 1924.
95 *performances.*
BOOK BY GUY BOLTON & P. G. WODEHOUSE; LYRICS BY WODEHOUSE.
Cast included: Queenie Smith, Frank McIntyre, Dwight Frye, Gertrude Bryan.
Principal songs: The Enchanted Train; A Year from Today.

DEAR SIR
Opened: Sept. 23, 1924.
15 *performances.*
BOOK BY EDGAR SELWYN; LYRICS BY HOWARD DIETZ.
Cast included: Genevieve Tobin, Oscar Shaw, Walter Catlett, Claire Luce.
Principal songs: All Lanes Must Reach a Turning; If You Think It's Love You're Right.

SUNNY
Opened: Sept. 22, 1925.
517 *performances.*
BOOK & LYRICS BY OTTO HARBACH & OSCAR HAMMERSTEIN II.
Cast included: Marilyn Miller, Jack Donahue, Clifton Webb, Mary Hay, Joseph Cawthorn, Paul Frawley, Cliff Edwards, Esther Howard, Pert Kelton, Marjorie Moss & Georges Fontana, George Olsen Orchestra.
Principal songs: Sunny; Who?; D'Ye Love Me?; Two Little Bluebirds; When We Get Our Divorce.

THE CITY CHAP
Opened: Oct. 26, 1925.
72 *performances.*

BOOK BY JAMES MONTGOMERY; LYRICS BY ANNE CALDWELL.
Cast included: Richard "Skeet" Gallagher, Betty Compton, Irene Dunne, George Raft, Frank Doane, George Olsen Orchestra.
Principal songs: Journey's End; Sympathetic Someone.

CRISS-CROSS
Opened: Oct. 12, 1926.
206 *performances.*
BOOK & LYRICS BY ANNE CALDWELL & OTTO HARBACH.
Cast included: Fred Stone, Dorothy Stone, Oscar Ragland, Lucy Monroe.
Principal songs: In Araby with You; You Will, Won't You; Cinderella Girl.

LUCKY
Opened: Mar. 22, 1927.
71 *performances.*
MUSIC ALSO BY HARRY RUBY; BOOK & LYRICS BY RUBY, BERT KALMAR & OTTO HARBACH.
Cast included: Mary Eaton, "Skeet" Gallagher, Walter Catlett, Ruby Keeler, Ivy Sawyer, Joseph Santley, Paul Whiteman Orchestra.
Principal Kern songs: When the Bo-Tree Blossoms Again; That Little Something.

SHOW BOAT
Opened: Dec. 27, 1927.
575 *performances.*
BOOK & LYRICS BY OSCAR HAMMERSTEIN II.
Cast included: Charles Winninger, Norma Terris, Howard Marsh, Helen Morgan, Edna May Oliver, Jules Bledsoe, Eva Puck, Sammy White, Aunt Jemima (Tess Gardella), Charles Ellis.
Principal songs: Make Believe; Ol' Man River; Can't Help Lovin' Dat Man; Life upon the Wicked Stage; You Are Love; Why Do I Love You?; Bill.

Recorded Versions
Columbia OL 4058 (O.C.) (1946).
RCA Victor LM 2008 (S.C.).
RCA Victor LOP 1505 / LSO 1505 (S.C.).
MGM E 3767 (F.V.) (1951).
Epic LN 3512 (S.C.).
Columbia's, with the 1946 revival cast, is the most theatrical version; the first RCA recording, with Patrice Munsel, Robert Merrill, and Risë Stevens, is the most complete; the second RCA recording, with Anne Jef-

freys, Howard Keel, and Gogi Grant, has the best sound. Keel is also heard on the MGM sound-track release, with Kathryn Grayson and Ava Gardner, which shares the LP with the sound track of Gershwin's *An American In Paris*. The Epic excerpts, featuring Doreen Hume and Bruce Trent, are backed by selections from Youmans' *No, No, Nanette*.

SWEET ADELINE
Opened: Sept. 3, 1929.
234 *performances.*
BOOK & LYRICS BY OSCAR HAMMERSTEIN II.

Cast included: Helen Morgan, Charles Butterworth, Robert Fischer, Irene Franklin, Robert Emmett Keane, Robert Chisholm, John D. Seymour, Violet Carlson, Max Hoffman, Jr.
Principal songs: Here Am I; 'Twas Not So Long Ago; Molly O'Donahue; Why Was I Born?; Don't Ever Leave Me; The Sun About to Rise.

THE CAT AND THE FIDDLE
Opened: Oct. 15, 1931.
395 *performances.*
BOOK & LYRICS BY OTTO HARBACH.

Cast included: Bettina Hall, Georges Metaxa, George Meader, Odette Myrtil, Eddie Foy, Jr., José Ruben, Doris Carson, Flora Le-Breton, Lawrence Grossmith.
Principal songs: The Night Was Made for Love; She Didn't Say "Yes"; One Moment Alone; Poor Pierrot; Try to Forget; A New Love Is Old; I Watch the Love Parade.

Recorded Version
Epic LN 3569 (S.C.).
The six selections on the record are well sung by Doreen Hume & Denis Quilley. Songs from Youmans' *Hit the Deck* are on the reverse.

MUSIC IN THE AIR
Opened: Nov. 8, 1932.
342 *performances.*
BOOK & LYRICS BY OSCAR HAMMERSTEIN II.

Cast included: Walter Slezak, Natalie Hall, Al Shean, Katherine Carrington, Reinald Werrenrath, Nicholas Joy, Tullio Carminati, Ivy Scott, Marjorie Main, Vivian Vance.
Principal songs: There's a Hill beyond a Hill; I've Told Ev'ry Little Star; And Love Was Born; One More Dance; In Egern on the Tegern See; I'm Alone; The Song Is You; We Belong Together.

Recorded Version
RCA Victor LK 1025 X.
This was to have been an original-cast release of the 1951 revival. However, as the show was not a success, RCA issued a collection of the lovely songs sung by Jane Pickens and chorus.

ROBERTA
Opened: Nov. 18, 1933.
295 *performances.*
BOOK & LYRICS BY OTTO HARBACH.

Cast included: Tamara, Bob Hope, Raymond Middleton, Fay Templeton, George Murphy, Sydney Greenstreet, Lyda Roberti, Fred MacMurray.
Principal songs: You're Devastating; Yesterdays; The Touch of Your Hand; Smoke Gets in Your Eyes; Let's Begin.

Recorded Versions
Columbia CL 841 (S.C.)
Decca DL 8007 (S.C.).
Capitol T 384 (S.C.).
MGM E 3230 (F.V.) (1952) X.
The best all-around version is on Columbia, which features Jack Cassidy, Joan Roberts, and Kaye Ballard. The Decca release stars Alfred Drake and Kitty Carlisle. On Capitol, Gordon MacRae and Lucille Norman sing excerpts on one side; Romberg's *The Desert Song* is on the reverse. On the MGM sound-track (called *Lovely to Look At*) Howard Keel, Kathryn Grayson, and the Champions are heard, with Kern's *Show Boat* on the other side.

VERY WARM FOR MAY
Opened: Nov. 17, 1939.
59 *performances.*
BOOK & LYRICS BY OSCAR HAMMERSTEIN II.

Cast included: Grace McDonald, Jack Whiting, Donald Brian, Avon Long, Richard Quine, Frances Mercer, Hiram Sherman, Eve Arden, Vera Ellen, Don Loper, Maxine Barrat, Hollace Shaw, Helena Bliss, June Allyson, Billie Worth, Matty Malneck Orchestra.
Principal songs: All the Things You Are; Heaven in My Arms; That Lucky Fellow; In the Heart of the Dark; All in Fun.

Irving Berlin

ZIEGFELD FOLLIES
Opened: June 26, 1911.
80 *performances.*
MUSIC & LYRICS ALSO BY OTHERS; SKETCHES BY GEORGE V. HOBART.

Cast included: Leon Errol, Walter Percival, Fanny Brice, Bessie McCoy, Dolly Sisters, Bert Williams, Lillian Lorraine, George White.
Principal Berlin songs: Ephraham; Woodman, Woodman, Spare That Tree.

WATCH YOUR STEP
Opened: Dec. 8, 1914.
175 *performances.*
BOOK BY HARRY B. SMITH.

Cast included: Vernon & Irene Castle, Frank Tinney, Harry Kelly, Justine Johnstone, Charles King, Elizabeth Brice, Sallie Fisher, Elizabeth Murray.
Principal songs: Play a Simple Melody; Settle Down in a One Horse Town; The Syncopated Walk; When I Discovered You; They Always Follow Me Around.

STOP! LOOK! LISTEN!
Opened: Dec. 25, 1915.
105 *performances.*
SKETCHES BY HARRY B. SMITH.

Cast included: Gaby Deslys, Justine Johnstone, Harry Fox, Marion Sunshine, Joseph Santley, Frank Lalor, Marion Davies, Marion Harris, James Doyle & Harland Dixon.
Principal songs: The Girl on the Magazine Cover; I Love a Piano; When I Get Back to the U.S.A.

THE CENTURY GIRL
Opened: Nov. 6, 1916.
200 *performances.*
MUSIC ALSO BY VICTOR HERBERT; HERBERT LYRICS BY HENRY BLOSSOM.

Cast included: Hazel Dawn, Sam Bernard, Leon Errol, Elsie Janis, Harry Kelly, Gus Van & Joe Schenck, Frank Tinney, John Slavin, Lillian Tashman, Irving Fisher.
Principal Berlin songs: The Chicken Walk; Alice in Wonderland; It Takes an Irishman to Make Love.

THE COHAN REVUE 1918
Opened: Dec. 31, 1917.
96 *performances.*
MUSIC & LYRICS ALSO BY GEORGE M. COHAN; SKETCHES BY COHAN.

Cast included: Nora Bayes, Charles Winninger, Irving Fisher, Fred Santley.
Principal Berlin songs: Down Where the Jack O'Lanterns Grow; King of Broadway.

YIP, YIP, YAPHANK
Opened: Sept. 2, 1918.
32 *performances.*
SKETCHES BY THE BOYS OF CAMP UPTON.

Cast included: Danny Healy, Harry Green, Bob Higgins, Sammy Lee, Benny Leonard, Irving Berlin.
Principal songs: Bevo; What a Difference a Uniform Will Make; Kitchen Police; Mandy; Oh, How I Hate to Get Up in the Morning; I Can Always Find a Little Sunshine in the Y.M.C.A.

ZIEGFELD FOLLIES
Opened: June 23, 1919.
171 *performances.*
MUSIC & LYRICS ALSO BY OTHERS; SKETCHES BY RENNOLD WOLF, GEORGE LEMAIRE, EDDIE CANTOR, GENE BUCK, DAVE STAMPER.

Cast included: Eddie Dowling, Mary Hay, Ray Dooley, Johnny Dooley, Fairbanks Twins, Delyle Alda, Marilynn Miller, Bert Williams, Gus Van & Joe Schenck, Eddie Cantor, John Steel, George Lemaire, Hazel Washburn, Billie Dove.
Principal Berlin songs: Bevo; Mandy; A Pretty Girl Is Like a Melody; You Cannot Make Your Shimmy Shake on Tea; I'm the Guy Who Guards the Harem.

ZIEGFELD FOLLIES
Opened: June 22, 1920.
123 *performances.*
MUSIC & LYRICS ALSO BY OTHERS; SKETCHES BY W. C. FIELDS, GEORGE V. HOBART, JAMES MONTGOMERY.

Cast included: Charles Winninger, Moran & Mack, Delyle Alda, Ray Dooley, Carl Randall, Fannie Brice, W. C. Fields, Bernard Granville, Gus Van & Joe Schenck, Mary Eaton, John Steel, Art Hickman Orchestra.
Principal Berlin songs: The Girls of My Dreams; Tell Me, Little Gypsy; The Syncopated Vamp; Bells.

MUSIC BOX REVUE
Opened: Sept. 22, 1921.
440 *performances.*
SKETCHES BY FRANCES NORDSTROM, WILLIAM COLLIER, THOMAS GRAY, GEORGE V. HOBART.
Cast included: William Collier, Wilda Bennett, Paul Frawley, Sam Bernard, Ivy Sawyer, Joseph Santley, Rose Rolanda, Emma Haig, Florence Moore, Brox Sisters, Margaret Irving, Chester Hale, Miriam Hopkins, Irving Berlin.
Principal songs: Everybody Step; Say It with Music; They Call It Dancing.

MUSIC BOX REVUE
Opened: Oct. 23, 1922.
330 *performances.*
SKETCHES BY FRANCES NORDSTROM, GEORGE V. HOBART, WALTER CATLETT, PAUL GERARD SMITH.
Cast included: Charlotte Greenwood, Grace LaRue, William Gaxton, Margaret & Dorothy McCarthy, Fairbanks Twins, John Steel, Bobby Clark & Paul McCullough, Margaret Irving, Robinson Newbold, Hal Sherman, Ruth Page.
Principal songs: Crinoline Days; Pack Up Your Sins and Go to the Devil; Lady of the Evening; Will She Come from the East?

MUSIC BOX REVUE
Opened: Sept. 22, 1923.
273 *performances.*
SKETCHES BY EDWIN BURKE, STANLEY BANK, IRVING STROUSE, GEORGE S. KAUFMAN, BERTRAM BLOCK.
Cast included: Frank Tinney, Joseph Santley, Ivy Sawyer, John Steel, Robert Benchley, Phil Baker, Charles Columbus, Grace Moore, Florence O'Denishawn, Brox Sisters, Florence Moore, Solly Ward.
Principal songs: Learn to Do the Strut; An Orange Grove in California; Tell Me a Bedtime Story; The Waltz of Long Ago; Little Butterfly.

MUSIC BOX REVUE
Opened: Dec. 1, 1924.
184 *performances.*
SKETCHES BY BERT KALMAR & HARRY RUBY, CLARK & McCULLOUGH, RALPH BUNKER, AND OTHERS.
Cast included: Fannie Brice, Bobby Clark & Paul McCullough, Oscar Shaw, Grace Moore,

Carl Randall, Ula Sharon, Brox Sisters, Hal Sherman, Claire Luce, Joseph Macaulay.
Principal songs: Don't Send Me Back to Petrograd; Tell Her in the Springtime; Unlucky in Love; Listening; Rock-a-Bye Baby.

THE COCOANUTS
Opened: Dec. 8, 1925.
276 *performances.*
BOOK BY GEORGE S. KAUFMAN.
Cast included: The Marx Brothers, Janet Velie, Georgie Hale, Margaret Dumont, Mabel Withee, Basil Ruysdael, Frances Williams.
Principal songs: Florida by the Sea; A Little Bungalow; Lucky Boy; Monkey Doodle-Doo.

ZIEGFELD FOLLIES
Opened: Aug. 16, 1927.
167 *performances.*
SKETCHES BY HAROLD ATTERIDGE & EDDIE CANTOR.
Cast included: Eddie Cantor, Andrew Tombes, Ruth Etting, Harry McNaughton, Dan Healy, Franklyn Baur, Claire Luce, Irene Delroy, Cliff Edwards, Brox Sisters, Edgar Fairchild & Ralph Rainger (duo-pianists).
Principal songs: It All Belongs to Me; It's Up to the Band; Oooh, Maybe It's You; Shaking the Blues Away; Rainbow of Girls.

FACE THE MUSIC
Opened: Feb. 17, 1932.
165 *performances.*
BOOK BY MOSS HART.
Cast included: Mary Boland, Hugh O'Connell, J. Harold Murray, Katherine Carrington, Andrew Tombes.
Principal songs: I Say It's Spinach; Let's Have Another Cup o' Coffee; On a Roof in Manhattan; Soft Lights and Sweet Music.

AS THOUSANDS CHEER
Opened: Sept. 30, 1933.
400 *performances.*
SKETCHES BY MOSS HART.
Cast included: Marilyn Miller, Clifton Webb, Helen Broderick, Ethel Waters, Leslie Adams, Jerome Cowan, Hal Forde, Harry Stockwell, José Limon, Letitia Ide, Hamtree Harrington.
Principal songs: Harlem on My Mind; Easter Parade; How's Chances?; Heat Wave; Not for All the Rice in China; Supper Time.

LOUISIANA PURCHASE
Opened: May 28, 1940.
444 *performances.*
BOOK BY MORRIE RYSKIND.

Cast included: William Gaxton, Vera Zorina, Victor Moore, Irene Bordoni, Carol Bruce, Nick Long, Jr., April Ames, Robert Pitkin, Hugh Martin, Ralph Blane, Georgia Carroll.
Principal songs: Fools Fall in Love; It's a Lovely Day Tomorrow; Latins Know How; Louisiana Purchase; You Can't Brush Me Off; You're Lonely and I'm Lonely.

THIS IS THE ARMY
Opened: July 4, 1942.
113 *performances.*

Cast included: Ezra Stone, Fred Kelly, Gary Merrill, Burl Ives, Philip Truex, Jules Oshins, Anthony Ross, Earl Oxford, James McColl, Robert Sidney, Irving Berlin.
Principal songs: This Is the Army, Mr. Jones; I Left My Heart at the Stage Door Canteen; I'm Getting Tired So I Can Sleep; Mandy; American Eagles; With My Head in the Clouds; Oh, How I Hate to Get Up in the Morning.

ANNIE GET YOUR GUN
Opened: May 16, 1946.
1,147 *performances.*
BOOK BY HERBERT & DOROTHY FIELDS.

Cast included: Ethel Merman, Ray Middleton, Marty May, Kenny Bowers, Betty Anne Nyman, William O'Neal, Ellen Hanley, Daniel Nagrin, Lubov Roudenko, Harry Bellaver, Christina Lind.
Principal songs: Doin' What Comes Natur'lly; The Girl That I Marry; You Can't Get a Man with a Gun; There's No Business like Show Business; They Say It's Wonderful; My Defenses Are Down; I'm an Indian, Too; I Got Lost in His Arms; I Got the Sun in the Morning; Anything You Can Do.

Recorded Versions
Decca DL 9018 (O.C.).
Capitol W 913 (TV) (1958).
MGM E 3768 (F.V.) (1950).
Your choice between the Decca and the Capitol releases depends largely on your preference for either Ethel Merman on the former or Mary Martin on the latter. Capitol, however, has the better sound. The MGM sound track excerpts with Betty Hut-

ton and Howard Keel are on one side of the LP, with Ruby and Kalmar's *Three Little Words* sound track on the other.

MISS LIBERTY
Opened: July 15, 1949.
308 *performances.*
BOOK BY ROBERT E. SHERWOOD.

Cast included: Eddie Albert, Allyn McLerie, Mary McCarty, Charles Dingle, Philip Bourneuf, Ethel Griffies, Herbert Berghof, Tommy Rall, Dolores (Dody) Goodman, Janice Rule.
Principal songs: A Little Fish in a Big Pond; Let's Take an Old-Fashioned Walk; Homework; Paris Wakes Up and Smiles; Only for Americans; Just One Way to Say I Love You; Give Me Your Tired, Your Poor.

Recorded Version
Columbia OL 4220 (O.C.).
There are many attractive pieces in this rather unappreciated score.

CALL ME MADAM
Opened: Oct. 12, 1950.
644 *performances.*
BOOK BY HOWARD LINDSAY & RUSSEL CROUSE.

Cast included: Ethel Merman, Paul Lukas, Russell Nype, Pat Harrington, Alan Hewitt, Henry Lascoe, Galina Talva, Muriel Bentley, Dolores (Dody) Goodman.
Principal songs: The Hostess with the Mostes' on the Ball; Marrying for Love; It's a Lovely Day Today; Something to Dance About; They Like Ike; You're Just in Love.

Recorded Versions
RCA Victor LOC 1000 (O.C.)X.
Decca DL 9022.
Ethel Merman's contract with Decca prevented her from making the original-cast disc for RCA, and she was replaced by Dinah Shore. However, she may be heard in the Decca set, supported by Dick Haymes.

George Gershwin

For other musicals with Ira Gershwin lyrics, see Two Little Girls in Blue *under Vincent Youmans;* Park Avenue *under Arthur Schwartz;* Ziegfeld Follies of 1936 *under Vernon Duke;* Life Begins at 8:40 *under Harold Arlen;* Lady in the Dark *and* The Firebrand of Florence *under Kurt Weill.*

LA LA LUCILLE
Opened: May 26, 1919.
104 *performances.*
BOOK BY FRED JACKSON; LYRICS BY ARTHUR JACKSON & B. G. DESYLVA.

Cast included: Janet Velie, John E. Hazzard, Helen Clark, Eleanor Daniels, Marjorie Bentley.
Principal songs: Tee-Oodle-Um-Bum-Bo; There's More to the Kiss Than the Sound; Nobody but You.

GEORGE WHITE'S SCANDALS
OF 1920
Opened: June 7, 1920.
134 *performances.*
SKETCHES BY ANDY RICE & GEORGE WHITE; LYRICS BY ARTHUR JACKSON.

Cast included: Ann Pennington, Lou Holtz, La Sylphe, Lester Allen, George "Doc" Rockwell, George White.
Principal songs: On My Mind the Whole Night Long; Scandal Walk; Idle Dreams; Tum On and Tiss Me.

GEORGE WHITE'S SCANDALS
OF 1921
Opened: July 11, 1921.
97 *performances.*
SKETCHES BY BUGS BAER & GEORGE WHITE; LYRICS BY ARTHUR JACKSON.

Cast included: Ann Pennington, Lou Holtz, Charles King, Aunt Jemima (Tess Gardella), George LeMaire, George White, Lester Allen, George Bickel.
Principal songs: South Sea Isles; Drifting Along with the Tide; She's Just a Baby.

GEORGE WHITE'S SCANDALS
OF 1922
Opened: Aug. 28, 1922.
88 *performances.*
SKETCHES BY GEORGE WHITE & W. C. FIELDS; LYRICS BY B. G. DESYLVA & E. RAY GOETZ.

Cast included: Jack McGowan, Winnie Lightner, George White, W. C. Fields, Lester Allen, Pearl Regay, Dolores Costello, Paul Whiteman Orchestra.
Principal songs: Cinderelatives; Where Is the Man of My Dreams; I Found a Four Leaf Clover; I'll Build a Stairway to Paradise; Argentina.

OUR NELL
Opened: Dec. 4, 1922.
40 *performances.*
MUSIC ALSO BY WILLIAM DALY; BOOK BY A. E. THOMAS & BRIAN HOOKER; LYRICS BY HOOKER.

Cast included: Mr. and Mrs. Jimmie Barry, Emma Haig, Olin Howland.
Principal songs: Innocent Ingenue Baby; Walking Home with Angeline.

GEORGE WHITE'S SCANDALS
OF 1923
Opened: June 18, 1923.
168 *performances.*
SKETCHES BY GEORGE WHITE & WILLIAM K. WELLS; LYRICS BY B. G. DESYLVA, E. RAY GOETZ, BALLARD MACDONALD.

Cast included: Johnny Dooley, Winnie Lightner, Margaret Breen, Lester Allen, Tom Patricola, Delyle Alda.
Principal songs: The Life of a Rose; Let's Be Lonesome Together; There Is Nothing Too Good for You.

SWEET LITTLE DEVIL
Opened: Jan. 21, 1924.
120 *performances.*
BOOK BY FRANK MANDEL & LAURENCE SCHWAB; LYRICS BY B. G. DESYLVA.

Cast included: Constance Binney, Irving Beebe, Marjorie Gateson, Franklyn Ardell.
Principal songs: Virginia; Someone Believes in You; The Jijibo.

GEORGE WHITE'S SCANDALS
OF 1924
Opened: June 30, 1924.
192 *performances.*
SKETCHES BY WILLIAM K. WELLS & GEORGE WHITE; LYRICS BY B. G. DESYLVA.

Cast included: Will Mahoney, Winnie Lightner, Lester Allen, Tom Patricola, The De-Marcos.
Principal songs: Somebody Loves Me; Night Time in Araby.

LADY, BE GOOD!
Opened: Dec. 1, 1924.
330 *performances.*
BOOK BY GUY BOLTON & FRED THOMPSON; LYRICS BY IRA GERSHWIN.

Cast included: Fred & Adele Astaire, Walter Catlett, Cliff Edwards, Alan Edwards, Ger-

344

ald Oliver Smith, Phil Ohman & Vic Arden (duo-pianists).
Principal songs: Hang On to Me; So Am I; Fascinating Rhythm; Oh, Lady Be Good!; "The Half of It, Dearie" Blues; Little Jazz Bird; Swiss Miss.

TELL ME MORE!
Opened: Apr. 13, 1925.
100 performances.
BOOK BY FRED THOMPSON & WILLIAM K. WELLS; LYRICS BY B. G. DeSYLVA & IRA GERSHWIN.

Cast included: Alexander Gray, Phyllis Cleveland, Andrew Tombes, Lou Holtz, Emma Haig, Portland Hoffa.
Principal songs: Tell Me More; Three Times a Day; Kickin' the Clouds Away; My Fair Lady; Why Do I Love You?

TIP-TOES
Opened: Dec. 28, 1925.
194 performances.
BOOK BY GUY BOLTON & FRED THOMPSON; LYRICS BY IRA GERSHWIN.

Cast included: Queenie Smith, Jeanette MacDonald, Robert Halliday, Allen Kearns, Andrew Tombes, Harry Watson, Jr., Phil Ohman & Vic Arden (duo-pianists).
Principal songs: Looking for a Boy; When Do We Dance?; These Charming People; That Certain Feeling; Sweet and Low-Down; Nightie-Night.

SONG OF THE FLAME
Opened: Dec. 30, 1925.
219 performances.
MUSIC ALSO BY HERBERT STOTHART; BOOK & LYRICS BY OTTO HARBACH & OSCAR HAMMERSTEIN II.

Cast included: Tessa Kosta, Guy Robertson, Greek Evans, Dorothy Mackaye, Russian Art Choir.
Principal songs: Cossack Love Song; Song of the Flame.

OH, KAY!
Opened: Nov. 8, 1926.
256 performances.
BOOK BY GUY BOLTON & P. G. WODEHOUSE; LYRICS BY IRA GERSHWIN.

Cast included: Gertrude Lawrence, Victor Moore, Oscar Shaw, Betty Compton, Gerald Oliver Smith, Fairbanks Twins, Constance

Carpenter, Harland Dixon, Phil Ohman & Vic Arden (duo-pianists).
Principal songs: Dear Little Girl; Maybe; Clap Yo' Hands; Do Do Do; Someone to Watch Over Me; Fidgety Feet.

Recorded Versions
Columbia CL 1050 (S.C.).
20th Fox FOX 4003/S-4003 (O.C.) (1960).
The only complete Gershwin score of the Twenties available on one record has been given a meticulous production. Jack Cassidy and Barbara Ruick head the fine cast. The excellent revival company heard on the 20th Fox disc dropped two numbers from the original score, changed the lyrics of "Don't Ask" and "Dear Little Girl," and added four other Gershwin tunes. David Daniels, Marti Stevens, and Bernie West are the leads.

FUNNY FACE
Opened: Nov. 22, 1927.
250 performances.
BOOK BY FRED THOMPSON & PAUL GERARD SMITH; LYRICS BY IRA GERSHWIN.

Cast included: Fred & Adele Astaire, Victor Moore, Allen Kearns, William Kent, Betty Compton, Phil Ohman & Vic Arden (duo-pianists).
Principal songs: 'S Wonderful; Funny Face; High Hat; Let's Kiss and Make Up; He Loves and She Loves; Tell the Doc; My One and Only; The Babbitt and the Bromide.

Recorded Version
Verve MG V 15001 (F.V.) (1957).
The film's sound-track, starring Fred Astaire and Audrey Hepburn, retains four songs of the original score, plus two others by Gershwin ("How Long Has This Been Going On" and "Clap Yo' Hands"), and two new ones by Roger Edens and Leonard Gershe. A delightful package.

ROSALIE
Opened: Jan. 10, 1928.
327 performances.
MUSIC ALSO BY SIGMUND ROMBERG; BOOK BY WILLIAM ANTHONY McGUIRE & GUY BOLTON; GERSHWIN LYRICS BY IRA GERSHWIN & P. G. WODEHOUSE; ROMBERG LYRICS BY WODEHOUSE.

Cast included: Marilyn Miller, Jack Donahue, Frank Morgan, Bobbe Arnst, Margaret Dale, Oliver McLennan, Clay Clement.

Principal Gershwin songs: How Long Has This Been Going On?; Say So!; Oh Gee! Oh Joy!

TREASURE GIRL
Opened: Nov. 8, 1928.
68 *performances.*
BOOK BY FRED THOMPSON & VINCENT LAWRENCE; LYRICS BY IRA GERSHWIN.

Cast included: Gertrude Lawrence, Clifton Webb, Walter Catlett, Mary Hay, Paul Frawley, Constance Cummings, Peggy Conklin, Phil Ohman & Vic Arden (duo-pianists).
Principal songs: I've Got a Crush on You; Oh, So Nice; I Don't Think I'll Fall in Love Today; Feeling I'm Falling; Got a Rainbow; Where's the Boy? Here's the Girl!; K-ra-zy for You.

SHOW GIRL
Opened: July 2, 1929.
111 *performances.*
BOOK BY WILLIAM ANTHONY McGUIRE & J. P. McEVOY; LYRICS BY IRA GERSHWIN & GUS KAHN.

Cast included: Ruby Keeler Jolson, Jimmie Durante, Lew Clayton, Eddie Jackson, Eddie Foy, Jr., Barbara Newberry, Harriet Hoctor, Frank McHugh, Joseph Macaulay, Doris Carson, Nick Lucas, Duke Ellington Orchestra.
Principal songs: Do What You Do; So Are You; Liza.

STRIKE UP THE BAND
Opened: Jan. 14, 1930.
191 *performances.*
BOOK BY MORRIE RYSKIND, BASED ON BOOK BY GEORGE S. KAUFMAN; LYRICS BY IRA GERSHWIN.

Cast included: Bobby Clark & Paul McCullough, Jerry Goff, Doris Carson, Margaret Schilling, Blanche Ring, Dudley Clements, Red Nichols Orchestra.
Principal songs: I Mean to Say; A Typical Self-Made American; Soon; Hangin' around With You; Strike Up the Band!; Mademoiselle in New Rochelle; I've Got a Crush on You.

GIRL CRAZY
Opened: Oct. 14, 1930.
272 *performances.*
BOOK BY GUY BOLTON & JOHN McGOWAN; LYRICS BY IRA GERSHWIN.

Cast included: Ginger Rogers, Willie Howard, Ethel Merman, Allen Kearns, Eunice Healey, William Kent, Antonio & Renée DeMarco, Roger Edens (pianist), Red Nichols Orchestra (including Benny Goodman, Gene Krupa, Glenn Miller, Jimmy Dorsey, Jack Teagarden).
Principal songs: Bidin' My Time; Could You Use Me?; Sam and Delilah; Embraceable You; I Got Rhythm; But Not for Me; Treat Me Rough; Boy! What Love Has Done to Me!

Recorded Version
Columbia CL 822 (S.C.).
Gershwin's slightly brittle score is softened by Mary Martin on five of the numbers, with the others sung by Louise Carlyle and Eddie Chappell.

OF THEE I SING
Opened: Dec. 26, 1931.
441 *performances.*
BOOK BY GEORGE S. KAUFMAN & MORRIE RYSKIND; LYRICS BY IRA GERSHWIN.

Cast included: William Gaxton, Victor Moore, Lois Moran, George Murphy, Dudley Clements, Florenz Ames, Grace Brinkley, June O'Dea.
Principal songs: Wintergreen for President; Love Is Sweeping the Country; Of Thee I Sing (Baby); Who Cares?; Hello, Good Morning; The Illegitimate Daughter; Because, Because.

Recorded Version
Capitol S 350 (O.C.) (1952) X.
Jack Carson and Paul Hartman may not be the ideal leads, but the score has been well preserved by the cast of the 1952 revival. Also included is "Mine" from *Let 'Em Eat Cake.*

PARDON MY ENGLISH
Opened: Jan. 20, 1933.
46 *performances.*
BOOK BY HERBERT FIELDS; LYRICS BY IRA GERSHWIN.

Cast included: Jack Pearl, George Givot, Lyda Roberti, Carl Randall, Barbara Newberry, Harry T. Shannon, Gerald Oliver Smith, Cliff Hall, Josephine Houston.
Principal songs: Lorelei; Isn't It a Pity?; My Cousin in Milwaukee.

LET 'EM EAT CAKE
Opened: Oct. 21, 1933.
90 *performances.*
BOOK BY GEORGE S. KAUFMAN & MORRIE
RYSKIND; LYRICS BY IRA GERSHWIN.

Cast included: William Gaxton, Victor
Moore, Lois Moran, Dudley Clements,
Florenz Ames, Philip Loeb, Edward H.
Robins, Consuelo Flowerton.
Principal songs: Wintergreen for President;
Mine; Down with Ev'rything That's Up;
Let 'Em Eat Cake; On and On and On; Blue,
Blue, Blue.

PORGY AND BESS
Opened: Oct. 10, 1935.
124 *performances.*
BOOK BY DuBOSE HEYWARD; LYRICS BY
HEYWARD & IRA GERSHWIN.

Cast included: Todd Duncan, Anne Brown,
John Bubbles, Ford Buck, Edward Matthews,
Georgette Harvey, Helen Dowdy, Ruby Elzy,
Warren Coleman, J. Rosamond Johnson.
Principal songs: Summertime; A Woman Is A
Sometime Thing; My Man's Gone Now; It
Take a Long Pull to Get There; I Got Plenty
o' Nuttin'; Bess, You Is My Woman Now; It
Ain't Necessarily So; What You Want with
Bess?; I Loves You, Porgy; There's a Boat
Dat's Leavin' Soon for New York; Oh,
Where's My Bess?; I'm on My Way.

Recorded Versions
Columbia OSL 162 (S.C.).
Bethlehem EXLP 1.
Verve MG V 4011-2 / MG V 6040-2.
Columbia OL 5410 / OS 2016 (F.V.)
(1959).
Decca DL 9024 (O.C.) (1942).
RCA Victor LOP 1507 / LSO 1507.
Decca DL 8854 / DL 78854.
RCA Camden CAL 500.
   Both the first Columbia and the Bethlehem
releases are on three records, and are the
most complete versions to date. However, the
Columbia set, featuring Lawrence Winters
and Camilla Williams, is far superior to the
Bethlehem (Mel Tormé and Frances Faye),
and is the best all-around version available.
Ella Fitzgerald and Louis Armstrong are on
the two-record Verve package, which is
recommended for Miss Fitzgerald's expressive singing. The Columbia sound track, with
Robert McFerrin and Adele Addison, is the
preferred recording among single-record
excerpts, even better than Columbia CL 922,
taken from the three-record album. The first
Decca, with Todd Duncan and Anne Brown,
is well sung and dramatic; the Victor spot-
lights the glossy techniques of Lena Horne
and Harry Belafonte; the second Decca features the hard-driving style of Sammy Davis,
Jr., and the clipped consonants of Carmen
McRae; the Camden entry is a welcome
reissue of the brilliant Gershwin-supervised
program starring Helen Jepson and Lawrence
Tibbett.

Vincent Youmans

TWO LITTLE GIRLS IN BLUE
Opened: May 3, 1921.
135 *performances.*
MUSIC ALSO BY PAUL LANNIN; BOOK BY FRED
JACKSON; LYRICS BY ARTHUR FRANCIS (IRA
GERSHWIN).

Cast included: Madeline & Marion Fairbanks,
Oscar Shaw, Fred Santley, Olin Howland,
Evelyn Law.
Principal Youmans songs: Oh Me! Oh My!;
Dolly; Who's Who with You?

WILDFLOWER
Opened: Feb. 7, 1923.
586 *performances.*
MUSIC ALSO BY HERBERT STOTHART; BOOK &
LYRICS BY OTTO HARBACH & OSCAR HAM-
MERSTEIN II.

Cast included: Edith Day, Guy Robertson,
Olin Howland, Esther Howard, Charles
Judels, James Doyle.
Principal songs: Wild-Flower; Bambalina;
April Blossoms.

MARY JANE McKANE
Opened: Dec. 25, 1923.
151 *performances.*
MUSIC ALSO BY HERBERT STOTHART; BOOK &
LYRICS BY WILLIAM CARY DUNCAN & OSCAR
HAMMERSTEIN II.

Cast included: Mary Hay, Hal Skelly, Stanley
Ridges, Kitty Kelly, Margaret & Elizabeth
Keene.
Principal Youmans songs: My Boy and I;
Toodle-oo; Flannel Petticoat Gal.

LOLLIPOP
Opened: Jan. 21, 1924.
152 performances.
BOOK BY ZELDA SEARS; LYRICS BY MISS SEARS
& WALTER DeLEON.
Cast included: Ada May, Zelda Sears, Irene
Dunne, Leonard Ceeley, Nick Long, Jr., Gus
Shy, Harry Puck.
Principal songs: Tie a String around Your
Finger; Take a Little One-Step; Going
Rowing.

NO, NO, NANETTE
Opened: Sept. 16, 1925.
321 performances.
BOOK BY OTTO HARBACH & FRANK MANDEL;
LYRICS BY HARBACH & IRVING CAESAR.
Cast included: Louise Groody, Charles
Winninger, Georgia O'Ramey, Wellington
Cross, Josephine Whittell, Mary Lawlor, Jack
(John) Barker, Frank Parker.
Principal songs: No, No, Nanette; Too Many
Rings around Rosie; I Want to Be Happy;
Tea for Two; You Can Dance with Any Girl
at All.
Recorded Versions
Epic LN 3512 (S.C.).
Pathé 30146 (French S.C.).
Highlights of the delightful score are well
sung by Doreen Hume and Bruce Trent on
one side of the Epic LP. Songs from Kern's
Show Boat are on the reverse. The French
version, backed by selections from Friml's
Rose-Marie, features a cast of five soloists.

OH, PLEASE!
Opened: Dec. 17, 1926.
75 performances.
BOOK BY OTTO HARBACH & ANNE CALDWELL;
LYRICS BY MISS CALDWELL.
Cast included: Beatrice Lillie, Charles Win-
ninger, Helen Broderick, Charles Purcell,
Kitty Kelly, Nick Long, Jr.
Principal songs: Nicodemus; I Know That
You Know.

HIT THE DECK
Opened: Apr. 25, 1927.
352 performances.
BOOK BY HERBERT FIELDS; LYRICS BY CLIF-
FORD GREY & LEO ROBIN.
Cast included: Louise Groody, Charles King,
Stella Mayhew, Madeline Cameron, Bobbie
Perkins, Brian Donlevy.

Principal songs: Join the Navy; Harbor of My
Heart; Why, Oh Why; Sometimes I'm
Happy; Hallelujah!
Recorded Versions
MGM E 3163 (F.V.) (1955).
Epic LN 3569 (S.C.).
Seven of the twelve songs on the MGM
sound track (with Tony Martin, Jane Powell,
and Debbie Reynolds) were in the original
show, with one, "Keeping Myself for You,"
dating from the first film version. The Epic
release features Doreen Hume and Denis
Quilley, and is paired with Kern's *The Cat
and the Fiddle*.

RAINBOW
Opened: Nov. 21, 1928.
30 performances.
BOOK BY LAURENCE STALLINGS & OSCAR
HAMMERSTEIN II; LYRICS BY HAMMERSTEIN.
Cast included: Allan Prior, Louise Brown,
Libby Holman, Charles Ruggles, Brian Don-
levy, May Barnes, Harland Dixon, Helen
Lynd.
Principal songs: I Want a Man; The One
Girl; I Like You as You Are; Hay, Straw.

GREAT DAY!
Opened: Oct. 17, 1929.
36 performances.
BOOK BY WILLIAM CARY DUNCAN & JOHN
WELLS; LYRICS BY WILLIAM (BILLY) ROSE
& EDWARD ELISCU.
Cast included: Mayo Methot, John Haynes,
Allan Prior, Walter C. Kelly, Miller & Lyles,
Maude Eburne, Ethel Norris, Lois Deppe,
Vanessi.
Principal songs: Happy Because I'm in Love;
Great Day; More Than You Know; Without
a Song.

SMILES
Opened: Nov. 18, 1930.
63 performances.
BOOK BY WILLIAM ANTHONY McGUIRE;
LYRICS BY HAROLD ADAMSON, CLIFFORD
GREY, RING LARDNER.
Cast included: Marilyn Miller, Fred & Adele
Astaire, Tom Howard, Paul Gregory, Eddie
Foy, Jr., Larry Adler, Clare Dodd, Georgia
Caine, Virginia Bruce, Bob Hope.
Principal songs: Time on My Hands; If I
Were You, Love.

THROUGH THE YEARS
Opened: Jan. 28, 1932.
20 *performances.*
Book by Brian Hooker; lyrics by Edward Heyman.

Cast included: Natalie Hall, Michael Bartlett, Charles Winninger, Reginald Owen, Nick Long, Jr.
Principal songs: Kinda like You; Through the Years; You're Everywhere; Drums in My Heart.

TAKE A CHANCE
Opened: Nov. 26, 1932.
243 *performances.*
Music also by Richard A. Whiting & Herb Brown Nacio; book by B. G. DeSylva & Laurence Schwab; lyrics by DeSylva.

Cast included: Jack Haley, Ethel Merman, Jack Whiting, June Knight, Sid Silvers, Robert Gleckler, Mitzi Mayfair, Oscar Ragland.
Principal Youmans songs: Should I Be Sweet?; Rise 'n' Shine; Oh How I Long to Belong to You.

Richard Rodgers and Lorenz Hart

POOR LITTLE RITZ GIRL
Opened: July 28, 1920.
119 *performances.*
Music also by Sigmund Romberg; book by George Campbell & Lew Fields; Romberg lyrics by Alex Gerber.

Cast included: Charles Purcell, Eleanor Griffith, Lulu McConnell, Andrew Tombes, Aileen Poe, Grant Simpson.
Principal Rodgers & Hart songs: Mary, Queen of Scots; You Can't Fool Your Dreams; What Happened Nobody Knows.

THE GARRICK GAIETIES
Opened: May 17, 1925.
211 *performances.*
Sketches by Benjamin M. Kaye, Morrie Ryskind, Sam Jaffe, & others.

Cast included: Sterling Holloway, Romney Brent, James Norris, June Cochrane, Betty Starbuck, Edith Meiser, Philip Loeb, House Jameson, Hildegarde Halliday, Lee Stras-

berg, Rose Rolanda, Alvah Bessie, Elizabeth (Libby) Holman, Sanford Meisner.
Principal songs: An Old-Fashioned Girl; April Fool; Manhattan; Sentimental Me.

DEAREST ENEMY
Opened: Sept. 18, 1925.
286 *performances.*
Book by Herbert Fields.

Cast included: Helen Ford, Charles Purcell, Flavia Arcaro, Harold Crane, Detmar Poppen.
Principal songs: War Is War; Cheerio; I Beg Your Pardon; Here in My Arms; Where the Hudson River Flows; Bye and Bye; Old Enough to Love; Sweet Peter; Here's a Kiss.

THE GIRL FRIEND
Opened: Mar. 17, 1926.
301 *performances.*
Book by Herbert Fields.

Cast included: Sam White, Eva Puck, June Cochrane, Frank Doane, John Hundley.
Principal songs: The Girl Friend; The Blue Room; What Is It?

THE GARRICK GAIETIES
Opened: May 10, 1926.
174 *performances.*
Sketches by Benjamin Kaye, Newman Levy, Herbert Fields, & others.

Cast included: Sterling Holloway, Romney Brent, Betty Starbuck, Edith Meiser, Philip Loeb, Bobbie Perkins, Hildegarde Halliday.
Principal songs: Mountain Greenery; What's the Use of Talking?; Keys to Heaven.

PEGGY-ANN
Opened: Dec. 27, 1926.
333 *performances.*
Book by Herbert Fields.

Cast included: Helen Ford, Lulu McConnell, Betty Starbuck, Lester Cole, Edith Meiser, Jack Thompson, Margaret Breen.
Principal songs: A Tree in the Park; A Little Birdie Told Me So; Where's That Rainbow?; Maybe It's Me.

BETSY
Opened: Dec. 28, 1926.
39 *performances.*
Book by Irving Caesar & David Freedman, revised by William Anthony Maguire.

349

Cast included: Belle Baker, Al Shean, Jimmy Hussey, Bobbie Perkins, Dan Healy, Allen Kearns, Madeleine Cameron, Barbara Newberry, Borrah Minevitch Harmonica Orchestra.
Principal songs: In Our Parlor on the Third Floor Back; If I Were You; This Funny World.

A CONNECTICUT YANKEE
Opened: Nov. 3, 1927.
418 *performances.*
BOOK BY HERBERT FIELDS.

Cast included: William Gaxton, Constance Carpenter, William Norris, June Cochrane, Jack Thompson, Nana Bryant.
Principal songs: My Heart Stood Still; Thou Swell; On a Desert Island with Thee; I Feel at Home with You.

SHE'S MY BABY
Opened: Jan. 3, 1928.
71 *performances.*
BOOK BY GUY BOLTON, BERT KALMAR, HARRY RUBY.

Cast included: Beatrice Lillie, Clifton Webb, Jack Whiting, Irene Dunne, Nick Long, Jr., William Frawley, Ula Sharon, Frank Doane.
Principal songs: You're What I Need; A Little House in Soho; A Baby's Best Friend.

PRESENT ARMS
Opened: Apr. 26, 1928.
155 *performances.*
BOOK BY HERBERT FIELDS.

Cast included: Charles King, Flora LeBreton, Busby Berkeley, Joyce Barbour, Franker Woods.
Principal songs: You Took Advantage of Me; Do I Hear You Saying "I Love You"?; A Kiss for Cinderella; Blue Ocean Blues.

CHEE-CHEE
Opened: Sept. 25, 1928.
31 *performances.*
BOOK BY HERBERT FIELDS.

Cast included: Helen Ford, William Williams, Betty Starbuck, George Hassell, Philip Loeb.
Principal songs: I Must Love You; Moon of My Delight.

SPRING IS HERE
Opened: Mar. 11, 1929.
104 *performances.*
BOOK BY OWEN DAVIS.

Cast included: Glenn Hunter, Lillian Taiz, John Hundley, Charles Ruggles, Inez Courtney, Joyce Barbour, Lewis Parker, Phil Ohman & Vic Arden (duo-pianists).
Principal songs: Yours Sincerely; With a Song in My Heart; Baby's Awake Now; Red Hot Trumpet; Why Can't I?; You Never Say Yes.

HEADS UP!
Opened: Nov. 11, 1929.
144 *performances.*
BOOK BY JOHN McGOWAN & PAUL GERARD SMITH.

Cast included: Barbara Newberry, Jack Whiting, Victor Moore, Betty Starbuck, John Hundley, Ray Bolger, Janet Velie, Robert Gleckler, Lewis Parker, Phil Ohman (pianist).
Principal songs: Why Do You Suppose?; It Must Be Heaven; My Man Is on the Make; A Ship without a Sail.

SIMPLE SIMON
Opened: Feb. 18, 1930.
135 *performances.*
BOOK BY ED WYNN & GUY BOLTON.

Cast included: Ed Wynn, Ruth Etting, Bobbe Arnst, Will Ahearn, Alan Edwards, Harriet Hoctor.
Principal songs: Send for Me; I Can Do Wonders with You; Ten Cents a Dance.

AMERICA'S SWEETHEART
Opened: Feb. 10, 1931.
135 *performances.*
BOOK BY HERBERT FIELDS.

Cast included: Harriette Lake (Ann Sothern), Jack Whiting, Gus Shy, John Sheehan, Inez Courtney, Jeanne Aubert, Dorothy Dare, Virginia Bruce, Jack Donohue.
Principal songs: I've Got Five Dollars; There's So Much More; We'll Be the Same; How About It?; Sweet Geraldine; Innocent Chorus Girls of Yesterday; A Lady Must Live.

JUMBO
Opened: Nov. 16, 1935.
233 *performances.*

BOOK BY BEN HECHT & CHARLES MAC-ARTHUR.

Cast included: Jimmy Durante, Gloria Grafton, Donald Novis, Poodles Hanneford, Bob Lawrence, Arthur Sinclair, Paul Whiteman Orchestra.

Principal songs: Over and Over Again; The Circus Is on Parade; The Most Beautiful Girl in the World; My Romance; Little Girl Blue.

ON YOUR TOES
Opened: Apr. 11, 1936.
315 *performances.*
BOOK BY RICHARD RODGERS, LORENZ HART, GEORGE ABBOTT.

Cast included: Ray Bolger, Tamara Geva, Monty Woolley, Doris Carson, David Morris, Luella Gear, Robert Sidney, Demetrios Vilan, George Church.

Principal songs: It's Got to Be Love; Too Good for the Average Man; There's a Small Hotel; The Heart Is Quicker Than the Eye; Quiet Night; Glad to Be Unhappy; On Your Toes.

Recorded Versions
Decca DL 9015 (O.C.) (1954).
Columbia CL 837 (S.C.) X.

Both these albums are recommended. Columbia's was made just before the 1954 revival and may have inspired it. Portia Nelson and Jack Cassidy are featured. Decca's recording of the revival cast includes the interpolated "You Took Advantage of Me."

BABES IN ARMS
Opened: Apr. 14, 1937.
289 *performances.*
BOOK BY RODGERS & HART.

Cast included: Mitzi Green, Wynn Murray, Ray Heatherton, Duke McHale, Alfred Drake, Ray McDonald, Grace McDonald, Harold & Fayard Nicholas, Robert Rounseville, Dan Dailey.

Principal songs: Where or When; Babes in Arms; I Wish I Were in Love Again; Way out West; My Funny Valentine; Johnny One Note; All at Once; The Lady Is a Tramp.

Recorded Version
Columbia CL 823 (S.C.).

This fresh, witty score probably contains more hit songs than any other by Rodgers & Hart. This recording, featuring Mary Martin, does them full justice.

I'D RATHER BE RIGHT
Opened: Nov. 2, 1937.
290 *performances.*
BOOK BY GEORGE S. KAUFMAN & MOSS HART.

Cast included: George M. Cohan, Joy Hodges, Austin Marshall, Taylor Holmes, Marion Green, Florenz Ames, Joseph Macaulay, Georgie Tapps, Mary Jane Walsh, Marie Nash.

Principal songs: Have You Met Miss Jones?; A Little Bit of Constitutional Fun; Sweet Sixty-Five; I'd Rather Be Right; Off the Record.

I MARRIED AN ANGEL
Opened: May 11, 1938.
338 *performances.*
BOOK BY RODGERS & HART.

Cast included: Dennis King, Vera Zorina, Vivienne Segal, Walter Slezak, Charles Walters, Audrey Christie, Charles Laskey, Casper Reardon (harpist).

Principal songs: Did You Ever Get Stung?; I Married an Angel; I'll Tell the Man in the Street; How to Win Friends and Influence People; Spring Is Here; A Twinkle in Your Eye; At the Roxy Music Hall.

THE BOYS FROM SYRACUSE
Opened: Nov. 23, 1938.
235 *performances.*
BOOK BY GEORGE ABBOTT.

Cast included: Jimmy Savo, Teddy Hart, Eddie Albert, Ronald Graham, Wynn Murray, Muriel Angelus, Marcy Westcott, Bob Lawrence, Robert Sidney, Burl Ives, George Church, Betty Bruce.

Principal songs: What Can You Do with a Man?; Falling in Love with Love; The Shortest Day of the Year; This Can't Be Love; He and She; You Have Cast Your Shadow on the Sea; Sing for Your Supper; Oh, Diogenes.

Recorded Version
Columbia CL 847 (S.C.) X.

This is a spirited rendition of Rodgers & Hart's superb score. The stars are Jack Cassidy, Portia Nelson, and Bibi Osterwald.

TOO MANY GIRLS
Opened: Oct. 18, 1939.
249 *performances.*
BOOK BY GEORGE MARION, JR.

Cast included: Richard Kollmar, Eddie Bracken Marcy Westcott, Desi Arnaz, Hal

LeRoy, Mary Jane Walsh, Leila Ernst, Ivy Scott, Diosa Costello, Van Johnson, James MacColl.
Principal songs: 'Cause We Got Cake; Love Never Went to College; Spic and Spanish; I Like to Recognize the Tune; I Didn't Know What Time It Was; Give It Back to the Indians.

HIGHER AND HIGHER
Opened: Apr. 4, 1940.
104 *performances.*
BOOK BY GLADYS HURLBUT & JOSHUA LOGAN.

Cast included: Jack Haley, Marta Eggert, Shirley Ross, Leif Erickson, Lee Dixon, Robert Chisholm, Billie Worth, Hollace Shaw, Robert Rounseville, Janet Fox, Jane Ball, Marie Nash, June Allyson, Vera Ellen.
Principal songs: From Another World; Nothing but You; Disgustingly Rich; Ev'ry Sunday Afternoon; It Never Entered My Mind.

PAL JOEY
Opened: Dec. 25, 1940.
374 *performances.*
BOOK BY JOHN O'HARA.

Cast included: Vivienne Segal, Gene Kelly, June Havoc, Jack Durant, Leila Ernst, Stanley Donen, Jean Casto, Van Johnson.
Principal songs: You Mustn't Kick It Around; I Could Write a Book; That Terrific Rainbow; Happy Hunting Horn; Bewitched, Bothered and Bewildered; The Flower Garden of My Heart; Zip; In Our Little Den of Iniquity; Take Him.

Recorded Versions
Columbia OL 4364 (S.C.).
Capitol S 310 (O.C.) (1952) X.
Capitol W 912 (F.V.) (1957).
The success of the Columbia release helped inspire the 1952 revival. The leads on the record, Vivienne Segal and Harold Lang, went into the new stage production. Capitol's LP has everyone else in the show, with Jane Froman and Dick Beavers substituting for Segal and Lang. The sound-track release is recommended only to Frank Sinatra fans.

BY JUPITER
Opened: June 2, 1942.
427 *performances.*
BOOK BY RODGERS & HART.
Cast included: Ray Bolger, Constance Moore,

Benay Venuta, Ronald Graham, Bertha Belmore, Margaret Bannerman, Mark Dawson, Ralph Dumke, Berni Gould, Vera-Ellen.
Principal songs: Jupiter Forbid; Life with Father; Nobody's Heart; Ev'rything I've Got; Careless Rhapsody; Wait till You See Her.

A CONNECTICUT YANKEE
(*revised version*)
Opened: Nov. 17, 1943.
135 *performances.*
BOOK BY HERBERT FIELDS.

Cast included: Dick Foran, Vivienne Segal, Julie Warren, Chester Stratton, Jere McMahon, Robert Chisholm.
Principal songs: My Heart Stood Still; Thou Swell; On a Desert Island with Thee; To Keep my Love Alive; Can't You Do a Friend a Favor?; I Feel at Home with You.

Cole Porter

SEE AMERICA FIRST
Opened: Mar. 28, 1916.
15 *performances.*
BOOK BY T. LAWRASON RIGGS; LYRICS ALSO BY RIGGS.

Cast included: Clifton Webb, Clara Palmer, Felix Adler.
Principal song: I've a Shooting Box in Scotland.

HITCHY-KOO 1919
Opened: Oct. 6, 1919.
56 *performances.*
SKETCHES BY GEORGE V. HOBART.

Cast included: Raymond Hitchcock, Florence O'Denishawn, Joe Cook, Lillian Kemble Cooper.
Principal songs: When I Had a Uniform On; My Cozy Little Corner in the Ritz; Old-Fashioned Garden.

GREENWICH VILLAGE FOLLIES
OF 1924
Opened: Sept. 16, 1924.
127 *performances.*
SKETCHES BY JOHN MURRAY ANDERSON; LYRICS ALSO BY IRVING CAESAR & ANDERSON.

Cast included: Dolly Sisters, Moran & Mack; Bobbe Arnst, George Rasely, Georgie Hale, Robert Alton, Vincent Lopez Orchestra.
Principal songs: I'm in Love Again; Two Little Babes in the Wood.

PARIS
Opened: Oct. 8, 1928.
195 *performances.*
MUSIC & LYRICS ALSO BY OTHERS; BOOK BY
MARTIN BROWN.

Cast included: Irene Bordoni, Arthur Margetson, Louise Closser Hale, Irving Aaronson's Commanders.
Principal Porter songs: Let's Do It; Two Little Babes in the Wood; Don't Look at Me That Way.

FIFTY MILLION FRENCHMEN
Opened: Nov. 27, 1929.
254 *performances.*
BOOK BY HERBERT FIELDS.

Cast included: William Gaxton, Genevieve Tobin, Helen Broderick, Jack Thompson, Betty Compton, Thurston Hall, Evelyn Hoey, Marie Valli (June Knight).
Principal songs: You Do Something to Me; You've Got That Thing; Find Me a Primitive Man; You Don't Know Paree.

WAKE UP AND DREAM!
Opened: Dec. 30, 1929.
136 *performances.*
MUSIC & LYRICS ALSO BY OTHERS; SKETCHES BY JOHN HASTINGS TURNER, RONALD JEANS, DOUGLAS FURBER.

Cast included: Jack Buchanan, Jessie Matthews, Tilly Losch, Dave Fitzgibbon, Frances Shelley.
Principal Porter songs: I Loved Him but He Didn't Love Me; What Is This Thing Called Love?; Which?; I'm a Gigolo; Looking at You.

THE NEW YORKERS
Opened: Dec. 8, 1930.
168 *performances.*
BOOK BY HERBERT FIELDS.

Cast included: Hope Williams, Jimmy Durante, Lew Clayton, Eddie Jackson, Ann Pennington, Frances Williams, Charles King, Richard Carle, Marie Cahill, Oscar "Rags" Ragland, Kathryn Crawford, Fred Waring Pennsylvanians.
Principal songs: Where Have You Been?; I'm Getting Myself Ready for You; Love for Sale; The Great Indoors; Let's Fly Away.

GAY DIVORCE
Opened: Nov. 29, 1932.
248 *performances.*
BOOK BY DWIGHT TAYLOR.

Cast included: Fred Astaire, Claire Luce, Luella Gear, Eric Blore, Erik Rhodes, Roland Bottomley.
Principal songs: After You; Night and Day; How's Your Romance?; I've Got You on My Mind; Mister and Missus Fitch.

ANYTHING GOES
Opened: Nov. 21, 1934.
420 *performances.*
BOOK BY GUY BOLTON & P. G. WODEHOUSE, REVISED BY HOWARD LINDSAY & RUSSEL CROUSE.

Cast included: William Gaxton, Ethel Merman, Victor Moore, Bettina Hall, Vivian Vance, Helen Raymond.
Principal songs: All through the Night; I Get a Kick out of You; You're the Top; Anything Goes; Blow Gabriel, Blow; Be like the Bluebird; The Gypsy in Me.

Recorded Versions
Decca DL 8318 (F.V.) (1955).
Columbia ML 4751.
  Bing Crosby, Donald O'Connor, Mitzi Gaynor, and Jeanmaire sing six Porter tunes (including "It's De-Lovely" from *Red, Hot and Blue!*) plus three written for the film by Van Heusen & Cahn. Columbia offers the serene Mary Martin (and chorus) gliding through six numbers—all from the show and all on one side—with songs from Schwartz and Dietz's *The Band Wagon* on the reverse.

JUBILEE
Opened: Oct. 12, 1935.
169 *performances.*
BOOK BY MOSS HART.

Cast included: Mary Boland, Melville Cooper, Charles Walters, June Knight, Margaret Adams, Derek Williams, Montgomery Clift, Jackie Kelk, Leo Chalzel, Olive Reeves Smith, Ted Fetter, May Boley, Mark Plant.
Principal songs: Why Shouldn't I?; The Kling-Kling Bird on the Divi-Divi Tree; When Love Comes Your Way; Me and Marie; Just One of Those Things; A Picture of Me without You; Begin the Beguine.

RED, HOT AND BLUE!
Opened: Oct. 29, 1936.
183 *performances.*
BOOK BY HOWARD LINDSAY & RUSSEL CROUSE.

Cast included: Ethel Merman, Jimmy Durante, Bob Hope, Paul & Grace Hartman, Polly Walters, Dorothy Vernon, Thurston Crane, Vivian Vance, Forrest Orr, Lew Parker.
Principal songs: Ours; Down in the Depths; You've Got Something; It's De-Lovely; Ridin' High; The Ozarks Are Calling Me Home; Red Hot and Blue.

YOU NEVER KNOW
Opened: Sept. 21, 1938.
78 *performances.*
MUSIC & LYRICS ALSO BY OTHERS; BOOK BY ROWLAND LEIGH.

Cast included: Clifton Webb, Libby Holman, Lupe Velez, Toby Wing, Paul & Grace Hartman, Rex O'Malley, Roger Stearns, June Preisser.
Principal Porter songs: You Never Know; At Long Last Love; For No Rhyme or Reason; From Alpha to Omega; What Shall I Do?

LEAVE IT TO ME!
Opened: Nov. 9, 1938.
291 *performances.*
BOOK BY BELLA & SAM SPEWACK.

Cast included: William Gaxton, Victor Moore, Sophie Tucker, Tamara, Mary Martin, George Tobias, Gene Kelly.
Principal songs: Get Out of Town; Most Gentlemen Don't Like Love; From Now On; My Heart Belongs to Daddy.

DU BARRY WAS A LADY
Opened: Dec. 6, 1939.
408 *performances.*
BOOK BY HERBERT FIELDS & B. G. DeSYLVA.

Cast included: Bert Lahr, Ethel Merman, Betty Grable, Benny Baker, Ronald Graham, Charles Walters, Janis Carter.
Principal songs: When Love Beckoned in Fifty-second Street; Do I Love You?; But in the Morning, No!; Give Him the Oo-La-La; Katie Went to Haiti; Well, Did You Evah!; It Was Written in the Stars; Friendship.

PANAMA HATTIE
Opened: Oct. 30, 1940.
501 *performances.*
BOOK BY HERBERT FIELDS & B. G. DeSYLVA.

Cast included: Ethel Merman, Arthur Treacher, James Dunn, Rags Ragland, Pat Harrington, Frank Hyers, Phyllis Brooks, Betty Hutton, Joan Carroll, Nadine Gay, Lipman Duckat (Larry Douglas), Janis Carter, June Allyson, Jane Ball, Betsy Blair, Lucille Bremer, Vera Ellen, Doris Dowling.
Principal songs: My Mother Would Love You; I've Still Got My Health; Fresh as a Daisy; Let's Be Buddies; Make It Another Old-Fashioned, Please.

LET'S FACE IT!
Opened: Oct. 29, 1941.
547 *performances.*
BOOK BY HERBERT & DOROTHY FIELDS.

Cast included: Danny Kaye, Mary Jane Walsh, Benny Baker, Eve Arden, Vivian Vance, Jack Williams, Nanette Fabray, Edith Meiser, Mary Parker & Billy Daniels, Jane Ball, Helena Bliss, Garry Davis, Joseph Macaulay.
Principal songs: Let's Face It; Farming; Ev'rything I Love; Ace in the Hole; You Irritate Me So; A Little Rumba Numba; I Hate You, Darling; Let's Not Talk about Love.

SOMETHING FOR THE BOYS
Opened: Jan. 7, 1943.
422 *performances.*
BOOK BY HERBERT & DOROTHY FIELDS.

Cast included: Ethel Merman, Bill Johnson, Betty Garrett, Paula Laurence, Allen Jenkins, Betty Bruce, Anita Alvarez, Jed Prouty, William Lynn, Frances Mercer, Bill Callahan, Murvyn Vye, Dolores (Dody) Goodman.
Principal songs: Something for the Boys; Hey, Good Lookin'; He's a Right Guy; Could It Be You?; I'm in Love with a Soldier Boy; By the Mississinewah.

MEXICAN HAYRIDE
Opened: Jan. 28, 1944.
481 *performances.*
BOOK BY HERBERT & DOROTHY FIELDS.

Cast included: Bobby Clark, June Havoc, George Givot, Wilbur Evans, Luba Malina,

Corinna Mura, Paul Haakon, Edith Meiser, Bill Callahan, Candy Jones.
Principal songs: Sing to Me, Guitar; I Love You; There Must Be Someone for Me; Abracadabra; Girls; Carlotta; Count Your Blessings.

SEVEN LIVELY ARTS
Opened: Dec. 7, 1944.
183 *performances.*
Sketches by George S. Kaufman, Moss Hart, Charles Sherman & others.

Cast included: Beatrice Lillie, Bert Lahr, Benny Goodman, Alicia Markova, Anton Dolin, Doc Rockwell, Dolores Gray, Nan Wynn, Mary Roche, Albert Carroll, Dennie Moore, Bill Tabbert, Jere McMahon, Billie Worth, Paula Bane, Teddy Wilson, Red Norvo, Helen Gallagher.
Principal songs: Ev'rytime We Say Goodbye; Only Another Boy and Girl; When I Was a Little Cuckoo; Hence, It Don't Make Sense.

AROUND THE WORLD IN EIGHTY DAYS
Opened: May 31, 1946.
75 *performances.*
Book by Orson Welles.

Cast included: Arthur Margetson, Orson Welles, Stefan Schnabel, Julie Warren, Larry Laurence, Mary Healy, Victoria Cordova, Jack Cassidy.
Principal songs: Look What I Found; There He Goes, Phileas Fogg; Should I Tell You I Love You?; Pipe-dreaming; If You Smile at Me.

KISS ME, KATE
Opened: Dec. 30, 1948.
1,077 *performances.*
Book by Sam & Bella Spewack.

Cast included: Alfred Drake, Patricia Morison, Lisa Kirk, Harold Lang, Lorenzo Fuller, Harry Clark, Jack Diamond, Annabelle Hill.
Principal songs: Another Op'nin', Another Show; Why Can't You Behave?; Wunderbar; So in Love; We Open in Venice; Tom, Dick or Harry; I've Come to Wive It Wealthily in Padua; I Hate Men; Were Thine That Special Face; Too Darn Hot; Where Is the Life That Late I Led?; Always True to You in My Fashion; Bianca.

Recorded Versions
Columbia OL 4140 (O.C.).

MGM E 3077 (F.V.) (1953).
RCA Victor LPM 1984/LSP 1984 (S.C.).
Capitol TAO 1267/STAO 1267 (S.C.).
The great Porter score is still best served by the original cast on Columbia. The film sound track features Howard Keel, Kathryn Grayson, and laundered lyrics. Keel is also heard on the imaginative RCA release with Anne Jeffreys and Gogi Grant. The capitol set reunites the original leads for a well-recorded though aggressively stereophonic production.

OUT OF THIS WORLD
Opened: Dec. 21, 1950.
157 *performances.*
Book by Dwight Taylor & Reginald Lawrence.

Cast included: Charlotte Greenwood, William Eythe, Priscilla Gillette, Barbara Ashley, William Redfield, George Jongeyans (George Gaynes), David Burns, Janet Collins.
Principal songs: Use Your Imagination; Where, Oh Where?; I Am Loved; Climb Up the Mountain; No Lover; Cherry Pies Ought to Be You; Nobody's Chasing Me; They Couldn't Compare to You; I Sleep Easier Now.

Recorded Version
Columbia OL 4390 (O.C.).
This is an unappreciated score with a rich variety of rhymes and rhythms.

CAN-CAN
Opened: May 7, 1953.
892 *performances.*
Book by Abe Burrows.

Cast included: Lilo, Peter Cookson, Hans Conried, Erik Rhodes, Gwen Verdon, Dania Krupska.
Principal songs: Never Give Anything Away; C'est Magnifique; I Am in Love; Allez-vous En; It's All Right with Me; I Love Paris.

Recorded Versions
Capitol S 452 (O.C.).
Capitol W 1301/SW 1301 (F.V.) (1960).
Not up to Porter's best, the score is nevertheless enlived by some spirited performances. The sound-track album, featuring Frank Sinatra, Shirley MacLaine, Maurice Chevalier, and Louis Jourdan, has cut six of the original songs. Replacing them are

"You Do Something to Me," "Let's Do It," and "Just One of Those Things."

SILK STOCKINGS
Opened: Feb. 24, 1955.
478 performances.
BOOK BY GEORGE S. KAUFMAN, LEUEEN McGRATH, ABE BURROWS.

Cast included: Hildegarde Neff, Don Ameche, Gretchen Wyler, Henry Lascoe, Leon Belasco, David Opatoshu, George Tobias, Julie Newmar.
Principal songs: Paris Loves Lovers; It's a Chemical Reaction; All of You; Siberia; Without Love; Silk Stockings.

Recorded Versions
RCA Victor LOC 1016 (O.C.) X.
MGM E 3542 ST (F.V.) (1957) X.
Two songs, "Fated to Be Mated" and "The Ritz Roll and Rock," were added to the film score, and one of the original songs, "As on through the Seasons We Sail," was cut. Otherwise, it is a decision between the original cast leads or the movie's (Fred Astaire and Cyd Charisse's "voice," Carole Richards).

Arthur Schwartz

For other musicals with Howard Dietz lyrics, see Dear Sir *under Jerome Kern;* Jackpot & Sadie Thompson *under Vernon Duke.*

THE GRAND STREET FOLLIES OF 1926
Opened: June 15, 1926.
55 performances.
MUSIC ALSO BY OTHERS; SKETCHES & MOST LYRICS BY AGNES MORGAN.

Cast included: Albert Carroll, Agnes Morgan, Dorothy Sands, Paula Trueman, Vera Allen, Jessica Dragonette.
Principal Schwartz songs: A Little Igloo for Two; Polar Bear Strut.

THE NEW YORKERS
Opened: Mar. 10, 1927.
52 performances.
MUSIC ALSO BY EDGAR FAIRCHILD & CHARLES SCHWAB; SKETCHES BY JO SWERLING; LYRICS BY HENRY MYERS.

Cast included: Tamara Drasin (later known as Tamara), Chester Clute, Mona Sorel.

Principal Schwartz songs: A Song about Love; Floating thru the Air.

THE LITTLE SHOW
Opened: Apr. 30, 1929.
321 performances.
MUSIC ALSO BY OTHERS; SKETCHES BY HOWARD DIETZ, FRED ALLEN, NEWMAN LEVY, MARYA MANNES, GEORGE S. KAUFMAN; LYRICS MOSTLY BY DIETZ.

Cast included: Clifton Webb, Libby Holman, Fred Allen, Romney Brent, Portland Hoffa, Bettina Hall, Helen Lynd, John (Jack) McCauley, Peggy Conklin, Constance Cummings, Adam Carroll & Ralph Rainger (duo-pianists).
Principal Schwartz songs: I Guess I'll Have to Change My Plan; I've Made a Habit of You; Hammacher Schlemmer, I Love You.

THE GRAND STREET FOLLIES OF 1929
Opened: May 1, 1929.
93 performances.
MUSIC ALSO BY MAX EWING; SKETCHES & MOST LYRICS BY AGNES MORGAN.

Cast included: Albert Carroll, Dorothy Sands, Paula Trueman, James Cagney.
Principal Schwartz songs: I Love You and I Like You; What Did Della Wear?; I Need You So.

THE SECOND LITTLE SHOW
Opened: Sept. 2, 1930.
63 performances.
MUSIC ALSO BY OTHERS; SKETCHES BY NORMAN CLARK & OTHERS; LYRICS MOSTLY BY HOWARD DIETZ.

Cast included: Al Trahan, J. C. Flippen, Gloria Grafton, Arline Judge.
Principal Schwartz songs: Lucky Seven; What a Case I've Got on You; I Like Your Face.

PRINCESS CHARMING
Opened: Oct. 13, 1930.
56 performances.
MUSIC ALSO BY ALBERT SIRMAY; BOOK BY JACK DONAHUE; LYRICS BY ARTHUR SWANSTROM.

Cast included: Evelyn Herbert, Robert Halliday, George Grossmith, Victor Moore, Jeanne Aubert, Douglass Dumbrille, Howard St. John, Duke McHale.
Principal songs: You; I'll Never Leave You.

THREE'S A CROWD
Opened: Oct. 15, 1930.
271 *performances.*
MUSIC ALSO BY OTHERS; SKETCHES BY HOWARD DIETZ, FRED ALLEN, LAURENCE SCHWAB, COREY FORD, GROUCHO MARX & OTHERS; LYRICS MOSTLY BY DIETZ.

Cast included: Clifton Webb, Libby Holman, Fred Allen, Tamara Geva, Portland Hoffa, Earl Oxford, Fred MacMurray.
Principal Schwartz songs: Something to Remember You By; The Moment I Saw You; Right at the Start of It.

THE BAND WAGON
Opened: June 3, 1931.
260 *performances.*
SKETCHES BY GEORGE S. KAUFMAN & HOWARD DIETZ; LYRICS BY DIETZ.

Cast included: Fred & Adele Astaire, Frank Morgan, Tilly Losch, Helen Broderick, Philip Loeb, John Barker.
Principal songs: Dancing in the Dark; New Sun in the Sky; Hoops; I Love Louisa; High and Low; Miserable with You; Where Can He Be?; White Heat; The Beggar Waltz.

Recorded Versions
MGM E 3051 (F.V.) (1953).
Columbia ML 4751.

Just three songs from the original production were kept in the MGM film of the same name, with seven other Schwartz & Dietz numbers added. Nevertheless, this is a scintillating album, with Fred Astaire, Nanette Fabray, and Jack Buchanan featured. On Columbia, Mary Martin and chorus sing eight songs from the show, backed by selections from Porter's *Anything Goes.*

FLYING COLORS
Opened: Sept. 15, 1932.
188 *performances.*
SKETCHES & LYRICS BY HOWARD DIETZ.

Cast included: Clifton Webb, Charles Butterworth, Tamara Geva, Buddy & Vilma Ebsen, Patsy Kelly, Larry Adler, Philip Loeb, Imogene Coca.
Principal songs: Two-Faced Woman; A Rainy Day; Mother Told Me So; A Shine on Your Shoes; Alone Together; Louisiana Hayride; Smokin' Reefers.

REVENGE WITH MUSIC
Opened: Nov. 28, 1934.
158 *performances.*
BOOK & LYRICS BY HOWARD DIETZ.

Cast included: Libby Holman, Charles Winninger, Georges Metaxa, Ilka Chase, Ivy Scott, Rex O'Malley, Joseph Macaulay.
Principal songs: You and the Night and the Music; If There Is Someone Lovelier Than You; When You Love Only One; Wand'ring Heart; Maria.

AT HOME ABROAD
Opened: Sept. 19, 1935.
198 *performances.*
SKETCHES MOSTLY BY HOWARD DIETZ; LYRICS BY DIETZ.

Cast included: Beatrice Lillie, Ethel Waters, Herb Williams, Eleanor Powell, Reginald Gardiner, Eddie Foy, Jr., Paul Haakon, James MacColl, Vera Allen.
Principal songs: That's Not Cricket; Hottentot Potentate; Paree; Farewell, My Lovely; Thief in the Night; Love Is a Dancing Thing; O Leo; What a Wonderful World; Loadin' Time; Get Yourself a Geisha; Got a Bran' New Suit.

VIRGINIA
Opened: Sept. 2, 1937.
60 *performances.*
BOOK BY LAURENCE STALLINGS & OWEN DAVIS; LYRICS BY ALBERT STILLMAN & STALLINGS.

Cast included: Gene Lockhart, Ronald Graham, Anne Booth, Mona Barrie, Ford Buck & John Bubbles, Dennis Hoey, Avis Andrews, Nigel Bruce, Patricia Bowman, Nora Kaye.
Principal songs: Goodbye, Jonah; You and I Know; An Old Flame Never Dies; If You Were Someone Else; I'll Be Sittin' in de Lap of de Lord; My Heart Is Dancing.

BETWEEN THE DEVIL
Opened: Dec. 22, 1937.
93 *performances.*
BOOK & LYRICS BY HOWARD DIETZ.

Cast included: Jack Buchanan, Evelyn Laye, Adele Dixon, Vilma Ebsen, Charles Walters, Tune Twisters.
Principal songs: I See Your Face before Me; Triplets; By Myself; I'm Against Rhythm; You Have Everything.

THE WORLD OF MUSICAL COMEDY

STARS IN YOUR EYES
Opened: Feb. 9, 1939.
127 *performances.*
BOOK BY J. P. McEVOY; LYRICS BY DOROTHY
FIELDS.
Cast included: Jimmy Durante, Ethel Mer-
man, Mildred Natwick, Tamara Toumanova,
Richard Carlson, Dan Dailey, Jr., Clinton
Sundberg, Nancy Wiman, Mary Wickes,
Walter Cassel, Roger Stearns, Nora Kaye,
Alicia Alonso, Jerome Robbins.
Principal songs: This Is It; A Lady Needs
a Change; Terribly Attractive; Just a Little
Bit More; I'll Pay the Check; It's All Yours.

PARK AVENUE
Opened: Nov. 4, 1946.
72 *performances.*
BOOK BY NUNNALLY JOHNSON & GEORGE S.
KAUFMAN; LYRICS BY IRA GERSHWIN.
Cast included: Leonora Corbett, Arthur Mar-
getson, Ray McDonald, Martha Stewart,
Robert Chisholm, Marthe Errolle, Charles
Purcell, Ruth Matteson, Raymond Walburn,
Mary Wickes, David Wayne, Kyle Mac-
Donnell.
Principal songs: Don't Be a Woman If You
Can; Land of Opportunitee; Sweet Nevada;
For the Life of Me; There's No Holding Me;
Goodbye to All That.

INSIDE U.S.A.
Opened: Apr. 30, 1948.
399 *performances.*
SKETCHES BY ARNOLD AUERBACH, MOSS
HART, ARNOLD HORWITT; LYRICS BY HOWARD
DIETZ.
Cast included: Beatrice Lillie, Jack Haley,
Herb Shriner, Valerie Bettis, John Tyers, Eric
Victor, Lewis Nye, Carl Reiner, Thelma Car-
penter, Estelle Loring, J. C. McCord, Rod
Alexander, Boris Runanin, Jack Cassidy,
Tally Beatty.
Principal songs: Inside U.S.A.; Blue Grass;
Rhode Island Is Famous for You; Haunted
Heart; My Gal Is Mine Once More; We
Won't Take It Back; At the Mardi Gras.

A TREE GROWS IN BROOKLYN
Opened: Apr. 19, 1951.
270 *performances.*
BOOK BY BETTY SMITH & GEORGE ABBOTT;
LYRICS BY DOROTHY FIELDS.
Cast included: Shirley Booth, Johnny John-

ston, Marcia Van Dyke, Nomi Mitty, Har-
land Dixon, Lou Wills, Jr., Jordan Bentley.
Principal songs: Mine till Monday; Make the
Man Love Me; I'm like a New Broom; Look
Who's Dancing; Love Is the Reason; If You
Haven't Got a Sweetheart; I'll Buy You a
Star; Growing Pains.
Recorded Version
Columbia OL 4405 (O.C.).
A score of great warmth and atmosphere,
this is probably Schwartz's finest work to
date.

BY THE BEAUTIFUL SEA
Opened: Apr. 8, 1954.
270 *performances.*
BOOK BY HERBERT & DOROTHY FIELDS;
LYRICS BY MISS FIELDS.
Cast included: Shirley Booth, Wilbur Evans,
Mae Barnes, Cameron Prud'homme, Richard
France, Warde Donovan.
Principal songs: Alone Too Long; Happy
Habit; I'd Rather Wake Up by Myself;
Hooray for George the Third; Hang Up!;
More Love Than Your Love.
Recorded Version
Capitol S 531 (O.C.)X.
Another period piece for Shirley Booth,
but the music has less appeal than that of
A Tree Grows in Brooklyn.

Vernon Duke

THE GARRICK GAIETIES
Opened: June 4, 1930.
170 *performances for two editions.*
MUSIC ALSO BY OTHERS; SKETCHES BY CAR-
ROLL CARROLL, SALLY HUMASON, BENJAMIN
M. KAYE, NEWMAN LEVY, GRETCHEN DAM-
ROSCH FINLETTER, & OTHERS; DUKE LYRICS
BY IRA GERSHWIN, E. Y. HARBURG, NEWMAN
LEVY.
Cast included: Albert Carroll, Edith Meiser,
Philip Loeb, Sterling Holloway, Nan Black-
stone, Ruth Chorpenning, Hildegarde Halli-
day, William Tannen, Roger Stearns, James
Norris, Imogene Coca, Ray Heatherton, Ted
Fetter. (For second edition, which opened
October 16, 1930, the following were added
to cast: Rosalind Russell, Katherine Carring-
ton, Donald Burr.)
Principal Duke songs: I Am Only Human
after All; Too Too Devine.

358

WALK A LITTLE FASTER
Opened: Dec. 7, 1932.
119 performances.
SKETCHES BY S. J. PERELMAN & ROBERT MACGUNIGLE; LYRICS BY E. Y. HARBURG.

Cast included: Beatrice Lillie, Bobby Clark & Paul McCullough, Dave Fitzgibbon, Evelyn Hoey, Donald Burr, John Hundley.
Principal songs: That's Life; April in Paris; So Nonchalant; Speaking of Love; Where Have We Met Before?; A Penny for Your Thoughts.

ZIEGFELD FOLLIES
Opened: Jan. 4, 1934.
182 performances.
MUSIC ALSO BY OTHERS; SKETCHES BY H. I. PHILLIPS, DAVID FREEDMAN, DAVID TURGEND, FRED ALLEN; DUKE LYRICS BY E. Y. HARBURG.

Cast included: Fannie Brice, Willie & Eugene Howard, Jane Froman, Everett Marshall, Vilma & Buddy Ebsen, Eve Arden, Cherry & June Preisser, Patricia Bowman, Victor Morley, Vivian Janis, Don Ross, Oliver Wakefield.
Principal Duke songs: Water under the Bridge; I Like the Likes of You; Suddenly; What Is There to Say?

ZIEGFELD FOLLIES
Opened: Jan. 30, 1936.
115 performances.
SKETCHES BY DAVID FREEDMAN; LYRICS BY IRA GERSHWIN.

Cast included: Fannie Brice, Josephine Baker, Gertrude Niesen, Harriet Hoctor, Bob Hope, Cherry & June Preisser, Eve Arden, Judy Canova, Stan Kavanaugh, Hugh O'Connell, Duke McHale, Nicholas Brothers, John Hoysradt.
Principal songs: Island in the West Indies; Words without Music; That Moment of Moments; I Can't Get Started.

THE SHOW IS ON
Opened: Dec. 25, 1936.
237 performances.
MUSIC ALSO BY OTHERS; SKETCHES BY DAVID FREEDMAN & MOSS HART; DUKE LYRICS BY TED FETTER.

Cast included: Beatrice Lillie, Bert Lahr, Reginald Gardiner, Mitzi Mayfair, Paul Haakon, Gracie Barrie, Charles Walters, Jack McCauley.
Principal Duke songs: Now; Casanova.

CABIN IN THE SKY
Opened: Oct. 25, 1940.
156 performances.
BOOK BY LYNN ROOT; LYRICS BY JOHN LATOUCHE.

Cast included: Ethel Waters, Todd Duncan, Dooley Wilson, Rex Ingram, Katherine Dunham, J. Rosamond Johnson, Helen Dowdy, Tally Beatty.
Principal songs: Takin' a Chance on Love; Cabin in the Sky; Do What You Wanna Do; My Old Virginia Home on the River Nile; Love Turned the Light Out; Honey in the Honeycomb.

BANJO EYES
Opened: Dec. 25, 1941.
126 performances.
BOOK BY JOE QUILLAN & IZZY ELINSON; LYRICS BY JOHN LATOUCHE & HAROLD ADAMSON.

Cast included: Eddie Cantor, Sally & Tony DeMarco, Lionel Stander, Audrey Christie, June Clyde, Morton & Virginia Mayo, Bill Johnson, Tommy Wonder, Doris Dowling, Shirl Thomas (Shirl Conway), Adele Jergens.
Principal songs: A Nickel to My Name; Not a Care in the World; We're Having a Baby; I'll Take the City.

THE LADY COMES ACROSS
Opened: Jan. 9, 1942.
3 performances.
BOOK BY FRED THOMPSON & DAWN POWELL; LYRICS BY JOHN LATOUCHE.

Cast included: Evelyn Wyckoff, Joe E. Lewis, Ronald Graham, Stiano Braggiotti, Gower Champion & Jeanne Tyler, Mischa Auer, Wynn Murray, Marc Platt, Morton L. Stevens, Hugh Martin, Ralph Blane, Lubov Rostova.
Principal songs: Summer Is A-Comin' In; You Took Me by Surprise; This Is Where I Came In; Lady.

JACKPOT
Opened: Jan. 13, 1944.
69 performances.
BOOK BY GUY BOLTON, SIDNEY SHELDON, BEN ROBERTS; LYRICS BY HOWARD DIETZ.

Cast included: Nanette Fabray, Allan Jones, Betty Garrett, Jerry Lester, Benny Baker, Mary Wickes, Wendell Corey, Billie Worth, Morton L. Stevens.
Principal songs: What Happened; Sugarfoot; I've Got a One-Track Mind; I Kissed My Girl Goodbye.

SADIE THOMPSON
Opened: Nov. 16, 1944.
60 performances.
BOOK BY HOWARD DIETZ & ROUBEN MA-MOULIAN; LYRICS BY DIETZ.

Cast included: June Havoc, Lansing Hatfield, Ralph Dumke, Beatrice Kraft, Doris Patston, Milada Miladova.
Principal songs: The Love I Long For; Poor as a Church Mouse; When You Live on an Island.

TWO'S COMPANY
Opened: Dec. 15, 1952.
90 performances.
SKETCHES MOSTLY BY CHARLES SHERMAN & PETER DEVRIES; LYRICS BY OGDEN NASH & SAMMY CAHN.

Cast included: Bette Davis, Hiram Sherman, David Burns, Bill Callahan, Nora Kaye, Ellen Hanley, Maria Karnilova, Tina Louise, Robert Pagent.
Principal songs: It Just Occurred to Me; Roundabout; Out of the Clear Blue Sky; Haunted Hot Spot; Just like a Man.

Recorded Version
RCA Victor LOC 1009 (O.C.)X.
Bette Davis' foghorn voice tends to obscure the attractiveness of many of the numbers in this revue.

THE LITTLEST REVUE
Opened: May 22, 1956.
32 performances.
MUSIC ALSO BY OTHERS; SKETCHES BY NAT HIKEN & BILLY FRIEDBERG, EUDORA WELTY, BUD MCCREERY & OTHERS; DUKE LYRICS BY OGDEN NASH.

Cast included: Joel Grey, Tammy Grimes, Charlotte Rae, Larry Storch.
Principal Duke songs: I Want to Fly Now (and Pay Later); Summer Is A-Comin' In; Good Little Girls; Love Is Still in Town; You're Far from Wonderful; Madly in Love.

Recorded Version
Epic LN 3275 (O.C.).
There are many bright touches in the score from Ben Bagley's off-Broadway revue.

Harold Arlen

EARL CARROLL VANITIES
Opened: July 1, 1930.
215 performances.
MUSIC ALSO BY JAY GORNEY; SKETCHES BY EDDIE WELCH & EUGENE CONRAD; ARLEN LYRICS BY TED KOEHLER; GORNEY LYRICS BY E. Y. HARBURG.

Cast included: Jimmy Savo, Jack Benny, Herb Williams, Harry Stockwell, Patsy Kelly, Faith Bacon.
Principal Arlen songs: Out of a Clear Blue Sky; Hittin' the Bottle; The March of Time.

YOU SAID IT
Opened: Jan. 19, 1931.
192 performances.
BOOK BY JACK YELLEN & SID SILVERS; LYRICS BY YELLEN.

Cast included: Lou Holtz, Mary Lawlor, Stanley Smith, Lyda Roberti, Benny Baker.
Principal songs: Sweet and Hot; You Said It.

LIFE BEGINS AT 8:40
Opened: Aug. 27, 1934.
237 performances.
SKETCHES BY DAVID FREEDMAN, ALLAN BAXTER, IRA GERSHWIN, E. Y. HARBURG & OTHERS; LYRICS BY GERSHWIN & HARBURG.

Cast included: Bert Lahr, Ray Bolger, Luella Gear, Frances Williams, Dixie Dunbar, Earl Oxford, Brian Donlevy, Robert Wildhack, Josephine Houston, James MacColl.
Principal songs: Shoein' the Mare; You're a Builder-Upper; Things; Fun to Be Fooled; What Can You Say in a Love Song?; Let's Take a Walk around the Block; I Couldn't Hold My Man.

HOORAY FOR WHAT!
Opened Dec. 1, 1937.
200 performances.
BOOK BY HOWARD LINDSAY & RUSSEL CROUSE; LYRICS BY E. Y. HARBURG.

Cast included: Ed Wynn, Jack Whiting, June Clyde, Vivian Vance, Paul Haakon, Leo Chalzel, Ruthanna Boris, Meg Mundy.

Principal songs: I've Gone Romantic on You; God's Country; Moanin' in the Mornin'; Down with Love; In the Shade of the New Apple Tree.

BLOOMER GIRL
Opened: Oct. 5, 1944.
654 *performances.*
BOOK BY SIG HERZIG & FRED SAIDY; LYRICS BY E. Y. HARBURG.

Cast included: Celeste Holm, David Brooks, Mabel Taliaferro, Joan McCracken, Dooley Wilson, Richard Huey.
Principal songs: When the Boys Come Home; The Eagle and Me; Right as the Rain; Sunday in Cicero Falls; Evelina; It Was Good Enough for Grandma; The Rakish Young Man with the Whiskers; I Got a Song.
Recorded Version
Decca DL 8015 (O.C.).
The Civil War, slavery, and women's rights are all dealt with in this attractive period score.

ST. LOUIS WOMAN
Opened: Mar. 30, 1946.
113 *performances.*
BOOK BY ARNA BONTEMPS & COUNTEE CULLEN; LYRICS BY JOHNNY MERCER.

Cast included: Ruby Hill, Harold & Fayard Nicholas, Rex Ingram, Pearl Bailey, June Hawkins, Juanita Hall, Lorenzo Fuller, Herbert Coleman.
Principal songs: Come Rain or Come Shine; Legalize My Name; Any Place I Hang My Hat Is Home; Cake Walk Your Lady; Sleep Peaceful, Mr. Used-to-Be; Leavin' Time; A Woman's Prerogative; Ridin' on the Moon.

HOUSE OF FLOWERS
Opened: Dec. 30, 1954.
165 *performances.*
BOOK BY TRUMAN CAPOTE; LYRICS BY CAPOTE & ARLEN.

Cast included: Pearl Bailey, Diahann Carroll, Juanita Hall, Ray Walston, Dino DiLuca, Rawn Spearman, Geoffrey Holder, Ada Moore, Enid Mosier, Dolores Harper, Frederick O'Neal, Don Redman.
Principal songs: A Sleepin' Bee; Bamboo Cage; Two Ladies in de Shade of de Banana Tree; I'm Gonna Leave Off Wearin' My Shoes; Has I Let You Down?; I Never Has Seen Snow; House of Flowers.

Recorded Version
Columbia OL 4969 (O.C.).
Possibly Arlen's supreme achievement is this exciting & exotic score.

JAMAICA
Opened: Oct. 31, 1957.
558 *performances.*
BOOK BY E. Y. HARBURG & FRED SAIDY; LYRICS BY HARBURG.

Cast included: Lena Horne, Ricardo Montalban, Adelaide Hall, Josephine Premice, Joe Adams, Erik Rhodes, Ossie Davis.
Principal songs: Savannah; Pretty to Walk With; Push the Button; Cocoanut Sweet; Pity the Sunset; Take It Slow, Joe; Ain't It the Truth?; Leave the Atom Alone; Napoleon; I Don't Think I'll End It All Today.
Recorded Version
RCA Victor LOC 1036/LSO 1036 (O.C.).
Arlen's melodic and rhythmic gifts are amply displayed in this showcase for Lena Horne.

SARATOGA
Opened: Dec. 7, 1959.
80 *performances.*
BOOK BY MORTON DaCOSTA; LYRICS BY JOHNNY MERCER.

Cast included: Howard Keel, Carol Lawrence, Odette Myrtil, Edith King, Warde Donovan, Carol Brice, Tun Tun.
Principal songs: Petticoat High; Why Fight This?; Game of Poker; Love Held Lightly; You or No One; The Man in My Life; Saratoga.
Recorded Version
RCA Victor LOC 1051/LSO 1051 (O.C.).
Though not a major work, Arlen's score captures much of the florid atmosphere of the story.

Burton Lane

EARL CARROLL VANITIES
Opened: Aug. 27, 1931.
278 *performances.*
MUSIC ALSO BY OTHERS; SKETCHES BY RALPH SPENCE & EDDIE WELCH; LANE LYRICS BY HAROLD ADAMSON.

Cast included: Will Mahoney, Lillian Roth, Jack Durant, William Demarest, Milton Watson.

Principal Lane songs: Have a Heart; Heigh-Ho, the Gang's All Here.

HOLD ON TO YOUR HATS
Opened: Sept. 11, 1940.
158 performances.
BOOK BY GUY BOLTON, MATT BROOKS, EDDIE DAVIS; LYRICS BY E. Y. HARBURG.

Cast included: Al Jolson, Martha Raye, Jack Whiting, Bert Gordon, Arnold Moss, Gil Lamb, Russ Brown, Jinx Falkenburg, Eunice Healey, Margaret Irving, Joanne Marshall (Joanne Dru), Constance Dowling.
Principal songs: The World Is in My Arms; Would You Be So Kindly?; Don't Let It Get You Down; There's a Great Day Coming Manana.

LAFFING ROOM ONLY
Opened: Dec. 23, 1944.
233 performances.
SKETCHES BY OLSEN & JOHNSON, EUGENE CONRAD; LYRICS BY LANE.

Cast included: Ole Olsen & Chic Johnson, Betty Garrett, Frank Libuse, Mata & Hari, J. C. McCord, Lou Wills, Jr., William Archibald, Willie West & McGinty, Fred Waring Glee Club.
Principal songs: Feudin' and Fightin'; This Is as Far as I Go.

FINIAN'S RAINBOW
Opened: Jan. 10, 1947.
725 performances.
BOOK BY E. Y. HARBURG & FRED SAIDY; LYRICS BY HARBURG.

Cast included: Ella Logan, Albert Sharpe, Donald Richards, David Wayne, Anita Alvarez, Robert Pitkin, Lorenzo Fuller, Lyn Murray Singers.
Principal songs: This Time of the Year; How Are Things in Glocca Morra?; If This Isn't Love; Look to the Rainbow; Old Devil Moon; Something Sort of Grandish; Necessity; When the Idle Poor Become the Idle Rich; When I'm Not Near the Girl I Love; That Great Come-and-Get-It Day.

Recorded Versions
Columbia OL 4062 (O.C.).
RCA Victor LOC 1057/LSO 1057 (O.C.) (1960).
One of Broadway's memorable scores has been well recorded by its original cast (Columbia) and the cast of the 1960 revival

(RCA). In addition to better sound, the Victor LP has Jeannie Carson, Howard Morris, and Biff McGuire.

E. Y. Harburg

EARL CARROLL'S SKETCHBOOK
Opened: July 1, 1929.
400 performances.
LYRICS ALSO BY OTHERS; SKETCHES BY EARL CARROLL, EDDIE CANTOR, SIDNEY SKOLSKY, EDDIE WELCH; HARBURG MUSIC BY JAY GORNEY.

Cast included: Will Mahoney, William Demarest, The Three Sailors, George Givot, Patsy Kelly, Faith Bacon.
Principal Harburg-Gorney songs: Kinda Cute; Like Me Less, Love Me More.

THE GARRICK GAIETIES
(*See* Vernon Duke).

EARL CARROLL VANITIES
Opened: July 1, 1930.
215 performances.
LYRICS ALSO BY TED KOEHLER; SKETCHES BY EDDIE WELCH & EUGENE CONRAD; HARBURG MUSIC BY JAY GORNEY; KOEHLER MUSIC BY HAROLD ARLEN.

Cast included: Jimmy Savo, Jack Benny, Herb Williams, Harry Stockwell, Patsy Kelly, Faith Bacon.
Principal Harburg-Gorney songs: I Came to Life; Ring Out the Blues.

BALLYHOO OF 1932
Opened: Sept. 6, 1932.
95 performances.
SKETCHES BY NORMAN ANTHONY; MUSIC BY LEWIS GENSLER.

Cast included: Willie & Eugene Howard, Jeanne Aubert, Lulu McConnell, Bob Hope, Paul Hartman.
Principal songs: Riddle Me This; Falling Off the Wagon.

AMERICANA
Opened: Oct. 5, 1932.
77 performances.
LYRICS ALSO BY JOHNNY MERCER; SKETCHES BY J. P. McEVOY; HARBURG MUSIC BY JAY GORNEY, VERNON DUKE, RICHARD MYERS, BURTON LANE, HAROLD ARLEN.

Cast included: George Givot, Albert Carroll, Lloyd Nolan, Georgie Tapps, Charles Weidman Dancers, Doris Humphrey Group, Rex Weber.
Principal Harburg songs: Brother Can You Spare a Dime? (Gorney); Let Me Match My Private Life with Yours (Duke); Whistling for a Kiss (Mercer-Myers); You're Not Pretty but You're Mine (Lane); Satan's Li'l Lamb (Mercer-Arlen).

WALK A LITTLE FASTER
(*See* Vernon Duke).

ZIEGFELD FOLLIES
(*See* Vernon Duke).

LIFE BEGINS AT 8:40
(*See* Harold Arlen).

HOORAY FOR WHAT!
(*See* Harold Arlen).

HOLD ON TO YOUR HATS
(*See* Burton Lane).

BLOOMER GIRL
(*See* Harold Arlen).

FINIAN'S RAINBOW
(*See* Burton Lane).

FLAHOOLEY
Opened: May 14, 1951.
40 *performances.*
BOOK BY HARBURG & FRED SAIDY; MUSIC BY SAMMY FAIN.

Cast included: Yma Sumac, Ernest Truex, Jerome Courtland, Edith Atwater, Irwin Corey, Barbara Cook, Bil Baird Marionettes, Fay DeWitt, Marilyn Ross, Nehemiah Persoff, Louis Nye, Lulu Bates.
Principal songs: You Too Can Be a Puppet; Here's to Your Illusions; Who Says There Ain't No Santa Claus?; Flahooley; The World Is Your Balloon; He's Only Wonderful; Jump, Little Chillun; The Springtime Cometh.

Recorded Version
Capitol S 284 (O.C.) X.
An unappreciated score of great charm.

JAMAICA
(*See* Harold Arlen).

Harold Rome

PINS AND NEEDLES
Opened: Nov. 27, 1937.
1,108 *performances.*
SKETCHES BY CHARLES FRIEDMAN, ARTHUR ARENT, MARC BLITZSTEIN & OTHERS.

Cast included: Members of the I.L.G.W.U.
Principal songs: Sing Me a Song of Social Significance; Sunday in the Park; One Big Union for Two; Chain Store Daisy; Nobody Makes a Pass at Me; It's Better with a Union Man.

SING OUT THE NEWS
Opened: Sept. 24, 1938.
105 *performances.*
SKETCHES BY CHARLES FRIEDMAN.

Cast included: Philip Loeb, Hiram Sherman, Mary Jane Walsh, Will Geer, Dorothy Fox, Michael Loring, Joey Faye, Rex Ingram, Richard Huey, Hazel Scott, June Allyson.
Principal songs: F.D.R. Jones; My Heart Is Unemployed; How Long Can Love Keep Laughing?; Yip-Ahoy; Plaza 6-9423.

LET FREEDOM SING
Opened: Oct. 5, 1942.
8 *performances.*
MUSIC & LYRICS ALSO BY OTHERS; SKETCHES BY SAM LOCKE.

Cast included: Mitzi Green, Betty Garrett, Lee Sullivan, Berni Gould.
Principal Rome songs: It's Fun to Be Free; Little Miss Victory Jones.

CALL ME MISTER
Opened: Apr. 18, 1946.
734 *performances.*
SKETCHES BY ARNOLD AUERBACH & ARNOLD HORWITT.

Cast included: Betty Garrett, Jules Munshin, Bill Callahan, Lawrence Winters, Harry Clark, Paula Bane, Maria Karnilova, Danny Scholl, Betty Lou Holland, Chandler Cowles.
Principal songs: Goin' Home Train; Little Surplus Me; The Red Ball Express; Military Life; The Face on the Dime; Yuletide Park Avenue; South America, Take It Away; Along with Me.

ALIVE AND KICKING
Opened: Jan. 17, 1950.
46 *performances.*

MUSIC & LYRICS ALSO BY OTHERS; SKETCHES BY RAY GOLDEN, HENRY MORGAN, JEROME CHODOROV, JOSEPH STEIN, WILL GLICKMAN, & OTHERS.
Cast included: David Burns, Bobby Van, Carl Reiner, Jack Cole, Gwen Verdon, Jack Gilford, Fay DeWitt, Jack Cassidy, Lenore Lonergan.
Principal Rome songs: Cry Baby Cry; French with Tears.

MICHAEL TODD'S PEEP SHOW
Opened: June 28, 1950
278 *performances.*
MUSIC & LYRICS ALSO BY OTHERS; SKETCHES BY BOBBY CLARK, H. I. PHILLIPS, WILLIAM ROOS, BILLY K. WELLS.
Cast included: Lina Romay, Lilly Christine, "Hi Wilberforce" Conley, "Bozo" Snyder, "Peanuts" Mann, "Red" Marshall, Clifford Guest.
Principal Rome songs: Pocketful of Dreams; I Hate a Parade.

BLESS YOU ALL
Opened: Dec. 14, 1950.
84 *performances.*
SKETCHES BY ARNOLD AUERBACH.
Cast included: Mary McCarty, Jules Munshin, Pearl Bailey, Valerie Bettis, Donald Saddler, Robert Chisholm, Byron Palmer, Jane Harvey.
Principal songs: I Can Hear It Now; Little Things Mean So Much to Me; A Rose Is a Rose; Summer Dresses; You Never Know What Hit You When It's Love.

WISH YOU WERE HERE
Opened: June 25, 1952.
598 *performances.*
BOOK BY ARTHUR KOBER & JOSHUA LOGAN.
Cast included: Sheila Bond, Jack Cassidy, Patricia Marand, Sidney Armus, Paul Valentine, Harry Clark, Florence Henderson, Larry Blyden, Phyllis Newman.
Principal songs: Wish You Were Here; Shopping Around; Could Be; Summer Afternoon; Where Did the Night Go?; Don José of Far Rockaway; Goodbye Love.
Recorded Version
RCA Camden CAL 621 (O.C.).
A light, lyrical score that ably catches the flavor of middle-class New Yorkers on a two-week vacation.

FANNY
Opened: Nov. 4, 1954.
888 *performances.*
BOOK BY S. N. BEHRMAN & JOSHUA LOGAN.
Cast included: Ezio Pinza, Walter Slezak, Florence Henderson, William Tabbert, Gerald Price, Nejla Ates.
Principal songs: Never Too Late for Love; Octopus Song; Restless Heart; Why Be Afraid to Dance?; Welcome Home; I Have to Tell You; Fanny; To My Wife; Love Is a Very Light Thing; I Like You.
Recorded Version
RCA Victor LOC 1015 (O.C.).
An ambitious, often moving work.

DESTRY RIDES AGAIN
Opened: Apr. 23, 1959.
473 *performances.*
BOOK BY LEONARD GERSHE.
Cast included: Andy Griffith, Dolores Gray, Scott Brady, Jack Prince, Libi Staiger.
Principal songs: Hoop-de-Dingle; Ballad of the Gun; I Know Your Kind; Anyone Would Love You; Fair Warning; Are You Ready, Gyp Watson?; That Ring on the Finger; I Say Hello.
Recorded Version
Decca DL 9075/DL 79075 (O.C.).
Rome on the range.

Kurt Weill

THE THREEPENNY OPERA
Opened: Apr. 13, 1933.
12 *performances.*
BOOK & LYRICS BY GIFFORD COCHRAN & JERROLD KRIMSKY, ADAPTED FROM THE ORIGINAL BY BERTOLT BRECHT.
Cast included: Steffi Duna, Robert Chisholm, Rex Weber, Rex Evans, Herbert Rudley, Burgess Meredith.
Principal songs: Legend of Mackie Messer; Wedding Song; Pirate Jenny; Soldier Song; Love Duet; Ballad of the Easy Life; Jealousy Duet; Song of the Aimlessness of Life.

JOHNNY JOHNSON
Opened: Nov. 19, 1936.
68 *performances.*
PLAY & LYRICS BY PAUL GREEN.
Cast included: Russell Collins, Roman Bohnen, Phoebe Brand, Sanford Meisner,

Bob Lewis, Lee J. Cobb, Art Smith, Albert Van Dekker, Elia Kazan, Luther Adler, Jules (John) Garfield, Morris Carnovsky, Joseph Pevney.

Principal songs: Johnny's Song; O Heart of Love; Song of the Goddess; O, the Rio Grande; Song of the Guns; Mon Ami, My Friend; Psychiatry Song.

Recorded Version

MGM E 3447 (S.C.).

Headed by Burgess Meredith, Hiram Sherman, and Lotte Lenya, a fine group of singers and actors admirably preserve the power of Weill's first American score.

KNICKERBOCKER HOLIDAY
Opened: Oct. 19, 1938.
168 performances.
BOOK & LYRICS BY MAXWELL ANDERSON.

Cast included: Walter Huston, Ray Middleton, Richard Kollmar, Jeanne Madden, Mark Smith, Clarence Nordstrom, Howard Freeman, Robert Rounseville.

Principal songs: There's Nowhere to Go but Up; How Can You Tell an American?; September Song; It Never Was You; The Scars.

LADY IN THE DARK
Opened: Jan. 23, 1941.
467 performances.
BOOK BY MOSS HART; LYRICS BY IRA GERSHWIN.

Cast included: Gertrude Lawrence, Macdonald Carey, Danny Kaye, Victor Mature, Bert Lytell, Evelyn Wyckoff, Donald Randolph, Margaret Dale, Natalie Schafer.

Principal songs: Oh, Fabulous One; One Life to Live; Girl of the Moment; This Is New; The Princess of Pure Delight; My Ship; The Saga of Jenny; Tschaikowsky.

Recorded Version

RCA Victor LM 1882 (TV) (1954) X.

Ann Sothern & Carleton Carpenter are the soloists in this remarkable work.

ONE TOUCH OF VENUS
Opened: Oct. 7, 1943.
567 performances.
BOOK BY S. J. PERELMAN & OGDEN NASH; LYRICS BY NASH.

Cast included: Mary Martin, Kenny Baker, John Boles, Paula Laurence, Teddy Hart, Sono Osato, Harry Clark, Lou Wills, Jr.,

Helen Raymond, Allyn Ann McLerie, Pearl Lang.

Principal songs: One Touch of Venus; How Much I Love You; I'm a Stranger Here Myself; Speak Low; West Wind; Foolish Heart; The Trouble with Women; That's Him; Wooden Wedding.

THE FIREBRAND OF FLORENCE
Opened: Mar. 22, 1945.
43 performances.
BOOK BY EDWIN JUSTUS MAYER; LYRICS BY IRA GERSHWIN.

Cast included: Earl Wrightson, Lotte Lenya, Melville Cooper, Marion Green, Beverly Tyler, John (Jack) Cassidy.

Principal songs: Sing Me Not a Ballad; A Rhyme for Angela; The Cozy Nook Trio; You're Far Too Near Me.

STREET SCENE
Opened: Jan. 9, 1947.
148 performances.
BOOK BY ELMER RICE; LYRICS BY LANGSTON HUGHES.

Cast included: Norman Cordon, Anne Jeffreys, Polyna Stoska, Brian Sullivan, Hope Emerson, Sheila Bond, Danny Daniels, Irving Kaufman, Juanita Hall.

Principal songs: I Got a Marble and a Star; Somehow I Never Could Believe; Ice Cream; Wrapped in a Ribbon and Tied in a Bow; Lonely House; Wouldn't You Like to Be on Broadway?; What Good Would the Moon Be?; Moon-Faced, Starry-Eyed; Remember That I Care; A Boy like You; We'll Go Away Together.

Recorded Version

Columbia OL 4139 (O.C.).

Weill's most operatic American score is a notable and moving achievement.

LOVE LIFE
Opened: Oct. 7, 1948.
252 performances.
BOOK & LYRICS BY ALAN JAY LERNER.

Cast included: Nanette Fabray, Ray Middleton, Johnny Stewart, Jay Marshall, Lyle Bettger.

Principal songs: Here I'll Stay; Progress; Green-Up Time; Economics; Love Song; Susan's Dream; Mr. Right.

LOST IN THE STARS
Opened: Oct. 30, 1949.

273 performances.
BOOK & LYRICS BY MAXWELL ANDERSON.

Cast included: Todd Duncan, Leslie Banks, Inez Matthews, Warren Coleman, Sheila Guyse, Frank Roane, Herbert Coleman, Georgette Harvey, Robert McFerrin.
Principal songs: The Hills of Ixopo; Thousands of Miles; Train to Johannesburg; The Little Grey House;. Trouble Man; Lost in the Stars; Stay Well; Cry the Beloved Country; Big Mole; A Bird of Paradise.

Recorded Version
Decca DL 8028 (O.C.).
This is a frequently impressive work, with brief bits of dialogue used on the record to bridge the musical selections.

THE THREEPENNY OPERA
Opened: March 10, 1954.
2,611 *performances.*
BOOK & LYRICS BY MARC BLITZSTEIN, ADAPTED FROM THE ORIGINAL BY BERTOLT BRECHT.

Cast included: Lotte Lenya, Scott Merrill, Martin Wolfson, Jo Sullivan, Charlotte Rae, Gerald Price, Beatrice Arthur.
Principal songs: The Ballad of Mack the Knife; Wedding Song; Pirate Jenny; Army Song; Love Song; Ballad of the Easy Life; Barbara Song; Jealousy Duet; Useless Song; Solomon Song.

Recorded Version
MGM E 3121 (O.C.).
The off-Broadway production has been given an excellent English adaption. Worthwhile recordings in the original German include: excerpts featuring the 1928 Berlin cast (Telefunken 66053), and the 1958 complete version on two records (Columbia 02L 257/C2S 201). Lotte Lenya is heard on all three.

Richard Rodgers and Oscar Hammerstein II

All books and lyrics by Mr. Hammerstein unless otherwise noted. See separate list for all musicals written by Mr. Hammerstein prior to his association with Mr. Rodgers.

OKLAHOMA!
Opened: Mar. 31, 1943.
2,212 *performances.*

Cast included: Betty Garde, Alfred Drake, Joan Roberts, Howard da Silva, Joseph Buloff, Celeste Holm, Lee Dixon, Katherine Sergava, Joan McCracken, Bambi Linn, George Church, Marc Platt, Diana Adams.
Principal songs: Oh, What a Beautiful Mornin', The Surrey with the Fringe on Top; Kansas City; I Cain't Say No; Many a New Day; People Will Say We're in Love; Pore Jud Is Daid; Out of My Dreams; All er Nothin'; **Oklahoma.**

Recorded Versions
Decca DL 9017 (O.C.).
Columbia CL 828 (S.C.).
Capitol WAO 595/SWAO 595 (F.V.) (1955).
Epic LN 3678/BN 562 (S.C.).
Decca's 78 rpm album started the vogue for original-cast releases. On an LP, it is still a worthy addition to any library, even though it is not so complete as Columbia's (Nelson Eddy, Virginia Haskins, Kaye Ballard), nor as well recorded as Capitol's sound track (Gordon MacRae, Shirley Jones, Gloria Grahame), or Epic's release (Stuart Foster, Lois Hunt, and Fay DeWitt).

CAROUSEL
Opened: Apr. 19, 1945.
890 *performances.*

Cast included: John Raitt, Jan Clayton, Jean Darling, Christine Johnson, Jean Casto, Murvyn Vye, Eric Mattson, Bambi Linn, Peter Birch, Pearl Lang, Russell Collins, Robert Pagent, Iva Withers.
Principal songs: Carousel Waltz; You're a Queer One, Julie Jordan; When I Marry Mr. Snow; If I Loved You; June Is Bustin' Out All Over; When the Children Are Asleep; Blow High, Blow Low; Soliloquy; This Was a Real Nice Clambake; What's the Use of Wond'rin'; You'll Never Walk Alone.

Recorded Versions
Decca DL 9020 (O.C.).
RCA Victor LPM 1048 (S.C.).
Capitol W 694/SW 694 (F.V.) (1956).
Epic LN 3679/BN 563 (S.C.)
Possibly the greatest of all R & H scores. The most complete version is on RCA, with Robert Merrill and Patrice Munsel, but both the Decca original cast (John Raitt, Jan Clayton) and the Capital sound track (Gordon MacRae, Shirley Jones) are also well

sung. The Epic, with Lois Hunt, Harry Snow, and Charmaine Harma, is rather dull.

ALLEGRO
Opened: Oct. 10, 1947.
315 *performances.*

Cast included: John Battles, Annamary Dickey, William Ching, John Conte, Muriel O'Malley, Roberta Jonay, Lisa Kirk, Kathryn Lee, Harrison Muller.
Principal songs: I know It can Happen Again; One Foot, Other Foot; A Fellow Needs a Girl; So Far; You Are Never Away; Money Isn't Ev'rything; The Gentlemen Is a Dope; Allegro.

SOUTH PACIFIC
Opened: Apr. 7, 1949.
1,925 *performances.*
BOOK BY HAMMERSTEIN & JOSHUA LOGAN.
Cast included: Ezio Pinza, Mary Martin, Myron McCormick, William Tabbert, Juanita Hall, Betta St. John, Martin Wolfson, Harvey Stephens, Dickinson (Richard) Eastham, Biff McGuire, Sandra Deel.
Principal songs: Dites-moi Porquoi; A Cockeyed Optimist; Some Enchanted Evening; Bloody Mary; There Is Nothin' like a Dame; Bali Ha'i; I'm Gonna Wash That Man Right Outa My Hair; I'm In Love with a Wonderful Guy; Younger Than Springtime; Happy Talk; Honey Bun; Carefully Taught; This Nearly Was Mine.
Recorded Versions
Columbia OL 4180 (O.C.).
RCA Victor LOC 1032/LSO 1032 (F.V.) (1958).
Rodgers & Hammerstein's most popular work is still heard at its best on the Columbia recording. The RCA sound-track release features Mitzi Gaynor and Giorgio Tozzi.

THE KING AND I
Opened: Mar. 29, 1951.
1,246 *performances.*

Cast included: Gertrude Lawrence, Yul Brynner, Dorothy Sarnoff, Doretta Morrow, Larry Douglas, Johnny Stewart, John Juliano, Gemze de Lappe, Michiko, Yuriko, Gloria Marlowe.
Principal songs: I Whistle a Happy Tune; My Lord and Master; Hello, Young Lovers; March of the Royal Siamese Children; A Puzzlement; Getting to Know You; We Kiss

in a Shadow; Something Wonderful; I Have Dreamed; Shall We Dance?
Recorded Versions
Decca DL 9008 (O.C.).
Capitol W 740/SW 740 (F.V.) (1957).
Philips BBL 7002 (London O.C.) (1953).
Epic LN 3680/BN 564 (S.C.).
Yul Brynner is heard on both the Decca and the Capitol versions of this lovely score. But the former does have Gertrude Lawrence, while the latter offers Deborah Kerr's "voice," Marni Nixon. The splendid English recording features Valerie Hobson and Herbert Lom. Epic has Lois Hunt, Samuel Jones, and Charmaine Harma.

ME AND JULIET
Opened: May 28, 1953.
358 *performances.*

Cast included: Isabel Bigley, Bill Hayes, Joan McCracken, Ray Walston, Mark Dawson, Jackie Kelk, Arthur Maxwell, George S. Irving, Helena Scott, Bob Fortier, Shirley MacLaine, Michael King, Barbara Carroll (pianist).
Principal songs: That's the Way it Happens; Marriage Type Love; Keep It Gay; The Big, Black Giant; No Other Love; It's Me; Intermission Talk; We Deserve Each Other; I'm Your Girl.
Recorded Version
RCA Victor LOC 1012 (O.C.)X.
A light, attractive collection of songs.

PIPE DREAM
Opened: Nov. 30, 1955.
246 *performances.*

Cast included: Helen Traubel, William Johnson, Judy Tyler, G. D. (George) Wallace, Mike Kellin, Ruby Braff, Patricia Wilson.
Principal songs: All Kinds of People; Ev'rybody's Got a Home but Me; A Lopsided Bus; Sweet Thursday; Suzy Is a Good Thing; All at Once You Love Her; Will You Marry Me?; The Next Time It Happens.
Recorded Version
RCA Victor LOC 1023 (O.C.)X.
The cast performs well, but this is the least impressive of all the masters' achievements.

FLOWER DRUM SONG
Opened: Dec. 1, 1958.
601 *performances.*
BOOK BY HAMMERSTEIN & JOSEPH FIELDS.

Cast included: Miyoshi Umeki, Pat Suzuki, Larry Blyden, Juanita Hall, Ed Kenney, Keye Luke, Arabella Hong, Jack Soo, Anita Ellis.
Principal songs: You Are Beautiful; A Hundred Million Miracles; I Enjoy Being a Girl; Like a God; Chop Suey; Don't Marry Me; Grant Avenue; Love, Look Away; Sunday.
Recorded Version
Columbia OL 5350/OS 2009 (O.C.).
Charming music, well sung and imaginatively orchestrated.

THE SOUND OF MUSIC
Opened: Nov. 16, 1959.
(Still running as of April 1, 1962)
BOOK BY HOWARD LINDSAY & RUSSEL CROUSE.

Cast included: Mary Martin, Theodore Bickel, Patricia Neway, Kurt Kasznar, Marion Marlowe, Lauri Peters, Muriel O'Malley.
Principal songs: The Sound of Music; Maria; My Favorite Things; Do-Re-Mi; Sixteen Going on Seventeen; The Lonely Goatherd; How Can Love Survive?; Climb Ev'ry Mountain; Edelweiss.
Recorded Versions
Columbia KOL 5450/KOS 2020 (O.C.).
Warner Bros. W 1377/WS 1377.
A work of much sweetness and light, this score is well sung by the original cast. There are even better voices on the Warner Bros. disc, which features members of the Trapp Family.

Oscar Hammerstein II

This list includes all Broadway musicals by Oscar Hammerstein II not written in collaboration with Richard Rodgers. All books and lyrics are by Mr. Hammerstein, unless otherwise noted.

ALWAYS YOU
Opened: Jan. 5, 1920.
66 *performances.*
MUSIC BY HERBERT STOTHART.

Cast included: Helen Ford, Walter Scanlan, Edouard Ciannelli, Julia Kelety, Ralph Herz, Bernard Gorcey, Anna Seymour.
Principal songs: Always You; Syncopated Heart; My Pousse-Café; The Tired Business Man.

TICKLE ME
Opened: Aug. 17, 1920.
207 *performances.*
BOOK WITH OTTO HARBACH & FRANK MANDEL; LYRICS WITH HARBACH; MUSIC BY HERBERT STOTHART.

Cast included: Frank Tinney, Vic Casmore, Allen Kearns, Marguerite Zender, Louise Allen, Frances Grant & Ted Wing.
Principal songs: Until You Say Goodbye; I Don't Laugh at Love Any More; Then Love Again; Tickle Me; If a Wish Could Make It So.

JIMMIE
Opened: Nov. 17, 1920.
71 *performances.*
BOOK WITH OTTO HARBACH & FRANK MANDEL; LYRICS WITH HARBACH; MUSIC BY HERBERT STOTHART.

Cast included: Frances White, Ben Welch, Paul Porcasi, Harry Delf, Hattie Burks, Don Burroughs.
Principal songs: Cute Little Two by Four; Baby Dreams; Jimmie.

DAFFY DILL
Opened: Aug. 22, 1922.
71 *performances.*
BOOK WITH GUY BOLTON; MUSIC BY HERBERT STOTHART.

Cast included: Frank Tinney, Guy Robertson, Marion Sunshine, Georgia O'Ramey, Irene Olsen, Frances Grant & Ted Wing, Margaret & Elizabeth Keene.
Principal songs: A Coachman's Heart; My Boy Friend; My Little Redskin.

QUEEN O' HEARTS
Opened: Oct. 10, 1922.
39 *performances.*
BOOK WITH FRANK MANDEL; ADDITIONAL LYRICS BY SIDNEY MITCHELL; MUSIC BY LEWIS GENSLER & DUDLEY WILKINSON.

Cast included: Nora Bayes, Harry Richman, Norma Terris, Max Hoffman, Jr., Arthur Uttry, Franker Woods, Georgie Brown, Edna Hibbard, Dudley Wilkinson, Consuelo Flowerton.
Principal songs: Dreaming Alone; You Need Someone; Tom-Tom.

WILDFLOWER
(See Vincent Youmans).

MARY JANE McKANE
(*See* Vincent Youmans).

ROSE-MARIE
(*See* Rudolf Friml).

SUNNY
(*See* Jerome Kern).

SONG OF THE FLAME
(*See* George Gershwin).

THE WILD ROSE
(*See* Rudolf Friml).

THE DESERT SONG
(*See* Sigmund Romberg).

GOLDEN DAWN
Opened: Nov. 30, 1927.
184 *performances.*
BOOK & LYRICS WITH OTTO HARBACH; MUSIC
BY EMMERICH KALMAN & HERBERT STOTH-
ART.

Cast included: Louise Hunter, Paul Gregory,
Marguerita Sylva, Robert Chisholm, Olin
Howland, Barbara Newberry, Gil Squires,
Hazel Drury, Archie Leach (Cary Grant),
Russian Art Choir.
Principal songs: When I Crack My Whip;
We Two; Dawn.

SHOW BOAT
(*See* Jerome Kern).

GOOD BOY
Opened: Sept. 25, 1928.
253 *performances.*
BOOK WITH OTTO HARBACH & HENRY
MYERS; MUSIC BY HERBERT STOTHART &
HARRY RUBY; LYRICS BY BERT KALMAR.

Cast included: Eddie Buzzell, Helen Kane,
Barbara Newberry, Charles Butterworth,
Sam Hearn, Effie Shannon, Dan Healy,
Borrah Minevitch, Evelyn Bennett.

THE NEW MOON
(*See* Sigmund Romberg).

RAINBOW
(*See* Vincent Youmans).

SWEET ADELINE
(*See* Jerome Kern).

FREE FOR ALL
Opened: Sept. 8, 1931.
15 *performances.*
BOOK WITH LAURENCE SCHWAB; MUSIC BY
RICHARD A. WHITING.

Cast included: Jack Haley, Tamara, Lillian
Bond, Vera Marsh, Peter Higgins, David
Hutcheson, Philip Lord, Seth Arnold, Benny
Goodman Orchestra.
Principal songs: I Love Him, the Rat; The
Girl Next Door; Not That I Care.

EAST WIND
(*See* Sigmund Romberg).

MUSIC IN THE AIR
(*See* Jerome Kern).

MAY WINE
(*See* Sigmund Romberg).

VERY WARM FOR MAY
(*See* Jerome Kern).

SUNNY RIVER
(*See* Sigmund Romberg).

CARMEN JONES
Opened: Dec. 2, 1943.
502 *performances.*
MUSIC BY GEORGES BIZET.
Cast included: Muriel Smith (alternating
with Muriel Rahn), Luther Saxon (with
Napoleon Reed), Carlotta Franzell (with
Elton J. Warren), June Hawkins, Cozy Cole,
Glenn Bryant, Inez Matthews.
Principal songs: Dat's Love; Dere's a Café
on de Corner; Beat Out Dat Rhythm on a
Drum; Stan' Up and Fight; Dis Flower; My
Joe; Our Man.

Recorded Versions
Decca DL 9021 (O.C.).
RCA Victor LM 1881 (F.V.) (1954).
 Hammerstein's resetting of Bizet's opera,
Carmen, makes for an excitingly theatrical
score. The voices on the sound track are
those of Marilyn Horn, LeVern Hutcherson,
Olga James, Pearl Bailey, and Diahann
Carroll.

Leonard Bernstein

ON THE TOWN
Opened: Dec. 28, 1944.
463 *performances.*
BOOK & LYRICS BY BETTY COMDEN & ADOLPH GREEN.

Cast included: Nancy Walker, Sono Osato, John Battles, Betty Comden, Adolph Green, Cris Alexander, Alice Pearce, Robert Chisholm, Herbert Greene.
Principal songs: New York, New York; I Can Cook, Too; Some Other Time; I Get Carried Away; Lonely Town; Ya Got Me; Lucky to Be Me.

Recorded Versions
Columbia OL 5540/OS 2028 (S.C.).
Decca DL 8030 (S.C.).
With Bernstein conducting, Nancy Walker, Betty Comden, and Adolph Green are featured on Columbia's definitive recording of this infectious work. Walker, Comden, and Green are also heard on the Decca release, on which they are joined by Mary Martin. (Raymond Scott's *Lute Song* score is on the reverse.)

WONDERFUL TOWN
Opened: Feb. 25, 1953.
559 *performances.*
BOOK BY JOSEPH FIELDS & JEROME CHODOROV; LYRICS BY BETTY COMDEN & ADOLPH GREEN.

Cast included: Rosalind Russell, George Gaynes, Edith Adams, Henry Lascoe, Jordan Bentley, Cris Alexander, Dody Goodman.
Principal songs: Christopher Street; Ohio; One Hundred Easy Ways; What a Waste; A Quiet Girl; Conga!; Swing!; It's Love; Wrong Note Rag.

Recorded Versions
Decca DL 9010 (O.C.).
Columbia OL 5360/OS 2008 (TV) (1958).
As both versions have Rosalind Russell it's a matter of whether you prefer the superior supporting cast on the former or the superior sound on the latter.

CANDIDE
Opened: Dec. 1, 1956.
73 *performances.*

BOOK BY LILLIAN HELLMAN; LYRICS MOSTLY BY RICHARD WILBUR & JOHN LATOUCHE.

Cast included: Max Adrian, Robert Rounseville, Barbara Cook, Irra Petina, William Olvis.
Principal songs: The Best of All Possible Worlds; Oh, Happy We; Glitter and Be Gay; You Were Dead, You Know; I Am Easily Assimilated; Eldorado; What's the Use?

Recorded Version
Columbia OL 5180 (O.C.).
Although a commercial failure, the score still possesses more real music than many of the box-office hits of recent years.

WEST SIDE STORY
Opened: Sept. 26, 1957.
734 *performances.*
BOOK BY ARTHUR LAURENTS; LYRICS BY STEPHEN SONDHEIM.

Cast included: Carol Lawrence, Larry Kert, Chita Rivera, Art Smith, Mickey Calin, Ken LeRoy.
Principal songs: Jet Song; Something's Coming; Maria; Tonight; Cool; America; I Feel Pretty; Somewhere; Gee, Officer Krupke!

Recorded Version
Columbia OL 5230/OS 2001 (O.C.).
The clashes between rival New York street gangs have inspired a score both explosive and tender. The ballet music has been recorded on one side of Warner Bros. B 1240/BS 1240 (orchestra conducted by Robert Prince), and on one side of RCA Victor LM 2340/LSC 2340 (Robert Russell Bennett and the RCA Victor Symphony Orchestra).

Alan Jay Lerner and Frederick Loewe

All books and lyrics by Mr. Lerner unless otherwise noted. For another musical with Lerner lyrics, see Love Life *under Kurt Weill.*

GREAT LADY
Opened: Dec. 1, 1938.
20 *performances.*
BOOK BY EARLE CROOKER & LOWELL BRENTANO; LYRICS BY CROOKER.

Cast included: Norma Terris, Tullio Carminati, Helen Ford, Irene Bordoni, Shepperd Strudwick, Joseph Macaulay, André Eglevsky, Walter Cassel, Dorothy Kirsten, Nora Kaye, Alicia Alonso, Paul Godkin, Jerome Robbins.
Principal songs: I Have Room in My Heart; There Had to Be the Waltz; May I Suggest Romance?

WHAT'S UP
Opened: Nov. 11, 1943.
63 *performances.*
BOOK BY LERNER & ARTHUR PIERSON.

Cast included: Jimmy Savo, Johnny Morgan, Gloria Warren, Sondra Barrett, Pat Marshall, Phyllis Hill, William Tabbert, Larry Douglas.
Principal songs: Joshua; You've Got a Hold On Me.

THE DAY BEFORE SPRING
Opened: Nov. 22, 1945.
165 *performances.*

Cast included: Bill Johnson, Irene Manning, John Archer, Tom Helmore, Pat Marshall, Estelle Loring, Hugh Laing, Mary Ellen Moylan.
Principal songs: A Jug of Wine; My Love Is a Married Man; I Love You This Morning; The Day before Spring; You Haven't Changed at All; God's Green World.

BRIGADOON
Opened: Mar. 13, 1947.
581 *performances.*

Cast included: David Brooks, Marion Bell, Pamela Britton, Lee Sullivan, George Keane, William Hansen, James Mitchell, Elliott Sullivan.
Principal songs: Brigadoon; Waitin' for My Dearie; I'll Go Home with Bonnie Jean; The Heather on the Hill; Come to Me, Bend to Me; Almost like Being in Love; There But for You Go I; My Mother's Wedding Day; From This Day On.

Recorded Versions
RCA Victor LOC 1001 (O.C.).
MGM E 3135 (F.V.) (1954).
Columbia CL 1132 (S.C.).
The most complete, best recorded, and best sung is the Columbia with Shirley Jones and Jack Cassidy. Gene Kelly does most of the singing on the sound track.

PAINT YOUR WAGON
Opened: Nov. 12, 1951.
289 *performances.*
Cast included: James Barton, Olga San Juan, Tony Bavaar, Gemze de Lappe, James Mitchell.
Principal songs: I'm on My Way; I Talk to the Trees; They Call the Wind Maria; I Still See Elisa; In Between; Carino Mio; There's a Coach Comin' In; Hand Me Down that Can o' Beans; Another Autumn; Wand'rin' Star.

Recorded Version
RCA Victor LOC 1006 (O.C.).
The lusty, flavorsome music of this goldmining saga is always a pleasure to listen to.

MY FAIR LADY
Opened: Mar. 15, 1956.
(Still running as of April 1, 1962)

Cast included: Rex Harrison, Julie Andrews, Stanley Holloway, Cathleen Nesbitt, Robert Coote, John Michael King, Christopher Hewett, Olive Reeves-Smith.
Principal songs: Why Can't the English?; Wouldn't It Be Loverly?; With a Little Bit of Luck; I'm an Ordinary Man; Just You Wait; The Rain in Spain; I Could Have Danced All Night; On the Street Where You Live; Show Me; Get Me to the Church on Time; A Hymn to Him; Without You; I've Grown Accustomed to Her Face.

Recorded Versions
Columbia OL 5090/OS 2015 (O.C.).
Columbia WL 155/WS 305 (Mexican O.C.).
Though you probably already have the original New York cast version, Columbia has obligingly offered a stereo edition of the London cast, and both mono and stereo versions of the Mexican cast sung in Spanish.

Jule Styne

HIGH BUTTON SHOES
Opened: Oct. 9, 1947.
727 *performances.*
BOOK BY STEPHEN LONGSTREET; LYRICS BY SAMMY CAHN.

Cast included: Phil Silvers, Nanette Fabray, Jack McCauley, Mark Dawson, Joey Faye, Johnny Stewart, Helen Gallagher, Paul Godkin, Sondra Lee.

Principal songs: Can't You Just See Yourself in Love with Me?; There's Nothing like a Model "T"; You're My Girl; Papa, Won't You Dance with Me?; On a Sunday by the Sea; I Still Get Jealous.

Recorded Version
RCA Camden CAL 457 (O.C.).
This low-priced ($1.98) reissue of the original 78-rpm album is an excellent buy.

GENTLEMEN PREFER BLONDES
Opened: Dec. 8, 1949.
740 *performances.*
Book by Joseph Fields & Anita Loos; lyrics by Leo Robin.

Cast included: Carol Channing, Yvonne Adair, Jack McCauley, Eric Brotherson, Alice Pearce, Rex Evans, Anita Alvarez, George S. Irving, Reta Shaw, Howard Morris, Peter Birch.
Principal songs: Bye Bye Baby; A Little Girl from Little Rock; Just a Kiss Apart; You Say You Care; Diamonds Are a Girl's Best Friend; Homesick Blues.

Recorded Versions
Columbia OL 4290 (O.C.)
MGM E 3231 (F.V.) (1953)X.
A good old-fashioned musical comedy score. The MGM sound track, backed by selections from Kern's *Till the Clouds Roll By*, offers little more than Marilyn Monroe and Jane Russell.

TWO ON THE AISLE
Opened: July 19, 1951.
281 *performances.*
Sketches & lyrics by Betty Comden & Adolph Green.

Cast included: Bert Lahr, Dolores Gray, Colette Marchand, Elliott Reid, Stanley Prager, J. C. McCord.
Principal songs: Hold Me, Hold Me, Hold Me; There Never Was a Baby like My Baby; Catch Our Act at the Met; If You Hadn't but You Did; How Will He Know?

Recorded Version
Decca DL 8040 (O.C.).
An amusing and lighthearted revue score.

HAZEL FLAGG
Opened: Feb. 11, 1953.
190 *performances.*
Book by Ben Hecht; lyrics by Bob Hilliard.

Cast included: Helen Gallagher, Thomas Mitchell, Benay Venuta, John Howard, Jack Whiting, Sheree North, Jonathan Harris, John Brascia.
Principal songs: I'm Glad I'm Leaving; Every Street's a Boulevard in Old New York; How Do You Speak to an Angel?; Everybody Loves to Take a Bow.

Recorded Version
RCA Victor LOC 1010 (O.C.)X.
Apart from "Every Street's a Boulevard," there is little to recommend here.

PETER PAN
Opened: Oct. 20, 1954.
152 *performances.*
Music also by Mark Charlap; play by James M. Barrie; Styne lyrics by Betty Comden & Adolph Green; Charlap lyrics by Carolyn Leigh.

Cast included: Mary Martin, Cyril Ritchard, Margalo Gilmore, Kathy Nolan, Heller Halliday, Sondra Lee.
Principal Styne songs: Never-Never Land; Mysterious Lady; Captain Hook's Waltz.

Recorded Version
RCA Victor LOC 1019 (O.C.).
Styne-Comden-Green & Charlap-Leigh have about half the songs apiece. A charming album.

BELLS ARE RINGING
Opened: Nov. 29, 1956.
924 *performances.*
Book & lyrics by Betty Comden & Adolph Green.

Cast included: Judy Holliday, Sydney Chaplin, Eddie Lawrence, Jean Stapleton, George S. Irving, Peter Gennaro.
Principal songs: It's a Perfect Relationship; On My Own; It's a Simple Little System; Is It a Crime?; Just in Time; Long Before I Knew You; The Party's Over; I'm Going Back.

Recorded Versions
Columbia OL 5170/OS 2006 (O.C.).
Capitol W 1435/SW 1435 (F.V.) (1960).
A bright, melodious collection of songs. Miss Holliday and Dean Martin are on the Capitol sound track.

SAY, DARLING
Opened: Apr. 3, 1958.

332 performances.
PLAY BY RICHARD BISSELL, ABE BURROWS, MARIAN BISSELL; LYRICS BY BETTY COMDEN & ADOLPH GREEN.
Cast included: David Wayne, Vivian Blaine, Johnny Desmond, Jerome Cowan, Constance Ford, Horace McMahon, Robert Morse, Matt Mattox, Mitchell Gregg, Robert Downing.
Principal songs: It's the Second Time You Meet That Matters; Say, Darling; Dance Only with Me; Something's Always Happening on the River.

Recorded Version
RCA Victor LOC 1045/LSO 1045 (O.C.).
   Pleasant, if undistinguished, music and lyrics.

GYPSY
Opened: May 21, 1959.
702 performances.
BOOK BY ARTHUR LAURENTS; LYRICS BY STEPHEN SONDHEIM.

Cast included: Ethel Merman, Jack Klugman, Sandra Church, Maria Karnilova, Paul Wallace, Lane Bradbury, Faith Dane, Chotzi Foley.
Principal songs: Let Me Entertain You; Some People; Small World; Little Lamb; You'll Never Get Away from Me; All I Need Is the Girl; Everything's Coming Up Roses; Together; You Gotta Have a Gimmick; Rose's Turn.

Recorded Version
Columbia OL 5420/OS 2017 (O.C.).
   An impressive achievement.

Frank Loesser

All music & lyrics by Mr. Loesser unless otherwise noted.

THE ILLUSTRATORS' SHOW
Opened: Jan. 22, 1936.
5 performances.
MUSIC MOSTLY BY IRVING ACTMAN; SKETCHES BY MAX LIEBMAN, HI ALEXANDER, KENNETH WEBB, OTTO SOGLOW & OTHERS; ACTMAN LYRICS BY LOESSER.

Cast included: Helen Lynd, Earl Oxford, Niela Goodelle, Gomez & Winona, O. Z. Whitehead, Otto Soglow.

Principal Actman & Loesser songs: Bang— the Bell Rang!; If You Didn't Love Me.

WHERE'S CHARLEY?
Opened: Oct. 11, 1948.
792 performances.
BOOK BY GEORGE ABBOTT.

Cast included: Ray Bolger, Allyn McLerie, Byron Palmer, Doretta Morrow, Horace Cooper, Jane Lawrence, Paul England.
Principal songs: The New Ashmolean Marching Society and Student Conservatory Band; My Darling, My Darling; Make a Miracle; Lovelier Than Ever; Pernambuco; Once in Love with Amy; At the Red Rose Cotillion.

Recorded Version
English Columbia 33SX 1085 (London O.C.) (1958).
   The only recording of this fondly remembered score is that of the splendid English company with Norman Wisdom.

GUYS AND DOLLS
Opened: Nov. 24, 1950.
1,200 performances.
BOOK BY JO SWERLING & ABE BURROWS.

Cast included: Robert Alda, Vivian Blaine, Sam Levene, Isabel Bigley, Pat Rooney, B. S. Pully, Stubby Kaye, Peter Gennaro, Scott Merrill.
Principal songs: Fugue for Tinhorns; The Oldest Established; I'll Know; A Bushel and a Peck; Adelaide's Lament; Guys and Dolls; If I Were a Bell; My Time of Day; I've Never Been in Love Before; Take Back Your Mink; More I Cannot Wish You; Luck Be a Lady; Sue Me; Sit Down, You're Rockin' the Boat; Marry the Man Today.

Recorded Version
Decca DL 9023 (O.C.).
   An outstanding blending of words and music provides a score that remains a classic in its field.

THE MOST HAPPY FELLA
Opened: May 3, 1956.
676 performances.
BOOK BY LOESSER.

Cast included: Robert Weede, Jo Sullivan, Art Lund, Susan Johnson, Shorty Long, Mona Paulee.
Principal songs: Somebody Somewhere; The Most Happy Fella; Standing on the

Corner; Joey, Joey, Joey; Rosabella; Abbondanza; Sposalizio; Happy to Make Your Acquaintance; Big "D"; Warm All Over; I Like Everybody; My Heart Is So Full of You; How Beautiful the Days.

Recorded Version

Columbia OL 3240 (O.C.).

This three-record set of the entire score reveals many facets of a distinguished musical talent. Highlights are on a single record, Columbia OL 5118.

GREENWILLOW
Opened: Mar. 8, 1960.
95 *performances.*
BOOK BY LESSER SAMUELS & LOESSER.

Cast included: Anthony Perkins, Cecil Kellaway, Pert Kelton, Ellen McCown, William Chapman, Lee Cass.
Principal songs: The Music of Home; Gideon Briggs, I Love You; Summertime Love; Walking Away Whistling; Could've Been a Ring; Never Will I Marry; Faraway Boy; Clang Dang the Bell; What a Blessing.

Recorded Version

RCA Victor LOC 2001/LSO 2001 (O.C.).

Loesser in a bucolic, frequently whimsical mood.

Richard Adler
and Jerry Ross

JOHN MURRAY ANDERSON'S
ALMANAC
Opened: Dec. 10, 1953.
229 *performances.*
MUSIC & LYRICS ALSO BY OTHERS; SKETCHES BY JEAN KERR, SUMNER LOCKE-ELLIOT, ARTHUR MACRAE, BILLY K. WELLS, HERBERT FARJEON, LAURI WYLIE.

Cast included: Hermione Gingold, Billy DeWolfe, Harry Belafonte, Orson Bean, Polly Bergen, Nanci Crompton, Carleton Carpenter, Alice Pearce, Celia Lipton, Elaine Dunn, Kay Medford, Monique Van Vooren, Tina Louise, Larry Kert.
Principal Adler & Ross songs: You're So Much a Part of Me; When Am I Going to Meet Your Mother?

THE PAJAMA GAME
Opened: May 13, 1954.
1,063 *performances.*

BOOK BY GEORGE ABBOTT & RICHARD BISSELL.
Cast included: John Raitt, Janis Paige, Eddie Foy, Jr., Carol Haney, Reta Shaw, Stanley Prager, Peter Gennaro, Shirley MacLaine.
Principal songs: Racing with the Clock; I'm Not at All in Love; I'll Never Be Jealous Again; Hey, There; Her Is; Once a Year Day; Small Talk; There Once Was a Man; Steam Heat; Hernando's Hideaway; 7½ Cents.

Recorded Versions

Columbia OL 4840 (O.C.).
Columbia OL 5210 (F.V.) (1957).

Both these releases have the same material and almost the same cast. The major change is Doris Day for Janis Paige on the sound track.

DAMN YANKEES
Opened: May 5, 1955.
1,019 *performances.*
BOOK BY GEORGE ABBOTT & DOUGLASS WALLOP.

Cast included: Gwen Verdon, Stephen Douglass, Ray Walston, Russ Brown, Shannon Bolin, Jimmie Komack, Robert Shafer, Jean Stapleton.
Principal songs: Goodbye, Old Girl; Heart; A Little Brains, a Little Talent; A Man Doesn't Know; Whatever Lola Wants; Who's Got the Pain?; Near to You; Two Lost Souls.

Recorded Versions

RCA Victor LOC 1021 (O.C.).
RCA Victor LOC 1047/LSO 1047 (F.V.) (1958).

There are a few minor changes in songs and lyrics on the sound-track, plus one major cast change in substituting Tab Hunter for Stephen Douglass.

Meredith Willson

THE MUSIC MAN
Opened: Dec. 19, 1957.
1,375 *performances.*

Cast included: Robert Preston, Barbara Cook, David Burns, Pert Kelton, The Buffalo Bills, Iggie Wolfington, Helen Raymond, Paul Reed, Eddie Hodges.
Principal songs: Rock Island; Trouble; Piano Lesson; Goodnight, My Someone; Seventy-Six Trombones; The Sadder-but-Wiser Girl; Marian the Librarian; My White

Knight; Wells Fargo Wagon; Shipoopi; Lida Rose; Will I Ever Tell You?; Gary, Indiana; Till There Was You.

Recorded Versions

Capitol WAO 990/SWAO 990 (O.C.).
Capitol T 1320/ST 1320.

Willson's skillful blending of corn and cacophony gets a remarkably fine aural production. The composer-lyricist is heard on the second Capitol set with his wife, Rini.

Bob Merrill

NEW GIRL IN TOWN
Opened: May 14, 1957.
431 *performances.*
BOOK BY GEORGE ABBOTT.

Cast included: Gwen Verdon, Thelma Ritter, George Wallace, Cameron Prud'homme, Mark Dawson, Lulu Bates.
Principal songs: Anna Lilla; Sunshine Girl; Flings; It's Good to Be Alive; Look at 'Er; Did You Close Your Eyes?

Recorded Version

RCA Victor LOC 1027/LSO 1027 (O.C.).
The atmospheric numbers capture the spirit of the tale better than the romantic ballads.

TAKE ME ALONG
Opened: Sept. 9, 1959.
448 *performances.*
BOOK BY JOSEPH STEIN & ROBERT RUSSELL.

Cast included: Jackie Gleason, Walter Pidgeon, Eileen Herlie, Robert Morse, Una Merkel, Susan Luckey, Peter Conlow.
Principal songs: I Would Die; Sid, Ol' Kid; Staying Young; I Get Embarrassed; We're Home; Take Me Along; Promise Me a Rose; Nine O'Clock; But Yours.

Recorded Version

RCA Victor LOC 1050/LSO 1050 (O.C.).
A score of much period charm and dramatic appeal.

Mary Rodgers
and Marshall Barer

ONCE UPON A MATTRESS
Opened: May 11, 1959.
470 *performances.*

BOOK BY JAY THOMPSON, MARSHALL BARER, DEAN FULLER.

Cast included: Joe Bova, Carol Burnett, Allen Case, Jack Gilford, Anne Jones, Matt Mattox, Harry Snow, Robert Weil, Jane White.
Principal songs: Many Moons Ago; In a Little While; Shy; Sensitivity; Normandy; Happily Ever After; Very Soft Shoes.

Recorded Version

Kapp KDL 7004/KDL 7004-S (O.C.).
Richard Rodgers' daughter, Mary, shows much promise in her first score, and the lyrics of Marshall Barer are especially bright.

Rick Besoyan

LITTLE MARY SUNSHINE
Opened: Nov. 18, 1959.
(Still running as of April 1, 1962)

Cast included: Eileen Brennan, William Graham, Elmarie Wendel, John McMartin, Mario Siletti, Elizabeth Parrish, John Aniston.
Principal songs: The Forest Rangers; Little Mary Sunshine; Look for a Sky of Blue; In Izzenschnooken on the Lovely Essenzook Zee; Tell a Handsome Stranger; Once in a Blue Moon; Every Little Nothing; Colorado Love Call; Do You Ever Dream of Vienna?

Recorded Version

Capitol WAO 1240/SWOA 1240 (O.C.).
The surprise off-Broadway hit receives a faithful interpretation in its recorded version, even though the musical accompaniment has been greatly enlarged.

Jerry Bock
and Sheldon Harnick

All lyrics by Mr. Harnick unless otherwise noted.

MR. WONDERFUL
Opened: Mar. 22, 1956.
383 *performances.*
BOOK BY JOSEPH STEIN & WILL GLICKMAN; LYRICS BY LARRY HOLOFCENER & GEORGE WEISS.

Cast included: Sammy Davis, Jr., Jack Carter, Pat Marshall, Olga James, Chita

Rivera, Hal Loman, Will Mastin, Sammy Davis, Sr.
Principal songs: Without You I'm Nothing; Mr. Wonderful; Ethel Baby; Too Close for Comfort.

Recorded Version
Decca DL 9032 (O.C.).
Sammy Davis, Jr., belts out this breezy score with an exuberance not completely warranted by the material.

THE BODY BEAUTIFUL
Opened: Jan. 23, 1958.
60 performances.
BOOK BY JOSEPH STEIN & WILL GLICKMAN.

Cast included: Mindy Carson, Steve Forrest, Jack Warden, Lonnie Sattin, Barbara McNair, Brock Peters.
Principal songs: Leave Well Enough Alone; Uh-huh, Oh, Yeah!; All of These and More; Summer Is; Just My Luck; A Relatively Simple Affair.

FIORELLO!
Opened: Nov. 23, 1959.
795 performances.
BOOK BY JEROME WEIDMAN & GEORGE ABBOTT.

Cast included: Tom Bosley, Patricia Wilson, Ellen Hanley, Howard DaSilva, Mark Dawson, Nathaniel Frey, Pat Stanley, Eileen Rodgers.

Principal songs: On the Side of the Angels; Politics and Poker; The Name's LaGuardia; I Love a Cop; 'Til Tomorrow; When Did I Fall in Love?; Gentleman Jimmy; Little Tin Box; The Very Next Man.

Recorded Version
Capitol WAO 1321/SWAO 1321 (O.C.).
New York's beloved Little Flower gets an affectionate and witty tribute.

Charles Strouse
and Lee Adams

BYE BYE BIRDIE
Opened: Apr. 14, 1960.
607 performances.
BOOK BY MICHAEL STEWART.

Cast included: Chita Rivera, Dick Van Dyke, Kay Medford, Paul Lynde, Dick Gautier, Michael J. Pollard, Susan Watson, Marijane Maricle.
Principal songs: One Last Kiss; One Boy; Baby, Talk to Me; Rosie; Put on a Happy Face; Kids.

Recorded Version
Columbia KOL 5510/KOS 2025 (O.C.).
A bright, humorous score that succeeds admirably in capturing the flavor of America's teenagers.

APPENDIX ADDENDA 1962

In order to keep the information as up to date as possible, the following Appendix Addenda has been added for this special edition of *The World of Musical Comedy*. Please note that the entries have been arranged in chronological order, and that important works by writers other than those discussed in the main body of the text have also been included.

THE FANTASTICKS
Opened: May 3, 1960.
(Still running as of April 1, 1962)
BOOK & LYRICS BY TOM JONES; MUSIC BY HARVEY SCHMIDT.

Cast included: Jerry Orbach, Rita Gardner, Kenneth Nelson, Richard Stauffer.
Principal songs: Try to Remember; It Depends on What You Pay; Soon It's Gonna Rain; Round and Round; They Were You.

Recorded Version
MGM 3872/S 3872 (O.C.).

There are many imaginative and appealing pieces in the score for this charming fantasy.

IRMA LA DOUCE
Opened: Sept. 29, 1960.
524 performances.
BOOK & LYRICS BY ALEXANDRE BREFFORT, ADAPTED BY JULIAN MORE, DAVID HENEKER, MONTY NORMAN; MUSIC BY MARGUERITE MONNOT.

Cast included: Elizabeth Seal, Keith Michell, Clive Revill, George S. Irving.
Principal songs: Valse Milieu; The Bridge of Caulaincourt; Our Language of Love; Dis-Donc; There Is Only One Paris for That.

Recorded Versions
Columbia OL 5560/OS 2029 (O.C.).
Columbia WL 177 (French S.C.).

This Parisian success that became equally popular in London and in New York contains a full complement of Gallic wit and verve. The French recording, featuring Jeanmaire lacks the spirit of the Broadway cast version.

TENDERLOIN
Opened: Oct. 17, 1960.
216 performances.
BOOK BY GEORGE ABBOTT & JEROME WEIDMAN; LYRICS BY SHELDON HARNICK; MUSIC BY JERRY BOCK.

Cast included: Maurice Evans, Ron Husmann, Wynne Miller, Eileen Rodgers, Rex

THE UNSINKABLE MOLLY BROWN *(1960). Harve Presnell and Tammy Grimes cavorting to "I Ain't Down Yet." (Costumes by Miles White; setting by Oliver Smith.)*

Everhart, Eddie Phillips, Lee Becker, Ralph Dunn.
Principal songs: Little Old New York; Artificial Flowers; The Picture of Happiness; Tommy, Tommy; How the Money Changes Hands; Good Clean Fun; My Miss Mary; My Gentle Young Johnny.

Recorded Version
Capitol WAO 1492/SWAO 1492 (O.C.)
 Though the musical had a rather muddled point of view in its tale of a vice-filled New York in the 1890s, Bock and Harnick's flavorsome score remains a delight. Maurice Evans does well enough in his first American musical, but it is Ron Husmann who wins the vocal honors.

THE UNSINKABLE MOLLY BROWN
Opened: Nov. 3, 1960.
532 performances.
BOOK BY RICHARD MORRIS; MUSIC & LYRICS BY MEREDITH WILLSON.

Cast included: Tammy Grimes, Harve Presnell, Cameron Prud'homme, Mony Dalmes, Edith Meiser, Mitchell Gregg.
Principal songs: I Ain't Down Yet; Belly Up to the Bar, Boys; If I Knew; My Own Brass Bed; Dolce Far Niente.

CAMELOT *(1960). Queen Guenevere (Julie Andrews) and courtiers offer a hoop-twirling tribute to "The Lusty Month of May." (Costumes by Adrian and Tony Duquette; setting by Oliver Smith.)*

DO RE MI *(1960). A bemused Phil Silvers listens as wife Nancy Walker details her mad, romantic life in "Adventure." (Costumes by Irene Sharaff; setting by Boris Aronson.)*

Recorded Version
Capitol WAO 1509/SWAO 1509 (O.C.).
The success of this work depended more on Tammy Grimes' ebullient performance than on its cumbersome book or routine score.

CAMELOT
Opened: Dec. 3, 1960.
(Still running as of April 1, 1962)
BOOK & LYRICS BY ALAN JAY LERNER; MUSIC BY FREDERICK LOEWE.

Cast included: Richard Burton, Julie Andrews, Roddy McDowall, Robert Coote, Robert Goulet, M'el Dowd, John Cullum, Bruce Yarnell, David Hurst.
Principal songs: Camelot; C'est Moi; The Lusty Month of May; If Ever I Would Leave You; What Do the Simple Folk Do?; I Loved You Once in Silence; Guenevere.

Recorded Version
Columbia KOL 5620/KOS 2031 (O.C.).
A distinguished score of melodic richness and lusty humor is brought to life by Richard Burton's rugged King Arthur, Julie Andrews' delicate Guenevere, and Robert Goulet's amorous Lancelot.

WILDCAT
Opened: Dec. 16, 1960.
171 *performances.*
BOOK BY N. RICHARD NASH; LYRICS BY CAROLYN LEIGH; MUSIC BY CY COLEMAN.

Cast included: Lucille Ball, Keith Andes, Paula Stewart, Edith King, Don Tomkins, Charles Braswell.
Principal songs: Hey, Look Me Over; You've Come Home; What Takes My Fancy; One Day We Dance; Give a Little Whistle; El Sombrero; Corduroy Road.

Recorded Version
RCA Victor LOC 1060/LSO 1060 (O.C.).
The Coleman-Leigh team made a more auspicious musical comedy debut than did star Lucille Ball, particularly with their exuberant hit, "Hey, Look Me Over."

DO RE MI
Opened: Dec. 26, 1960.
400 *performances.*
BOOK BY GARSON KANIN; LYRICS BY BETTY COMDEN & ADOLPH GREEN; MUSIC BY JULE STYNE.

Cast included: Phil Silvers, Nancy Walker, John Reardon, David Burns, George

Mathews, George Givot, Nancy Dussault.
Principal songs: I Know About Love; Cry Like the Wind; What's New At the Zoo?; Adventure; Make Someone Happy.

Recorded Version
RCA Victor LOCD 2002/LSOD 2002 (O.C.).
Mr. Kanin's comedy about jukebox racketeers inspired an only average score, except for Miss Walker's wildly funny "Adventure."

THE HAPPIEST GIRL IN THE WORLD
Opened: April 3, 1961.
96 performances.
BOOK BY FRED SAIDY & HENRY MYERS; LYRICS BY E. Y. HARBURG; MUSIC BY JACQUES OFFENBACH.

Cast included: Cyril Ritchard, Janice Rule, Dran Seitz, Bruce Yarnell.
Principal songs: The Happiest Girl in the World; Shall We Say Farewell?; Vive la Virtue; Adrift on a Star; Five Minutes of Spring.

Recorded Version
Columbia KOL 5650/KOS 2050 (O.C.). The familiar Offenbach melodies used here seem strangely out of place in E. Y. Harburg's satirical approach to the *Lysistrata* legend.

CARNIVAL
Opened: April 13, 1961.
(Still running as of April 1, 1962)
BOOK BY MICHAEL STEWART; MUSIC & LYRICS BY BOB MERRILL.

Cast included: Anna Maria Alberghetti, James Mitchell, Kaye Ballard, Pierre Olaf, Jerry Orbach, Henry Lascoe, Anita Gillette.
Principal songs: Direct from Vienna; Mira; Theme from *Carnival;* Yes, My Heart; Beautiful Candy; Always Always You; The Grand Imperial Cirque de Paris.

Recorded Version
MGM 3946 OC/S 3946 OC (O.C.).
There are many attractive things in Bob Merrill's score, though Gower Champion's staging made it a show that must be seen to be fully appreciated. The drama critics voted it the best musical of the season.

SAIL AWAY
Opened: Oct. 3, 1961.
167 performances.
BOOK, MUSIC & LYRICS BY NOEL COWARD.

Cast included: Elaine Stritch, James Hurst, Margalo Gillmore, Alice Pearce, Patricia

CARNIVAL *(1961). When his vision of a "Grand Imperial Cirque de Paris" gets slightly out of hand, Pierre Olaf leads the*

Harty, Grover Dale, Charles Braswell, Betty Jane Watson.
Principal songs: Sail Away; The Passenger's Always Right; Later than Spring; Something Very Strange; The Little Ones' ABC; When You Want Me; Why Do the Wrong People Travel?

Recorded Versions
Capitol WAO 1643/SWAO 1643 (O.C.).
Capitol W 1667/SW 1667.
Noel Coward's first musical written especially for Broadway may have been a bit old-fashioned, but his words and music continue to be timeless. On the second Capitol set, Mr. Coward r-r-rips through the score himself in elegant style.

writers for the musical stage. Always true to its Israeli setting, the work is marked by sincere warmth and deep understanding.

HOW TO SUCCEED IN BUSINESS WITHOUT REALLY TRYING
Opened: Oct. 14, 1961.
(Still running as of Apr. 1, 1962)
BOOK BY ABE BURROWS, JACK WEINSTOCK, WILLIE GILBERT; MUSIC & LYRICS BY FRANK LOESSER.

Cast included: Robert Morse, Rudy Vallee, Bonnie Scott, Virginia Martin, Charles Nelson Reilly, Claudette Sutherland.
Principal songs: The Company Way; A Secretary Is Not a Toy; Grand Old Ivy; Been a Long Day; Paris Original; Rosemary; I Believe in You; The Brotherhood of Man.

PHOTO BY FRIEDMAN-ABELES

PHOTO BY FRIEDMAN-ABELES
embers of a second-rate carnival troupe in exultant dance. (Costumes by Freddy Wittop; setting by Will Stevens Armstrong.)

MILK AND HONEY
Opened: Oct. 10, 1961.
(Still running as of April 1, 1962)
BOOK BY DON APPELL; MUSIC & LYRICS BY JERRY HERMAN.

Cast included: Robert Weede, Mimi Benzell. Molly Picon, Tommy Rall, Lanna Saunders, Juki Arkin, Thelma Pelish.
Principal songs: Shalom; Milk and Honey; There's No Reason in the World; That Was Yesterday; I Will Follow You; Hymn to Hymie; It's As Simple As That.

Recorded Version
RCA Victor LOC 1065/LSO 1065 (O.C.).
Jerry Herman's initial Broadway score quickly established him among the top young

HOW TO SUCCEED IN BUSINESS WITHOUT REALLY TRYING (1961). *Alma mater "Grand Old Ivy" is ardently sung by old-grad J. B. Biggley (Rudy Vallee) and would-be young-grad J. Pierrepont Finch (Robert Morse).*

Recorded Version
RCA Victor LOC 1066/LSO 1066 (O.C.).

Though short on melody, Frank Loesser's songs for this blockbusting satire on big business have a number of genuinely comic ideas. However, they are less effective on record than they are on the stage.

KWAMINA
Opened: Oct. 23, 1961.
32 performances.
BOOK BY ROBERT ALAN AURTHUR; MUSIC & LYRICS BY RICHARD ADLER.

Cast included: Sally Ann Howes, Terry Carter, Rex Ingram, Brock Peters, Ethel Ayler.
Principal songs: Cocoa Bean Song; Welcome Home; Nothing More to Look Forward To; Ordinary People; What's Wrong with Me?; What Happened to Me Tonight?; Another Time, Another Place.

Recorded Version
Capitol W 1645/SW 1645 (O.C.).

The struggles of an emerging African country have produced a richly colorful score that makes excellent use of native rhythms.

THE GAY LIFE
Opened: Nov. 18, 1961.
114 performances.
BOOK BY FAY & MICHAEL KANIN; LYRICS BY HOWARD DIETZ; MUSIC BY ARTHUR SCHWARTZ.

Cast included: Walter Chiari, Barbara Cook, Jules Munshin, Loring Smith, Elizabeth Allen, Jeanne Bal, Yvonne Constant.
Principal songs: You're Not the Type; Magic Moment; Who Can? You Can!; Oh, Mein Liebchen; Something You Never Had Before; Come A-Wandering with Me.

Recorded Version
Capitol WAO 1560/SWAO 1560(O.C.).

Dietz and Schwartz have returned after a thirteen and a half year absence to provide a gay and lilting musical accompaniment for this version of Schnitzler's *Affairs of Anatol.* Barbara Cook's singing is especially noteworthy.

SUBWAYS ARE FOR SLEEPING
Opened: Dec. 27, 1961.
(Still running as of April 1, 1962)
BOOK & LYRICS BY BETTY COMDEN & ADOLPH GREEN; MUSIC BY JULE STYNE.

Cast included: Sydney Chaplin, Carol Lawrence, Orson Bean, Phyllis Newman.
Principal songs: Girls Like Me; I'm Just Taking My Time; Ride Through the Night; Be a Santa; Comes Once in a Lifetime.

Recorded Version
Columbia KOL 5730/KOS 2130 (O.C.).

Some rather attractive songs are sung adequately by Carol Lawrence and atrociously by Sydney Chaplin. The musical was based on Edmund Love's book about New York's warm-hearted vagrants.

NO STRINGS
Opened: Mar. 15, 1962.
(Still running as of April 1, 1962)
BOOK BY SAMUEL TAYLOR; MUSIC & LYRICS BY RICHARD RODGERS.

Cast included: Richard Kiley, Diahann Carroll, Noelle Adam, Alvin Epstein, Mitchell Gregg, Polly Rowles.
Principal songs: Loads of Love; La La La; Nobody Told Me; Look No Further; No Strings; The Sweetest Sounds.

Recorded Version
Capitol WAO 1695/SWAO 1695 (O.C.).

ALL AMERICAN
Opened: Mar. 19, 1962.
(Still running as of April 1, 1962)
BOOK BY MEL BROOKS; LYRICS BY LEE ADAMS; MUSIC BY CHARLES STROUSE.

Cast included: Ray Bolger, Eileen Herlie, Ron Husmann, Anita Gillette, Fritz Weaver, Bernie West, Betty Oakes, Mort Marshall.
Principal songs: We Speak the Same Language; Once Upon a Time; The Real Me; What a Country!

Recorded Version
Columbia CL 1790/CS 8590 (O.C.).

Index